BY THE SAME AUTHOR:

The Secret Search for Peace in Vietnam
(with David Kraslow)

DEFEATED

INSIDE AMERICA'S
MILITARY MACHINE

RANDOM HOUSE NEW YORK

DEFEATED

INSIDE AMERICA'S MILITARY MACHINE

BY STUART H. LOORY

Library of Congress Cataloging in Publication Data

Loory, Stuart H.
Defeated; inside America's military machine.
Includes bibliographical references.
   1. United States—Armed Forces. I. Title.
UA23.L69   355.3'0973   73-5102
ISBN 0-394-48025-2

Manufactured in the United States of America

First Edition

For Joshua Alan, Adam Edward and Miriam Beth
and, again,
Marjorie

CONTENTS

DEFEATED

INSIDE AMERICA'S
MILITARY MACHINE

INTRODUCTION

In the winter of 1969, a national magazine commissioned me to pinpoint the locations throughout the country where nuclear weapons were manufactured, tested, stored and deployed. The search took me from coast to coast and, during its course, my eyes opened for the first time to the pervasiveness of the American military machine—its nonnuclear as well as nuclear components—in society.

It was not the overbearing numbers of weapons themselves that gave me an uneasy feeling. As a reporter covering science, technology, national politics and foreign affairs for fifteen years, I had grown used to the idea that this was an unsafe world in which such tools as missiles, airplanes, ships and tanks were necessary in great numbers to defend the nation and our way of life.

The 1969 trip taught me how the military establishment had insinuated itself throughout civilian society and had come to dominate dozens of localities. At the highest level, the federal budget, with 37 percent of it going to military uses, testified to the increasing domination of the military over civil society. But there were other signs uncovered on that trip. The commander of the Polaris Submarine Facility outside Charleston, South Carolina, like any Main Street businessman, had hung a plaque on his wall identifying himself as a member of the local Chamber of Commerce. The symbiotic relationship suggested by that plaque spoke volumes about a change in American attitudes toward the military over the decades since townspeople had posted signs reading "no dogs or soldiers allowed" at the city limits. The American people had embraced

3

the military as their defender, and in turn, the military had turned the embrace into a stranglehold—or so it seemed. In central New Jersey, the Navy had built a private railroad that carried ammunition right through the backyards of an affluent suburb from inland bunkers to a pier in Lower New York Bay. Along the Atlantic Coast in North Carolina, the Marine Corps controlled a stretch of federal highway. Motorists driving the scenic coastal route could negotiate the stretch only at the sufferance of Marine sentries stationed in guard houses at either end. Storage sites for chemical warfare material crept right up to the end of the runway at Denver's commercial airport and were visible from jets landing and taking off. A nuclear weapons design laboratory operated for the Atomic Energy Commission by the University of California grew out of the vineyards in northern California's Livermore Valley. In dozens of suburbs of the major cities, nuclear-tipped Nike Hercules antiaircraft missiles became familiar sights to children at play.

My tour indicated that the historic servant-master relationship, which once put the military under strict civilian control, was undergoing a transformation. In the skewed scheme of things, the military machine was assuming a greater importance than the society it protected.

I began to look at the Vietnam War, then at its height, not as an aberration in American policy but as an inevitable result of a militaristic policy that had been pursued since the end of World War II. I began to think of our nation as a bastion of militarism that, instead of contributing to a peaceful stability in the world, encouraged instability.

The tour stimulated my interest in the American military establishment as an institution. When the opportunity presented itself, I decided, as a journalist and as a citizen concerned that his country had taken a wrong turn, to conduct a more thorough investigation. This book is the result.

In the summer of 1971, I left the Washington Bureau of the Los Angeles *Times* to work full time on the project. In addition to extensive reading, I interviewed hundreds of officers and enlisted men in all the services as well as civilians closely connected with the military machine. In the winter of 1971–1972, I toured military installations throughout the world, armed with a telegram from the Department of Defense asking officers at the bases to extend to me normal courtesies and a letter from the Center for Constitutional Rights in New York to its "Dear Brothers in Peace" asking that its antimilitary representatives in the Far East cooperate with me. I sought out, listened to, recorded and evaluated

4

viewpoints from all the wavelengths on the spectrum of thought and experience within the military machine.

This was not an easy book to write. It was difficult emotionally because I knew as I worked that inevitably it would be taken as an attack against men and their profession when it was really intended as an indictment of the system in which they worked. Over the course of my research I developed many new and cherished friendships with men in uniform. These are sensitive, concerned, intelligent, patriotic Americans drawn to the profession of arms for all the same reasons I was drawn to journalism, and now it gives me some pain to produce a work questioning the import of their careers.

This book could not have been written without a generous grant from the Woodrow Wilson International Center for Scholars. The center, headquartered in the Smithsonian Institution Building, was chartered by Congress as a living memorial to the nation's twenty-eighth President. Special thanks must go to Benjamin H. Read, the center's first director; Albert Meisel, deputy director; William M. Dunn, administrative officer; Mary Anglemyer and Marcella Jones of the library staff; and Frances Hunter and Frances Tompkins, who typed the manuscript. Army Lieutenant Colonel Zeb B. Bradford was a Fellow at the Center concurrently. He and several of his friends, particularly Army Lieutenant Colonel William L. Hauser, were invaluable in steering me on the right track during the course of my research and writing. Although they will almost certainly not agree with much that is written here and bear no responsibility for it, I would like to acknowledge their contribution. I am proud to call them my friends.

Throughout the world I received help, encouragement, information and comfort from dozens of men and women in uniform, and civilians. I can name some; others preferred to remain unmentioned. Among others, I am indebted to the following:

In Washington, Gregory Marus, Henry Ohrenberger and Susan Soper for research; Harry Zubkoff of the Defense Department who made his daily clipsheet files available; Dennis Britton, Lucy Lazarou and Joann Wilson of the Los Angeles *Times;* Wendy Sigal of the Washington *Post;* David Wise; Frederick Asselin of Senator Abraham Ribicoff's staff; Army Captain Stephen Hurwitz; Janice and Bill Fain of Consolidated Analysis Centers, Inc., for allowing me to audit their course on systems analysis; Army Major Paul Miles; Francine Berkowitz and Ann H. Krafthofer of the Smithsonian Institution, and Louise Platt.

New York: Rick Wagner of the Center for Constitutional Rights and Robert D. Loomis of Random House, my editor; West Point, New York: Major Josiah Bunting and his wife, Diana, and Major Carl Mc-Carden; Newport, Rhode Island: Lieutenant Commander Beth F. Coye of the Naval War College; Jacksonville, Florida: Martin Crotts of the Florida *Times-Union;* Madison, Wisconsin: Dave Zweifel of *The Capital Times;* Waltham, Massachusetts: William W. Moss of the John F. Kennedy Library; Oakland, California: Eric Meskaukas, editor of *Overseas Weekly;* Los Angeles, California: William Ellet of the Los Angeles *Times;* Fairbanks, Alaska: L. W. Morgan of *The Tundra Times;* Honolulu, Hawaii: Lyle Nelson of the Honolulu *Star-Bulletin;* Tokyo: Eric Seitz of the Center for Constitutional Rights; Seoul: Norman Thorpe, James C. Wade and John C. Stickler; Okinawa: Mark and Carol Amsterdam; Saigon: Dave and Kate Miller and the staff of the CBS News Bureau; USS *Coral Sea:* Lieutenant Randy Anderson; Bangkok: Jack and Florence Foisie of the Los Angeles *Times;* Frankfurt: Charles Cooper of *Overseas Weekly;* London: Navy Captain Robert Bathurst and his wife, Jean, and Sidney and Rosemary Weiland of Reuters.

In addition, there were dozens of public affairs officers from all the services whose help was invaluable.

Washington, D.C.
March 4, 1973

PART ONE

THE ASSEMBLY-LINE GENERATION GOES TO WAR

1

A MACHINE AT REST AND THE RADARMAN SECOND CLASS

Stretched along lines of supply and communication girdling the globe, the American military machine today is in a troubled rest. The world's most powerful fighting force is wounded, confused, drugged, demoralized, feeling betrayed, its lifeblood clogged in hardened bureaucratic arteries, its reflexes numbed by political intervention.

From remote Army camps in the Far East and Central Europe to stateside garrisons, Vietnam veterans from general to grunt—and newer recruits for whom the war is only legend—are caught up in a make-work boredom. They face a future rendered uncertain by a confusion over their mission. They are wondering, almost as one man, What am I doing here?

At dozens of air bases around the world, pilots indoctrinated with a belief in their own invincibility ponder the matter of why it was that all the nation's nonnuclear air power could not bring a fourth-rate nation to its knees.

From the Straits of Taiwan to the Bosporus, an aged, tradition-bound Navy wonders whether it will be up to the challenge of a young and virile Soviet Navy.

In the meeting rooms of the Joint Chiefs of Staff at the Pentagon, the nation's highest military officers struggle to regain their self-confidence and prestige.

On Capitol Hill, the always staunch and once all-powerfull defenders of the military face an upstart and increasingly successful opposition from lawmakers more interested in domestic priorities and even join the attack themselves.

There was, in the early 1970s, a long catalog of malaise:

Blacks rose up almost to the point of mutiny in an institution that for a generation had been taken as a model for dealing with problems of desegregation and promoting good race relations; young whites in increasing numbers went AWOL or deserted in despair; career-minded young officers complained of the failure of the organization to give back loyalty they had given it; older officers indicted the lying ways they say they must adopt to succeed in the bureaucracy; some critics from within attacked the indolent bureaucratic methods of an organization that must have eight backup men for every fighting man it fields; others complained of the careerism that made "a small war but the only war we've got" a test bed for new methods and a training ground for officers who knew they needed combat experience to get ahead; corruption crept into the cadre; officers and men in what was once essentially a people's army began to mouth the same "I was only following orders" justification for war crimes that marked the defenses of World War II enemies on trial; drugs became a way of life for thousands who might otherwise have been unexposed; discipline broke down to the point that some superiors began to fear for their safety; crime became a major problem on several military bases; enlisted men were forced by inadequate pay to go on welfare.

The meaning of all this is disturbing in its simplicity. The American military machine today is not qualified to protect the nation's vital interests in situations short of nuclear exchange. There is some question that it could function properly even in that ultimate holocaust.

The American military machine is defeated.

No matter what the outcome of the Vietnam War in diplomatic terms, the military machine, though it won many a battle and kept an enemy from achieving a battlefield victory in Southeast Asia, lost a war —a war in which the Vietnam conflict was but one theater.

The war this book talks about is another conflict—one the machine had been fighting with itself since the end of World War II as the United States moved onto the world's stage as policeman of order and protector of the faith. That move legitimized a change in the national

10

character that forsook the traditional skepticism over a strong military in favor of a deep concern that without a monstrously large military machine the nation would not survive.

Monstrously large is what the military became. A generation of American parents surrendered 5,042,975 of its sons to the involuntary servitude of the draft between January 1, 1946, and June 30, 1972. All told, during that period 17.6 million men and women served in uniform.

The military bragged that, behind the Soviet Union and the People's Republic of China, it was the third-largest planned economy in the world. Its PX system, with $3.5 billion in sales in 1969, was the third-largest American retailer, behind Sears, Roebuck & Company and J. C. Penney Company, and ahead of such giants as F. W. Woolworth and Montgomery Ward. The military, in June 1971, owned or controlled 41,184 square miles of real estate in the United States alone—a total square mileage equal to that of the thirty-fifth-largest state, Ohio. Overseas, it owned or controlled another 4,198 square miles, an area equal to twice the size of the state of Delaware. All told, the value of this land and improvements on it—housing for troops and their families, maintenance facilities, airfield pavements, roads, operating facilities on land, electrical facilities, test facilities, covered storage areas and office space —is carried on the Pentagon's books at $40.5 billion. That figure does not include the cost of all the weapons, planes, ships, tanks, and missiles worth tens of billions more. By comparison, General Motors, the nation's —and the world's—largest manufacturing corporation, valued its real estate, plant and equipment at the end of 1971 at only $5.57 billion.

In 1970, the United States alone spent 37.6 percent of all the money budgeted by all the world's nations for defense.

The American military machine, instead of serving the nation, had made the nation its servant. Its demands were insatiable. It demanded and received from the federal treasury hundreds of billions of dollars which other sectors of society could have used handily. It drew upon the nation's pool of human talent, taking what it needed of the best minds and strongest bodies, leaving the rest for civilian endeavors. It confiscated vast stretches of seashore and acres of prairie, desert and mountains for its exclusive use. It hoarded its own stockpiles of scarce raw materials. When a conflict over any of this arose between the military machine and civilian society, the arbiters decided in favor of the machine.

11

Once the machine started rolling, it could not be stopped. It burrowed into the Midwestern plains, planting a crop of nuclear rockets capable of killing hundreds of millions. It hollowed out the Rocky Mountains and filled the cavity with a nerve center capable of controlling warfare throughout the continent. In other caves it stockpiled an inventory of nuclear weapons that seemed never-ending in its growth. It spanned the oceans to bases ringing the Communist world. Its submarines cruised previously uncharted depths. Its planes, for a time carrying nuclear weapons, patrolled the skies covering much of the planet. It hurled spy satellites into space orbits. It planted sensors on remote jungle trails and in the Arctic wastes to track movements of the enemy. Its weapons were stockpiled in Europe, Africa, on Pacific islands and in Asia.

It grew and grew, and even after its builders had forgotten its fundamental purpose, it continued to grow. Finally it overwhelmed the men who were operating it. Where before they justified their careers as protectors of the American Way, now they were worshiping their machine, the maintenance of which they saw as an end in itself. By the 1970s, the American military machine was hobbled by a size that made it unable to cope with the real world around it. It had grown unmanageable.

By the early 1970s, a handful among the more than two million men in uniform had begun to understand the overbearing nature of the machine and question the need for it. General David M. Shoup, a former commandant of the Marine Corps and member of the Joint Chiefs of Staff, was one such man. He wrote and spoke eloquently on the new militarism that pervaded the country. Another was Vice Admiral Gene LaRoque, who retired from a strategic planning job in the Pentagon to head a group that would serve as watchdog over Pentagon spending. At West Point, thirty-three faculty and staff members, among them some of the most highly regarded young men in the Army, resigned because they saw no good future for themselves in the service. There were other resignations up and down the chain of command and, among many who did not resign, there was a feeling of bitterness and despair. They were trapped by forces they could not control, and they made little effort to understand them.

One young Navy man made some effort at understanding. His story is revealing.

In the early spring of 1971, John T. Watts, then only twenty-one years old, began to think of himself as a killer. At the time, the young Navy radarman second class was serving aboard the destroyer *Everett F. Larson* (DD830) cruising off the coast of South Vietnam in the Gulf of Thailand. His job consisted of sitting at a radio set, maintaining contact with a Marine forward air controller, and taking down coordinates and passing them along to the ship's gun batteries which, day after day, lobbed shells into South Vietnam's U-Minh forest area and at supposed enemy shipping traffic in his area.

John T. Watts: the son of a career Navy petty officer; a boy scout well drilled in the importance of old-fashioned, flag-waving patriotism; a former Methodist choirboy. Now, sitting at his radio console, jolted with the report of each five-inch gun salvo leaving the barrels of the *Larson*'s three two-gun turrets, listening to the Marine spotter's hollow voice on the radio describing damage to "structures" on shore and "waterborn logistics craft" afloat, the thought that he was still a murderer, no matter how remote he was from the damage and the killing, weighed heavily on his mind.

It was not easy for Watts to articulate his thoughts. He had had only a high school education in Glendale, California, and writing did not come easily. But in his off hours, working on foolscap, he began to put his thoughts on paper. Just the physical act of writing on a destroyer of the United States Navy in the early 1970s was no easy job. He would stand in the aisleway of his berthing space deep belowdecks, leaning on his bunk, the center berth in a three-tiered unit. The lighting was dim. Weeks before, in response to the Navy's new emphasis on making life more comfortable for enlisted men, bunk lights had been installed, but they were not yet wired. Every time one of his shipmates wanted to pass by, he had to straighten up. Other times, he would sit in the ship's Combat Information Center, writing by the green glow of the radar sets.

"Some of my letters," he would say later, "were not in very good hand because of that. There wasn't any place to write. There were tables on the mess deck, but they were never available. They were always being used for meals, clean-up, movies and other activities."

By April 22, 1971, he had one document in shape. A friend had typed it, and Watts mailed out copies to President Richard M. Nixon; California's two senators, Alan Cranston and John Tunney; and Representative H. Allen Smith, his congressman. Here is Watts's letter, as addressed to Tunney:

22 April 1971
USS *E. F. Larson* (DD 830)
FPO San Francisco
California 96601

The Honorable John Tunney
United States Senate
Washington, D.C. 20510
Dear Senator Tunney:

The outcome of the Calley case has raised controversy over whether or not people in the higher ranks should be held responsible for this type of incident. There are those who believe that senior people not actually involved in incidents such as My Lai do not know the facts of what is going on in the field and so are innocent. I would like to relate to you some things I have learned while serving aboard a destroyer, the USS *Everett F. Larson* (DD830), in the Viet Nam area, which make me believe that there may be a great deal of covering up going on in this war.

During the month of February 1971, the *Larson* was conducting shore bombardment a few thousand yards off the U-Minh forest area of South Viet Nam in the Gulf of Thailand. My job at the time was as radio communicator with the marine spotter flying around in an airplane calling for our fire. After each mission we received Gun Damage Assessments describing what the results of our firing had been. The terminology used in these G.D.A.'s is very vague and general and may sound something like this; 8 structures damaged, 1 waterborn logistics craft damaged. I spent a great deal of time wondering just what a "structure" was and what a "waterborn logistics craft" was. I was able to find out one day when a marine sergeant, one of the spotters, came aboard for a visit. He told me that a "structure" could be anything from a villager's hut to a Viet Cong hospital. He said that he had in fact "blown away" a Viet Cong hospital using another ship. Do enemy hospitals come within the terms of the Geneva Convention as artillery targets? The "waterborn logistics craft" I had been wondering about, he told me, had been a sampan loaded with supplies. He said he had to report it as a "waterborn logistics craft"

14

because he is not allowed to call in fire on sampans. He also added that he thought we had had 2 KIA (killed in action) from that sampan but that he couldn't report them over the radio because he thought they had been women. Does killing women not actually involved in combat come within the terms of the Geneva Convention? It is also common knowledge that the use of white phosphorous rounds is frequent in naval gunfire support. The word "smoke" is used over the radio to cover up the use of this abhorrent weapon. The sergeant seemed to feel that though there was a large civilian population in the area, they were all subject to being "blown away" because they were Viet Cong sympathizers. It was my opinion that we are in Viet Nam to free these people from the clutches of the Communists, not to kill them off because the Communists happen to have control over their area.

If there is nothing to be covered up, why do the senior military people allow such vague terminology as "structure" and "waterborn logistics craft" to be used?

Very possibly we do need a comparably nonpartisan commission to explore the whole question of American conduct of the Vietnam War.

I hope this letter will give you some small help in your heavy burden of decision making.

Sincerely,
John T. Watts

That was one of many letters Watts wrote. To salve his guilt, he not only wrote letters but he also refused to take money for his job, and at one point he petitioned for a demotion from his petty officer's rating.

By the time Watts's doubts overwhelmed him, he was already serving his second tour in Vietnam's coastal waters. During the first tour, from January to July, 1969, the impressions of his country acquired in his youth still strong, he believed in and supported the cause. But two years later, that had changed.

"I was sure that the war was wrong," he said. "I felt that it was not right for me to profit from a war I do not believe in. For this reason I kept most of my basic military pay except during those weeks when we were actually firing into the countryside of Vietnam. When we did, I also gave away this money."

In February 1971, he leaned on his bunk in that dark aisleway and wrote a letter to the women of the First United Methodist Church of Glendale, where he had once sung in the choir.

> Ladies,
> Here is my combat pay for the month of February which I was given for helping to kill people in Vietnam. Please give it to the board of missions so that it may be used to help people and to stop some of the feelings and beliefs of mankind which allow us to kill one another. John T. Watts.

In March, he sent $65 to Project Hope and $150 to a sick child in Tujunga. In May, he sent $65 "to President Nixon for redistribution to a peaceful cause." A month later, he received a letter from then Assistant Navy Secretary Robert A. Frosch which said:

> Dear Petty Officer Watts:
> On behalf of President Nixon, I am replying to your letter of May 23 regarding the Vietnam conflict.
> The contents of your letter were fully noted. I can assure you that it is the President's determined desire to end this war and to achieve a lasting peace in the entire Pacific area. He believes he is taking every reasonable step to bring an end to the fighting on the basis of a permanent and equitable settlement. In this regard, the recent redeployments of U.S. troops are positive demonstrations of his desire to achieve such a peace.
> I am returning your money order to dispose of as you wish.
> Sincerely,
> Robert A. Frosch
> Assistant Secretary of the Navy

By the time Watts received that reply, he had only a few days left to serve in the Navy. The following month, returned to civilian life, he tried once again to make a donation for peace to the White House, working hard this time to reword his letter "so as not to offend his administration and its policies." Once again the money order came back with this letter:

Dear Mr. Watts:

Thank you, on behalf of President Nixon, for your letter of July 10. He appreciates your interest in writing again and is grateful for your expressions of confidence and support.

The President also appreciates your thoughtfulness in enclosing a money order for $65.00, but a longstanding policy of the White House does not permit him to accept funds as you have requested. I am confident that you will understand why it is necessary to return your generous contribution.

You may be assured the President shares your concern about our continued commitment in Vietnam, and he feels that the course he has set will lead to a lasting, rather than a temporary peace. In a recent speech, the President said: "We all pray for a time when military strength will be unnecessary, but as long as strength is essential, we shall maintain the preparedness which is essential to protect the peace."

With the President's best wishes,

Sincerely,
Michael B. Smith
Staff Assistant

It was a frustrating time for John T. Watts. The President would not accept his money. The two California senators answered his April letter, thanking him for his comments on the "Calley Case" without ever bothering to note the deeper, more pervasive issues he had raised about the military's conduct in Southeast Asia.

Given the complexity of modern-day society, there is something miraculous in the way John Watts's attitude toward the Vietnam War developed and in the steps he took to right what he perceived to be wrongs. It was as if an assembly-line worker at General Motors suddenly were to take full responsibility for the defects in the cars he was helping to produce. It had the same unreality as a trash collector feeling guilt for the dirty streets of New York City. Or a policeman feeling remorse for the crime in Chicago. Or a teacher taking on blame for the lack of education in the ghettos of New Orleans.

As the twentieth century comes to a close, wars are fought the same way we turn out automobiles and furniture and pension checks, sandwiches and sailboats and skyscrapers. Wars are fought with assembly lines. And as a result, no one individual, from the highest general to the lowliest rifleman, is made to bear the responsibility for his acts, though those at the top can feel pride in their achievements.

Most modern-day warriors do not participate in battle. Save for the relatively few riflemen who patrolled the jungles and paddies of Southeast Asia, war has become a remote business. A warrior these days is more likely the grimy seaman on the flight deck of an aircraft carrier, his back bent into a forty-knot wind as he lugs a heavy bag of chains used to snub a fighter bomber down to a catapult, or a bomb handler at an Air Force base attaching a white phosphorous cluster bomb to the wing of a B-52. He is a helicopter repairman in a remote camp on the Korean peninsula, a tank driver in Germany, a garrison soldier in the United States, a deck hand in the Mediterranean, a communications specialist in Ethiopia, a warehouseman in Turkey, an aircraft maintenance man at any one of dozens of air bases throughout the world. He guards an embassy in Moscow or Paris. He cops dope in a grimy bar in Wrightstown, New Jersey. He mans a desk and phone in a Tokyo press liaison office. He drives a scooter up and down the Pentagon halls in Washington, alternately filling in-baskets and emptying those marked "out." He is John T. Watts, peering at his radarscope or listening to the phone. All, one way or another, exist to play a part in killing. None of them are killers.

The system has been designed, almost certainly with inadvertence, to keep all these men clear of conscience.

General William C. Westmoreland, while he was the Army Chief of Staff, once told an audience that he did not lose any sleep while he was the commander of all American forces in Vietnam, during a period when hundreds of Americans and thousands of Asians were dying cruel deaths each week.

If General Westmoreland did not lose any sleep, why should anyone else? War is a job. The advancement of the nation's foreign policies is the product. Death is an unfortunate by-product like the smog that was the result of the automobile assembly line.

John T. Watts—and thousands of young men like him—could not bring themselves to view the situation in the same manner as the general.

Out of the Navy, Watts rejoined the First United Methodist Church of Glendale in the hope of clarifying his "idea of God" and "because I wanted to be part of an organization which had social concerns." He found the church wanting. "It has got a budget of $300,000," he said. "The money going to health and welfare is $100 and the money to social concerns is $125. But they pay a music director $8,500 a year. It's a case of mistaken priorities."

Unlike Westmoreland, Watts had lost sleep over Vietnam, and now he was losing sleep over concerns in civilian society as well.

By then, Watts, who had earlier dropped college preparatory courses in high school to take shop work as better education for the Navy, had enrolled as a liberal arts major in Glendale Community College. In his own time, he relaxed in his apartment, surrounded by maps, prints, a portrait of Sitting Bull, and a poster of overripe color and wording with the message:

> Love is above all
> The gift of oneself.

He had drawn up his own reading list and was plowing through Paul Tillich, Eric Bonhoffer, Aldous Huxley, Henry David Thoreau and George Orwell.

Slouching in an easy chair, his long hair and beard framing his thin face, some newly purchased hiking equipment behind him, he said, "The notion of Tillich's that God is the depth of our experience intrigues me."

John Watts's experience in the Navy had been defeating. True, he had returned to Glendale alive while 55,000 other Americans had died; his body was whole where tens of thousands of others were maimed, scarred, disfigured or otherwise punished by the war. But the damage to his psyche left him one of the casualties of the war and of the military experience in modern-day America. His values had been challenged, and they did not stand up to examination. Neither did those of society.

As the summer of 1972 approached, he was seeking a brakeman's job on the Santa Fe Railroad. He could expect no special treatment because he was a veteran. In fact, his veteran's status might be held against him. In April 1972, the unemployment rate for what the Bureau of Labor Statistics calls "Vietnam Era Veterans" in the twenty- to twenty-four-year-old category was 12.7 percent, well over two times the national average of 5.9 percent. That statistic was an indication of the lack of obligation civilian society felt to continue support for the machine. Americans traditionally showed their appreciation for defense efforts by welcoming returning fighting men generously after previous wars. The absence of generosity toward Vietnam veterans was a symptom of the nation's failure to support the war. Failure to support the war soon became a reluctance to support the military machine that waged it. The machine faced defeat at home.

John T. Watts, former radarman second class, now a college dropout collecting unemployment, was caught up in that defeat along with thousands of others. What were the forces playing on them?

The forces that brought about the defeat of the American military machine did not grow out of the Vietnam War. The Vietnam War was a symptom of the defeat or, perhaps, a result, but not a cause. Rather, the causes of the defeat originated in the dramatic growth of the machine beginning after World War II. The growth alone resulted in a new impersonality that motivated men to take a greater than usual interest in themselves. Officers coming from a tradition that taught, with justifiable pride, the virtues of duty-honor-country now found themselves caught up in a system whose new trinity was me-myself-and-I.

Military leaders became so engrossed with their own career progress and with nurturing the seductive growth of the machine that they never realized what was happening in the enlisted ranks. The enlisted men were exploited. The nation was militarized on their backs. As a result, social grievances festered unchecked.

All this could only occur because of a conscious deception practiced at every level in the chain of command. Deception was tolerated and, at times, even demanded. There was deception between enlisted men and their noncommissioned officers, between NCOs and junior officers, between junior officers and their seniors, between senior officers and generals, between generals and the civilian leadership of the Defense Department, between the Defense Department and the rest of the executive branch of government, between the executive branch and Congress, between the government and the people. The situation grew so intolerable that, ultimately, nobody—or so it seemed—believed anyone else. And without trust, the military machine, like any other huge bureaucracy, could not function effectively.

Careerism among the officers bred a generation of yes men. Failure to show proper concern for enlisted men led to a generation of exploited men. The lying that prevaded the military machine resulted in a generation of deception. All this, interacting, brought about the defeat of the American military machine.

PART TWO

A GENERATION OF YES MEN

A Defense Department news release of May 14, 1970, read as follows:

FOR CORRESPONDENTS: *May 14, 1970*   *No. 406-70*

The Medal of Honor was presented today to Captain Paul W. Bucha, United States Army, by President Richard Nixon, in the name of Congress, in ceremonies at the White House.

The citation that followed told the story of the three-day exploit as commander of Company D, 3d Battalion (Airborne), 187th Infantry, 3d Brigade, 101st Airborne Division, that brought Bucha to the White House. On March 16, 1968, the eighty-nine officers and men of Delta Company were inserted by helicopters into a suspected enemy stronghold area near Phuoc Vinh in South Vietnam's Binh Duong Province. They had been in Vietnam for four months and, though the enemy's Tet offensive had already run its course, they had not yet suffered a single casualty. For two days the company moved through the area, destroying enemy fortifications and base areas, eliminating scattered resistance as it moved. On March 18, Delta's lead element ran into an enemy force estimated at battalion size. The men were pinned down by fire from heavy automatic weapons, machine guns, small arms, rocket-propelled grenades and Claymore mines. Bucha, with complete disregard for his safety, moved into the attacked area to direct the defense and place reinforcements. He crawled outside the company perimeter, through a hail of enemy fire, to single-handedly destroy a machine-gun bunker with grenades, receiving a painful shrapnel wound in the process. Returning to the perimeter, he saw that Delta Company could not hold its position. He ordered a withdrawal to a better position from which he could direct artillery fire on the charging enemy. When one of his elements, retrieving casualties, was ambushed and cut off from the rest

22

of the company, Bucha ordered them to feign death. Then he directed artillery fire around them. During the night of the 18th, Bucha moved among his men, distributing ammunition, providing encouragement and ensuring the strength of the defense. He also directed artillery, helicopter gunship and Air Force gunship fire on the enemy, throwing smoke grenades as markers. Using flashlights in complete view of enemy snipers, he directed the evacuation of three air-ambulance loads of seriously wounded men. At daybreak, he led a rescue party to recover the dead and wounded members of the ambushed element. Although the citation did not say so, Delta Company, which Bucha had formed and trained back at Fort Campbell, Kentucky, nine months before, suffered eight dead and fifty-four wounded.

"We went through that ordeal as a group," Bucha said later. "It was not only me, it was 'we' who did it."

The citation read before the gathering at the White House concluded:

During the period of intensive combat, Captain Bucha, by his extraordinary heroism, inspirational example, outstanding leadership and professional competence, led his company in the decimation of a superior enemy force which left one hundred and fifty-six dead on the battlefield. By his conspicuous gallantry at the risk of his own life in the highest traditions of the military service, Captain Bucha has reflected great credit on himself, his unit, and the United States Army.

In April 1972, two years after President Nixon snapped the wide blue ribbon holding the nation's highest award around Bud Bucha's neck, the young hero, then only twenty-eight years old, resigned from the service. After seven years on active duty, he had decided that the Army was not really for him. Between January 1971 and June 1972, thirty-two other West Point faculty and staff members, the elite of the Army's younger generation, resigned with him.

Bucha's was not an easy decision. He came from a military family. His father was a retired Army colonel, and Bucha had grown up on military posts in Germany, Japan and Indianapolis before his father retired and the family settled in St. Louis.

In 1961, Bucha received a Presidential appointment to West Point where he graduated four years later as a "distinguished cadet." He stood in the top three percent academically. During his senior year, he was captain of the swimming team (and an All-American), a regimental commander, and the first recipient of the Association of Graduates Award for "excellence in all areas of cadet endeavor."

After graduation, he attended the Stanford University Graduate School of Business, earning a master's degree in June 1967. During his summer recess, he went to Fort Benning, Georgia, to go through Ranger and airborne training. Qualification for those two patches on a uniform as a youngster are virtually mandatory if one has plans to become a general someday.

In the summer of 1967, he was assigned to the 101st Airborne Division, the famous Screaming Eagles that General William C. Westmoreland himself had once commanded, at Fort Campbell, Kentucky. In the manpower crush of those years of the Vietnam War's escalation, he spent only two months as a platoon leader—a job in which a young lieutenant might expect to spend a year or more in peacetime—and was then elevated to create and command Delta Company.

Bucha built his new unit from scratch in much the same way the manager of a major-league baseball expansion team must operate.

"First there was me," he recalled four years later, "then an executive officer and then we got nine troops. Then nine more troops from the stockade and a sergeant and we started training. We were sort of a laughing stock. We looked like a large squad with four lieutenants for twenty men. But soon we filled up. We were given rejects from Fort Bragg and from Fort Campbell. We were sent fillers from the stockade. They sent us clerks and typists. We worked for four months and taught each other things. None of us had any experience. All the other company commanders in the battalion had already been to Vietnam once."

When the Screaming Eagles deployed to Vietnam in December 1967, Delta Company was on the roster. What it lacked in experience it made up for in spirit. Shortly after the action near Phuoc Vinh, Bucha was relieved of Delta Company's command. It was now time, under the Army's system, for some other young officer to be given command experience. Then, after service in a staff job, Bucha reutrned to Fort Knox, Kentucky, in December 1968 to attend a course in armor.

"Until that point, I had enjoyed every minute of my life," he said. "I never really had occasion to stop and reflect on anything. Then, when I entered the armor course, I discovered they were preparing me for Vietnam when I had already been there. I began reading every word

24

about the war in the Louisville Courier-Journal *and a dissatisfaction set in. I saw that we were making a mess of things."*

The dissatisfaction gnawed within Bud Bucha, and all the honors he received did nothing to ease the discomfort. In August 1969, he was assigned to West Point as an instructor in the Department of Social Sciences, a prestigious billet for a young officer: a tip-off that the Army had big things in mind for him. Later in the year, he was named a member of the Council on Foreign Relations in New York, giving him an entrée into the foreign-policy establishment. Then the Jaycees listed him as the youngest of their ten outstanding young men for 1970, among whom were White House Press Secretary Ronald Zeigler and rock-and-roll star Elvis Presley. The singer and the soldier became friendly, and Bucha still wears an Elvis Presley wrist watch under the sleeve of his Hong Kong-tailored suit.

Despite all the honors and the promise of an unusually successful career ahead, Bucha continued to feel an emptiness in his life. In the fall of 1971, he was approached by a group of upstate New York Republican Party leaders who asked him to consider running for Congress. That started him thinking about the possibility of a nonmilitary career, one in either the law or politics.

"If I stay," he said during that period of soul-searching, "it is important that I explore seriously that which I am turning down. It is important that each man in the Army first choose not to go into other things. It is important to understand he is accepting a life style and a profession rather than just a job.

"I have become impatient. I have a real desire to get involved and be in a position to influence events. I know that the opposite will happen in the Army, that advancement will be slower. I have no desire for a major's leaf or a general's star as such, but I do want the responsibility that comes with higher rank.

"I have been encouraged by the Army to be different, to be independent. Now I have become a victim of that.

"I think the goal of the United States Army should be to provide a service to society. It's a body of highly trained, efficient and committed labor and skill available to do that which society wants it to do. We should use it for social good.

"Of course all this should be with the understanding that we will always be there first and foremost to provide for the national defense.

25

But if our primary mission can be fulfilled without doing our primary activity, let's do it. Let's help Mayor Lindsay lift all those abandoned vehicles off the streets of New York, for example; let's develop chemicals for peace and not war.

"We've got a body of labor that just isn't being used properly."

By April 5, 1972, Captain Paul W. Bucha, Medal of Honor winner, decided he had little chance of making his views prevail in today's defense establishment as an Army officer. He was the kind the Army needed to help guide the institution into the twenty-first century. By 1995 he would have been in line, by normal standards of career progression, to become Chief of Staff.

Instead he submitted his resignation after seven years of service.

"It was seven years of protesting things," he said, "of questioning those men who stressed a merely cosmetic performance."

2

THE STATIONS OF THE CROSS
AND THE NEEDLE'S EYE

Lieutenant General William R. Peers has seen it all. After graduating from the University of California at Los Angeles in 1937, he joined what was then known as the "Pineapple Army" as a second lieutenant and served in peacetime posts. By 1942, he was deeply involved in the exotic Office of Strategic Services operation in Burma and China, working under Brigadier General Joseph W. ("Vinegar Joe") Stilwell. At the end of World War II, he directed the liberation of Americans from Japanese prisoner-of-war camps, and he parachuted into Nanking at the head of a Chinese unit to occupy that city.

He has served in high-level, prestigious staff jobs at the Pentagon and in Europe. He worked in the innermost sanctums of the Joint Chiefs of Staff and at the platoon level in garrisons. He commanded a division and field force in Vietnam and also served a tour as special assistant to the Chief of Staff of the Army for special warfare activities, which is to say he had charge, in 1964, of all the Army's "dirty tricks" or covert activities.

As a thirty-two-year veteran, Lieutenant General Peers was the man the Army selected in 1969 to lead the investigation of the My Lai massacre. On March 15, 1970, when he turned in his now-famous report on the massacre, he also handed a little-known, top-secret memorandum to General William C. Westmoreland, the Army Chief of Staff, that shook the Chief as much, if not more, than the My Lai investigation itself.

The Peers Report on My Lai was subsequently well publicized. But the memo—even its existence—was never made public. The Army did not want the public to know that even it felt that the issues raised by the My Lai matter had far broader ramifications than the question of war crimes.

"The memo pointed out that on the basis of the more than four hundred interviews his commission had conducted with Army officers in investigating My Lai, Peers had come to the conclusion that there was something deeply and basically wrong with the moral and professional climate of the Army officer corps," Major General Franklin M. Davis, Jr., later noted.

"The memo," Davis continued, "shook Westy to the core."

That Peers, writing in 1970, should have produced a document about the state of the Army officer corps so perturbing to his boss was in itself an indication of the utter isolation in which most of the nation's top-ranking military officers were living as the decade of the seventies dawned.

The officer corps in each of the services had long since evolved into a stultified bureaucracy, rife with dissatisfaction, composed mainly of individuals motivated by little but the desire to climb the ladder within the chain of command, forgetful of their responsibilities to their troops, fearful at each level of incurring wrath from above by passing up bad news.

A drug problem was growing within the services. The generals of the Army, Air Force and Marine Corps, and the admirals of the Navy would take few steps to deal with it until a year after the Peers Report when it burst into the public consciousness through the press. Similarly, an incipient race problem was written off as the doings of dissatisfied blacks bringing their yearnings from civilian society into uniform. Antiwar sentiment among enlisted men was viewed as troublemaking by a few radicals.

In hundreds of different kinds of jobs, officers were lying—lying to themselves about the honor of their profession, lying to their civilian masters about the capabilities of their services, lying to the public about the nature of their accomplishments.

For the most part, the officer corps had lapsed into a bureaucracy of "ticket punchers," men who scurried about frantically from one billet to another, filling up their personnel files with prestigious-looking assignments, buttering up their superiors so that they would get topnotch performance ratings, seeking commands not because they really wanted to lead troops in battle but because without such experience they could not go still higher up the ladder.

For the most part, they were honorable and moral men caught up in a dishonorable and immoral situation. The worst of them accepted their plight unthinkingly, not interested in the meaning of it all, approaching their jobs from the same career-oriented viewpoint as middle-level executives in private industry. The best of them recognized the trap that the system had sprung on them and looked for ways to extricate themselves—and the system—with honor. Some of the worst and some of the best were resigning, retiring or being released from duty as the services took advantage of the post-Vietnam force-level cutbacks to purge their ranks. But those cutbacks in themselves left the character of the system unchanged.

It could only change if the leaders of the services were willing to consider alternatives to the old ways of doing business. That was difficult. The leaders were, after all, products of the system. They had met it on its terms, mastered it, survived and climbed to the top. Therefore, it could not have been all bad. And so, in the spring of 1972, the leaders were still concerned with such superficialities as hair length and mustache styles when combat readiness was at a low point. They were concerned with what kinds of posters could be put on walls when barracks were crumbling. They were struggling to improve services at the PXs when thousands of service families were living below the poverty line. They were re-ordering boxes on the officer-efficiency report forms when the whole promotion system itself was, with exquisite insensitivity, elevating mediocrity to the top of the scale and frustrating the best intentions of those sensitive to the problems.

If the American Military Establishment, after Vietnam, was a defeated organization, the reasons for that defeat lay in the headquarters buildings of the troop units spread around the world; in the E-Ring of the Pentagon; on the bridges of the ships; at Pearl Harbor, Heidelberg, Seoul, Okinawa, Naples and all the other top-level headquarters areas. The troops may have participated in the defeat, but they did not perpetrate it. The civilian masters of the military—in a system where the military has always been subordinate to civilian authority—may have preordained the defeat with unwise policies, but it was the officer corps which promised the wherewithal to accomplish the task and which promised results. As the military professionals, who should have known better, they presided over the defeat.

In 1959, a philosopher and World War II veteran by the name of J. Glenn Gray, after reflecting on his military experiences for thirteen years, put his finger on the problem that is basic to the officer corps today. Gray wrote:

> Not at all certain whether they will later be considered by their own people as heroes or as scoundrels, great numbers find it simpler to ignore the moral problems by thinking of them as little as possible. Better to let the conscience sleep, to do as the others are doing and as one is told to do, and the future will bring what it will. Who knows what the future will bring anyway? Most soldiers in wartime feel caught in the present so completely that they surrender their wills to their superiors and exist in the comforting anonymity of the crowd.[1]

That comforting anonymity survived World War II and lay, like a security blanket, over the officer corps throughout the Cold War, throughout the Korean War and the Vietnam War as well. There were attempts underway to shake it off in the 1970s, but whether they would succeed was uncertain. History was not on the side of quick reform. After World War II, complaints about the military establishment similar to those heard today were voiced, and the Army impaneled the Doolittle Board, named after its chairman, Lieutenant General James H. ("Jimmy") Doolittle, to look into relationships between officers and enlisted men.

The Doolittle Board recommended a number of reforms that were never enacted. It urged better selection and training of officers, proper assignments, promotion on the basis of merit, a more effective internal policing system to prevent abuses of privilege, steps to break down the caste system and the chasm between officers and enlisted men, equality of pay, stricter punishment for dereliction of duty for men of higher rank than lower rank, and the elimination of the terms "officer" and "enlisted man."[2]

There is a tendency within the officer corps of each of the services to write off today's problems within the military by saying they have not changed since the establishment of armies. We have antiwar demonstrations today? Look at the Civil War draft riots in New York, they say. We have a moral and discipline breakdown in the services today? Remember the Doolittle Report of 1946, they answer. Prostitution is running rampant in and near the United States' garrisons overseas? Julius Caesar had the same problem with his Roman legions, they point out. Soldiers will be soldiers. The failure to cope in the past becomes the rationale for refusing to cope in the present.

That argument might have had some validity in past years. But today's American military machine is far greater than any previous fighting force ever assembled, in terms of destructive capacity; its demands on the society it protects are much greater than they have ever been in peacetime. For these reasons, problems within the military machine cannot be regarded as isolated situations of little concern to the rest of society. And neither can they be regarded as untreatable situations that are endemic to all military organizations throughout the ages. The problems affect not only the relatively small number of men living in military isolation, but they spill over into civilian society. Failure to even consider the problems, much less find solutions, has affected the nation's foreign policy in the past quarter century. Needless deaths have been suffered by Americans as well as foreign friends and enemies. At home, the new militarism contributed to the shredding of the fabric of civilian society in the 1960s.

Too many military professionals today took upon the machine's problems as age-old conditions only magnified by the Vietnam War. Now that the war has ended, they think, the machine will cure itself without making deep reforms. Dissent from this viewpoint is treated with distrust within the system when it is tolerated at all. When the dissent grows too vocal and becomes noticed outside the military, the dissenters find themselves in deep trouble with their superiors within the system. Consider the case of the man who was known as the Army's most decorated soldier.

The street was on the fringe of Washington's DuPont Circle area, the capital's little hippie kingdom. The building was a nondescript white brick and glass high rise containing dozens of overpriced furnished apartments inhabited by transients looking for some after-hours solace to relieve the frustrations of their tangle with the federal bureaucracy. The lobby was decorated with plastic shrubbery, ersatz antique mirrors and heavy-duty Spanish provincial furniture, made specially for the hotel trade in North Carolina. The name on the mailbox for apartment 6E read "Omar Khayyam."

"Just disregard the name," Colonel David H. Hackworth, USA (retired), said over the phone. "That's our apartment. Bring your wife along. We've got a lot of odds and ends of booze to drink up. We're leaving in two days for Spain. We're going to spend a year there, and then Jennifer and I are going to settle in Australia. I don't know what I'm going to do. Probably go into business of some sort."

Hackworth, at forty, had just a few days before completing twenty-five years in the United States Army—he enlisted at fifteen after lying about his age—and had retired.

He was, at the time of his retirement, on everybody's list to become a general. He was known as the most-decorated soldier in the United States Army, and yet the end of his career—the last seventy-seven days—had been spent virtually in hiding, livng behind the door marked Omar Khayyam, first dodging the Army and then waiting to see if the Army was going to prosecute him. According to Hackworth, he had picked up indications through the grapevine that the Army was looking into the possibilities that he had misappropriated funds, had stolen government property, had run a house of prostitution on his base in the Delta region of South Vietnam, and was practicing adultery.

It was an unlikely place to interview one of the nation's real war heroes, that sterile high rise. And it was under unlikely circumstances.

Dave Hackworth is the stuff patriotic movie scenarios were made of in bygone years. And the final scene should have been Hackworth, the chest of his dark-green tunic ablaze with all his medals, retiring before a guard of honor at some garrison, smiling stiffly at the pomp, taking a final salute, and then meeting the press to pay one last tribute to the Army to which he had given so much and which had honored him in return.

Hackworth did go out with one of those final press interviews, but in it he paid no encomiums to his Army. On a nationwide television program, he noted that three years before he had been asked by General William C. Westmoreland to critique the Army's performance in Vietnam, and he had found it grossly lacking. The interviewer then asked if in the three years there had been any improvement.

"No, I don't think so," Hackworth said in the valedictory, continuing: ". . . There have been no viable reforms. . . . The corruption that exists in Vietnam, the graft, the failure to produce continues to exist. . . . The military has not established any strategic goals, nor had there been any tactical concepts developed to support the strategic goals which were not developed and announced.

". . . We sent an Army to Vietnam that was not prepared to fight the war. We sent an Army that was top-heavy in administrators and logisticians and . . . fighters not trained for the war. . . . We didn't understand the nature of the war in the military. . . . Just everything we had done in Vietnam had been done wrong."

Those words were aired on the ABC television network on Sunday afternoon, June 27, 1971, throughout the United States. The next morning, a team of Army Criminal Investigative Division men descended on his headquarters at Cao Lanh near the Cambodian border and began searching his records.

David Hackworth's was neither a typical life nor a typical military career. Born in 1930, he was orphaned at the age of one and grew up in institutions, foster homes or, for a time, under the care of a grandmother. At the age of thirteen he joined the merchant marine, and during the height of World War II, he sailed the Pacific. At fifteen, he lied his way into the Army, serving a tour in Italy in 1946. By 1950, he had risen to sergeant and was sent to Korea with a reconnaissance unit after war broke out there. Lusting for action, he went AWOL from his unit, joined an infantry battalion, and three months later, he was awarded a battlefield promotion to lieutenant. Between February and November, 1951, he was wounded four times, taking a bullet wound in the skull; grenade fragments in the face, chest and hands; shrapnel in the back and, finally, in the last incident, bullet and grenade fragments in his left arm, chest and face.

He came out of the war a most highly regarded soldier indeed.

During the Cold War peacetime years of the 1950s, the Army sent him to school in California and then seasoned him with a company command and staff work. In 1959, he was assigned to Germany, where he was officer-in-charge of a VIP bureau at Seventh Army headquarters. He spent his time escorting important visitors around Europe, impressing them by his very presence with the best of the Army. When the Communists constructed the Berlin Wall in 1961 and President John F.

Kennedy reacted by reinforcing the Berlin garrison, Hackworth led the spearhead company of reinforcements into the West Berlin enclave, and the unit received commendations for its performance from officials ranging from JFK down.

In the early 1960s, he finished his schooling, earning a B.S. degree and attending all the service schools necessary to keep a promising career in good standing. In May 1965, he shipped out to Vietnam with the 1st Brigade of the 101st Division. He spent the year in battalion- and brigade-level posts and then, still only a major in May 1966, he was awarded a battalion command, a job every infantry officer covets. Usually, those positions are given to lieutenant colonels. He kept the battalion command only two months, after which, in a pattern of personnel turnovers that plagued the Army, he was transferred to a staff job in Washington for only two months. Then he was returned to Vietnam to train selected officers in how to conduct after-action interviews.

By now, he was virtually a trans-Pacific commuter. In March 1967, he returned to the United States to coauthor with Brigadier General S. L. A. Marshall a book for the Army named *The Vietnam Primer*.

In early 1969, Hackworth made his third trip to Vietnam, once again as a battalion commander. He was wounded once a month for the next four months by enemy bullets and shrapnel, establishing himself as a most unusual battalion commander. Most of his colleagues remained literally above the battle, exercising their commands from helicopters hovering in immunity above the fighting. In June, he said, at the express order of General Creighton Abrams, Jr., the American commander in South Vietnam, Hackworth was removed from his command because of all the wounds. He served the next six months as operations adviser to the South Vietnamese Army in the II Corps area, and then, his one-year tour ended, he volunteered to spend another six months as a deputy senior adviser to a South Vietnamese airborne division.

By this time, he had become a living legend, known not only to newsmen but throughout the Army as the most articulate, seasoned field-grade expert extant on the Vietnam War. He was the complete commander. He spoke his mind. People listened. He had a glorious future.

Three times he was ordered back to the United States to attend the Army War College, a one-year course any officer must attend (save for chaplains, staff judge advocates and doctors) before he can become a general. Twice he refused out of an urge to remain where the action

34

was. From 1970 to 1971, he served as senior adviser to the Vietnamese 44th Special Tactical Zone, a composite organization made up of American and Vietnamese special forces and Vietnamese Rangers. He was advising 44,000 Vietnamese troops.

By July 1971, the breast of his dress jacket was ablaze with color: ribbons representing two Distinguished Service Crosses, nine Silver Stars, four Legions of Merit, eight Bronze Stars, eight Purple Hearts; four Army Commendation Medals, four Vietnam Crosses of Gallantry, a Distinguished Flying Cross, about forty Air Medals (some for valor) and, as Hackworth himself once put it, "a bunch of Vietnamese good-fellow awards."

But by July 1971, he had also had his fill. He grew too outspoken, went before the television cameras and realized his career was at an end. He refused, for the third time, the orders to War College. He retired instead.

Dave Hackworth's biography did not exactly jibe with the assessment current in the Army's hierarchy at the time. Once a hero so highly regarded that he was trotted out to impress VIPs, Hackworth, since his apostasy, was privately denigrated in extreme terms. Shortly before I went to Hackworth's apartment for an interview, one general told me, "Hackworth is a complete bum."

He then leveled a series of charges. They were not proven. They were never even brought except in the whispering campaign to try to discredit Hackworth.

This is not to say that the Army did not try to bring the charges. Hackworth was on terminal leave in the United States when he heard the investigation at Cao Lanh was underway. The rumor mill produced information that he would be ordered back to Vietnam to face charges and that his retirement would be held up.

"Dave's first impulse was to go underground. After all, he was trained in counterinsurgency," a friend said. "He had the idea that he could skip around the country, staying one step ahead of the process server and then show up at Fort Lewis on September 30 and say, 'Well, here I am reporting for retirement,' pick up his papers and leave."

Cooler heads prevailed. Hackworth retained Joseph Califano, a Washington lawyer not unfamiliar with the workings of the Pentagon—

he had been the Defense Department's general counsel and President Lyndon B. Johnson's chief domestic aide—who advised the colonel to turn himself in and to find out what was going on.

Hackworth called the Pentagon and was ordered to report immediately to Fort McNair in Washington where he was to turn in all his personal gear in preparation for return to Vietnam. Califano, learning this, called the Army's general counsel and demanded that Hackworth be kept in Washington, near his lawyer. "If there are going to be any charges in Vietnam, I will be happy to go out there to defend my client," Califano told the government.

The threat loomed of still another embarrassment to the Army in the wake of My Lai, the PX scandals, the drug crisis, the morale and discipline breakdown, the "fragging" or attempted murder of superiors by disaffected enlisted men, and the rupture in race relations. The Army relented and assigned Hackworth to Fort Meade, Maryland, which during the wind-down of the Vietnam War had become a holding area for an assortment of men giving the Army problems—deserters, drug users, race agitators, conscientious objectors and men accused of carrying out war crimes or covering them up.

The Army's handling of the Hackworth matter is indicative of an institutional paranoia that had set in. At one point, Califano had to extract from Army lawyers a promise that Hackworth's phone would no longer be tapped. The day that Hackworth was ordered back to Vietnam, the officer who served the order remained in the motel lobby to monitor Hackworth's movements. The colonel spotted him, went to a pay phone, called the motel operator and said, "This is Colonel _____ speaking. Is my man still there monitoring Colonel Hackworth's phone calls?"

"Oh, no, sir, he's not monitoring the calls, he's only getting a list of them."

"Thank you very much," Hackworth replied.

When Hackworth's retirement day rolled around, the Army discharged him honorably, bringing no charges. But the general who had denounced him to me hinted darkly that civil action might be taken against the erstwhile hero. The general's attitude left one matter unclear. If his assessment of Hackworth's activities and character was correct, how did it happen that Hackworth was elevated to such high positions? And why, before he turned sour on the Army, were his superiors pressing him to go even higher up the ladder? Where other officers were clamoring to receive an important assignment to the War College, Hackworth three times spurned the opportunity despite the Army's urgings.

Two conclusions can be drawn: (1) Hackworth was a far better soldier than the Army made him out to be at the parting, or, (2) despite all the rhetoric to the contrary, the military establishment was willing to put up with any possible character defects as long as men such as Hackworth continued to perform as the system demanded.

When he retired, Dave Hackworth still had a boyish look and a boyish enthusiasm about him that gave him the aura of, if not a boy scout, at least a scoutmaster. His grin was wide, quick and genuine. His voice was soft and well modulated. His face was round and handsome. His hair was neat but verging on the modish.

The military grapevine is an awesome device and the careerists who hang on it keep close tabs on their competitors. Mention the name of a "hard charger"—say, a bright young lieutenant colonel on the Pentagon staff—to a remote base commander in Korea, and the colonel will say, "Oh, yes, I know him. He's going to go all the way. He'll be a general." Similarly, a battalion commander in Germany will offer a comment on the prospects of a division staff member in Korea, and everyone knew who had the key positions in Vietnam during the height of the war.

Thus, mention Hackworth's name anywhere in the Army to a professional officer in midcareer, and the officer would shoot back, "Dave Hackworth. Sure, I know him. He's going to be a general."

Instead, at the end, he had to take refuge behind the door marked Omar Khayyam. In a few days, he would leave his homeland to go first to Spain to write a book and then to Australia to take up permanent residence. When last heard from in January 1973, he was a waiter in an Australian Gold Coast resort known as Surfer's Paradise. "I'm here," he said, "because I like peace."

It would be easy to describe Hackworth as bitter. But it would be inaccurate. His had been a twenty-year love affair with the Army, and like many a thoughtful rejected lover, he was trying hard to understand, trying desperately to look at the cause for the breakdown within himself. But try as he might, it was the Army that had let him down. He could reach no other conclusion.

"If they called you up tomorrow and said 'Come on back and be Chief of Staff,' what would you do with the Army?" I asked.

Laughing, he answered, "Well, I think the best thing for the United States Army right now is probably to disband and start all over again. It's just a real sick organization, and it's sick because, in my judgment, the people who are running it—that would be the three-star generals and above—are inadequate. I'm talking now about Westmoreland and all his cronies. His cronies are in every key slot.

"I think I'd just start at the three-star level. Not categorically all three-star heads would roll, but I'd say 99 percent of them. There are a few good three-stars around, I suppose, but I just didn't meet any of them. I think one of the things there—it's a fundamental thing—is that the people who are all three-stars now started out in the Army between 1936 and 1940. Westmoreland graduated from the Military Academy in '36; Abrams is '36, I believe. O.K. World War II broke out, and they spent a year as first lieutenant. Suddenly they got a company to command. They had maybe two and a half years of service and they were lieutenant colonels. The war ended and young Westmoreland, who was not yet thirty, was a bird colonel [a full colonel]. His present cronies were then twenty-three- and twenty-four-old battalion commanders.

"Well, in 1945 came the great emphasis on management, and so a lot of them dashed off, got their highfaluting degrees in systems analysis and all the rest of it, how to run an Army by computer, by the proven modern management systems that businesses use, which is devoid of the human being.

"But the Army runs on human beings. Leonidas, at Thermopylae, with 300 guys lopped off the heads of something like 10,000 Persians.* There was no systems analysis there. There was motivation and leadership and dedication. A small group of guys, in my judgment, can win. And I think that all these great systems which the Army has used, right down to the efficiency report and all the rest of it, has just got to damn them and it will damn them.

"It has produced a group of very, very shallow yes men."

When Hackworth gets going on the Army, conversation turns to monologue—names, dates, places and anecdotes—as a career is relived. Personal experiences provide examples.

---

* History is vague on just how many Persian casualties the forces of the King of Sparta did inflict in that famous 480 B.C. battle, but the Greeks did fight to the last man for three days before the superior manpower of the Persians overwhelmed them.

"Am I going too fast?" he asks. And though he is, his listeners, engrossed in the performance, urge him on.

Now the monologue turns to a discussion of how the United States military has always relied on superior firepower and supplies to wear down an enemy: "We have tried to win wars by the magic outflow of our assembly lines, not through tactical skill or our ability. You can even go back past World War I, go back to the Civil War. We didn't win the Civil War by any great skill on the part of Grant and all of his flunkies. We won it just because we could out-produce and out-assemble and put more people in blue and march them down the road and keep them supplied.

"In a word: logistics.

"And that's the thing we found to be so humiliating in Vietnam—our great assembly line did not help us one bit. All of our technology and so on didn't help us defeat a scroungy little country of eighteen million people that were fighting for an ideal, a country they believe in. They were highly motivated, really dedicated people.

"I remember a German lieutenant captured at Salerno who I was guarding in 1946 at a prisoner-of-war camp. He was a real tough-looking kraut and I was a young punk, a pimply-faced kid. He could speak perfect English, and I was riding him. I said, 'Well, if you're so tough, if you're all supermen, how come you're here captured and I'm guarding you?'

"And he looked at me and said, 'Well, it's like this. I was on this hill as a battery commander with six 88-millimeter antitank guns, and the Americans kept sending tanks down this road. We kept knocking them out. Every time they sent a tank, we knocked it out.

" 'Finally, we ran out of ammunition and the Americans didn't run out of tanks.'

"And that's it in a nutshell."

Hackworth's is a very personal analysis, of course. But there is a growing body of data to document his beliefs. Retired Army Colonel Trevor N. DuPuy, a military historian now working with the Historical Evaluation and Research Corporation near Washington, for the past several years has been attempting to marry the art of the military historian and the science of the systems analyst, which Defense Secretary Robert S. McNamara introduced to the Pentagon with such a vengeance in the

1960s. In a sentence, DuPuy has developed mathematical formulae and has programmed a computer to study World War II battles in the hope of discovering just how well the United States Army really performed.

A study of the Italian campaign of 1943 and 1944 does not offer much comfort to the United States and Air Force officer corps. DuPuy's studies show that the American and British successes in Italy had nothing at all to do with superior generalship or a better strategy. Superior firepower made the difference. Dupuy's studies completely back up the conclusion of that officer young Hackworth guarded.

DuPuy's formulae were set up to measure the "effectiveness" of six German divisions that took part in sixty selected battles on the Italian boot against five American and three British divisions. After all the computer runs were completed, DuPuy said that only one of the American divisions was as effective as any of the German divisions. Here are the figures:[3]

TENTATIVE ESTIMATES AVERAGE DIVISION COMBAT EFFECTIVENESS ITALY, 1943–1944

Allied Divisions	%	German Divisions	%
88th Infantry (US)	86.18	3d Panzer Grenadier	94.81
3d Infantry (US)	82.65	65th Infantry	93.60
1st Infantry (Br)	76.91	Hermann Goering Panzer	89.72
34th Infantry (US)	76.91	15th Panzer Grenadier	87.50
46th Infantry (Br)	76.40	16th Panzer	86.94
85th Infantry (US)	76.01	94th Infantry	85.28
45th Infantry (US)	72.70		
56th Infantry (Br)	64.82		

For comparison's sake Colonel DuPuy arbitrarily assumed a 90 percent average efficiency rating for the German divisions, but he did not assume that the German divisions were better than the Allied. If, for example, he had assumed an average 50 percent efficiency rating for the German divisions, the Allied divisions, with the exception of the 88th, still would have fallen below the ratings for the Germans.

One wonders what Colonel DuPuy's analytical techniques will show about American performance in Southeast Asia if they are ever used by future historians. Among other conclusions that can be drawn from

DuPuy's analysis is that without superior firepower, the American officer is not the equal of his counterparts in other armies.

If Colonel DuPuy's mathematics and Colonel Hackworth's observations are correct, then the officer corps of the United States military establishment has not been doing its job well at all, not only in the Vietnam War, but dating back to World War II. How did the leaders of what has always been thought to be the most powerful fighting machine ever assembled come to such a state? There are many different views. But they all boil down to a simple proposition.

The leaders of the armed services these days—and those aspiring to leadership—have been far too "careerist" and not all "professional" as they grasp their way up the ladder the military calls "the chain of command."

Marine Corps General David M. Shoup, who rose to the top of the ladder—commandant of the Corps and member of the Joint Chiefs of Staff before retiring in 1963—is the most stunning critic of careerism. In the April 1969 issue of *The Atlantic Monthly,* Shoup, writing on "The New American Militarism," said:

> . . . Military professionals cannot measure the success of their individual efforts in terms of personal financial gain. The armed forces are not profit-making organizations, and the rewards for excellence in the military profession are required in less tangible forms. Thus it is that promotion and the responsibilities of higher command, with the related fringe benefits of quarters, servants, privileges, and prestige, motivate most career officers. Promotions and awards also frequently result from heroic and distinguished performance in combat, and it takes a war to make a military hero. Civilians can scarcely understand or even believe that many ambitious military professionals truly yearn for wars and the opportunities for glory and distinction afforded only in combat. A career of peacetime duty is a dull and frustrating prospect for the normal regular officer to contemplate.

Scholars such as Morris Janowitz in *The Professional Soldier* and Samuel P. Huntington in *The Soldier and the State* have devoted a large part of their careers to trying to define worthy professionalism as opposed to unsavory careerism, and their abstract definitions leave something to be desired for the working warrior. The pages of the military journals are replete with long, soul-searching analyses of the problem. Young military men, like any other group of concerned, achievement-oriented idealists, spend much of their time wondering, What am I doing here?

But when all the moralizing is stripped away, the essence of careerism, the fuel on which much, if not most, of the uniformed officer corps operates today, is easy to describe.*

"Careerism" means placing one's own goals ahead of those which are best for the organization. It means conniving to be at the right place at the right time to further one's own future rather than sticking at a job which the organization needs to have done for its good. It means comforting a superior with good news even when poor conditions require a more brutally frank report. It means paying attention to superficialities rather than to problems with deep-rooted origins.

Gilbert and Sullivan captured the essence of careerism in one line of *H.M.S. Pinafore:* "I polished up that handle so carefully that now I am the ruler of the Queen's Navee!"

Not every young officer wants to be a careerist. Some, like Hackworth, rebel and find themselves used up. Others fight the system from within and suffer for it. Still others resign early. And others still play the game and suffer silently.

I encountered one such silent sufferer in Korea at Camp Casey, the headquarters of the 2d Infantry Division. He was tall, handsome and very alert. He was a young officer on the staff of the division commander, and when I encountered him, he was waiting with his fellow staff members in the commanding general's outer office. The daily staff meeting was to begin in a moment.

"Oh, I'd like very much to sit down and talk with you about your project," the major said. "I've been doing a lot of thinking and have some ideas on what needs to be done to the Army."

Time did not allow us to get together, but he agreed to write to me.

---

* When criticized for their careerist attitudes, many military men offer the same rejoinder: "Things are just the same in private industry, so why take us to task?" Though that argument may hold some truth, the fact remains that industry does have measures of success that are absent in the military. Salesmen and production experts have quotas to meet; executives must achieve profit goals. On the other hand, in the military, particularly in peacetime, measures of success are far more subjective. Thus the military career man is far more susceptible to toadyism than his counterpart in private industry.

By the time I left Camp Casey an hour and a half later, the young major had written out his thoughts and had passed them along to my escort in a sealed envelope. He wrote:

THOUGHTS ON THE ARMY OFFICER CORPS

An army officer must be a well-rounded personality with:

1. Human understanding to cope with the problems of his men.
2. A high degree of physical fitness.
3. Well-maintained family relationships.
4. A broad understanding of national and international politi-, cal considerations affecting the employment of the military to achieve national objectives.
5. The ability to express himself clearly and concisely orally and in writing.
6. The motivation to pursue not only the specialized requirements of his particular assignment but also a greater understanding of the civilian community and how its problems and aspirations affect the military.
7. [An understanding of] the role any institution receiving the majority of the national budget has on a society such as ours.

At present the Army Officer Corps has not achieved these goals.

At the upper echelon there are those who understand these requirements and are attempting to achieve them through the VOLAR [Volunteer Army Program]. Although I cannot agree with the entire program I recognize that it is a start to recognize individual dignity and develop a professional army, one that trains instead of raking leaves or cutting grass.

At the troop unit level, however, we are still suffering from those middle and senior grade officers who sincerely believe that loyalty, not ability, should be the sole criterion for advancement.

These individuals work their subordinates unbelievable hours on projects which have immediate and highly visible results, but which contribute little to long-term improvement. In other words, because they will occupy these positions of authority for only a short time they are compelled by a driv-

43

ing personal ambition to demonstrate immediate results to their superiors. To the loyal subordinate who works the long hours required on such projects, neglecting true improvement and the broadening of his horizons beyond his own narrow military specialty, go the rewards. It is my sincere hope to be in this Army long enough to achieve a position of authority which will allow to me a voice in the correction of our inadequacy. For this reason I request my identity remain undisclosed, but please feel free to make any use of these thoughts you consider necessary.

The major's numbered points are concise statements of the ideals by which all officers should live. His criticisms depict the reality within the officer corps at present.

The ideal is an officer corps devoted to selfless service to country. The reality is an officer corps composed of men mostly scheming to get ahead.

The ideal is leaders spending every working hour at the job of keeping their men happy, well motivated, in good condition and highly trained. The reality is a preoccupation with appearances—superficialities such as the length of one's hair, the shine on one's shoes, the nature of posters on the walls in the barracks, the height of the grass on the battalion parade grounds.

The ideal is a leader in such close rapport with his troops that their grievances quickly reach him through the chain of command. The reality is a situation in which troops grouse and gripe about major and minor problems while their leaders think all is well with the world or at least getting better.

The ideal is the issuance of an unequivocal command carried out with dispatch. The reality is the issuance of such a command and the discovery much later by the commander that his men never received the order.

The ideal is an atmosphere in which subordinates can voice vigorous disagreement with their superiors over policies and prospective orders (in other than combat situations) and not have their loyalty impugned. The reality is a system so rigid that anyone who voices such disagreement runs the risk of a less than outstanding efficiency report, which is enough to stifle a career.

Most importantly, the ideal is the establishment of a system in which officers are kept in jobs which they do best and promoted along lines to keep them in related tasks. Most seriously, the reality is a belief that every officer should be a generalist and that only those with combat experience or experience as troop leaders can advance to the highest ranks in the services.* This final reality is the key to the ticket-punching problem.

Much has been written about the ticket punching in the officer corps since the height of the Vietnam War. At that time, each officer assigned to Vietnam in the combat arms actually served not one tour of one year's duration but two tours of six months each. One of those tours was in a combat job, leading men in battle, and the other was in a staff job, helping to plan and direct or administer the operations.

Dr. Morton H. Halperin, one of the Whiz Kids in Robert S. Mc-Namara's Defense Department and later one of the earliest members of Henry A. Kissinger's national security staff in the White House, once said, "One of the reasons the Army fought the war the way it did in Vietnam was to give as many officers as possible some combat experience."

Former Lieutenant Colonel Edward L. King, a regular Army officer who retired after twenty years of service because of his "opposition to the unnecessary, poorly commanded, no-win war in Vietnam," described the debilitating effects of ticket punching on combat units this way: †

* The Navy has taken the lead in this regard with the establishment of a few specialities for officers in which they can advance from ensign to admiral as specialists in, for example, public relations and intelligence; but generally, even in that service, if you want to be an admiral you must first drive ships or airplanes.

† King enlisted in the Army in 1946, fought in Korea in response to President Truman's call for volunteers in 1950, won a competitive direct commission in the regular Army, served for three years on the staff of the Joint Chiefs of Staff and was working as a Joint Chiefs-Defense Department representative on a National Security Council study group at the time of his retirement. He had received orders to Vietnam and did not want to go for reasons stated in the text. Once cited by a commanding officer for "the highest standards of professional competence, enthusiasm and professional stature reflecting great credit on you and the Department of the Army," King, after voicing his beliefs, was removed from his Joint Chiefs job and ordered to take a psychiatric examination. The reason: "grave doubts as to his integrity." His case is evidence of an institutional schizophrenia within the armed services. On the same day that he took his mental test, he was ordered to appear at the Pentagon to receive the Presidential Legion of Merit "for exceptionally meritorious conduct in the performance of outstanding

45

There has . . . been hot competition for combat commands. In fact, there were fewer command slots than applicants, so it was decided to rotate command assignments. After only six months of combat command, officers were assigned to staff or advisory jobs. This enabled more officers to qualify for promotion by getting combat command time on their records. But it by no means provided the most effective leadership for combat units consisting of draftees. Many officers who volunteered for combat command had never commanded a unit, or had not done so for years. It is not possible for a combat commander to get to know his men, and also be fully oriented to local combat conditions in less than 30 or even 90 days. Nevertheless, the rotation system has moved commanders when they had barely learned their job, and replaced them with new, untried officers.

The men who have to serve in such units for one year bear the brunt of eager, green commanders, who "lead" them into battle by circling overhead in a helicopter, issuing profane commands. This system gets quite a few professional West Point officers promoted. It also gets more draftees killed than need be.

The two-star commander of the division that assaulted Hamburger Hill was on his second voluntary tour of duty in Vietnam. Officers who undertake extra tours may of course be motivated by patriotism and a desire to serve. But they also know, as did this new three-star lieutenant general, that one of the unwritten conditions for promotion to three-star Army rank is command of a division and preferably one in combat. And there are some who, to promote their own careers, would gladly continue a war that is corrupting and destroying the U.S. Army.[4]

Not all officers who agree with King's point of view are quitting the Army. Others are remaining in uniform and dedicating themselves to the task of urging reforms from within. They play the game, they get

---

services" while working for the Joint Chiefs. The Army later resolved its own conflict, releasing King "in the best interests of the service" and noting "a complete reversal of the previously highly rated attitude and motivation reflected during your career."

their tickets punched, and they live on the hope that when they have finally climbed the ladder and are in positions of authority, they will be able to change things. They recognize the reality. They yearn for the ideal.

Two such men are Lieutenant Colonel Zeb B. Bradford, a paratrooper, and Lieutenant Colonel William Cody, a field artilleryman. Both are West Pointers, Vietnam combat veterans and concerned, dedicated, patriotic officers. But they know just what the situation is and do not hide the facts.

BRADFORD: "If you want to get ahead in the Army, there are certain stations of the cross you must attain—six or seven of them after the service academy. You must get a company command, attend graduate school, get some combat experience, attend the command and general school at Fort Leavenworth, command a battalion, be selected for War College and serve on the Department of the Army staff or at a higher level."

It is a long and arduous pilgrimage, and only a few go the whole route.

CODY: "You get a battalion command by going to the Office of Personnel Operations at Fort McNair. You talk to the Jesuits there. You ask, 'What do I have to do to save my soul?' You say, 'I want a battalion. I will go anywhere.' Then you get some idea of where the battalions are open, and you look for friends at the general officers' level in the divisions. You call one up and tell him you would like a battalion, and you can get it if he requests you by name. It's a question of who you know."

Battalions are the basic maneuver element of the United States Army. A typical infantry battalion commander has some thirty-five officers and about eight hundred men in his command, divided into four companies (three fighting and one headquarters company), and an independent platoon or two for heavier weapons than the basic rifles carried by the grunts, antitank weapons or reconnaissance.

An ambitious, eager battalion commander is usually in his mid- or late thirties. Some are a little younger, some are a little older. Such is their prestige and power within the Army that they are known, sometimes affectionately, to their troopers as "the old man." An infantry battalion commander in Vietnam was one of those who got to circle overhead in a helicopter, barking the orders to his company commanders and platoon leaders on the ground, conferring with his operations officer, usually a young, ambitious major, through the aircraft's intercom, coming and going like the lord of a feudal manor. His fire base was his castle; the jungles, mountains or paddies, his estates; the young grunts, his minions.

Battalions are the last testing ground of the stations of the cross.

BRADFORD: "Once you get a battalion, you must get a good efficiency report. With one of those, the War College selection board will take a look at you. The board consists of seven or eight men, representing each branch of the service. A brigadeer general is in charge. The others are colonels. All lieutenant colonels are eligible who have the permanent rank of major. Selections must be made between the fifteenth and twentieth years of service.

"The sooner, the better. A man selected in, say, the nineteenth or twentieth year knows that he's only going to get hard assignments after that, and he hasn't got much chance of making general.

"A good estimate is that one in five War College graduates makes general, zero non-War College graduates make it."*

I asked the two what officers learn at War College.

CODY: "That's not important. You can string beans, peel potatoes or play tennis. The important thing is that you've been there."

After War College, the records of the graduates are segregated from those of the lieutenant colonels who have not matriculated. They are moved to a separate file cabinet at Fort McNair, and only that cabinet is consulted for the filling of certain jobs. A chief of staff is needed for one of the thirteen divisions in the Army, for example. That job is filled only from the War College file. Ditto, a division artillery commander, a brigade commander, a department head at West Point, a War College instructor or a division chief on the Department of the Army Staff in the Pentagon.

BRADFORD: "Without a War College diploma, you can't compete for stars. Your file is in the wrong cabinet. No matter how good you are, you can't make it. The problem with the system is that the War College experience comes too late. Such selection should be made earlier in an officer's career so that he can be better prepared for higher command."

CODY: (talking about conduct at the last of the stations of the cross): "Once you get assigned to a post–War College job, it doesn't

---

* The number is not quite zero. Of 519 generals in the Army in 1972, two had not attended War College.

pay to stay in it too long. You should get a good efficiency report and move on. If possible, you should get a job on the staff of General Bruce Palmer, who was United States Army commander in Vietnam [a subordinate to General William C. Westmoreland, who was overall commander] and is now vice chief of staff [having moved back to Washington with Westmoreland]. His guys seem to get their stars.

"Finally," Cody concluded, "the system has ground down all the rough edges. You have always been filing through the eye of a needle. All of the men are in good physical condition. They all have good teeth. They are all emotionally stable. They all wear their uniforms well. You get your star and then you wonder what it's all about."

Numbers give some idea of how much smaller the eye of that needle grows. In fiscal year 1971, the services commissioned 42,342 lieutenants and ensigns. In the same year, only 7,380 men were promoted by all four services to the rank of lieutenant colonel or its Navy equivalent, commander; only 2,681 made colonel (captain in the Navy); and, the needle eye now getting minuscule, 195 were awarded their first stars.*

Many an officer today, like Edward L. King, wonders how the service can retain an ideal of public service when the system is so corrupt. The stations of the cross, remember, are not traversed in a single pilgrimage lasting only a few weeks or months or even years. By the time a man steps forward to receive the first star, he is usually in his mid- or late forties and has been soldiering for twenty-five years. He has

---

* This table shows, by services, the intensity of competition for higher rank in the military:

PROMOTION TO SELECTED GRADES

Fiscal Year 1971

Lieutenant (Ensign)		Lieutenant Colonel (Commander)	Colonel (Captain)	Brigadier General (Rear Admiral)
Army	18,688	1,987	806	94
Air Force	11,800	3,610	1,107	54
Navy	9,795	1,636	603	38
Marines	2,059	147	138	9
Total	42,342	7,380	2,681	195

Table compiled from figures supplied by Defense Department Office of the Assistant Secretary of Defense for Public Affairs.

taken as much abuse as a raw recruit. He has stood ramrod-stiff and has kowtowed before his superiors. And he has forced his subordinates to do the same. He has lied and cheated a thousand times, usually in small ways, sometimes in very large ways, and has justified the means he used by the ends he achieved. He may have suffered an alcoholic wife and neurotic children. He has shuttled back and forth around the world, leaving roots nowhere.

One of the most poignant experiences one can imagine is to ask a field-grade Army officer where he's from and have him wince and pause and think and then say, "Well, just about everywhere. I was born in Walla Walla, Washington, but my home of record is Syracuse, New York. I taught ROTC there once, and there are good tax advantages for military men there."

It is not easy to fit through the eye of a needle over and over and over again.

3

"THE BEST OFFICER I HAVE EVER SEEN"

In the summer of 1970, Lieutenant Colonel Robert Leider, a member of the faculty of the National War College, grew concerned over the alarmingly high rate of resignations in the West Point class of 1966. Obligated to four years of military service in return for their education, 23.1 percent of the graduates who entered the Army turned in their resignations at the earliest opportunity.* Leider decided to try to find out why, in a carefully constructed survey of one hundred of the resigners. During the course of his research, he discovered a man identified in the study only as Captain X.

Less than a year after X graduated from West Point, he received his first assignment—that of a platoon leader in a tank battalion in Germany. This was during 1967 when the Vietnam War escalation was continuing rapidly and the Army in Germany was being used as a replacement depot for the Southeast Asian effort. X's immediate superior, his company commander, was another young lieutenant. Among his jobs was the completion of officer efficiency reports for his subordinates.

On two different occasions, he filled out ratings on X, stating that the West Pointer was "a very fine young lieutenant," an assessment that X thought was fair enough.

---

* By December 1971, that figure rose to 31.8 percent. Almost one out of three graduates had resigned five and a half years after graduation.

51

In time, the company commander moved on to a new job, and X remained, learning, developing his talents, soon becoming an outstanding officer. His platoon was rated so highly that it was awarded a one-week paid holiday at the recreation area at Garmisch in the Bavarian Alps, which the Army operates for troops in Europe. The platoon also figured strongly in the battalion's performance at the Grafenwoehr training site where it broke existing tank gunnery records.

X's part in all this was recognized. His new commanders rewarded him with superlative efficiency ratings. He was moved out of the tank platoon and made a general's aide, a plum for a young officer, the kind of job reserved for men whose careers prosper. Then he was reassigned to Vietnam.

On his way to the Far East, he passed through Washington and, like any ambitious young officer, he made the pilgrimage to the Fort McNair "Jesuits"—the men at the Office of Personnel Operations (OPO) who were keeping track of his career. X wanted to know what his prospects were for the future.

The assignment officer at OPO spun a lazy susan containing thousands of young officers' files, picked out X's, read the two early efficiency reports—the others had not yet arrived—and solemnly told X he was an average officer with an average career potential ahead of him.

A pragmatic young man, X reasoned that if, as the most successful tank platoon leader in all Europe, he had only average prospects ahead of him, then there was not much he could do to insure success in the future. Sitting in the OPO office with all those files bearing down on him, he reached his decision to resign from the service.

He left the building, moved on from Washington to South Vietnam, distinguished himself in combat, won four awards for heroism, and then, in June 1970, when he had completed the minimum obligation for his West Point education, he resigned his commission.

When last heard from, he was considering a career in politics.

The lesson to be drawn from Captain X's story is that there is no room for mere fairness in the services' career-rating systems. If X's career was going to be launched properly, his first rater should have listed him as "The best officer I have ever seen."

That's the way all the other young company commanders were rating all the other young platoon leaders in the Army who wanted to make a career out of the service. The military refers to the phenomenon —benignly—as report inflation. It is just one more example of the corruption within the officer corps. Captain X was penalized because his first superior, also inexperienced, took the descriptions on the officer efficiency report seriously. That was a mistake.

Few other officers in the service do.

Each of the services has an officer-rating system, and though the descriptions and arrangement of boxes vary from Army to Navy to Air Force, the general form—and the result—are pretty much the same.

Consider the Navy's form. The top rating for a Navy man is "Outstanding. ONE out of 100. Exceeds all others."

Below outstanding, the ratings on the Navy form proceed like this:

"Exceptional. One of the next top FEW. Extraordinary."

"Superior. ABOVE the great majority."

"Excellent. EQUAL to the majority."

"Acceptable. BELOW the majority."

"Marginal. Barely satisfactory."

"Unsatisfactory."

A rating officer must give one of these grades in each of the following categories:

(a) Professional knowledge (comprehension of all aspects of the profession)

(b) Moral courage (to do what he ought to do regardless of consequences to himself)

(c) Loyalty (his faithfulness to his shipmates, his command, the service, and the nation)

(d) Force (the positive and enthusiastic manner with which he fulfills his responsibilities)

(e) Initiative (his willingness to seek out and accept responsibility)

(f) Industry (the zeal exhibited and energy applied in the performance of his duties)

(g) Imagination (resourcefulness, creativeness, and capacity to plan constructively)

(h) Judgment (his ability to develop correct and logical conclusions)

(i) Reliability (the dependability and thoroughness exhibited in meeting responsibilities)

(j) Cooperation (his ability and willingness to work in harmony with others)

(k) Personal behavior (his demeanor, disposition, sociability, and sobriety)

(l) Military bearing (his military carriage, correctness of uniform, smartness of appearance and physical fitness)

(m) Self-expression (oral) (his ability to express himself orally)

(n) Self-expression (written) (his ability to express himself in writing)

Honestly used, such forms would provide a detailed record of officers as they progressed through the system. But continued abuse now means officers must be rated "ONE out of 100" just to get promoted.

"There's a situational ethic being applied here," remarked Lieutenant Colonel Dandridge M. Malone, a faculty member of the Army War College. "Each officer knows what his colleagues are doing, so he doesn't mind telling a little lie."

"It's at the point where the modal efficiency report—the modal, the point on the curve where the most officers are grouped—is 'the best officer I have ever seen,'" said Dr. Donald Penner, a civilian professor of behavioral sciences at the Army War College. "The whole thing has been inflated to the point where, if you're rated above 75 percent of all the other officers in the corps, your career is ruined. You're damned with faint praise."

The Air Force, like the other services, suffers from inflated reports. The third ranking description on the Air Force form was "Excellent. Seldom Equaled." "Rate a guy that way and he won't even get promoted to captain," one Air Force colonel said. "You'd ruin a man with that kind of rating." Most of the Air Force men scored in the top rating: "Absolutely superior. Unequaled."

The inflation in the efficiency reporting system leads to several kinds of corruption.

For one thing, it is the primary reason for the yes-man syndrome. Few subordinates will risk offending their superiors, who are doing the rating, for fear that disagreement with them or failure to cater to their whims might mean that a career-crippling low mark—say, only a "Superior. ABOVE the great majority"—will show up in something like reliability or military bearing.

Some men do refuse to go along, and their careers are stunted. Air Force Colonel Everest E. Riccioni is a case in point. In the winter of 1971–1972, Colonel Riccioni was the operations and training officer for the 314th Tactical Air Division at Osan Air Force Base, Korea. It was a backwater job if ever there was one for a man who thought in grand concepts, who had definite ideas on just what was wrong with the Air Force and its equipment, who had dedicated himself to trying to put "my Air Force" (it was always "my Air Force" as opposed to "the Air Force" or "the United States Air Force" to Riccioni) on the right track for the future.

Riccioni was serving a year in exile, doing penance. In a Pentagon slot, he had ruffled too many feathers, stumping for the development of a new, lightweight, maneuverable tactical fighter plane.

> The officer has the obligation [Riccioni once wrote], in serving his country, to remind a superior if any disparity exists between the going fashion of thought and that which is militarily sound. This item is brought to light only because all officers are human and some recognize the personal (selfish) aspect of going along with a commander's current view or ideas. The officer-soldier must overcome this trap, else he will someday fail to overcome the enemy. This phenomenon of the junior officer agreeing with his commander for personal rather than logical reasons and the commander's belief that he has a valuable, loyal junior officer because he compliments him through agreement, will hereafter be referred to as "incestous amplification."[1]

Talk to any general about yes men and he will deny that he has them on his staff. General Michael S. Davison, the commander-in-chief of the United States Army in Germany, said of the yes-men problem: "When you say 'pleasing his commander,' the inference of putting it that way is that the subordinate is in a position of apple-polishing and catering to his commander. I just don't believe this as being the general operative rule in the officer corps. Now, it's been my observation that while there are ass-kissers in any organization, the basic orientation of the officer corps is mission-oriented and is to get the job done. And the best way to get a good efficiency report is to get the job done. Mission accomplished."*

---

* General Davison and I talked for over an hour one morning in his huge office in Heidelberg. We were alone except for a public-affairs officer who ran a tape recorder. When the interview ended, the general went to lunch and then returned to his office for an interview with a newsman. I went to interview another general.

Mission accomplished. When a commander issues an order, the assumption is that the mission is always accomplished. Sometimes it really is. Oftentimes it is not.

In Korea, Brigadier General Pat W. Crizer provided a cogent example of how missions are not always accomplished in keeping with a general's orders. We were discussing the toilet-paper problem: the fact that very seldom is there toilet paper in enlisted men's latrines anywhere in the military.

Crizer was most sympathetic to the need. "A few months ago, I visited a latrine where the toilet paper was all suspended from a closet pole over the entrance to the commode area rather than on the rollers in each stall. Now I can understand why that was done. The paper is always slopping down onto the floor and getting wet. Men use too much of it. But still, when a man needs a piece of toilet paper, he needs it, and he shouldn't have to get up and go hunting for it. So I gave an order that toilet paper should be put back into all the stalls and the men trained on how to use it."

"Was your order carried out, General?" I asked.

"Well, I haven't been back to check. But I assume so."

"Let's you and I go back to that latrine and see if there's toilet paper in each stall."

"Well, I don't know if I can find the exact one."

A few minutes later, we left to tour a barracks area in the 2d Infantry Division, which is garrisoned between Seoul and the boundary line between North and South Korea. Crizer is deputy commander of the division.

When we entered a latrine, Crizer immediately recognized it as the one he had visited previously. "Now let's see about the toilet paper," he said.

We walked behind a partition to the area containing the commodes, and there, over the entranceway, was a closet pole containing eight roles of toilet paper. The general's order had been ignored.

Colonel Frederick W. Best, Jr., commander of a trouble-ridden base called Camp Humphreys, south of Seoul, had a similar illustration

---

When I left the afternoon interview, I was handed a message asking me to call a colonel on General Davison's staff. The colonel explained that General Davison had been talking at lunch about my questions concerning yes men. "The general asked me to call you to reassure you that he doesn't have any yes men on his staff," the colonel said.

of how orders did not survive passage through the chain of command. Black soldiers on Best's base believed they were suffering discrimination and were growing mutinous. Among other complaints, the blacks felt they were receiving punishment for infractions that were overlooked when committed by whites. When a group of whites brawled in a downtown bar, they were court-martialed. Best ordered that news of the punishments be read at company formations to be conducted throughout the base.

"Two weeks later, I had a meeting of my Human Relations Council," he recalled later. "There were twenty-five members. I walked in and said something like, 'Well, I guess now you know that we don't punish only blacks.' And you know, twenty-one of the twenty-five members of the council had not heard about the punishments. My order had not been carried out."

Not only are missions not accomplished, but often, when they are, they are not carried out in the way intended.

Major C. Powell Hutton, who at thirty-four must have been one of the Army's youngest tank battalion commanders, if not the youngest, related a story about how tank battalions in Germany are combat-qualified each year. Such qualification is an important mission accomplishment. "The idea is to get as many tanks qualified as possible from each battalion," Hutton, a West Point graduate, Rhodes Scholar, and member of a distinguished military family, said. "And we are always shorthanded on crews. We never have enough men. So all the battalion commanders put their staff officers into the tanks as well. Now you just know that those staff officers are not going to be in the tanks if a war ever comes."

Once again, the mission has been accomplished. The records have been made to look as good as possible. For the purposes of the efficiency report, the officers have performed well.

But that does not obscure the fact that the original purpose of the tank qualification mission—to make sure that as many tanks as possible are available to fight a war in Europe, if necessary—has not been accomplished.

From the layman's viewpoint, it would seem that the mission would stand a better chance of accomplishment if the battalion commanders were to tell their superiors they could not qualify enough tanks because of a lack of personnel. Then the generals could take steps to remedy the manpower shortage.

In today's military, things do not work that way. The American military machine is a can-do organization. No officer wants to tell a superior he cannot do.*

The can-do syndrome is not unique to any of the services. Retired Commander Charles McIntosh, a 1951 Naval Academy graduate, has told the story of can-doism in the Navy exquisitely in the *U.S. Naval Institute Proceedings.* McIntosh reported on a squadron of ships that had just returned from a long cruise, expecting to spend time in port. Instead the admiral who commanded the squadron summoned the ship commanders together and informed them that it would be necessary to make an immediate new deployment to fulfill the plans of "a distraught State Department and a harried President." The admiral had already told his superiors that his squadron could carry out the mission. At the meeting, he asked his skippers if their ships were up to it.

The ships, according to McIntosh, who was an officer in the squadron, were in bad condition. He reported one ship had men enough for only one qualified steaming watch out of the six that are normally necessary to keep a ship underway for twenty-four hours. The other five watches did not simply lack trained men but were actually short of bodies. Another ship was operating on only two emergency fuel feed pumps, its other four being out of commission. A third ship was in such bad shape that it needed time in a shipyard for extensive repairs. All the ships, McIntosh wrote, "had severe problems of personnel shortages, urgent need for leaves and liberties, schools, and other people-type things."

These problems were all ignored at the squadron meeting. Instead, McIntosh wrote:

> To a man, the captains swallowed, smiled, and assured the admiral that they, their crew and their ships were ready to go —anywhere, anytime, for any duty.[2]

Why did the skippers not speak up? McIntosh said that the admiral

---

* The can-do syndrome, incidentally, afflicts even those at the uppermost levels of the chain of command. General William C. Westmoreland, who commanded the American forces for three years in Vietnam, has privately complained about the restraints placed upon him by the civilian leadership. But, in the face of those restraints, he gave assurances that he could do the job anyhow. It was the old can-do spirit. Generals pay lip service to the idea of always being willing to turn in their stars if they see a political leader making a bad military decision. But few of them ever do.

58

was a man who had accomplished the impossible many times himself and that any skipper who had pointed out the difficulties to him would have jeopardized his own career.

A second kind of corruption results from the efficiency reporting system. It is the favoritism shown to some yes-man officers by their superiors. Before the choice few are selected out after War College, how do you pick and choose among all the thousands of officers in the services for the assignments in jobs where they will be able to display their talents? You find the answer to that question by visiting the records rooms maintained by the "Fort McNair Jesuits." They work in a row of nondescript yellow temporary buildings of World War II vintage on the perimeter of Fort McNair in a rundown section of southwestern Washington. Within those buildings are kept the career records, each in a thick file, of every officer in the Army.

Everything is carefully ordered. There is a building for each branch of the Army—infantry, artillery, armor, ordnance and the like. Within each building, there is a bay for each grade of officer. Inside each building, everything goes by rank. In one branch, all the lieutenants of infantry can find their files, all neatly stacked on dozens of huge lazy susans. A file for each man, each file like the other in outward appearance. Only the little check marks in the boxes on the efficiency report differentiating one from the other. A few feet farther down the corridor, another bay, this one for captains. Once again, the same revolving tables laden with files, each one a little more dog-eared now, for each has been fingered a few years longer. A little more dog-eared and a little thicker. In the lower grades, the progression is somewhat automatic. In the Army's infantry branch, for example, each lieutenant becomes a platoon leader and a company executive officer before promotion to captain. In that higher rank, he serves as a company commander. After sufficient time in grade, he can count on automatic promotion to major and a job on a battalion, brigade or division staff.

Weeding out begins when officers become majors. Based on the accumulation of efficiency reports and other data, some majors are ordered to civilian graduate schools to earn advanced degrees. From this elite, a few will be assigned to teach at West Point or to staff jobs in the Pentagon. They become front runners in the promotion race. At OPO, the Jesuits pay close attention to the reports on these newly developing elite groups of young men.

When the folders for a particular "year group"—a group of men who entered the service at roughly the same time—are transferred to the lieutenant colonel's bay, competition for battalion command—the last station of the cross—develops.

In the early 1970s, the man in charge of assigning infantry lieutenant colonels to new jobs was Lieutenant Colonel Lester E. Bennett. Though some might call him a Jesuit, a more accurate description for Bennett and his OPO colleagues would be keepers of the career tickets. Bennett and the rest were responsible for matching up talent with positions.

Bennett's specific job was the assignment of 3,300 lieutenant colonels of infantry, filling requests for men from commands and agencies throughout the nation and around the world. Theoretically, he did his job by consulting those dog-eared folders to match the most suitable officer up for reassignment at any given time with the available job for which he was qualified.

"The efficiency reports are the most important single element in the file," Bennett said as he leafed through a typical folder. "They demonstrate the personal qualities. Drinking habits and all the personal traits show up in those reports."

But if the reports are mostly the same, ranking almost every man at the very top of the scale, how can they be of any value?

"In spite of the inflation, the front runners are obvious," Bennett said. "A man who is a dud—somewhere along the line someone is going to call him a dud." Thus Bennett confirmed the possibility that a career could be stifled by one bad comment.

In effect, OPO is an employment agency. The officers awaiting assignment are job hunters and the military outfits with positions open are clients. Just as civilian job seekers besiege employment agencies personally, so do the military officers.

"We get anywhere from a half dozen to a dozen visitors a day," Bennett said. "In addition, we get telephone calls from all over the world from officers inquiring about their next assignment. We encourage officers to ask for specific jobs. If what a person is asking for is consistent with Army's needs, we give him the assignment. There's no harm done. If it does not give one person an advantage over all the others, it's okay with us."

But gaining such an advantage is the essence of ticket punching. Each lieutenant colonel awaiting assignment is hoping for an advantage over his 3,299 colleagues. Infantry lieutenant colonels do not want just any job. They want battalion commands. At the beginning of 1972, Bennett had only 250 commands to assign. The men sought those positions not because they really wanted to do the job and for the satisfactions command offered but because command was necessary for promotion. In Bennett's words: "Without a battalion command, you cannot get a brigade, and without a brigade, you cannot make general."

The scarcity of infantry command jobs is mirrored in the Army's other combat arms—field artillery and armor—as well as in the other services. The Air Force equivalent of a battalion command is an aircraft squardon command. In 1972, there were 17,000 Air Force lieutenant colonels competing for 2,300 squardon command jobs. The Navy equivalent is command of an aircraft squardon, a destroyer or a submarine. In 1972, there were 5,300 Navy commanders (the equivalent of lieutenant colonel in the other services) competing for 634 command positions in these units.

The talent pool is virtually unlimited. The records on most of the competing men read almost identically. And so a kind word to the assignment officer from a man of high rank can help tilt the scales in favor of one individual over many others. Generals and admirals often intercede for their favorites, and the assignment officers—men of lower rank such as Bennett—grant the men wearing the stars their wishes.

As Bennett said, "Generals call all the time in favor of an individual. If a three- or four-star general intercedes for a man, I won't fight it."

Why should he? Bennett might have been serving a tour as a ticket keeper, but he, like all other officers, is also a ticket puncher, and as such, he cannot afford to offend a general who might someday rate him.

Just as favoritism can help one officer get ahead faster than his contemporaries, the arbitrary enmity of a superior can shatter the career of a subordinate. Although most officers receive exceptionally high efficiency reports, a few are given very poor reports without justification. During his investigation of the high resignation rate in the West Point class of 1966, Lieutenant Colonel Leider discovered Captain Y, who had received poor efficiency ratings.

Assigned to Europe after graduation, Captain Y became a company executive officer and was quickly promoted to company commander. Shortly after his promotion, the commander of his battalion was changed. The new commander, meeting him, said, "You are a West Point graduate. Don't expect any special consideration from me." Y told Leider that despite this remark, he continued to do his work, performing acceptably in every respect. He was never told otherwise.

But the battalion commander, after ten months and without telling Y, recommended that the young officer not be promoted with his contemporaries. Two months later, he relieved Y of command, filling out a devastating efficiency report. He never gave Y any reasons for the relief.

Later, a division staff member showed Y his efficiency report. Y claimed it contained at least three lies concerning events that had never occurred. How could the youngster rebut the report? No one in his unit knew. Finally Y found a warrant officer who had heard of a form that could be used to appeal. Several phone calls produced the form. No one knew how to fill it out. Y and the warrant officer wrote and rewrote, developing what they thought was an acceptable document. The appeal was submitted and disapproved on technicalities before it got to a level where the merits of the case could be judged.

While Y was still seeking a hearing, he was transferred to Vietnam. While he fought the enemy, he continued to fight also a rear-guard action against the bureaucracy. And the bureaucracy continued to be as intractable as the enemy; Y finally surrendered to the bureaucracy. He resigned his commission at the earliest opportunity, not because of the bad report but because he could not get an official judgment on the justice of the report.

The Army's personnel system, Y told Leider, is "highly inflexible" with "little consideration for the feelings of the individual."

Leider can be given to understatement. In summarizing the attitudes of the men he interviewed on the matter of efficiency reports, he wrote, "Interviewee opinion on OER's was that the system is not sufficiently pure to serve as a basis for career-influencing decisions. In their judgment, the system is essentially one-sided. It allows seniors to use it in a vendetta without fear of recourse."[3]

The Fort McNair Jesuits only deal with assignments. Technically they have nothing to do with promotion. That is handled by special boards convened at regular intervals at Bailey's Crossroads, Virginia, in a building across the street from a store named Toys Я Us.

Major General Franklin M. Davis, Jr., described a typical promotion board selection process. "We were picking colonels," he said. "We

62

had 1,300 slots to fill, and we had 3,000 candidates. Picking the best and weeding out the worst was easy. There were four men on the board. Each file had to be read by three of them. We used a rating system from zero to six, and we each worked with a different color pencil. Anybody who got three sixes was automatically selected and anybody who got three zeros was automatically rejected.

"It was when we got down to the three point fives that we had a problem. And here, if someone on the board knew the candidate, it helped."

In that kind of situation, it pays to make oneself known, and this is done most easily through the assignments one gets. Thus the OPO operation presided over by Bennett and his colleagues has a great bearing on promotion. As Bennett said, "It is our job to get these men promoted to colonel."

His colleagues down the hall who are in charge of assigning colonels have a yet more sensitive job. They have to make sure that as many men as possible in the infantry branch are promoted to general.

A general, as the rank implies, is not a specialist. He is a generalist. Once a man gets his stars, it is presumed that he can do almost anything. He can command, he can administer, he can think big thoughts as a policy planner, he can be a public relations expert.

Generals do not wear the insignia of the branch in which they advanced on their collars. They wear only the insignia "U.S." So, whereas competition from lieutenant to colonel is within one's branch, the competition for promotion to general is Army-wide. And in this competition, each branch tries to get more of its own promoted than the other branches.

A newly promoted general becomes a patron for his branch. Once the beneficiary of those calls to OPO, he is now in a position to make the calls.

The system is set up to foster concern for the individual. Instead, it encourages favoritism. Lieutenant Colonel Leider discovered in his survey that the resigning West Pointers felt that OPO was impersonal, vague and not aware of individual needs.

The efficiency reports are intended to rate men objectively. Instead, objectivity goes out the window in favor of either vindictiveness or false inflation of a man's capabilities. The men who use the reports say this is not necessarily so, that inflation is controlled because somewhere along the line, one person will tell the truth. What they see as a virtue, others regard as an evil. Lieutenant Colonel Leider, for example, has suggested that, when it comes to promotion consideration, an officer's lowest efficiency report be discarded, much the way a teacher will often discard a student's lowest test score in giving a final grade. In that way, Leider said, not only would vindictiveness be overcome, but officers would be encouraged to evaluate a subordinate fairly, knowing that if his rating was low, it would not count if it were mistaken or atypical over the course of a career.

From time to time there have been several suggestions put forth for changing the rating system. West Point uses a peer rating system in which cadets rate each other. The Academy claims the students are far more frank in judging classmates than superiors are in their evaluations.

Some officers, such as Lieutenant Colonel Paul Suplizio, who was detailed to work on one of the Army's numerous professionalism studies in the early 1970s, have been so bold as to suggest that subordinates be given the opportunity to rate their superiors. That idea has gained little favor. It smacks of troops electing their officers, an idea that cannot be seriously entertained in an organization that depends on strict discipline.

If ticket punching is going to be ended—and there are few left in the military these days who speak well of the system—the services must consider some drastic alternatives not only in the officer-rating system but in the entire system of career management. In the past, the services have tried to take care of the problem simply by re-ordering boxes on the forms, changing descriptions raters must checkmark, and making other revisions in the paperwork.

Such superficial changes are nowhere near enough. They always produce the same results: continued inflation of ratings.

The more drastic approach involves an attack on the idea that every young lieutenant is a potential chief of staff, that jobs exist only as stepping stones to other jobs at higher rank, that career satisfaction is found not in doing a job well but in gaining promotion and decoration.

These changes can be accomplished, but only if the system is willing to overthrow years of tradition.

4

CENTRAL PARK SOUTH GOES TO WAR

The generals and admirals of the American military machine are the survivors of the ticket-punching system. They have met the system on its own terms, mastered it and turned it to their own use. They see little of a fundamental nature wrong with it, and precious few of their subordinates will risk telling them. Even when they lead men in combat, the generals and admirals live in a splendid isolation.

In the winter of 1971–1972, Rear Admiral James E. Ferris commanded an aircraft carrier task force on Yankee Station in the South China Sea washing the coast of North Vietnam. The admiral's mission was to conduct the bombardment of North Vietnam with the wing of aircraft stationed aboard his flagship CVA–43, the *Coral Sea*. Ferris' quarters, known as "admiral's country" aboard ship, were more like a New York Central Park South luxury apartment than the command center of a powerful carrier task force waging war against an enemy nation.

From the flight deck a few stories below, dozens of aircraft took off each morning, their bellies and wings laden, as the expression goes, with death and destruction. Admiral Ferris could witness this spectacle from picture windows in his quarters, or he could tune it all out. "Tune out" means he could retire to his study, a windowless little room obviously appointed by an interior decorator.

A huge green plant grew against one wall, providing a little life. The planter rested on thick beige carpeting that helped deaden the bone-shaking noise of aircraft launching and recovery operations. There was not a stray bit of dust on the glass-topped coffee table nor an ash in any of the heavy glass ashtrays. The thought was inescapable that orderlies were ever present, waiting for the tiniest bits of refuse to accumulate, sweeping them up as soon as the admiral left the room. On one wall, a walnut credenza held a stereo tape player. The admiral's desk was set against the opposite wall.

The sofa was covered in a nubby white fabric. It was functional but soft, enveloping a visitor in instant comfort and security. Just outside the doorway to the study, a Marine aide stood attentively, if not always at attention, waiting to carry out the admiral's every wish. In the small galley, two Filipino messmen were preparing a chicken dinner for the evening.

The admiral's dining room—it was to a mess what the private dining room in the White House is to a government worker's cafeteria—could seat ten comfortably around an oval table covered with starched white linen. The silverware was heavy and glistening. The meals were served with painstaking etiquette by white-coated attendants.

In the midst of a war, there was this incredible luxury and gentility. Below the admiral, 4,000 officers and men bent to the task of keeping the planes flying, of keeping the bombs, missiles and napalm canisters falling on a backward country. In the waters around the behemoth, a group of destroyers circled endlessly, protecting the carrier from the prospect of surprise attack and standing ready to provide search and rescue for downed flyers.

In admiral's country, all that could be forgotten. The admiral need not hear of all the problems. Commander Morton D. Kiefer, chief of the *Coral Sea*'s engineering department, noted that 75 percent of the carrier was inadequately air-conditioned. Admiral's country, of course, was within the comfortable 25 percent. Belowdecks, the crew was jammed together, 150 men to each open, windowless, poorly lighted, ill-ventilated bay. They lived one atop the other, three bunks high, with no privacy and little storage space, with the constant noise of the ship's operations jarring them. They took their meals in windowless, low-ceilinged mess spaces that doubled as warehouses for the bombs and rockets the airplanes would use.

The admiral not only had that stylish dining room; he slept each night between white sheets in a proper bed someone else made up for him.

Admiral Ferris was not born to this kind of luxury. He could make no hereditary claim to membership in the exclusive admiral's club like some of his colleagues; neither was he a member of any "old boys' network" composed of friendships formed at the Naval Academy. He had not attended the Academy. Born in England in 1919, he immigrated to the United States with his family at the age of three and grew up in Kearny, New Jersey, a seamy industrial town on the New Jersey meadows outside New York City. His father was a worker at the Kopper's Company, coke manufacturers, and his brother became a fireman in the town. Ferris grew up building model airplanes and eventually he learned to fly. He did his share of barnstorming before World War II. He attended but did not graduate from Elon College in North Carolina, and in October 1941, when the Japanese were making final preparations for the attack on Pearl Harbor, he enlisted in the Navy.

He was commissioned as a fighter pilot in August 1942, and joined the air wing aboard the USS *Saratoga*, where he fought in the Solomon Islands campaign and later in other actions in World War II. He also flew during two tours in the Korean War and rose steadily through the ranks, commanding a squadron, a wing and, finally, the *Coral Sea* itself, winning a caseful of medals and awards along the way.

At fifty-three, he was lean and trim, his craggy face handsome in the John Wayne manner. He was generous, articulate and friendly to one who had arrived unexpectedly in his domain. Leaning back in his upholstered swivel chair, he addressed himself to the problems facing the military machine as seen from the flag bridge of an aircraft carrier task force.

A few months before, the *Coral Sea* had almost been prevented from sailing from the West Coast to Yankee Station by a small but vocal antiwar movement in the crew. On the same day that I visited the ship, a representative from Admiral Elmo R. Zumwalt's staff was on board investigating reports of racial discord in the crew. Sailors talked openly of the drugs they bought and used when the ship made calls at Far Eastern ports. Rumors abounded that some crewmen had stashed drugs for use while the ship was conducting operations. The working conditions for the men who kept the ship running, the planes in condition, and the aircraft operations running smoothly, resembled a mythical inferno: the heat, noise, vibration, backbreaking jobs and danger—the constant, intense danger—all combining to glaze the eyes, dull the minds and weary the bodies of the thousands of men involved.

These conditions, which brought to a modern-day fighting force aspects of life in a medieval armada, resulted from the serious problems confronting the task force on Yankee Station and all the other units in the military machine. But the admiral did not recognize that. His sphere of problems was circumscribed by what he could see from his bridge and what he heard from the men who visited his quarters. From the bridge, he saw the operations—the planes taking off and landing with a precision that would do a ballet master proud. In his quarters, he talked with the elite on the ship, the flyers—men who were, for the most part, emulating him in building their careers. Like the admiral, the pilots were concerned with the aircraft operations aboard the ship. When they talked to their leader, it concerned these matters. So the admiral, dealing mostly with the flyers, did not hear much about what went on within the ship's crew. And when he ventured out of admiral's country to visit other areas, it was usually with forewarning, giving the ship's officers time to present conditions in the best possible light.

The comfort of the surroundings, the perquisites of his position and the responsibilities that went with his power were all inducements to stay in admiral's country, an area foreign to the real world of the aircraft carrier, an isolated enclave. The enlightened self-interest of his subordinates, many of whom someday wanted to live in admiral's country themselves, dictated that they keep the admiral as ignorant as possible of conditions on the ship.

The problems, then, as the admiral saw them, related not to what the services had done to the men on the ship. Instead, they arose from what society had done to the military.

Admiral Ferris said, "The stereotype of the military mind is one who wants a bigger and bigger military establishment, more and more military junk. Frankly, I resent that. I'm in this business because I get a great satisfaction out of associating with the others in it. I'm in it for adventure. I enjoy the hazard of flying planes off of ships.

"I am no more militaristic than any graduate of a liberal arts college. I am no more narrow nor no more broad. But somehow, I've gotten typed as the military mind, and I'm cast as a villain. What I want to know is what would the nation do without us?"

The admiral sat there in the luxury of his surroundings, talking about how the Army made everything too easy for its men during the Vietnam War. He decried the personnel turnover system in which each

Army man spent only a one-year tour in Vietnam. He ridiculed the rest-and-recreation program that allowed each Army man in Vietnam a week off from the war to visit one of the pleasure domes of Asia or to return to Hawaii.

Leaning back in the well-upholstered easy chair, drawing deeply on a cigarette, butting it in an ashtray that an attendant would empty and polish in a few minutes, the admiral said of the luxuries enjoyed by others, "It all suggests we've made a mockery of this war."

Others feel that an excess of perquisites granted to general- and flag-rank officers is one of those factors that helped make a mockery of the system.

In theory, there's nothing wrong with perquisites. Those who have achieved high rank are entitled to a few extra privileges. They need aides, orderlies and drivers to ease the burden of coping with life's little time-consuming annoyances. Certain comforts and conveniences are necessary to enable high-ranking officers to use their time efficiently and perform their jobs well. But when the perquisites work to isolate the man of responsibility from the real world—a world full of problems—that becomes another matter.

Army general officers have their own dimly lighted, tastefully appointed, quiet private dining room in the Pentagon. "The chef is a warrant officer who has traveled all over the world gathering recipes," one general tells a guest. "He's really topnotch."

A white-coated waiter serves sherry to start the meal. A dessert cart stacked with fruits, pastries and puddings is part of the decor. The menu includes an array of dishes from exotic places. Mints and cigars are served to end the meal.

"It's one of the best-kept secrets in the Pentagon," the general said of the dining room, with a sly smile.

The dining room also works to reinforce a system in which generals talk only to generals, colonels to colonels, majors to majors and so on down the line. There is little enough communication of other than a formal nature upward and downward through the chain of command. Many are the generals who announce proudly to their troops at a formation that "if you have any problems, remember that my door is always open." In fact, however, the door is carefully guarded by aides who discourage visits from subordinates if not prevent them altogether. Institutions such as that private Pentagon dining room make it even more difficult for the generals to develop any meaningful feeling for the world in which their subordinates live.

In Vietnam, Brigadier General Joseph C. McDonough, the commander of the 196th Light Infantry Brigade—the "Chargers"—lived in a hilltop home outside Danang that was air-conditioned and equipped with hot and cold running water which never failed. The officers and men of his command, one of the last combat units to be phased out of Vietnam, lived on the hillside below, fighting malarial mosquitoes, eating in drab surroundings, shaving in droplets of water that occasionally dripped out of an inadequate plumbing system, and grousing, in the winter of 1971–1972, about the nature of the war. President Nixon had said American troops were no longer on the offensive in Vietnam, but every day they were sending patrols into the jungle around Danang to find the enemy. Though they had not made contact in months, they were still suffering occasional casualties from American support fire that sometimes landed short. At one fire base, some enlisted men were circulating a petition to the general asking him to reconcile the brigade's activities with the President's statement.

The general received no inkling of the incipient morale problem. To confess a morale problem, Lieutenant Colonel Frederick H. Mitchell, the thirty-nine-year-old, chunky, cigar-smoking battalion commander in charge of that fire base, would have to confess his own failure as a leader within the terms of the system. (A precept of the system is that good leaders do not have morale problems). That, in turn, would count heavily against him in any future consideration for promotion. So the symptoms went unrecognized, or, if they were seen, they went unreported. Mitchell, landing at his fire base's helipad, would alight quickly and, carrying his modified M-16 (the wooden stock had been removed) like an attaché case, he would hurry through the compound to his command bunker, making small talk to the men along the way.

His men might grumble to visitors about their assignment; about the rats that infested their bunkers; about middle-of-the-night "mad hours" in which, for no reason perceptible to them, the commander ordered round after round of artillery and mortar fire into the surrounding jungle; about demands for radio silence and floodlights burning throughout the night, but he would hear nothing of it. Or, if he heard, he did not listen.

In December 1971, I sat in Mitchell's command bunker, burrowed into the hilltop ridge, thickly protected with sand bags. There was no luxury here, save for a couple of boxes of expensive cigars Mitchell's wife had sent him. Mitchell slept on a canvas cot; he sat in a metal folding chair; he worked in an eye-spoiling dim light. You could feel the pressure of immediate responsibility for 900 lives on him in the surroundings and the more remote pressure of searching the jungles for the elusive enemy rocket men who, every once in a while, silently infiltrated the defenses and moved down the lush valleys to launch a rocket or two or more into Danang, South Vietnam's second largest city. It was a responsibility not to be taken lightly, and sitting there, he evoked sympathy. You could understand if he had a passion for overcaution that might rankle his less sophisticated troops.

And yet you wondered at his failure to make the needs of the situation known to the troops and felt by them.

"These men are the best in the Army," he said. "I have absolutely no complaint with them except that I practically have to march them to the barbershop to get a haircut. I have not had the problems I thought I would when I came over here. The battalion, particularly out in the bush, has had extremely high morale. I just have not had the excessive problems other people appear to have had. My soldiers want to do a good job. I have to hold them back. They all want to get the combat infantry badge.

"We have never had any semblance of a refusal to fight here."

Four months later, the Chargers made front-page news during the 1972 North Vietnam offensive. Transferred north from Danang to Phubai to protect an American airfield there, Mitchell's battalion was assigned a patrolling mission.

Dozens of men from one company complained bitterly about the assignment but went reluctantly. About 50 out of 142 men in another company refused for an hour and a half to move out.

"We're not going. This isn't our war. We're not going out in the bush. Why should we fight if nobody back home gives a damn about us?" the men shouted.

Finally they did move out.

Exasperated, Lieutenant Colonel Mitchell, his career hanging in the precarious balance of the moment, turned on the press who witnessed the incident, saying, "All you press are bastards. I blame you for this and you can quote me on it."[1]

The reluctance to look within the system upon which officers are so dependent is great. As a result, those at the top, who might be able to deal with the problems, seldom find out the problems are there—until it is too late. If Mitchell, living on a fire base with his men, had no feeling for the morale problem in his unit, the chances were even less that General McDonough, in those relatively comfortable quarters back at Danang, could find out what was going on.

Occasionally the men who wear the stars see something that disturbs them, and that only reinforces the attempts by the men below to keep the leaders isolated.

When admirals, for example, come and go from their ships, the fact is announced over the squawk box. Preparations are made. Men along the route are alerted. When they arrive on board, a covey of officers stands on the quarter-deck to greet them. Not only is courtesy involved here, but all those staff members act as a shield. Admirals should see only what their subordinates want them to see.

One day in 1971, Vice Admiral Gerald E. Miller, commander of the United States Sixth Fleet, stationed in the Mediterranean, walked through the living quarters of the enlisted men on his own flag staff aboard the stately old guided-missile cruiser *Springfield*. The ship is the Sixth Fleet flagship and, tied up to the pier in the little resort town of Gaeta, Italy, its home port, it is an impressive projection of American seapower, its masts competing with the spires of the town's churches for a share of the skyline, its guns recalling the days of the great battle-wagons, long since departed from the oceans.

On board, every piece of brass is shined to a mirror finish. Deckhands chip away at what appears to be good paint to apply even newer paint. The rope work is immaculate. A visitor walking the main deck feels he could safely eat off the spotless teak underfoot.

But the day Admiral Miller walked through those crew quarters was not a happy one. The area was unsuitable to him. Clean, maybe, but not clean *enough*. Angered at what he saw, tthe admiral returned to his quarters and announced over the intercom that he was restricting himself to the ship until that area was cleaned up.

His self-confinement meant his entire staff would not be able to leave the ship, and that was a hardship, since most of the men lived on shore, using their quarters on board only when the *Springfield* was at sea. Confinement of the flag staff meant confinement of the ship's entire crew.

The admiral's intended lesson was cleanliness. The lesson his subordinates drew from the incident instead was that they must do a better job of isolating the admiral.

A chance encounter, like Admiral Miller's with the dirt, is something to be avoided if at all possible.

And on down the line, officers at each level in the chain of command are doing their best to insulate those above them from the unhappy truths. That also helps make a mockery of the system.

What also helps is simply that the military establishment these days has so many generals and admirals that it sometimes seems as if it does not know what to do with them. In areas of the world where the National Defense Establishment has had time to entrench itself, the number of general and flag-rank officers has proliferated to the point where it also seems as if there are more chiefs than Indians. Korea is a good example. At the height of the Korean War in the early 1950s, there were, within the so-called United Nations Command, 302,483 American troops in Korea. The overall command for the Americans was the Eighth Army, which a number of distinguished American generals headed at one time or another. The Eighth Army was divided into three Army Corps; each corps, at the high point, had six divisions. (There was also a Marine division under the overall command of the Eighth Army commander.)

Today, there are only some 30,000 troops left in Korea, including only one combat division—the 2d. But much of the old structure still remains. There was, in 1972, an Eighth Army headquarters at Seoul, command by a four-star general, General John H. Michaelis, known as "Iron Mike," a battlefield hero and paratrooper who took part in the Normandy Invasion and the Battle of the Bulge in World War II and the toughest part of the Korean War fighting.

As a four-star general, Iron Mike did not see much of the training grounds in Korea any more. He had no fewer than eleven other generals in his headquarters in Seoul helping him with the task of balancing three hats of command on his head—one for the Eighth Army, one for the United Nations Command and one for the command of all American forces, Air Force and Navy as well as Army, in Korea. About twenty miles north of Seoul, in the little city of Uijongbu, Lieutenant General Glenn D. Walker commanded the I Corps Group, which had control over the only American division left in the country. To make the rationale for the command sound a little more credible, officials maintained that it also had control over "several" Korean divisions. Walker had another general helping him.

Another twenty miles farther up the road, in Tongduchon, Major General Jeffrey G. Smith (two stars), assisted by two brigadier generals (one star each), commanded the 2d Division.

In the rear areas, south of Seoul, there were assorted other generals and two admirals, making the roster of generals and admirals in Korea total twenty-two in all.

That's a lot of brass for a relatively few men. When you consider that each one of those men had his own staff, his own aides and orderlies, his own drivers, and could call upon the active units to provide special details of one sort and another when needed, that adds up to a lot of nonproductive labor devoted to the care and feeding of rank. By comparison, Thailand had about the same number of American uniformed personnel who were able to get alone with only five generals (no admirals) on board, even though the largest part of the Indochina War —the air war—was being waged from Thai air bases at the time. The commitment was newer in Thailand, and the bureaucracy had not grown as entrenched.

Vietnam is the most interesting case of all. President Nixon's 1969 Vietnamization program, in which he gradually withdrew American forces, did not apply equally to generals and others.

In April 1969, when the number of American ground troops in South Vietnam was at its peak—543,400 in all—the Army, Air Force, Navy and Marines had 67 generals and admirals in the country leading them. A few months later, President Nixon began the withdrawal program. By January 1970, when troop strength had dropped 11 percent to 475,000, the number of generals and admirals in the country dropped only 7 percent to 62. By January 1972, when the number of troops had dropped 71 percent to 157,000, there were still 57 generals and admirals in South Vietnam. Their number had dropped only 15 percent.

It all seemed to confirm the facetious saying attributed to the ambitious men in the officer corps—"it's not much of a war, but it's the only war we've got." The military had gone from an avowed policy of more bang for the buck to a real policy of more brass to spend the bucks.

Back at the Pacific Area Command headquarters in Hawaii, the situation was not much better. CINCPAC, as it is known, is situated high above Pearl Harbor on the island of Oahu, and from that lofty perch, Admiral John S. McCain, Jr., commanded all the military forces stretching from North Pole to South Pole and from a few hundred miles off the west coast of North and South America to just off the east coast of Africa, including the Aleutian Islands and the Arctic Ocean north of Siberia. In all, McCain, in 1972, had responsibility for 94 million square miles of the earth's surface, and he had a lot of brass from the Army, Navy, Air Force and Marines to help him exercise it.

At McCain's headquarters there were stationed no fewer than fifty-three generals and admirals. There were four four-star officers, six three-stars, nineteen two-stars and twenty-four one-stars, making it the biggest concentration of brass outside the Pentagon.

Now, most generals and admirals, like most successful corporation executives, are among the more conservative members of society, in the traditional sense of the word. If you were to accuse them of feather-bedding in the way that the plumbers' or printers' unions demand featherbedding clauses in their contracts, the generals and admirals would probably respond by accusing you of unpatriotic motives. And yet the numbers indicate that the generals and admirals in Vietnam, in Korea and in Hawaii have been feathering their billets very nicely.

They showed no disposition to change, either. According to the office of the Defense Department controller, the four services planned to make large reductions in manpower in the two years between June 30, 1971, and June 30, 1973, when President Richard M. Nixon's all-volunteer force was to go into effect. The Army planned to cut the number of enlisted men from 971,871 to 720,054 during that period—a reduction of 26 percent. But it planned to reduce its officers in the top grades—lieutenant colonels and above—from 21,021 to 18,840, a reduction of only 10.3 percent. Thus, in relative terms, the Army, as its need for troops dropped with the Vietnam War wind-down, planned to become even more brass-heavy. It planned to become particularly top-brass-heavy, reducing its number of generals from 497 to 488, a reduction of less than 2 percent.

The Navy was a little less egregious in its plans for all brass, scheduling a 3.4 percent reduction in enlisted personnel as opposed to a 1.7 percent cut in the grades of commander and above. But it too was taking care of the admirals. It had actually programed a small (less than 1 percent) increase in the number of admirals, from 312 to 315.

The Air Force appeared to be grinding away at the brass. It scheduled a 4.6 percent reduction in enlisted personnel as opposed to a

9.1 percent reduction in lieutenant colonels and above. But it was also taking care of the generals, reducing them by little more than 2 percent.*

Only the Marines were making reductions across the board. While it was reducing its lean, mean corps of enlisted men by 6.1 percent, from 190,604 to 178,832, it was reducing the brass by 9.7 percent; that is, like the Air Force, at a rate greater than its reductions in enlisted men. At the same time, unlike the Air Force, it planned to reduce its generals from 77 to 72—a 6 percent reduction that equaled the reduction in enlisted men. The Marines, obviously, were not in the feather-bedding business. They were adopting an outlook as startling in context as that of a modern-day labor union willing to aid management in the introduction of labor-saving automation techniques.

The situation was getting so bad that even the military's old and good friends on Capitol Hill could no longer stomach it. On November 11, 1971, the Appropriations Committee of the House of Representatives submitted its report on the 1972 Defense Department Appropriations Bill.[2] For years, the committee, within limits, could be counted on to give the Pentagon what it wanted. But now it was showing signs of impatience. The report said:

Proliferation of Generals and Colonels

The Committee reviewed in depth the promotion practices and the officer grade structure of the Armed Services. The review revealed that there are more three and four star generals and admirals in uniform today than there were at the height of World War II when there were over 12 million men and women in uniform. Even more startling is a comparison of the number of individuals serving in the grades of Colonel,

---

* Though the Air Force was reducing its chiefs-to-Indians ratio over the two years in question, it was not making the reductions happily. In fact, it has been carrying on a campaign for years to win from Congress authorization to increase the number of brass in the organization. The Air Force generals have been arguing that, as the youngest service, established after World War II, it did not have its fair share of top-ranking officers. Congress has responded warily, giving the Air Force only temporary increases in top billets. The 1973 figure represents the amount of brass the Air Force will have if Congress does not again grant a temporary or permanent increase in the ceiling. But the Air Force will be lobbying on Capitol Hill for more, even in the face of widespread criticism in Congress about the top-heaviness the services already have.

Lieutenant Colonel and Navy Captain or Commander. Today there are 900,000 fewer officers in uniform than there were in 1945 but we have 6,000 more Colonels, Navy Captains and Commanders.

An equally interesting comparison can be drawn by comparing our peak officer strength during the Korean War with our officer strength today. At the peak of the Korean War we had 3.6 million men in uniform and today we have only 2.7 million. However, we have 190 more Generals and Admirals today than we had at the height of the Korean War. Even more amazing is the fact that today we have over 16,000 more Colonels and Navy Captains and Commanders than when we had a million more men in uniform.*

The changes in relative size at the top and bottom of the military hierarchy from World War II through Korea to the present day can best be illustrated by the graph, adapted from the committee's report (see page 78).

It was not until December 1944, less than a year before World War II was to come to an end, that the proliferation of brass really became alarming. At that time, with 8 million men already in uniform, the United States Military establishment had only six four-star generals and nine admirals in uniform. Then Congress established the five-star grade of general of the Army and admiral of the Fleet, and seven men

* This is the full table presented in the committee report:

OFFICER GRADE STRUCTURE

Rank	WWII June 30, 1945	Korea June 30, 1952	Today June 30, 1971
General or Admiral	38	25	45
Lieutenant General or Vice Admiral	101	65	145
Major and Brigadier General or Rear Admiral	1,929	1,052	1,145
Subtotal	2,068	1,142	1,330
Colonel or Captain	14,989	12,490	17,388
Lieutenant Colonel or Commander	36,967	28,927	40,431
Subtotal	51,956	41,417	57,819
Total officers	1,260,109	375,829	371,416
Total enlisted	10,795,775	3,245,310	2,329,754
Total personnel	12,123,455	3,635,912	2,714,727

WORLD WAR II   **KOREA**   **1971**

were promoted to that grade.* Those few promotions to super-rank opened the door to dozens of promotions to four-star rank which in turn allowed the creation of hundreds more generals, thousands of colonels and tens of thousands more officers down the line. Prior to World War II, only four men in history had ever held the permanent grade of four stars. They were Ulysses S. Grant, William T. Sherman and Philip H. Sheridan of Civil War fame and General John J. Pershing of World War I. Congress created the four-star rank for George Washington, but he was never promoted to it.

The House committee attributed much of the proliferation of high-ranking officers to the assignment of uniformed men to jobs that should be held by civilians. "Every few years the Department of Defense announced a 'Civilization' program, the intention of which is to reduce the number of military personnel assigned to civilian type jobs," the

---

* They were, in order of rank, Admiral William D. Leahy, chairman of the Joint Chiefs of Staff and chief of staff to President Franklin D. Roosevelt; General George C. Marshall, Chief of Staff of the Army; Admiral Ernest J. King, Chief of Naval Operations; General Douglas MacArthur, commander-in-chief of the Southwest Pacific Area; Admiral Chester W. Nimitz, commander-in-chief of the Pacific Area; General Dwight D. Eisenhower, commanding general of the European Theater of Operations, and General Henry A. Arnold, commanding general of the Army Air Forces. After the war, five-star rank was also conferred on Admiral William F. Halsey and General Omar N. Bradley. If it had not been for Marshall, Congress might have created the grade of "field marshal" to give American commanders rank equivalent to their British counterparts, but it was decided that the United States could have no "Field Marshal Marshall."

committee noted. "However, what has evidently happened over the years is a rather rapid and drastic 'Civilianization in reverse' or 'militarization' of many of the higher level jobs in the Department of Defense." The committee pointed to the Defense Supply Agency (DSA) which has 21 authorized generals on its rolls. Why, the committee asked, did it need any such officers? DSA's manpower was decreasing by 5,355 over a two-year period, the committee said, but it was adding 127 more colonels and above during the same period. "This continual upgrading of personnel apparently is happening throughout the entire Defense Department," the committee said.

Whereas it might be cheaper for the military to use drafted, rather than civilian labor at the lower levels, this is not so in the high-brass grades. According to the committee:

"The need to let civilians do civilian jobs in the Department of Defense becomes increasingly important as the cost of military personnel continues to increase. Not only do some high ranking officers cost more in terms of salary and benefits than their civilian counterparts but there is the added cost of first having to train them for a new job and then having to move them to another new assignment after two or three years."

One point the committee did not mention is that the competition to get to those high grades is so intense that the ticket-punching system keeps men on the move throughout the services. This, in turn, creates huge retraining and education costs not only for men doing jobs that should be civilianized in the Pentagon but also for military jobs around the nation and the world. Another erstwhile good friend of the military interested in rank proliferation was Representative Otis Pike, the veteran New York Democrat. He headed a House Armed Services special subcommittee on manpower utilization which held hearings on grade escalation. His findings:

Rank has been escalating in the officer corps of the services rapidly. In 1946, the services had 315,000 more people than 1971's 2.7 million in uniform, but today's force has 26,000 more captains, 21,000 more majors, 15,000 more lieutenant colonels and 4,000 more colonels. Meanwhile, down at the bottom of the pile, there are 120,000 fewer lieutenants.

The military structure, Pike said, had changed from the traditional pyramid shape to that of a "top-heavy balloon." He, too, was interested in what this did to the military budget. If the United States used today's pay scales and the 1946 rank structure, it could save 2.7 billion a year. Representative Teno Roncalio, a Wyoming Democrat and combat hero of World War II in Sicily, North Africa and France (he won a Silver Star and still belongs to the First Infantry Division Association) told his constituents in a newsletter that with today's pay scale and the 1946 rank structure, we could add 51,000 more officers and 315,000 more enlisted men and still save $760 million a year.

Control of rank inflation is central to the solution of many problems. Not only does rank inflation create a situation in which underlings have to kowtow to many more men in pursuing their own careers, but it also creates a superannuated officer corps. "I am already too old for my command," Brigadier General Paul Francis Gorman, deputy commander of the Army's infantry school at Fort Benning, Georgia, said in the spring of 1972, "and I'm one of the youngest brigadier generals in the Army." Gorman, then forty-three, was talking at a seminar at the Woodrow Wilson International Center for Scholars chaired by retired Lieutenant General James M. Gavin. "People don't realize that General Gavin was only thirty-seven years old when he was commanding a division. Now we have men older than that commanding battalions, and they're too old for their jobs. Down at Fort Benning, I have seventy-five full colonels on my staff doing the work that twenty colonels should be doing. They're just sitting there waiting to retire."

Ticket punching, kowtowing, rank inflation, superannuation, featherbedding, attention to meaningless missions, overuse of perquisites. Now the question becomes, What can be done about it? Some uniformed officers have ideas, and they are not at all as drastic as Colonel David Hackworth's disband-it-all-and-start-over-again suggestion.

In the Navy, suggestions for change came—as orders—from the top.

5

A TIME FOR ICONOCLASTS

On April 13, 1971, teletype machines in communications centers of Navy bases and ships around the world came to life to clatter out an unclassified message headed "From SECNAV to ALNAV." Navy Secretary John H. Chafee was informing the Navy of the instructions he had given to Admiral Bernard A. Clarey, president of the 1971 board that would select line admirals. On the last page of the four-page cable, Chafee said:

> I would hope that you would select a few iconoclasts— original, provocative thinkers who could stimulate the Navy to constantly re-examine its premises and whose selection would encourage those in the lower ranks to do likewise, with the realization that they are not just tolerated but in fact welcomed.

Actually the Navy already had an iconoclast for a leader. Almost a year before that memo was drafted, President Nixon reached thirty-six places down the Navy seniority list and selected Vice Admiral Elmo R. Zumwalt, Jr., then commander of Navy forces in Vietnam, to become the Chief of Naval operations. "Bud" Zumwalt was not yet fifty years old at the time and was the youngest man ever named a full admiral in the United States Navy.

There is nothing in Zumwalt's background to suggest iconoclasm. The only unconventional feature of his career had been the rapidity with which he climbed the ladder from Naval Academy graduate in 1942 to the top. That in itself should be enough to classify him anti-iconoclastic.

As a lieutenant junior grade, he took part in the classic Battle of Leyte Gulf, embarked in a destroyer that made torpedo attacks on Japanese battleships. When the war ended, he took command of a Japanese river gunboat and skippered it up the Whangpoo River to Shanghai. His was the first ship flying the American flag since the beginning of World War II to make that voyage. (In Shanghai, he met and married his wife, the former Mouza Coutelais-du-Roche, a White Russian who had grown up in Manchuria.) During the Korean War, he was a navigator aboard one of the last of the battleships, the USS *Wisconsin,* bombarding the coast of North Korea. After the war, he commanded the first of the Navy's guided-missile destroyers. In the early 1960s, Zumwalt worked as a desk officer in the Defense Department's Office of International Security Affairs (the Pentagon's own little State Department) and for the Chief of Naval Operations, as the organizer of the Navy's counterattack against Robert S. McNamara's Whiz Kids. He directed the establishment of the Navy's own systems-analysis division. He left that job to take command in Vietnam.

In a system that called for perfection in the art of ticket punching, Zumwalt's file was a model. Despite his youth (as viewed from the perspective of a flagship), there was nothing to indicate he would betray his own kind, the other members of the admiral's club.

But the betrayal was not long in coming. As Chief of Naval Operations (CNO), almost from the beginning he showed a marked impatience with the cumbersome chain of command and initiated a whole series of messages to the Navy, the impact of which was to say that the CNO was listening and he was hearing noises from below indicating all was not well with the Navy. The messages were dubbed "Z-Grams," and their originator soon became known to the Navy as "The Z" or "Zumie."

Z-Gram Number One, issued only two weeks after he became CNO, pointed the way. It began: "No other problem concerns me as deeply as reversing the downward trend of Navy retention re-enlistment rates and I am committing myself to improving the quality of Navy life in all respects and restoring the fun and zest of going to sea."

In the following weeks, salvo after salvo of Z-Grams issued from the fifth floor of the Pentagon. They ordered improvements in check-cashing facilities, the establishment of an ombudsman for Navy wives,

the granting of compensatory time off in port for men who were at sea
on holidays, the deletion of formal dress uniforms for young officers,
improvements in commissary operations, creation of better shower and
locker facilities for men doing dirty work, and the creation of a Pentagon office headed by a rear admiral to which men anywhere in the world
could bring personal complaints.

In the belowdecks living spaces of ordinary ships' crewmen, The
Z quickly established himself as a hero. Among the senior petty officers,
on the bridges and in some of the more stuffy wardrooms, the new programs were treated with skepticism.

But Zumwalt knew the need for what he was doing. Not only did
it show in the statistics—retention rates had fallen to the point where
it would become virtually impossible to run a complex Navy—but Zumwalt had also seen for himself what was going on in Vietnam. As commander of all Navy forces there, he did not have the big ships of the
fleet in his command. He had charge of the small units, the so-called
brown-water Navy that patrolled the inland waterways and policed the
shorelines in small boats. He was not isolated from his command by a
shield of lesser admirals and captains. He was dealing directly with
young commanders and lieutenant commanders. In other words, he was
able to get a close, personal look at the horrendous and deepening personnel problems in his service. All this helped to explain the revolution
by telegram that he and many of his key staff members from Vietnam
wrought when they returned to Washington to take over the Navy.

Z-Gram 57 was to become the high-water mark of the Zumwalt
revolution. Issued on November 10, 1970, and headed, with character-
istic bureaucratese, "DEMEANING OR ABRASIVE REGULATIONS, ELIMINA-
TION OF," its message set in motion changes that rocked the Navy from
stem to stern, from fo'c'sle to flag bridge, from wardroom to engine
room. It began:

> Those demeaning or abrasive regulations generally referred
> to in the fleet as "Mickey Mouse" or "Chicken" regs have, in
> my judgment, done almost as much to cause dissatisfaction
> among our personnel as have extended family separation and
> low pay scales. For this reason, shortly after taking command
> I requested a comprehensive review of current Naval policies
> and regulations. I desire to eliminate many of the most abra-
> sive policies, standardize others which are inconsistently en-

forced, and provide some general guidance which reflects my conviction that if we are unable to place the importance and responsibility of "the person" in proper perspective in the more efficient Navy we are seeking, the worth and personal dignity of the individual must be forecefully reaffirmed . . . When visiting fleet units, I not only do not wish to see fresh paint applied strictly because of my visit but consider that rusted surfaces hastily painted over are a reflection of poor command discretion. This type of preparation for any senior officer visit shall be prohibited.

Z-57 struck at everything from painted surfaces to hairstyles, from leave regulations to the use of motorcycles on base, from civilian clothing to the dress of line handlers on deck when a ship is entering port. It was the kind of document that let a hundred flowers of criticism bloom in the Navy. Bloom they did. The Z and his staff of hard-driving, newly created young admirals set up hothouses for nurturing ideas, composed of special "retention boards" to bring complaints to the surface, and then a special office in the Bureau of Personnel to investigate each complaint, make a recommendation to The Z and ultimately transmit his corrective order on green striped paper. "Greenstripers" soon became as familiar a form in the Navy chain of command as the Z-Grams themselves.

The Navy's was a guided revolution from the fifth floor of the Pentagon's E Ring. It might not have been going fast enough to please everyone. The younger officers and enlisted men continued, with reason, to complain. The Z-Gram changes were not always enacted locally. But the complaints, curiously, excused The Z. He was identified as a man trying to set things straight, as a man hampered by all the old, insensitive, traditionalist admirals and lesser officers below him. There was skepticism over whether the Z's programs would work. A typical comment was: "There's lot of guys just going through the motions, sitting around in their jobs, knowing that Zumwalt won't be there forever."

And some were even more outspoken. When Admiral John J. Hyland retired as commander of the Pacific Fleet a few months after the Z-Gram Revolution began, he stood on the flight deck of the aircraft carrier *Oriskany,* and, warning of bleeding hearts, he posed this rhetorical question: "How far can we permit absolute freedom of speech, deportment and dress—and still hang on to the indispensable element of discipline?"

A year and a half later, there were plenty of changes. Civilian clothes were hanging in the living spaces belowdecks, where they had never been permitted on ships before. The flight decks of carriers and the companionways of lesser ships were resplendent with beards, mustaches, sideburns and long hair in the tradition of the men-o'-war commanded by John Paul Jones. Navy men no longer had to change clothes a half dozen times a day.

Contrary to the dire predictions of many, the fleet remained afloat despite the Z-Grams. But that does not mean that the revolution prospered. In fact, the Zumwalt program ran into the expected counterrevolution. And just as Mao had to back down, so did The Z.

The Navy's counterrevolutionaries, like Mao's Communists, were the hard-liners—the senior petty officers and the career officers who could not adjust to the new ways, who saw comfort in traditionalism. Used to giving orders and receiving quick compliance, they were miffed at having to explain *why* in the new Navy. Used to old standards of dress and appearance, they equated the new standards with a permissiveness that was translated into lack of patriotism. They made their complaints known.

In Iceland, the traditionalists refused even to post some of the Z-Grams at the Naval base. In Naples, petty officers ignored many of them.

The Z recognized the strains he was creating. Thirteen months after he promulgated Z-57, he sent out, in December 1971, Z-102:

RESPONSIBILITY FOR STANDARDS OF SMARTNESS

1. During recent visits to ships and stations throughout the Navy, I have seen indications that a few of our people are interpreting some of the initiatives we have introduced as indicative of a shift to a permissive Navy, allowing a relaxation of traditional standards of smartness and cleanliness. In addition, a recent retention study group unanimously stated that there is a need for further definition of acceptable grooming and clothing standards so that this matter can be laid to rest, and all hands can get on with more substantive issues.

2. As an example, Z-57, concerning the elimination of de-

meaning and abrasive regulations, has been erroneously interpreted by some to suggest that saluting and other military
courtesies can be dispensed with. Also, instances are still
observed of men in public with dirty or torn uniforms, haircuts and beards which are below Z-70 standards. Therefore, I
wish to reemphasize once again, that our new initiatives do
not lower our standards of smartness and cleanliness.

3. I have stressed the need to place increased trust in each
individual and want to continue and expand this recognition of
confidence in him. In return, each individual must assume
added responsibilities for his own appearance, conduct, and
performance. . . .

It was not only the internal objectors who gave Zumwalt trouble.
In the spring of 1972, one of his staff members was asked why the
admiral had found it necessary to backtrack. He answered: "Congress.
We're asking for a lot of money this year, and a lot of the men up on the
Hill do not like what they consider to be permissiveness."

Thus, a key part of the backdown came when the Navy, reacting to
criticisms by Representative F. Edward Hébert, the Louisiana Democrat
who headed the House Armed Services Committee, agreed not to send
its men to graduate school at universities that had thrown ROTC off
campus.

Hébert's pressure was simple. He said he would not give the Navy
any funds if it continued the practice.

But nonetheless, a lively debate continued as part of the Zumwalt
revolution. The United States Naval Institute in Annapolis, an old-line,
traditionalist organization dedicated to promoting the Navy's interests
and the nation's supremacy on the seas, dedicated its journal to the
debate. The pages of the *U.S. Naval Institute Proceedings* were opened
to several iconoclastic authors as well as to traditionalists. Vice Admiral
Hyman G. Rickover, the granddaddy of iconoclasts-in-blue, who had
spurned the magazine for years, even deigned to give it praise. Typical
of the reform literature was an article by Lieutenant Malcolm S. Harris,
a young reserve officer who had spent almost four years on active
duty aboard ships in the Pacific and Mediterranean. He then left active
duty to return to law school, giving the Navy a few things to think about
in an article about why the Navy is unable to keep as many junior
officers as it would like:

More than 80 per cent of Navy surface officers choose to return to civilian life at the end of their first tour of obligated service. . . . As late as 1965, naval aviators "shipped over" at the rate of 56 per cent; they now make a second tour at a rate of only 26 per cent. Retention of nuclear submarine officers has fallen from 84 per cent to 45 per cent in the same period.

Obviously, the Navy is not providing the sort of environment in which today's young man wants to pursue a career.[1]

Noting that money alone—either in salary or security-oriented fringe benefits—did not keep young men in uniform, Harris indicted many other aspects of the system.

The automatic promotion of young officers without regard to capabilities "removes what could be a great source of better performance and increased satisfaction," he said. Instead of such uniformity, he suggested promoting lieutenants junior grade to lieutenants according to ability— 20 percent early, 40 percent on time (after three years), 20 percent late and 20 percent not at all. He asked that the so-called Navy Way in which the slogan "Don't Give Up the Ship" has been replaced by "Don't Rock the Boat" be discarded, saying:

The key to success (at least to the level of captain) seems to be the ability to "stay out of trouble." . . . One of the most unfortunate by-products of all this is the homogenizing influence it exerts on the personalities involved. To the junior officer, most senior officers seem, at best, bland; at worst mediocre.

He called for a revision of the Officers Candidate School curriculum to fill "the cerebral void." He asked for an overhaul of the personnel management system, which he describes as "chaotic." He said:

An officer did not attend four years of university and undergo the rigors of the Naval Academy, NROTC or OCS to end up . . . supervisor of fantail sweepdowns. Contrary to popular opinion, what the junior officer really wants is a demanding schedule of relevant work.

And then, harping on the situation that was so apparent aboard Admiral Ferris' *Coral Sea,* he discussed "priorities":

One continually witnesses a tragic system of priorities which places the design and maintenance of machines above the needs of the men who operate them. Electronics spaces are air-conditioned to keep equipment cool, but men in staterooms and berthing compartments continue to swelter in all but the most modern ships. Millions of dollars were spent in programs which modernized the weapons and electronics systems of ships but did virtually nothing to improve their habitability. The reversal of this philosophy must be assigned a high priority.

Then he discussed "life styles," noting that politics, along with women and religion, is taboo for discussion in wardroom's according to OCS curriculum, creating "political monasticism." He criticized the isolation of Americans stationed abroad, called for an end to wasteful procurement of weapons systems, and said junior officers now see the Navy as "an organization which is satisfied with sweeping its internal problems under the rug instead of forcefully attacking them."

Almost a year after The Z had taken command of the Navy, Harris called for "a handful of leaders who have the imagination, compassion and moral courage to undertake a dramatic and convincing shake-up . . . The planning and execution of these reforms must be undertaken with a clean sheet of paper. A patchwork pattern of cosmetic touch-ups can no longer suffice in dealing with the immense retention problem now facing the Navy. Anything less than a completely fresh attitude seems doomed to be defeated by the very system it is trying to improve."

It was not only the youngsters in the Navy who spoke out. A nuclear submariner who was one of the crew of the USS *Triton,* which made the first submerged circumnavigation of the world, wrote to disclose "The Quiet Crisis in the Silent Service." Said Captain Tom B. Thamm, a 1952 Naval Academy graduate:

In less than 20 years, the submarine service has been transformed from a military service with a waiting line to get in, to one with a waiting line to get out.

Thamm took a sociological point of view, comparing the new nuclear submarine service with the old diesel service of World War II fame. The new service, he found, lacks cohesion among the officers. Instead, men are more wedded to their jobs and to the equipment over which they have charge than to their fellow crew members and the ship as a whole. The old service, he said, was characterized by a camaraderie that went from job to wardroom to on-shore activities. It was a free-wheeling spirit typified by the initiation rite an officer endured to win his "gold dolphins," the submariner's equivalent of a pilot's wings. Dolphins, in the old Navy, were sunk in a tall tumbler of whiskey the initiate had to consume before the badge was pinned on his blouse. The new Navy abolished the practice after tests showed the tumbler represented "a potential lethal dose." Thamm continued:

> The cohesiveness of the submarine wardroom has deteriorated because it no longer has the forces of attraction and retention it once had. Its attraction and retention have declined because this group satisfies fewer human needs than before. The group satisfies fewer needs today because its properties have changed as the result of impersonal technological change. Lastly, because it satisfies fewer needs, first-tour officers are seeking other groups that can better satisfy these needs.

The Navy came up with an answer to the retention problem among nuclear submarine officers. It was a good American answer: money. On April 2, 1969, Congress passed a law enabling the Navy to pay $15,000 bonuses to any officer who would reenlist. The bonuses were to be paid in monthly installments, so that, among other things, it meant that some junior officers were earning more than their skippers in the undersea boats.

How did this go over in the Navy? "Expressions of concern over salary conditions are often used to camouflage other considerations," Thamm said.[2]

Commander McIntosh—he who criticized the can-do syndrome—was more direct. He labeled the bonuses "a bribe."

While the Navy's experiment in guided revolution chugged along, the Army was going through a kind of carefully staffed evolution toward the same goals—a service more responsive to the needs of the individual. The focus for change in the Navy could be found right in the CNO's office. Meanwhile, General William C. Westmoreland, the Army Chief, had become typed as a resister to change. In the McLuhan era when image counts, the matter of whether or not Westmoreland had been accurately typed was beside the point. "Westy has all these bright young men working for him, telling him just what he needs to be done, sending him pieces of paper, but he's just afraid to do anything," one bright young Army officer complained.

Nonetheless, dozens of bright young officers and many bright, somewhat older but still not elderly officers like Brigadier Generals Paul Gorman and Robert Gard, who was placed in charge of the Army's drug, discipline and deserter problems in 1971, and Lieutenant General George Forsythe, who was mandated to create a "modern volunteer army," were straining for the Chief's attention.

Study groups at the Army War College and in the Pentagon's general staff were working on the problem. At Fort Benning, the home of the Infantry, and Heidelberg, Germany, the headquarters of the Seventh Army in Europe, effort was underway. But generally, it was the quick, ad hoc fix that was being made while the real problem, the integrity of the officer corps, received lots of attention but far too little in the way of correction.

There were no Westy-Grams in the Army.*

When Westmoreland received the obiter dictum on My Lai from Lieutenant General Peers—the memo calling to his attention the deep moral and professional degeneration in the officer corps—he decided the time had come to act.

So he ordered the Army War College at Carlisle, Pennsylvania, to conduct a deeper study to determine whether the Peers Commission findings really stood up. The War College team surveyed the cream of the Army officer corps—students at the Command and General Staff College at Fort Leavenworth, Kansas, and at the War College itself at

---

* Although there were no Westy-Grams, there were Westy-Letters—one to each Army officer in 1969 on integrity, in which he said: "I want to make it clear beyond any question that absolute integrity of an officer's word, deed, and signature is a matter that permits no compromise"; one in April 1971, giving guidance on leadership: "We must all be constantly concerned and involved with the welfare of our troops"; and one in October 1971, on special trust and confidence. "We must further rejuvenate the meaning of 'special trust and confidence' as we develop a professional force of the highest quality." The effort was not taken very seriously. "Westy thought he could write a letter saying we must have integrity and we would have integrity," one officer said. On a field trip, a major general known as an apple-polisher told Westy he thought so much of the letters that he had had them printed up in a little booklet and distributed throughout the division. The Chief returned to the Pentagon and mentioned what good work the major general was doing. As a result, in 1972, the Army published a fancy little pamphlet with the three letters, entitled "Chief of Staff's Guidance to the Officers of the Army."

Carlisle. The students at those institutions, by definition, were men the Army respected. And yet, as they answered the questionnaires, they showed a deep contempt for the system, confirming what Peers had written.

The results were presented to Westmoreland at a briefing. And now he was really shaken.

He sent a directive to his deputy chief of staff for personnel, ordering him to draw up a plan to redress the professionalism-careerism imbalance within the officer corps; to, in effect, reestablish integrity within the system.

DCS/PERS (pronounced "despers") complied, and within a year the office had produced a massive, wide-ranging program for revolutionizing the officer corps career patterns. The study became known as OPMS—for Officer Personnel Management System—and many of the young, concerned hard chargers in the Pentagon seized upon it as the answer to the Army's post-Vietnam problems.

OPMS was not intended to attack the question of *who* eventually made it to the top. It was, after all, drafted by officers who had succeeded within the system. And, though the system had forced mediocrity to the top in many cases—or at least men mismatched to their jobs—it had also rewarded a high percentage of capable, sensitive officers. OPMS did, however, deal with the question of *how* people made it, what they had to endure, how it crippled their thought processes, corrupted their viewpoints and ultimately made the officer corps a dead weight within the system rather than a guiding light.

OPMS struck at the system's most serious problem—the frenetic competition for command jobs that produced the ticket punching. It put forth the radical, for the Army, proposition that an officer could become a general without having to serve tours in command jobs. It suggested that specialists in such subjects as personnel administration, automatic data processing, intelligence and logistics, to name a few, could hold jobs in those career fields and still hope that someday they would win the right to wear stars on their shoulders. At the same time, its authors proposed that troop command itself—the leading of combat men—be made a separate and distinct specialty within the Army.

Under OPMS, a much smaller group of officers than at present would have been singled out as majors for future command assignments, and from that point on, they would have pursued careers taking them to battalion command as lieutenant colonels, brigade command as

91

colonels and division command as major generals. In this manner, the system would have ensured selection of highly qualified men for intense training and experience in the important command jobs. It would also have lessened pressure by others to obtain those jobs, allowing a stabilization of troop-unit leadership. At present, because there are so few command jobs available and so many officers seeking them, any individual officer's tour is limited in time. After receiving a minimum of experience, he must give way to another officer who also needs experience. Never mind that troop units suffer for this constant turnover in command. At times it seems as if all those men have been summoned into uniform simply to act as pawns for commanders seeking experience.

OPMS had other features intended to restore integrity and bring stability to the officer corps. It would have done away with the distinction between reserve and regular Army officers above the rank of major (allowing many talented reserve officers who are otherwise forced to retire at the rank of lieutenant colonel to remain in service if they wished), and it would have allowed regular Army officers to leave service with a lump-sum separation allowance (not a lifetime pension) after twelve years of service. The reasoning behind this proposal was the belief that the Army had far too many field-grade officers just waiting out their time until retirement and, like Brigadier General Gorman's colonels at Fort Benning, taking up jobs that should have gone to younger men.

Supporting these changes were proposals for a drastic revision of the Army's educational, training and promotion programs for the officer corps.

All neatly tied together in one document, OPMS was submitted to key officers throughout the Army for their comments. And, as a result, toward the end of 1971, OPMS was killed.

"Two groups of critics killed it," said one officer who had a hand in drafting OPMS. "First there were the old generals who took the attitude that there's nothing wrong with the system. 'We made it,' they said, 'so it can't be very bad.' Then there was the group of old colonels who did not make it. 'If we couldn't do it,' they said, 'nobody else will either.' Everyone took the attitude that OPMS was the doing of some young punks looking for a new way to milk the system."

A debate over OPMS raged internally, by memorandum, all the memos piling up on the desk of General Westmoreland. Only once did it break out into the open. In the December 1971 issue of *Army,* the monthly publication of the Association of the U.S. Army, Lieutenant Colonels William L. Hauser, a field artillery officer, and Zeb B. Bradford, an infantryman, published an article entitled "Officer Corps Reform is Our Job." The article was a last-ditch effort to save OPMS, and the authors had clearance from their superiors in the Pentagon. They said:

> We must realize that the Army, like the nation, has reached a turning point in civilian-military relations. The honeymoon begun at Pearl Harbor lasted a long time, but, regretfully, it is over. People aren't taking anything on faith anymore. We are going to be held accountable for every dollar and every soldier to a degree we have never before experienced. We must gear up for the next generation of service to our country. It is going to be a lot tougher. We are going to have to be a lot better and we aren't going to make it if we don't get moving.

Shortly after the article appeared, OPMS was revived, though it was much trimmed down in scope. Much of the language that had rankled its critics, and many of the programs, were excised. A plan was devised for putting the system into effect piecemeal and, now known as OPMS II, it was approved in concept by General Westmoreland and Army Secretary Robert F. Froehlke.

Even the new, less ambitious program, already the result of much thought and discussion, could not be put into effect immediately. That was just not the Army's way. Instead, General Westmoreland set up a new study board to study the new OPMS study. Groups went to work on how to implement it. A decision was made that phase one of the implementation would be the creation of a new, centralized selection board for command at the colonel and lieutenant colonel levels. The boards each year would select only enough officers to fill command jobs opening during the coming year. In other words, if there were only twenty-five brigade command positions opening up, the board would select only twenty-five colonels to fill them. A colonel not selected for command under the new system knew that the opportunity would be denied him permanently. Previously, hundreds of colonels would be hounding OPO—and beseeching prestigious generals to do some hounding for them as well—to win brigade command jobs. With OPMS II in effect, men selected for command knew they would get a job and men not selected knew that whatever amount of pressure they brought to bear on OPO would be useless. Near the very top, at least, ticket punching had been cut down.

But nonetheless, OPMS II was less than half a loaf. It still did not provide for early identification and selection of potential commanders, thus leaving the young officers with the need to scamper from billet to billet, pressuring OPO for command experience. Command experience itself was still a necessity for promotion to the highest ranks.

Along with the establishment of the command selection board, the Army took steps to stabilize command by making tours in battalion- and brigade-level jobs eighteen to twenty-four months. Commanders, in other words, were expected to stay with their troops, not just obtain the minimal experience—get their tickets punched—and move on. Not all high-ranking officers were happy with the new system; there was still pressure for fast rotation.

"I'm afraid we'll have this new system for a year or so and then it will go right back to the old way," one officer said.

With recognition of the importance of specialists still not adopted, the Army clearly intended to award the stars to the troop commanders.

"That's what the game is all about," one officer on General Westmoreland's staff said, ignoring the fact that a successful troop commander—say, a man like General George S. Patton, Jr., of World War II fame—does not necessarily make the best chief of staff of the Army or member of the Joint Chiefs of Staff, jobs which call for a great deal more cerebration and greater capacity to think abstractly about roles and missions, about national purpose and overall security than troop commanders must.

It was with knowledge aforethought that the military projected successful bomber pilots, aircraft carrier skippers and division commanders to the top of the heap. They are good at leading men in battle. They are not necessarily so good at devising defense policy for the nation. In fact, the two aptitudes may work at cross purposes. A successful national security adviser may, at times, perform his job better by recommending that men not be called to action. One who has made a career of leading men, on the other hand, inevitably calls on his past experience to help in solving a contemporary problem.

So, in the last analysis, the greatest tangible failing of the system, other than its own corruption, may be the projection of commanders to the top, to membership on the Joint Chiefs of Staff.

6

THE FLIMSY BUFF-GREEN-RED-STRIPED NIGHTMARE

The meetings of the Joint Chiefs of Staff convene as regularly as a West Point course in political science—and they are about as important to the overall operation of the Defense Establishment. Every Monday, Wednesday and Friday afternoon, the top-ranking officers in each of the four armed services and their chairman—five four-star officers in all—take their places around an oval walnut conference table in a little-known room called "The Tank" situated just inside the Mall entrance to the Pentagon.

The deputies to the Joint Chiefs have carefully prepared the scene. The thick gold carpeting has been swept clean and its pile fluffed high. The necessary papers have been laid out on the table in front of each chair. Someone has thought to fill a couple of glass bowls with an assortment of penny candy on which the Joint Chiefs have traditionally munched and sucked as they deliberate the affairs of the world and the needs of their services. "We like to keep the Chiefs happy," an aide said in commenting on the penny candy touch. "They pretty much get what they want."

Five four-star officers: Five regulation neckties carefully knotted. Five shirts freshly starched. Five breasts emblazoned with row upon row of campaign and awards ribbons representing the achievements of a lifetime. Five jackets securely brass-buttoned without a wrinkle among them all. Five pairs of trousers pressed to a fine crease by enlisted aides —service-provided valets, actually—each morning. Five pairs of shoes brought to a mirror-bright shine. These are the outward signs of professionalism. A military professional is known by the attention he pays to detail. Lack of attention to detail could someday mean the loss—needlessly—of lives under one's command, and so all five of these men, since their earliest days in the service as plebes at the service academies, have been taught to abhor the speck of dust, the scuff mark or the wrinkle that betrays lack of attention to detail.*

They are professionals all: firm of jaw, trim of figure, possessed of the social graces, articulate, precise of movement. They epitomize what thousands of other officers someday hope to become. And now they take their seats around that table.

Their chairman, in 1972, was Admiral Thomas Hinman Moorer, sixty, a jocular Alabaman who was a veteran of the Annapolis gridiron and the Japanese attack on Pearl Harbor, where, on December 7, 1941, he was stationed as a young flying-boat pilot. Shot down by the Japanese while flying another patrol in the Dutch East Indies in 1942, he was rescued and decorated for "courage and leadership" during a subsequent enemy attack that sunk the rescue ship. He was a member of the post-World War II team that conducted the famous Strategic Bombing Survey to determine how much damage air raids had done to the Japanese home islands. Promoted to rear admiral at the age of forty-five, he commanded the Atlantic Fleet in the mid-1960s, served as Chief of Naval Operations from 1967 to 1969 and was named Chairman of the Joint Chiefs of Staff by President Nixon in 1970.

Representing the Army was General William Childs Westmoreland, fifty-eight, a South Carolinian who graduated from West Point in 1936 as first captain of the corps of cadets, announcing soon after to his fel-

---

* Professional military men make a fetish of appearance. Ernest B. Furgurson, the biographer of General William C. Westmoreland, met an Army chaplain who had served with Westmoreland as a young man. In *Westmoreland, The Inevitable General,* published by Little, Brown and Co. in 1968, Furgurson quotes the chaplain this way on page 97:

> He [Westmoreland] was a meticulous dresser, changed uniforms every day, looked as sharp and smart at night as in the morning. He deplored sloppy dress, not so much because of its hygienic and aesthetic aspects as because he reasoned it was a manifestation of an indifferent, sloppy attitude. He would often say that by his dress you can tell if a man has a positive or negative attitude. . . .

low second lieutenants of field artillery that he expected one day to become Army Chief of Staff. By the age of twenty-eight, he was commanding a battalion. He commanded a full division before he turned thirty-
one. He was a veteran of combat in North Africa, Sicily, France, Bel-
gium and Germany. He forsook the field artillery in 1946 to earn his
paratrooper's wings and transfer to the airborne infantry. During the
Korean War, he commanded an airborne regimental combat team. In
1953, he attended the Harvard Business School for a short course. Then
he served successively as secretary of the Army General Staff, commander of the elite 101st Airborne Division (the "Screaming Eagles"),
superintendent of West Point, commander of the XVIII Airborne Corps
at Fort Bragg, North Carolina, and then deputy commander and later
commander of the U.S. Military Assistance Command in Vietnam. The
prototypical ticket puncher, the man against whom thousands of other
officers subsequently measured their careers—going through jump
school to become "airborne," applying for graduate school, seeking battalion command—Westy assumed his seat at the walnut table in The
Tank on July 3, 1968.

General John Dale Ryan, fifty-seven, of Cherokee, Iowa, the Air
Force Chief of Staff, graduated from West Point in 1938 where, like
Moorer at Annapolis, he was a distinguished football player. In fact, in
1962, *Sports Illustrated* named him to a Silver Anniversary All-American
Team composed of former college stars who had done well in their
chosen professions. Ryan never saw combat at a level lower than lieutenant colonel, a grade he achieved at age twenty-seven after progressing from first lieutenant to lieutenant colonel in two years. A bomber
pilot, he became commander of the Strategic Air Command in 1964,
commander of the Pacific Air Forces in 1967 and Chief of Staff of the
Air Force in 1969.

Admiral Elmo R. Zumwalt, Chief of Naval Operations, was the
Navy's member.

Finally, the most junior member of the group was General Robert
E. Cushman, Jr., Marine Corps Commandant and a protégé of Richard
M. Nixon. Cushman, fifty-eight, is a native of St. Paul, Minnesota, and a
1935 graduate of Annapolis. Like Moorer, Cushman was at Pearl
Harbor on December 7, 1941. He was commanding the Marine detachment aboard the battleship *Pennsylvania* which was attacked by Japanese planes in the harbor and severely damaged. Later he commanded
a battalion that stormed across the beaches of Bougainville, Guam and

Iwo Jima in the campaign to regain strategic Pacific islands from the Japanese. Although Cushman accumulated all the traditional tickets for an officer of his age—World War II combat, command at battalion, regimental and division levels, staff jobs in Washington, service-school education—he also worked in two unusual jobs. From October 1949 to May 1951, he served a tour with the CIA in a capacity his official biography does not detail. In 1957, he was assigned to the staff of then Vice President Nixon as assistant for national security affairs, a position in which he served four years. During the height of the Vietnam War, he served as deputy commander and then commander of all the Marines in Vietnam. In April 1969, President Nixon named him deputy director of the CIA,* and in January 1972, the President appointed him Commandant of the Marine Corps. Thus of the five men sitting at the table in The Tank, only Cushman could approach his work with the benefit of a background widened by service in other than strictly military situations.

Of the five officers dealing with political and social questions of a world-wide nature, not one had served overseas in a capacity other than troop leader. Not one had ever studied overseas. Not one had ever been a military attaché. If one of them had ever traveled abroad in a nonprofessional capacity, that fact was not deemed important enough to mention in the official biography sheets (as General Westmoreland mentioned that his hobbies were water-skiing and tennis). With the exception of Westmoreland's three months at the Harvard Business School, not one had ever taken advantage of higher education.

The five men who gathered around that table in The Tank to reflect on the state of the world three times a week were all men of action asked to serve in a thinker's role. They were leaders of men asked to become analysts of ideas. They were commanders serving as advisers.

---

* During his second CIA tour, Cushman, a long-time associate and favorite of President Nixon, gave agency support to White House domestic espionage agents despite legal restraints on such activity by the agency. (It is only chartered to operate overseas.) At his direction, the CIA provided disguises, forged documents and the paraphernalia of spying to White House-hired men investigating Daniel Ellsberg, the man who made the Pentagon Papers public. The White House men burglarized the office of Ellsberg's psychiatrist, looking for records. When nothing was found, the agency's specialist started to draw up a psychiatric profile of Ellsberg. When Cushman saw that he was drawing the agency in too deeply, he withdrew the support. But that he even gave that much astounded many. Cushman's rationale: The White House requested the help and he was only following orders.

And, at their level, they could refer to no step-by-step service manuals to detail for them, in precise language, just how to do their jobs.

Just what was that job? In service-manual terms, that question could be answered easily:

It was the duty of the Joint Chiefs of Staff to provide the President, the National Security Council and the Secretary of Defense with the best possible advice on matters affecting the military strength of the nation. Secondarily, it was their duty to make certain that the orders of the President and the Secretary of Defense—the civilian masters of the Joint Chiefs—to the military were carried out efficiently and in keeping with the spirit of the Presidential dictates.

Over the years, the Joint Chiefs have amassed a staff of assistants now almost two thousand men strong and have developed a form of decision-making, unparalleled in Washington in its ritualism, to help them in supposedly designing, building and operating the military machine. The purpose of all those men and the ritualism is to protect the interests of each of the military services in the decision-making process and to enable the combined services to wage bureaucratic war against the civilians in the Defense Department and in the other departments of the government.

The irony is that as the organization has grown more and more elaborate, the influence of the Joint Chiefs within the national security bureaucracy in Washington has grown steadily weaker. Today, the five top military leaders in the land are reduced to presiding over hundreds of top-flight officers who perform little but make-work. The history of the organization sheds some light on how this all came to pass.

President Harry S. Truman struck upon the idea of the unification of the military services after World War II to avoid an organizational nightmare: the continued growth of three separate War Departments—one for land, one for sea, one for air—all, in the name of national defense, working at cross purposes. His campaign resulted in the creation in 1947 of a unified National Defense Establishment, headed by a secretary of defense, but still containing cabinet-level departments of the Army, Navy and Air Force. Since that creation, the unified Defense Establishment itself has become an organizational nightmare—an actual evil that replaced an anticipated evil—and still no one has been able to straighten it out.

The conventional wisdom is that Robert S. McNamara, the Defense

Secretary under Presidents John F. Kennedy and Lyndon B. Johnson, made great strides in untangling all the threads of that bad dream. But the legacies of the McNamara years—the transport and fighter planes he bought that pilots are afraid to fly, the ships he ordered that sailors dislike sailing, the communications systems he installed that send important messages intended for the Mediterranean instead to the Far East, the ground forces designed under his supervision to counter insurgency in backward countries that failed so dismally in Vietnam—all deny the truth of that evaluation.

McNamara found the Defense Department a nightmare. He left it that way. And it remained a nightmare under Defense Secretary Melvin R. Laird. The Joint Chiefs of Staff represent only one aspect of that bad dream. In the nightmarish organization of the defense establishment, the practice has been for civilians more and more to make purely military decisions without ever counseling with the Joint Chiefs. Thus Lyndon Johnson and his advisers, much of the time without any military men present, each Tuesday over a lunch table in the White House selected the targets his airplanes would bomb in North Vietnam. No Joint Chiefs were invited to dine during the early months of the process. Nixon delegated to an organizational creation of his administration—the Washington Special Actions Group (abbreviated WSAG and pronounced "wasag")—the authority for planning and overseeing the Cambodian invasion of 1970 and the renewed air war in North Vietnam in the spring of 1972. The chairman of the Joint Chiefs attended those meetings but none of his colleagues. Back in 1960 and 1961, Presidents Eisenhower and Kennedy allowed the Central Intelligence Agency to plan the invasion of Cuba—which ended in the Bay of Pigs fiasco—without calling on the Chiefs for more than cursory comment on the plans.

All this grew out of what was intended as a very rational process in which the Joint Chiefs were to play an important role. On paper, the national security apparatus in Washington appears most rational. The Central Intelligence Agency is the keystone of an intelligence community that provides and analyzes information. The State Department exercises a diplomatic function in keeping the nation's relations with foreign countries on an even keel. The powers of the Defense Department are called upon only when diplomatic tools fail in furthering the nation's vital interests. Superimposed on these agencies—and others such as the Agency for International Development, which dispenses foreign aid, and the

United States Information Agency, which dispenses an image of America—is the National Security Council, which was established as a top-level policy-making and advisory group to the President.

The actualities of usage have not lived up to the rationalities of design. Instead you find the CIA raising, supporting and committing armies (all foreign) to battle; the Defense Department developing its own little State Department; the National Security Council falling into disuse except as a body to ratify decisions already made more informally, and the State Department, in the Nixon Administration, being stripped of even its fundamental role as diplomatic representative of the nation abroad. All this is indicative of the imperfections Presidents find in an ever-growing bureaucracy that does not respond to the varied styles of the men elected to head it. It is also reflective of an internecine warfare conducted without abatement inside the bureaucracy to make certain that not only are the vital needs of the nation met but that they are met in a manner which does not hinder the continued growth of each bureaucratic element.

The bureaucratic wars are fought on many levels: CIA against Defense Department; Pentagon against the State Department's Arms Control and Disarmament Agency; State Department against the CIA and/or Pentagon. Inside the Pentagon, they are also fought on several levels: military against civilians; service against service; one civilian bureau against another; branch of service against another branch of the same service. The problem with all this warfare is that too often, the vested interests of the separate bureaucratic elements are placed above the best interests of the nation in formulating policy and resolving difficulties.

The planning and execution of the invasion of Cuba at the Bay of Pigs in April 1961 stands as the classic case of how intrabureaucratic warfare not only failed to help advance the nation's foreign policy but actually dealt it a severe setback. That operation was conceived, planned and executed by the Central Intelligence Agency which, initially, kept the planning so secret that even the Joint Chiefs of Staff were not advised of what was under way.

The Joint Chiefs uncovered the CIA's plans first by chance and then by piecing together bits of stray information. More than a decade after the abortive invasion of Cuba, Admiral Arleigh Burke, who was Chief of Naval Operations at the time, recalled that he first heard of the imminent invasion in the winter of 1960–1961 from Naval intelligence

101

sources who reported the clandestine training of a band of Cubans in Nicaragua. About the same time, General David M. Shoup, then Commandant of the Marine Corps, noticed one day on a visit to a Marine depot in Albany, Georgia, that thousands of rifles were being removed from a warehouse, cleaned and packed for shipping to an Army base in Texas.

"We were being relieved of 3,000 rifles," Shoup recalled in the spring of 1972. "Obviously those weapons had been commandeered, and I knew nothing about it previously." When Shoup returned to Washington, he found that none of the deputies knew of the transfer either. The rifles were being shipped to the CIA, which was turning them over to the Cuban invaders, and the only two men who knew of the transaction, according to Shoup, were a captain in the Pentagon "and the man who was cleaning the rifles for shipment" in Albany.

At this point, the Joint Chiefs pooled the intelligence-gathering capabilities of their services to mount a clandestine campaign against the CIA. Experts in the techniques of amphibious warfare, the Chiefs were nonetheless excluded from the early planning and were reduced to spying on their fellow bureaucrats to keep informed of a military operation their own government was organizing. When the CIA ran into difficulty with the planning of the logistics for the invasion, the Joint Chiefs were finally called in for consultation. President Kennedy asked them to review the plan.

They did and sent a memo to the White House, according to Burke, which said that the operation had only a "fifty-fifty chance" of success if the logistics problems could be cleared up. Subsequently, for political reasons, the landing site was switched from the city of Trinidad to the Bay of Pigs. Now the Joint Chiefs told the President the plan had "less than a fifty-fifty chance of success."

The Chief's admonition that the plan was more likely to fail than succeed was ignored by both the CIA and the White House, leading Burke to say, in 1972, "The President had been used to more spectacular words. Looking back, we should have insisted on the Bay of Pigs being a military operation, and we should have insisted that once the President approved of the operation that he keep his hands off, which he wouldn't do."

But the Chiefs did not pursue that course. Like officers throughout the chain of command, they were trapped in a system where orders are orders or, to be even more precise, where *presumed* orders are orders;

where a subordinate bends to a superior's will even though he knows that the course chosen means disaster. Of course, in any highly organized bureaucracy, men must, within reason, follow orders. But in other bureaucracies, the consequences of adhering to bad orders are far less than in the military. They could result in great losses of profit, in distasteful advertising campaigns, in uncomfortable work stoppages, in a transitory damage to the environment. But allowing bad orders to go forward without vigorous protest in the military results in needless loss of life and the infliction of unjustified suffering on thousands of human beings who would be better off left alone. In an organization that measures a man's ability to pay attention to detail by the manner in which his valet keeps his clothes in condition, the manner in which it trains subordinates to overlook major mistakes of superiors and accept them without objection is striking.

"We are pragmatic men," Burke said in trying to explain why the Joint Chiefs did not object more vigorously to the Bay of Pigs plans in 1961. "Words do not mean the same thing to us that they do to other people. The Chiefs did not realize that when President Kennedy used such phrases as 'we will do this' that he had not yet really made up his mind. The Chiefs took those phrases to mean that a Presidential decision had been made and that it was our responsibility to support it and not argue with it. Similarly, Kennedy did not understand the full import of the language the Chiefs were using."

Burke's recollections illuminate the manner in which communication can break down within the national security bureaucracy either accidentally or through design. (There is one school of thought in Washington which holds that the Joint Chiefs deliberately underplayed their forebodings out of a desire to see the CIA-led Bay of Pigs operation fail.)

After the Bay of Pigs failure, Kennedy empaneled a committee chaired by General Maxwell D. Taylor, a former Army Chief of Staff who came out of retirement to do the job, to investigate the fiasco. The committee included Burke; Robert F. Kennedy, then Attorney General; and Allen Dulles, director of the CIA. The committee took testimony from hundreds of witnesses and, following the President's orders, submitted its report in only one copy. Among other criticisms of the operation, the report indicted the Joint Chiefs for not giving the President candid enough advice, and Kennedy, disregarding the many other faults in the operation, seized upon that point, heaping the blame on the

Chiefs. The Chiefs, in fact, remained a convenient whipping boy for a decade as historians glossed over the fact that the Chiefs had told Kennedy the operation had a greater chance of failure than success.*

After Taylor's post-mortem, Kennedy, the general said, went to the Pentagon and met with the Joint Chiefs in The Tank. "It was a blunt meeting," according to Taylor. "The President told the Chiefs they should no longer give narrow professional advice. He told them he wanted their best judgment on economic, political and psychological matters as well as strictly military matters. The Chiefs asked him to put that in writing, and he did in a National Security Council memorandum."

According to Taylor, President Johnson, when he took office, reaffirmed the highly classified memo, which is now the most current known document detailing just how Presidents expect the Joint Chiefs to operate. More than a decade after it was written, the memo remains classified, not because it contains sensitive information but to maintain the principle that all national security council documents are free from declassification. Thus it has been made impossible for the American public to learn even the theoretical ground rules under which Presidents expect their Joint Chiefs of Staff to operate.

It is not only the narrowness of their own outlook and the timidity of their advice that renders the output of the Joint Chiefs unacceptable, as it did at the time of the Bay of Pigs. They suffer also from the complexity of their own bureaucracy and the manner in which the whole Organization of the Joint Chiefs of Staff fits into the larger national security bureaucracy.

During the years leading up to the inauguration of John F. Kennedy as President, money was the prize over which many an internecine battle was fought in The Tank. With strategic weapons—nuclear bombs and warheads, and the planes, rockets and submarines to carry them—gobbling up ever larger chunks of the government's funds, the services each fought long and hard for their share. With the jurisdictional problems over the control of forces settled, the services began to fight over equipment. The Air Force and Navy squared off in a fight over bombers

---

* In 1972, Professor Lyman B. Kirkpatrick, Jr., a professor at Brown who was CIA inspector general at the time of the Bay of Pigs, somewhat belatedly said his old agency, and not the Joint Chiefs of Staff, was to blame for the failure. He spoke at the Naval War College.

versus aircraft carriers, each fearful that if Congress chose to buy one weapons system, it would not buy the other. The Army and Air Force fought over who would control continental air defense. The Army claimed that antiaircraft and antimissile defenses were but an extension of traditional field and shore artillery defenses. The Air Force said you needed airplanes to shoot down other airplanes and that the ground weapons were only secondary defenses. The Army and Navy fought over the matter of troop transport, the Army wanting to preserve its own fleet of transport ships to move its troops overseas. These are only examples. There was hardly a question that was not subjected to this kind of scrutiny in The Tank, and the fights were fierce.

McNamara changed that. In the pre-McNamara days, each service was awarded a fixed budget ceiling each year and had to plan its spending within that ceiling. McNamara discarded that idea, replacing it with a scheme for setting force levels regardless of cost on the basis of mission requirements. In other words, if one service prospered in the Mc-Namara system, it would not necessarily be at the expense of another. The new way led the Joint Chiefs into a delicate log-rolling process in The Tank in which, instead of bitterly disagreeing, they began to support each other and produce unanimity. The Air Force dropped its objections to the Army's antiballistic missile system when it saw that construction of such a system would not mean fewer airplanes. The Navy began to support the system in the hope that it would become the forerunner of a Navy shipborne ABM program.

In addition the Joint Chiefs united to fight the new generation of civilians whom McNamara brought to the Pentagon to analyze and evaluate military spending programs. They were the systems analysts or "Whiz Kids" who soon became hateful to the military. They were interested in data to support conclusions. The Joint Chiefs were used to making conclusions based on their less tangible personal experience. The Whiz Kids spoke a language that the Joint Chiefs at first did not understand. The generals united against the common enemy as they would have against any invading horde. They regrouped, studied the new tactics being used against them, fought a rear-guard action, and finally adopted the ways of the enemy.

The Joint Chiefs developed their own capacity for systems analysis.

McNamara loaded the Joint Chiefs apparatus down with studies, keeping the Chiefs and their Indians—as the Joint Staff members are known—busy with make-work. The results of all their studies were generally ignored as the civilians increased their control over the decision-making process in the Pentagon.

The pressure was on the Joint Chiefs to agree among themselves. If they could not, they thought, then the Defense Secretary or the President would make decisions for them, and none of the services would be happy.*

The Pentagon offices of the civilian controller, of systems analysis and of international security affairs (the Pentagon's little State Department) grew as powerful—if not more so—than The Tank. As the years wore on, political appointees infiltrated deeper and deeper into the bureaucracy, first under Kennedy and then under Lyndon Johnson. They usurped more and more of the authority that belonged to the Joint Chiefs and the uniformed officers working under their direction.

One man who watched all this happen was a bright young colonel by the name of Alexander Haig who, himself, was favored by the civilian appointees and thus could watch from a good vantage point. Haig worked for one of the more important of the civilian employees, Joseph Califano, a young Whiz Kid who was to move from McNamara's Pentagon staff into the White House where he became Johnson's number one adviser and operative on domestic affairs. After Califano left Defense, Haig went to work for Army Secretary Cyrus L. Vance, and when Vance was elevated to the number two job in the Pentagon, deputy secretary, Haig remained with him.

Haig was one of a small group of uniformed men working in the civilian bureaus of the Pentagon in the sixties who gained the unqualified respect of their civilian superiors. (Zumwalt, one of those men who had become knowledgeable about systems analysis, was another.) Haig was given more and more responsibility.

As the Vietnam War escalated, Haig, like all other ambitious young officers of the period, wanted a Southeast Asian tour. With a war on, the only sure way for advancement was through action in the field. But McNamara and Vance thought him too valuable in Washington, and his requests for transfer were refused. So he remained behind and watched with disappointment as his civilian masters gathered in more and more power which he felt should remain in the hands of the Joint

---

* In 1964, General Taylor, by then himself the chairman of the Joint Chiefs of Staff, talking to the American Bar Association, noted that the Joint Chiefs, in the consideration of 7,300 different questions in the five years 1958 through 1963, disagreed on only 128 items, less than one quarter of 1 percent.

Chiefs. "The President does not have to agree with the Joint Chiefs," Haig told a friend, "but he should at least listen to what they have to say."

Finally the time came for service in Vietnam, and Haig left Washington. Just before his departure, he wrote a tough memorandum to the civilians deploring the fact that even General Earle G. Wheeler, chairman of the Joint Chiefs of Staff at the time, was being excluded from the White House Tuesday lunch sessions, the key decision-making meetings on the war. Johnson invited McNamara and Secretary of State Dean Rusk to those sessions. Richard Helms, the CIA director, attended, and so did Walt W. Rostow, the President's national security affairs adviser. Bill D. Moyers, and later, George Christian, the White House press secretaries, attended. They were civilians all. There was not a military man among them as they pored over maps and reports, making decisions down to such minute detail as the type of bombs that would be used in attacks on particular targets and the flight plans the aircraft would fly.

Although there may be no cause-and-effect relationship, shortly after Haig submitted his memo, Johnson began inviting Wheeler to the Tuesday lunch sessions.

Haig finished his year in Vietnam and then went to West Point to become deputy commandant of the Academy, the position he held when the Nixon Administration took office. After Nixon hired Dr. Henry A. Kissinger as his national security adviser, the former Harvard professor began recruiting a staff. He asked each of the services to nominate a candidate to take charge of running the White House Situation Room, that nerve center from which the President is kept abreast of important happenings around the world. The Army nominated Haig. His candidacy was given an important push by Fritz Kraemer, an old friend and early mentor of Kissinger who was working as a political-military consultant to Westmoreland. Haig was hired, and slowly, to the consternation of the civilians on Kissinger's staff, he established himself as Kissinger's deputy. He was one soldier who, over the year, had learned something about how to deal with civilians.

When Haig was promoted to brigadier general, President Nixon himself pinned the star on his shoulder. When Haig was promoted to major general, the President pinned on the second star as well. Only forty-seven, and one of the most junior generals in the Army, Haig had established himself as the most influential Army man and one of the most influential military men in Washington. Haig met often with the President. Westmoreland, nominally the Army's top man, met with the President only on ceremonial occasions. Westy did, at times, have the opportunity to meet with Kissinger. Those sessions were arranged by Haig. Haig led the advance party that arranged the details of President Nixon's extraordinary 1972 trip to China. Haig made several quick trips to Vietnam to check, for the President, on the reports filtering up through the chain of command. And finally, in the summer of 1972, Haig was skipped over dozens of his seniors, promoted from two to four stars, and named vice chief of staff of the Army.*

Meanwhile, Defense Secretary Melvin R. Laird was at least listening to the Joint Chiefs. After he took office, he established a policy of attending each of the Monday meetings in The Tank and as a result quickly earned the approval of the Joint Chiefs. Stories began appearing in the press that the Joint Chiefs, "down" in the Kennedy and Johnson years, were once again on their way up. Actually that was far from the case.

Haig was the military man who counted in Washington while he was in the White House and, ironically, he was making himself a prime candidate to one day soon take a place at the walnut conference table in The Tank. Whether he would enjoy the same influence as Army chief of staff that he enjoyed as a young major general with an office in the White House remained to be seen. His was one of the few careers that had broken out of the mold dictated for all the other ticket punchers. It was a career that suited him admirably for service in The Tank. And ultimately, his membership on the Joint Chiefs would provide a test of whether the problem with that body is systemic or whether it is background career deficiencies of the men themselves that must be held responsible for the Joint Chiefs' failures.

Whatever the reason, those failures went unrecognized within the organization itself. Despite the fact that no one was listening, the Organization of the Joint Chiefs of Staff continued to work at a frenzied pace.

---

* In April 1973, after Haig had been in his new job less than six months, he was summoned back to the White House to replace H. R. ("Bob") Haldeman as President Nixon's chief of staff when Haldeman was implicated in the Watergate scandal. So the President's political needs were assigned precedence over the Army's intense need for reform as Haig was "temporarily" detached from military duty. Several weeks later, he resigned from the Army altogether.

Joint Staff members are called "purple suiters" to denote the idea that the colors of all their uniforms—the green of the Army, the dark blue of the Navy, the light blue of the Air Force and the khaki of the Marines—would blend into a single, unified color representing all the services without partiality. It was a nice intention. In fact, the colors do not mix. The men working for the Joint Chiefs do not rise above the parochial interests of their individual services, as intended. They instead become protectors of their services within the Joint Chiefs of Staff organization.

For years it has been fashionable to say in Washington that "the Supreme Court deliberates, Congress debates and the Joint Chiefs bicker." That is no longer really the case. The big fault with the Joint Chiefs is not bickering so much as the process developed to avoid bickering. That process is an unbelievable rite of compromise which precludes any meaningful difference from leaking out of The Tank on all but the rarest of occasions.*

Compromise, as practiced by the Joint Chiefs of Staff, requires manpower. In 1958, Congress authorized the Chiefs to recruit a "Joint Staff" of 400 officers from the three services, the Marine members to be included in the Navy's allotment. So that no service would receive an advantage over the others, the Joint Staff has actually been fixed at

---

* How the Joint Chiefs can compromise their differences was illustrated in 1970 in an incident that has not been previously reported. It occurred when the Army general commanding all American troops in Europe requested a change in operational plans to allow him to order the firing of intermediate range ballistic missiles in wartime without consulting higher authority. The change made sense militarily, and it went through the cumbersome deliberative process to be detailed later in this chapter. At the last moment, the Air Force made what it called an "editorial change" in the sentence reading "CINCEUR shall have the authority to fire IRBMs." The change was the insertion of the word "not." The Navy supported the Air Force change. At issue, of course, was the Army's gaining the opportunity to hit targets in Eastern Europe with surface-to-surface missiles, taking away jobs from both land- and sea-based aircraft. A split paper was threatened, which would have meant that Defense Secretary Melvin R. Laird would be called upon to make the decision. Admiral Thomas H. Moorer, the Joint Chiefs of Staff chairman, refused to countenance a split. "We're not going to have one. We've already had three splits in this fiscal year," he said, according to a Joint Staff member who attended the JCS session. Compromise was in order. The Army suggested its own editorial change, insertion of the phrase "under certain circumstances" into the sentence, making it read: "CINCEUR shall, under certain circumstances, have the authority to fire IRBMs." The certain circumstances were never spelled out, making the new policy meaningless. Thus do the Joint Chiefs finesse their responsibility to provide military advice to their civilian masters.

399, a total divisible into three equal parts. Since 1958, the Joint Chiefs have been able to circumvent easily the Congressional limitation on size. It created a bureaucracy known as the "Organization of the Joint Chiefs of Staff," which has employed over 2,100 officers, enlisted men and civilians.

This organization is supposed to provide the Chiefs with impartial information on which they may base their decisions. Once delegated to work for the Joint Chiefs, officers from the services theoretically subordinate their loyalty to their own service in favor of loyalty to the entire defense establishment. It is a nice theory. It does not always work. Too many of the officers assigned to the organization of the Joint Chiefs use their positions to act as advocates of their service's viewpoint. Even this, however, is not satisfactory to the services. Each maintains a large staff of officers in its headquarters to work with the staff of the Joint Chiefs in conducting studies.

The meaning of this in bureaucratic terms is staggering. When the Joint Chiefs initiate a study, each of the services sets up a companion study of the same problem. Each study is considered at three different levels within the Organization of the Joint Chiefs—by colonels, low-ranking generals and lieutenant generals—before it is tabled in The Tank. Simultaneously, each study is considered at the same three levels in the headquarters of each service. The procedure is so complicated that the staff men use color-coded paper to remind them what stage a study is in. Colonels work on flimsy paper, low-ranking generals on buff paper, lieutenant generals on green. Amendments to the studies are called "purples" because they were once submitted on purple paper, a practice that has now been abandoned in the interest of sight-saving. Once a study has been approved and its content made military policy, it is issued on red-striped paper.

The studies are of problems ranging from the most picayune to the most all-encompassing. The Chiefs once spent weeks discussing the design of the uniform for the Air Force when that service separated from the Army. They use the same procedure for that kind of study that they employ to develop long-range military policies for the nation.

The purpose of all this debate at the lower levels is the protection of the five Chiefs against the embarrassing necessity to disagree among themselves. When agreement is reached by the staff members—the "Indians," as they are called—the Chiefs rubber-stamp the position, often without debate. There is only one subject they insist on considering themselves. No recommendation for the Medal of Honor goes to the President without the personal approval of the five members of the Joint Chiefs of Staff.

Shortly after his inauguration in 1969, President Nixon appointed a panel to study the management of the Defense Department. A year later the so-called Blue Ribbon Defense Panel, headed by Gilbert W. Fitzhugh, chairman of the board of the Metropolitan Life Insurance Company, published a report that could have been written by a New Left group.

Despite all the civilians who had been insinuated into the military machine at lower and lower levels, the civilian leadership lacked effective control over the military, the panel said. It called civilian control over military operations "critically" impaired by a lack of experience within the office of the Defense Secretary on the conduct of military operations.

Though by theory and by law, the Joint Chiefs of Staff were supposed to be advisers on military matters to the Defense Secretary and the President and not commanders in military operations, the civilian leadership had delegated too much authority to them to carry out military operations, the panel said. The civilians, according to the panel, were left with no expert monitors of what the Chiefs were doing in the operations.

At the same time, the panel found, the Joint Chiefs, because of that cumbersome organization under them, were improperly staffed to carry out their work effectively.

The panel made two important recommendations. First, it suggested that the Joint Chiefs be relieved of all operational authority and that this be given to a new military officer working for the Defense Secretary in his office. Second, it urged a cutback in the size of the Joint Staff from the 2,100-man level to 250 officers, enlisted men and civilians. All those men, the panel said, helped to create a system that was "awkward and unresponsive," providing a "forum for inter-service rivalries to be injected into the decision-making process for military operations" that inhibited the "flow of information between the combatant commands and the President and the Secretary of Defense, often even in combat situations." In other words, the panel found that the

111

Commander-in-chief and his Defense Secretary did not get good information on which to base *their* decisions.

Historically there was reason for this situation. Congress deliberately created a cumbersome staff structure within the military out of the traditional American fear that a strong military represented a threat to democracy. In trying to vitiate that threat, however, it has created a machine of such bureaucratic complexity that, at important times, there is a danger it can run out of control. In fact, it has developed a bureaucracy in which objective consideration of issues has been replaced by politically oriented consideration.

As the Joint Staff structure grew more and more awkward, their studies became more and more compromised. As a result, the Joint Chiefs grew more unresponsive to the civilian leadership. Because of that, their advice, as it was in the Bay of Pigs, was ignored.

Politically, however, they remained formidable powers. They were the military machine personified on Capitol Hill. President Kennedy considered their political power so important that, in the 1963 debate over the limited nuclear test-ban treaty, he took the trouble to persuade all the Chiefs, though they had great reservations, to support the Soviet-American initiative to ban the atmospheric testing of nuclear weapons. Had the Chiefs not concurred, the possibility of Senate ratification would have diminished.

McNamara, though he opposed construction of an ABM system, in 1967 reluctantly gave in to the Chiefs' pressure for the system, realizing that he could not veto the Chiefs on every issue. He then turned his attention to devising an ABM system that would be as harmless as possible. The Chiefs sat by complacently as he worked, satisfied that no matter what kind of system was approved initially, they could exert pressure for expansion later. President Nixon and Laird, even as the Nixon Administration opened intensive negotiations with the Soviet Union to limit the development of ABMs, played the same game. Though the Nixon Administration reached an agreement with the Soviet Union to limit deployment of the antimissile missiles to the protection of their capitals and one other strategic missile site, he allowed millions of dollars to be spent for construction at four missile sites. It was said publicly that this was necessary as a bargaining chip in the complex negotiations with the Soviet leadership. The Soviets did not find it necessary to use such chips, and one must conclude that the President acted on the ABM to assuage the feelings of the Joint Chiefs at a time when he was cutting down on the Vietnam commitment.*

Long before he himself rose to eminence as White House adviser and operative of unique position in the nation's history, Dr. Henry A. Kissinger, as a young academic, put his finger on the problem facing the Joint Chiefs of Staff when he wrote:

> One of the paradoxes of an increasingly specialized, bureaucratized society is that the qualities rewarded in the rise to eminence are less and less the qualities required once eminence is reached. . . .
> . . . While the head of an organization requires a different outlook from that of his administrative subordinates, he must generally be recruited from their ranks. Eminence thus is often reached for reasons and according to criteria which are irrelevant to the tasks which must be performed in the highest positions. Despite all personnel procedures and perhaps because of them, superior performance at the apex of an organization is frequently in the deepest sense accidental.[1]

Though not written specifically about the Joint Chiefs, Kissinger's elegant formulation of the Peter Principle applies splendidly to them. They should be the nation's soldier-statesmen, the only real professionals at the highest level of government with the expertise to relate the needs of national security, broadly speaking, to the more technical capabilities of the military establishment. Yet one of their major failings has been their inability to join successfully the necessarily broad world outlook of the statesman and their own operational experience. For more than twenty-five years, a succession of Joint Chiefs advised the civilian leadership on how to "contain" Communism. None of them had a good, firsthand knowledge of just what it was they were trying to contain.

---

* Shortly after President Nixon took office in 1969, he revised the Johnson ABM program into one that would protect specific ICBM missile sites. By the time Nixon completed the strategic arms limitation agreement in Moscow in May 1972, work had been 85 percent completed at Grand Forks, North Dakota, 5 percent completed at Malmstrom Air Force Base, Montana, and test borings had been made at Whitman Air Force Base, Missouri, and Warren Air Force Base in Colorado. Only the Grand Forks project will be completed. The others will be scrapped.

113

Years after the first cracks appeared in the Moscow-Peking Axis, the Joint Chiefs still perceived Communism as a monolithic, Moscow-directed force. Unmindful of a long history of antipathy between the Vietnamese and the Chinese, they debated American policies in Southeast Asia in terms of whether or not the Chinese would come into the Vietnam War as they had in Korea. They could have sensed that antipathy by strolling the streets of Saigon. They could not get it from the rear seat of an escorted, air-conditioned sedan motoring from the Military Assistance Command Vietnam headquarters to the American Embassy or the Cercle Sportif, the old French colonial tennis club.

Before promotion to a position in The Tank, all of a prospective Joint Chief's experience relates to mastering the details of "countering threats" (along with a mastery of the outward details of professionalism). Prior to taking a seat in The Tank, prospective Joint Chiefs have never been under any pressure to think through the problem of just what the threats to the nation's security are.

A man like Brigadier General Joseph W. ("Vinegar Joe") Stilwell of World War II fame had a good idea of the threats to American security in Latin America and Asia. Between the two World Wars, he traveled extensively in those areas, keeping notebooks, checking his impressions and refining his ideas. Stilwell would have been considered too much of a maverick to sit on the Joint Chiefs of Staff.

Presidents have a limited pool of talent from which to select Joint Chiefs, that pool being the lists of successful generals and admirals. Air Force General Curtis E. LeMay is the man most often cited by his colleagues as a poor choice for membership on the Joint Chiefs. He was a man of great courage, a leader who inspired subordinates to perform at highly efficient levels, an organizer who whipped the Strategic Air Command into a shape that the nation could rely upon to exercise the role of nuclear deterrent. He was a plain-speaking, cigar-chomping bomber pilot who did not have the analytical turn of mind to sit in The Tank. One of LeMay's colleagues told me, however, "President Kennedy had to appoint him Air Force Chief of Staff. To have done anything else would have been affront to the Air Force and a great blow to its morale."

Other Joint Chiefs may not have been so colorful in their lack of qualification, but it existed—and continues to exist—nonetheless.

General Taylor, after serving a tour as Army chief of staff but before becoming chairman of the Joint Chiefs, wrote in the foreword to *The Uncertain Trumpet* in 1959:

> I was asked recently what in my past experience had been most helpful to me as Chief of Staff. Was it attendance at the Command and General Staff College and the Army War College? Was it service alongside General Marshall at the time of Pearl Harbor? Was it command of the 101st Airborne Division in Europe in World War II or of the Eighth Army in Korea? I never hesitated in replying, "My most valuable preparation was membership in the Northeast High School Society of Debate in my pre-West Point days in Kansas City." The subsequent chapters will show the reader why.

Twelve years later, retired after a forty-seven-year career in which he went on to become chairman of the Joint Chiefs of Staff, ambassador to Saigon, and a principal adviser to Presidents Kennedy and Johnson, the general greeted me in the living room of his Washington apartment. All the memorabilia of the career surrounded the man—the medals in a glass case, art objects and valuable furniture purchased in Europe and Asia, gifts of appreciation from foreigners and friends, all suitably inscribed, a huge portrait of the younger general hanging on a wall over the sofa. I asked the general if he had been kidding when he wrote the foreword. He grew serious and produced a handwritten list of qualifications for a Joint Chief, from which he spoke. (A man who always did his homework, he had known beforehand some of the topics I wanted to touch on in the interview and had prepared himself.)

"A candidate," he said, "should have gone through his own service school system and the National War College. In his own service schools he obtains a thorough knowledge of his own service's capabilities. At the War College he gains general knowledge of the other services. Then he should have extensive service in both Europe and Asia. Finally he should have senior service in the Pentagon, preferably on the Joint Staff where he gets to see how the government works, a feeling for the capital, a look at how Congress works. He should pay some attention to the State Department. He should have respect for his own service but should not be a 'palooka' for it. He should read widely in history and foreign affairs. He should be able to speak clearly and persuasively— honestly, as well."

Like the major in Korea who gave his thoughts on what an ideal officer was, Taylor had eloquently represented his views on what the ideal member of the Joint Chiefs should be. And the official biography sheets of just about all the men who held seats in The Tank for the past quarter century indicate they passed muster—superficially. That is another way of saying they all had their tickets punched.

But assignment in Europe and Asia, rather than becoming an experience in which a prospective chief has learned something about those areas, has almost in every case been with an American military unit. This means that the young officer's attention has been directed inward toward the organization rather than outward toward the countries and areas in which he has been stationed.

Many who have attended War College say that while there they are exposed to little more than college-freshman-level courses in political science and foreign relations.

As for the meaning of service on the Joint Staff as experience for bigger jobs, as we have seen, it is a make-work existence that bears little relationship to reality.

As a result of all this, the men of the American military machine today live a sublime nightmare: thousands of officers rushing year after year from station to station, seeking the advantages that will propel them ahead of their colleagues into membership on the Joint Chiefs of Staff at some future time. Those few who, after thirty years, do arrive in The Tank will have been intellectually crippled by the procedure they endured to get there. Once seated at the walnut table, it will be to undertake a job the President and Secretary of Defense do not consider very important anyhow. And, even if attention were paid, the Chiefs, by virtue of their training and education, are ill-equipped to perform properly.

The sublime nightmare corrupted the officer corps, creating a generation of yes men. That was problem enough in itself. But it also helped to deflect attention from two equally serious problems: the exploitation of millions of enlisted men in the services and the deception of the nation over the matter of just what it was that the military machine could really do to help preserve American democracy.

PART THREE

A GENERATION OF EXPLOITED MEN

As commanding general of the 3d Armored Division in West Germany, Major General William R. Kraft, Jr., had one of the more difficult jobs in the United States Defense Establishment in the early 1970s. First of all, there was the mission: The 3d Armored—or Spearhead—Division was headquartered in a suburb of Frankfurt, and its units sat astride one of the traditional invasion routes from the East into the industrial heart of West Germany and the other NATO nations beyond.

Secondly, Kraft's 15,000 men, like the rest of the Army, Navy and Air Force of the period, were wracked by the turmoil caused by racial conflict, drug and alcohol use, demoralization, a push for individual rights, and slum living conditions. Keeping his troops prepared to meet the enemy under these conditions was described by division officers as a difficult task. To an outside observer talking to uniformed men at all levels and looking at the conditions dispassionately, it appeared more to be an impossible task.

But William Kraft, fifty-three years old and looking ten years younger, was not brought up to think in terms of professional impossibilities.

It was not through taking an impossible view of things that the Spearhead Division distinguished itself during World War II in the drive to the Elbe. Kraft's picture hangs on a wall at headquarters, the latest in a long row of successful generals who had commanded the Spearhead with distinction, and clearly, he could not think of impossibilities. Tradition denied such thought. So did education and training. A West Point graduate (class of 1942), a World War II combat veteran, a West Point instructor, a Vietnam veteran, Kraft is imbued with the can-do spirit.

"I sense that my company commanders, battalion commanders and brigade commanders really get depressed at the magnitude of the prob-

lems," Kraft said one January afternoon in 1972. "It's kind of hard for them to get the right perspective. We have a mission in Germany. There's a threat—twenty-two divisions on the other side of the interzonal boundary. If those Soviet divisions weren't there, there would be no reason for us to be here. By our presence and the credibility of our presence—the way we train and act—we deter them from something.

"Preparedness to fight is part of deterrence. But we have another threat—the internal threat. Automobile accidents among our troops detract, racial tension detracts, people on drugs are ineffectual. Then we get characters who come in who are felons; they shouldn't be in the service but they have been given moral waivers . . .

"What bothers commanders is that they have so many balls in the air at once. It's hard to see the relationships between the mission and internal threats.

"But in the end, everything else is secondary to good training and a disciplined environment. . . . The hardest thing to grab hold of is consistently good training in all of our units. A lot of other problems would disappear or be minimized if we had good training. But our young sergeants and officers don't put a lot of effort and imagination into training. Getting them to work hard at it is like pushing a piece of wet spaghetti across the table."

Later I asked the general how well qualified the 15,000 men in his command were to defend the nation's interests if an enemy attack were to come as we talked. I asked him to rate the training of his division on a scale of zero to a hundred.

"If you take seventy-five as a passing score," he said, "of twenty-three battalions in the division, five or six are above passing. The rest would be below seventy-five in various degrees; none would be real low."

The general was admitting that three quarters of his division was incapable of fighting adequately. Training, of course, could cure that problem.

But the fact was that in Germany, in early 1972, it was hard to find a meaningful training program under way in an Army that was supposed to be prepared to fight at a few moments' notice.

7

TRAINING: A MIXTURE OF FACT AND FANTASY

QUESTION: If the Soviet divisions in Eastern Europe moved across the "interzonal boundary" (née Iron Curtain) in Germany tomorrow, would the United States Seventh Army be ready to repel them?

ANSWER: No.

QUESTION: If the Soviet Union's Mediterranean Squadron engaged the ships of the United States Sixth Fleet in the Mediterranean, which President Nixon has called the mightiest fighting force ever assembled by man, would the American ships respond decisively?

ANSWER: No.

QUESTION: If Soviet aircraft were to attempt to establish air superiority over the European continent, would the best and most expensive fighters in the American inventory be up to stopping them?

ANSWER: No.

Despite the assurances of the leaders to the contrary, the American military machine, designed to counter such eventualities, is simply unprepared for them. The reason: The hundreds of thousands of men who comprise the most important single resource of the establishment—the manpower—are not sufficiently trained to do the job.

Not only are they not trained. They are not even in good enough physical condition.

To some extent, this is a vestige of the Vietnam War, a period in

120

which the American military machine throughout the world was canni-balized to resupply the war effort in Southeast Asia. To a greater extent, the lack of preparedness is the result of personnel turbulence in which officers and enlisted men were always *coming* and *going* from assign-ments but never really *in* one long enough to learn a job and then re-main prepared to carry it out.

In Korea, Lieutenant General William R. Peers (who, after head-ing the My Lai investigation, became deputy commander of the Eighth Army in Korea) said in the winter of 1971–1972 that the one remaining combat division there was training at the individual level—that is, that fighting men in the division were busy relearning what they were already supposed to have learned in the basic training camps and in the ad-vanced individual training they had gone through back in the United States. They were not up to the task of maneuvering in company- or battalion-sized groups.

In the Mediterranean, hardly a line officer on the ships of the Sixth Fleet did not complain that training was impaired by severe fuel limita-tions. To stay within its budget, the Navy had ordered that ships could not cruise at speeds fast enough to go through training exercises. Thus the Fleet was cruising slowly from port to port in "the Med," paying courtesy calls, showing the flag, giving the men the opportunity for lib-erty in exotic places.

In Germany, enlisted men complained that, when their superiors had the choice between levying men for work details and filling up head-quarters slots, or assigning them to training missions, the first two always won out over the last.

In England, at the only air base overseas where the all-weather, $14.9-million F-111 fighter-bomber was deployed in early 1972,* the Air Force command had deliberately instituted a hold-down on the number of hours the planes could be flown each month. Given the

---

* Ask an Air Force spokesman how much an F-111 fighter costs and he answers: "Take your pick, either $11.8 million or $14.9 million." The first price, he says, is the simple "fly-away" cost of one airplane coming out of the General Dynamics plant in Forth Worth. The second price is the "per-program unit" cost which includes the cost of all the research and development, the cost of maintenance facilities, spare parts, special ground equipment needed for the planes, and the like. Cost number two is arrived at by taking all the money spent in the TFX-F-111 program and dividing it by the more than four hundred planes built. That seems like a reasonable way of doing things. Later in 1972, the F-111 was de-ployed to Southeast Asia where three planes were lost in its first weeks of en-gagement.

choice between flying them and keeping them grounded, the command almost always opted for keeping them on the runway. Why? Because the trouble-ridden aircraft, known to the public in its controversial earlier days as the TFX, was considered so expensive and so unpredictable that commanders feared a crash when the planes were airborne. A crash meant a black mark on the commander's record. Thus it was the better part of valor not to fly them. As a result, pilots did not gain as much experience with their aircraft as they should.

On the island of Okinawa, the men of the 3d Marine Division and the Army's Special Forces Group, the only combat troops on the island, complained that they had to spend so much time guarding all the military installations on the island against anti-American demonstrations that they had no time to train.

"We spend two or three days getting ready for a demonstration. We have to draw different equipment, get it ready, practice riot control," one Marine said. "Then we go on duty for a few days or a week. Then we come back and spend two or three days standing down from the duty. We start getting ready for some training and then we get a call to prepare for another demonstration."

The situation reflected an important aspect of the military machine's defeat in the 1970s. Okinawa was retained after World War II as a forward Far Eastern base on which the United States could garrison quick-reacting troops and supplies for use in global peace-keeping operations. The garrison instead had grown so preoccupied with the protection of its own existence that it could not remain prepared for its primary mission.

In September 1971, years after that part of the Army not slated for Vietnam duty had lapsed into inactivity, the situation came to the attention of General William C. Westmoreland, then the Chief of Staff.

He reacted by appointing a board of officers to study the situation. He named it the Board for Dynamic Training (taking the title from an article he had written himself in 1960 about the dynamic training procedures he had instituted as commander of the 101st Airborne Division) and charged it to complete a study in three months.

The board was headed by one of the Army's newest and youngest generals, Brigadier General Paul Francis Gorman, a member of the West Point class of 1950. Gorman represents a new generation of leadership in the Army, one for which the experiences of World War II are simply recent history and nothing personal.

Gorman grew up in an Army committed to fighting cold war and its hot outbreaks. Within weeks after the graduation of his class of 670 new second lieutenants from the Academy, the North Korean Army streamed over the thirty-eighth parallel on a remote Asian peninsula that many well-educated Americans could not even identify on a map, and a United Nations police action had begun. Gorman's class suffered fearsome casualties. Of the graduates that June, thirty-nine were to die in the fighting in the next three years and two others would die in North Korean prisoner-of-war camps. Gorman survived but won a Purple Heart for wounds he suffered.

As a cold warrior, he became one of the Army's best-known young strategists, a student of threat and counterthreat. Herman Kahn, one of the preeminent nuclear strategists of the era, once said of Gorman that if the Army would only leave him alone with his studies, he could become one of the great strategic thinkers of our time.

But the Army did not leave him alone, nor is there evidence that he wanted such a scholarly career exclusively. Gorman served two tours in Vietnam—in 1966–1967 as a battalion commander for six months and a division staff officer for six months, and in 1970–1971 as a brigade commander: jobs every infantry officer must hold if he wants to become a general.

In between, he served as a policy planner, working with Robert S. McNamara's Whiz Kids in the Pentagon's "little state department," the office of International Security Affairs, and for almost two years, as a military adviser to the Paris delegation seeking a negotiated settlement to the Vietnam War. After the second Vietnam tour, Gorman was looking forward to spending a year in New York as a fellow at the Council on Foreign Relations where he could continue as a policy planner. Instead, Westmoreland tabbed him as one of the bright young men needed to help sift out the chaos in the Army, promoted him to the rank of brigadier general and made him assistant commandant of the Army Infantry School at Fort Benning, Georgia. His first job was to head the Board for Dynamic Training.

In his charge to the board, Westmoreland attributed the Army's training problems to what he called "the Vietnam strait jacket." He meant the Army had an overbearing need in the late 1960s to concentrate all its efforts on supplying troops to the Southeast Asian War. This need, he thought, left the service incapable of keeping up training in other areas. If that view had prevailed, then the Pentagon could think that it had cured the training problem simply by developing a better educational program for the Army's cadre of trainers. Once the trainers were trained better, they would in turn do a better job of training troops.

The Gorman board found a host of other obstacles to good training, and without saying so directly, placed the blame for the problems at the doorstep of General Westmoreland and his high-ranking deputies. Contrary to "the Vietnam strait jacket" hypothesis, the board developed the idea that "the Army has marginally adequate training not because of inadequate trainers but because of systemic difficulty in assigning and articulating training objectives for its trainers and providing them *requisite resources.*"[1]

In simpler terms, the Army had no good idea of what it wanted its trainers to teach and failed to give the trainers the equipment they needed to do the job. Furthermore, it was institutionally unable to solve the training problem because the chain of command did not function properly and because "high-level staffs"—the generals—were not doing their jobs. Tactfully, Gorman appeared to be telling his superiors that unless they did their jobs better, training could not improve, even after the Vietnam War ended.

The Gorman board visited 103 active and 35 reserve Army units. It held conferences with 99 officers representing 58 units stationed throughout the world. It conducted a scientific training management survey of more than 2,600 men and consulted with representatives of 16 foreign military establishments and 9 retired American generals. From that work, the board distilled this picture of how the Army's system of training support was viewed from the field:[2]

Source of Support for Unit Training	Should Provide	Actually Provides
Army Training Literature	—Planning guidance —Doctrine	—Irrelevant guidance —Out-of-date,
—Field Manuals	(what to teach)	incomplete doctrine
—ATP, Subject Schedules	—Techniques of tng (how to teach)	—Little or no technique
—DA Circulars, Pamphlets		

Source of Support for Unit Training	Should Provide	Actually Provides
Service Schools	—Trained trainers —Correspondence courses —Technique of tng	—Ill-prepared trainers —Little or no technique
Training Aids Center Audio-Visual Centers	—Devices —Audio-visual support	—Outmoded in medium and message
Higher Commander	—Missions Goals Priorities —Resources men, money, equipment, facilities, ammo, ranges, etc.	—Distractions from tng —Constraints on tng

Even in such a fundamental skill as marksmanship training, the board found grave deficiencies. The report said:

If there is one training subject which the Army traditionally emphasizes, and on which it expects high training proficiency in units, it is shooting. Yet here, too, "replacement-training" tunnel vision is the norm. A young officer setting out today to conduct a "dynamic" range session for his unit is confronted with a tough job which is analogous to a maze. The M-16 rifle is the subject of one manual (FM 23-9), while marksmanship is treated in another (FM-23-71). The latter is written around the M-14 rifle and the Trainfire Range. If he can count on a Trainfire Range, and his only objective is to fire his men through that individual training course, all well and good. But if he wants to conduct meaningful fire team shooting, he will find little in the manuals on appropriate training technique options. . . . He needs an old-fashioned exposition on the technique of training in musketry. Even an old-fashioned manual would be a step in the right direction.[3]

The board found that except in the rarest of cases, it took a minimum of eighteen months to produce a field manual. Oftentimes by the
time a manual was published, its material was out of date.

But the training crisis in the combat arms of the Army was not
only one of educational materials. The board also found an emphasis
on out-dated techniques (despite the increasing urbanization of the
world, for example, there was no training given in door-to-door fighting
within a city) and too much of a stress on ideal situations (field manuals were written for exercises involving full squads despite the fact that
rarely could a full squad be mustered for an exercise).

The biggest factors in producing poorly trained units, according
to the board, were "personnel turbulence," low manning levels in combat units, inadequate budget and lack of qualified noncommissioned
officers to serve as trainers.

"Personnel turbulence" was the term the Army used in the 1970s
to describe the situation in which, in the course of a year, a unit might
have a turnover of more than 100 percent. That is, that of all the men
present in, say, an infantry company garrisoned in Germany on January
1 of any given year, none of them would be present the following year.
And in fact some of the replacements coming in during the year would
be transferred again before the end. In one division stationed in the
United States in 1968, there had been 50,000 job changes among its
15,000 men in just twelve months. Part of this was due to the Vietnam
War and its insatiable manpower requirements. But another part was
due to ticket punching—keeping key men moving to give them experience—and the need to shore up an establishment intended to meet
inflated objectives (Robert S. McNamara thought it could fight "two
and a half wars" at once) with inadequate manpower resources.*

---

* An Air Force first sergeant in Thailand provided the best example of what
all this movement means. I encountered him one night standing behind a counter
in the Bangkok offices of Tommy's Tourist Agency, the Thai firm that had a
contract with the United States military in Southeast Asia to provide hotel and
tour services for men on "R and R" (rest and rehabilitation) from Vietnam.
The sergeant was one of two men manning a military liaison office at Tommy's
on the night shift. "If old Proxmire only knew what I was doing now, he'd have
a fit," the sergeant said, referring to Senator William D. Proxmire, the Wisconsin
Democrat who was the scourge of military cost overruns. The sergeant then
related how he had spent three years training to maintain the electronics and
hydraulic systems of the controversial new C5A troop transport. He spent all
that time at Lockheed's Marietta, Georgia, plant following the new plane through
its early days of construction. Then he was transferred to Dover Air Force Base

Personnel turbulence is such an important factor that the services actually request more men than they need to absorb some of the impact of movement. For 1973, they asked for 88,000 more men than they needed, and together, the services admitted that they would be making 1.1 moves during the year for each man in uniform. (Put another way, each man would be moved every eleven months.) The Navy and the Air Force were actually planning more moves with smaller forces in 1973 than in 1972. The Senate Armed Services Committee was sharply critical of all the moves, saying:

> Moves solely for the purposes of providing broadened career opportunity, retraining for the convenience of the individual or those associated with promotion are potential areas for reduction. At the current cost of manpower, we cannot afford the luxury of theoretically preparing each and every individual to reach the highest position in his Service. More selective and efficient ways of providing career opportunities need to be explored.[4]

Even with the extra 88,000 men there were still not enough men to go around. A tank battalion commander in Europe would meet that problem by putting his staff men from headquarters into his tanks. But more often, it was the other way around. If a battalion was short of men, the commander would always fill his headquarters company—the paper shufflers, drivers, typists, administrators, planners—and let the fighting units suffer. If the commanding officer wanted a letter typed, he always had his enlisted man clerk-typist on the job to do it. If a company commander could not train his unit because he was short of men, well, that was too bad.

The Senate Armed Services Committee found in 1972 that all the

---

in Delaware where he was to be an instructor for other maintenance men. A few weeks after he arrived, he received orders to Thailand to work on ground crews for the C-130 gunships stationed there. All his training for the new job had gone out the window. He was replaced by another sergeant in his instructor's job. The new sergeant had no training at all in the C5A's problems. The sergeant in Thailand was trying to help him over the hump by correspondence. To make matters even worse, after arriving at the Thai base, the sergeant was detailed to Bangkok where he functioned at Tommy's as little more than a clerk in a travel agency. "I tried to tell someone. But my name came out of the computer and I had to go. My training made no difference," the sergeant, who refused use of his name, said.

services combined had 140,000 men asigned to command and head-quarters jobs. The committee produced this breakdown:

Army	35,000
Navy	35,000
Marine Corps	8,000
Air Force	62,000

"This would be enough military manpower to man nearly nine Army divisions," the committee said, noting that these men were assigned only to higher headquarters staffs: Army corps and divisions, numbered Air forces and Air divisions, ship squadrons and divisions, and for all the services, higher headquarters on up to the Pentagon. The committee said it was difficult to estimate the number of men employed in headquarters and command jobs at lower levels (battalions, wings, ships), but that the number was substantial. In all, the committee estimated that one out of every four men in uniform was involved in commanding or supporting the commanders of the other three, and asked the Defense Department to study this situation. It also recommended an arbitrary cut of 25 percent in all headquarters personnel.[5]

The Senate committee discovered that the Army apparently, at any given time, does not really know how many men it has in uniform. The report said that, for a whole series of reasons, including dilatory action by Congress on the 1972 budget, the Army delayed in cutting back its force in 1972 to the 861,000-man ceiling demanded by Congress. In the winter of 1971 and the spring of 1972, it began releasing men rapidly many months early. When the "early out" program was completed, the Army had released 31,000 men or more—too many. "There is reason to believe that there is some room for improvement in the Army's personnel data system," the Senate committee said dryly.[6]

In 1970, the controller of the Army surveyed a cross section of Army units to determine how commanders used the efforts of their troops. The study showed that company and battalion commanders *planned* to spend roughly three quarters of their units' effort on the primary task—training—with the other one quarter devoted in almost equal parts to administration and maintenance. In *actuality*, however, those commanders were spending only one third of the effort on training, one half on administration and one fifth on maintenance. Commenting on this study, the Gorman board wrote:

128

One could generalize that trainers were spending less than half the time they planned for on training and receiving less than one-third of usable effort.*

The figures, of course, also show that the commanders were spending three or four times more than they had scheduled on administration, receiving one half of all the effort of their men for this purpose. The 5th Mechanized Division at Fort Carson, Colorado, did a study in 1970 which showed what happens when manning levels drop below those planned. The study was boiled down, in the Gorman report, to these numbers:

PERCENT UNIT EFFORT

Percent Present for Duty	Training	Maintenance	Administration
100	37	31	32
76	16	41	43

In other words, if a unit's manpower decreases by a quarter, the amount of time it can spend training decreases by more than half, and the amount of time it spends on maintaining its equipment and administering itself goes up by a third.

Just looking at the numbers, it would be hard to fault the Army for spending so much time taking care of its equipment. It was all purchased by the taxpayers and should be kept in good shape. But that's not what maintenance really means. The controller of the Army study discovered that what was going under the guise of maintenance was really preparation for inspections.

---

* Quoted from page 74 of the *Report of the Board for Dynamic Training*. Here, adapted slightly from the report, are the Army controller's findings in tabular form:

COMMANDER'S USABLE EFFORT

	Primary Task (training)	Administrative Support	Maintenance
Company, Planned Use	78%	12%	10%
Company, Actual Use	36%	47%	17%
Battalion, Planned	74%	16%	10%
Battalion, Actual	30%	53%	17%
Average, Co & Bn, Actual	33%	49%	18%

The controller's briefing stated: "One half of the inspections [a unit commander] undergoes are believed to be measures of his personal capabilities. Excellent performance in these is essential to his professional advancement." So high marks in inspections help the commander. They do nothing to insure that a unit will be ready and trained to fight when it has to. That proficiency cannot be—or is not—measured by superiors in the same way that inspectors can judge whether toothpaste has been lined up properly with the razor in a kit bag or whether oil stains have been scrubbed clean from a truck park. All this, the controller noted, has an effect on the troops:

> The evidence supports a conclusion that unit members have lost the feeling that they are most involved in the primary mission they were trained to do, and their unit was organized to do; thus a reduction in sense of worth, an increase of frustration and an adverse impact on morale.[7]

Undoubtedly, a large factor in the morale problem was what the board termed "a crisis of confidence" among noncommissioned officers. Many of the best NCOs were killed in the Vietnam War. Others, caught between the Army's demands to maintain discipline and the assertions of enlisted men for more personal freedom, simply gave up and retired. Still others tried to hold the line and suffered either a lack of support from their young company-level officers (whose views were more in sympathy with the enlisted men than the NCOs), or if they were backed up, received trouble from the enlisted men. Still other NCOs were promoted to their positions in combat in Vietnam and did not possess the experience to lead men in peacetime garrisons. The NCO corps, like the officer corps, had its ninety-day wonders.

The big complaint the board found among the NCOs was the centralized testing procedure used to promote them. Each year they were required to take written tests that were centrally graded. Their problem was that the field manuals used to study for such tests were in short supply. On many bases, a black market in manuals developed. An NCO who took his leadership responsibilities seriously—who was, in other words, performing his primary job well and whose promotion should have been based on this—did not have as much time to study for the tests as his counterpart who ignored his troops to further his own career. Such was the incredible web in which the military system entangled its men.

All this led Gorman to write, in the letter accompanying his report:

> . . . the Board discovered no managerial "quick fix," nor magic gadgetry that will swiftly and surely lead to such improvement. . . . In a matter so close to the heart of its professionalism, the Army must take particular pains to avoid rhetoric unmatched by action. The Board calls attention to the fact that its recommendations, even if fully accepted, would impact on unit training only after many months—conceivably years—of concerted effort at all echelons of the Army.[8]

Westmoreland, following one of Gorman's recommendations, established a new board at Fort Benning to improve training in the combat arms. Gorman then embarked on a round of briefings to sell his ideas throughout the Army and settled into his job at the Infantry School to do his share in the years of concerted effort needed to turn the situation around. His plans were big; his ideas were many. Visitors to Fort Benning in the late spring of 1972 were struck with the vitality of the operations. Among other things, he was developing a farseeing center for programed learning that might ultimately supplant the staid, old, out-of-date field manuals with a multimedia learning approach consisting of television and voice tape cassettes, films, slides and programed textbooks that could be used in small units.

Just as the program was getting under way, personnel turbulence struck again. In July 1972, after he had been on the job less than a year and had made himself one of the acknowledged experts on the Army's training problems, Paul Gorman was transferred back to Washington, where he was detailed to the Department of Justice to help the government prosecute its case against Daniel Ellsberg, the man who leaked the Pentagon Papers to the public. Later, when the trial was postponed, he was made assistant division commander of the 5th Mechanized Division at Fort Carson. He thus had three different jobs in less than six months.

What was true for the United States Army's combat arms, according to the Gorman report, was true for the other services as well, including the fabled "lean, mean" Marine Corps. Publicly, the image of the Corps is one of a small, tough fighting force ever ready to protect the nation's interests from the Halls of Montezuma to the Shore of Tripoli, on land, sea or (as a postscript to the Marine Corps Hymn) in the air. In the early 1970s, the Marine Corps was the only service that *wanted* to re-duce its size and return to a small, disciplined, tightly controlled band of elite, Spartan fighters. The Corps's goal in 1970 and 1971 was to reduce from its Vietnam War peak strength of 317,000 men to 222,000 men. While Army recruiting posters advertised "Today's Army Wants to Join You" and projected that message with pictures of modish young men sitting at Paris cafés with attractive blondes, the Marines advertised "We Don't Promise You a Rose Garden" or "The Marines Are Looking for a Few Good Men." While the Army experimented with liberalized basic training (beer in the barracks, weekend passes, abandonment of reveille, replacing the "kill-kill" shout in bayonet practice with "yah-yah," semiprivate rooms in the barracks) to attract new volunteers, the Marines remained true to the old procedures (shaved heads, shouting drill instructors, reference to the recruits as "hogs," copious punishment, grueling physical training and withdrawal from the outside world).*

The Marines stationed one of their three divisions on the island of Okinawa as a quick-reacting force capable of projecting American power anywhere in the Orient. A visit there in December 1971 showed that the few good men of the Corps on that island fortress were in no better shape than the Army.

* The Army's liberalized basic training program was part of the new Volunteer Army or "Volar" concept designed to encourage enlistments after the end to the draft in 1973. At the height of the liberalization in mid-1971, not only were there all the amenities mentioned above. Also, punitive push-ups were discarded (de-merits were substituted for the Sad Sacks, which resulted in loss of weekend passes), training was lightened out on the theory that clerk-typists did not have to know how to fight, midnight inspections were abandoned and recruits were al-lowed to voice complaints to a "trainee council" that was in constant touch with commanding officers.

Even some of the recruits objected to the relaxation. A survey at Fort Leonard Wood, Missouri, basic training camp showed two out of three recruits thought the training not as tough as expected. One in five wanted more physical exercise. In February 1972, the Army abandoned much of the experiment, return-ing to open-bay barracks, removing the beer machines and toughening training for everyone, even the clerk-typists. But reveille was not reinstituted and the weekend passes continued to be granted.

On the other side, the Marines have loosened up a bit. Shaken by disclosures of brutality going all the way back to 1956 when a drill sergeant forced seventy-five recruits into a nighttime march in which six drowned, and more than sixty courts-martial of drill instructors for brutality between 1965 and 1971, the Marines have reinforced their rules. DIs are no longer able to touch a recruit except to adjust a military position. As Henry Allen, a Washington *Post* writer, put it, today "brutality to the Marines is like usury to Jews—a nightmare that threatens their very existence."

Okinawa is the home of the III Marine Amphibious Force which moved out of South Vietnam in 1971 as part of President Nixon's withdrawal from the war. The force includes a combat division, a helicopter air wing and all the support elements necessary to get the men into combat. The men of the III MAF are garrisoned and trained in a complex of fifteen different installations on the island which together comprise about 42,000 acres.

From the top of the chain of command, the problems of the force seemed under control.

Brigadier General Robert S. Barrow, forty-nine, a native of Baton Rouge, Louisiana, relaxed easily in his office and spoke of how the force was in "a high state of readiness." He said that two battalions from the division were always afloat with the United States Seventh Fleet ("we fight on land and ride at sea"), undergoing six weeks of training exercises. Noting the discontent among the enlisted men, he said, "We are spending a lot of money improving the living conditions of the Marines. You have to be in the Corps to get a feel for what's happening. I am a complete and utter optimist about the future of the Marines. There are still enough young people in the Corps who want to identify with the kind of Spartan, stern, disciplined life to insure a future for the Corps."

Were a congressman to sit on the colorful rattan furniture in Barrow's bright, airy, hilltop office and listen to the general, he would come away reassured. Barrow is straight-talking; he is earnest; he is articulate; he is sincere.

But the picture begins to change as you go down the chain of command. Colonel Robert J. Perrich was commander of the 4th Regiment of the 3d Division, one of the key combat forces in the III MAF.

I asked him if his regiment was ready to fight.

"One battalion is at 90 percent of its strength," he answered. "Another is getting ready. It has only 65 percent of its people. The third, on paper, looks good, but many of its people will be leaving soon. We can take to the field and do the job but not without a great deal of difficulty. Our problems are related to the quantity of men and their training. One of our battalions has over a hundred men out doing other jobs on the base. We have trouble filling all the slots with the people we've got."

In just a few short sentences, Perrich confirmed that he had the same problems in keeping his men ready that the Gorman board found in the Army—turbulence, low manning levels, assignments to duty other than the primary task.

But the forty-six-year-old colonel's recitation was not yet completed. In his throaty voice he continued: "Ten years ago, when I was a battalion commander, I could focus most of my energies on mission-oriented training. A battalion commander today has to do 20 percent more paperwork than I did. A relatively small part of this increase is due to the 'people problems' (drugs, race, morale). Their major effort is in feeding the computers. You can't have idle time on the computers, so my battalion commanders have to fill up the vacuum. Honest to God, that's the way it appears from here. They can give you statistics on anything, including the number of times a marine moves his bowels each week."

Once again, Perrich revealed that the Marines had a problem similar to the Army's. In his judgment, the demands of high-level staffs were responsible for excess attention to administration at lower levels.

Major William Von Harten, thirty-nine, a massive, youthful-looking redhead from Beaufort, South Carolina, served as one of Perrich's battalion commanders. The huge insignia of the "Thundering 3d Bn., 4th Reg't" hung behind his desk. From his vantage point, the new "liberalism" and "permissiveness" of society were "affecting the ability of the Marines to perform our mission." Enlisted men today, he said, "start imposing some of their own values on the system, their impression of what's right and what's wrong. They want to discuss matters further when an order is given, and that causes a drag on execution. We get a disobedience of orders, and that increases our disciplinary problems."

I asked him what kind of orders were disobeyed.

"Any legal military order. For example, you order a man to report to the armory at 1300. He says, 'I don't want to do it, I had armory duty yesterday. I won't go, so screw you.' Little nit-picky stuff like that takes up a lot of time."

On Major Von Harten's desk were six cases involving men who refused to obey orders.

How can it be that the lean, mean, disciplined, Spartan Marines, all of whom volunteered for the service, could refuse orders?

Captain John R. Clickner, thirty-one, from Springfield, Illinois, a company commander in Von Harten's battalion with eight years of service to his credit, answered that question. "Our men do not find what they expect when they get into the Marine Corps. So they develop an antimilitary feeling. Budgetary and personnel turbulence as a result of the Vietnam War and our heavy commitment schedule mean that we cannot devote as much time as we should to tight training. We are not challenging our men. And they want a challenge. We can't make the training interesting. Every time we stand two days of riot control duty, we have to block out a week of training."

Continuing down the chain of command, Lieutenant Timothy L. Burfield, twenty-three, of Baltimore, Maryland, a platoon leader in Clickner's company, saw the problem from a more philosophical point of view.

"Motivation and interest are the big problems," he said. "Most of the people coming into the Marines are romantics, and romanticism is a mixture of a sense of virility, patriotism and a longing for excitment. They come into the Marines and don't receive fulfillment. They don't see any direct connection between defending life, liberty and the pursuit of happiness and being stationed on Okinawa. Their duties are very ordinary every day.

"My job is to keep my men motivated. Most of them enlisted with the idea of going to 'Nam and they didn't get a chance to go. They joined the Marines because it was a builder of men. There was a lot of fantasy associated with it, and now they find in day-to-day life that it's just not that way."

Clickner and Burfield had an imaginative solution for the problems. "We should have a smaller force with a higher level of stability," Clickner said. "Our men don't get to know each other, there's so much turnover."

"We need a continuity in service and in units like the British have," said Burfield.

"We should all be living aboard ships. We should have mobile sea bases with constant training, landing exercises and liberty in various ports. We haven't been off the island once in the past year. No one has been anywhere except Okinawa," Clickner added.

And finally, Burfield said, "Mobile sea bases would fulfill more of a sense of continuity, better personal relationships. Interest. Excitement. The excitement of travel, the excitement of training."

But meanwhile, there was only the boredom of garrison life. And no one experienced the boredom more than the individual enlisted man —the sons of World War II's Willie and Joe, the present-day Sad Sacks.

By the time the discussion had reached down to the bottom of the chain of command, the "high state of readiness" seen by Brigadier General Barrow or the ability to "get the job done with some difficulty" mentioned by Perrich had disappeared. Instead, Lance Corporal Ricky Schack, a twenty-year-old from Littleton, Colorado, with only one year in service, said, "We ain't in no way ready."

Sergeant Thomas Hutton, twenty-seven, an eight-year veteran from Galena, Mississippi, added, "I don't think there is a company in the battalion that has four platoons. And the men don't have the right jobs. We have four people in our platoon working in the office who should be weapons men. My friend has been a welder for five years; now he's assigned to recoilless rifles. They make us go by the book, and the book's got a lot of mistakes in it. A lot of people pay for those mistakes too. We've got three officers in our company who can't read a map or a compass, and they will tell you that. Yet they give instructions in how to read maps and compasses. They've got the wrong people giving classes. They don't know what's going on."

At the lowest level in the division, the privates felt little sense of purpose. Private First Class Jeffrey Smith, twenty, of Salt Lake City, Utah, for example, said, "Our purpose in life is to provide work parties. I don't smoke. Why should I have to go around picking up someone else's cigarette butts? We do too many work parties."

And Private First Class Dennis Christensen, nineteen, of Window Rock, Arizona, who had ten months in service: "We don't do any training. Even when we went to Japan for field exercises, we were supposed to fire 1,000 rounds each in the 45 days we were there. We each had 700 rounds left over. We spent our time there in work parties."

From the general to the grunts, none of these men were deliberately sought out as dissidents. In fact, all of them were selected by the Marine information officer on the island, whose candid instruction to the men was simply to answer questions truthfully and speak their minds.

The interviews left one wondering why the Marines bothered to keep a garrison on Okinawa at all.

Elsewhere, the situation was no different. In Naples, Lieutenant Commander Kenneth Galkin, executive officer of the USS *Hammerberg*, a destroyer escort with intelligence-gathering duties, told me, "I think the best thing that could happen to the Sixth Fleet is to have someone fire a shot at it. Then the Navy would be able to tell just how combat-ready the Fleet is. The possibility exists that it is very unready because of deficient training and a lack of good arms."

Aboard the USS *Springfield,* the light guided-missile cruiser which serves as the flagship of the Fleet, a young radarman complained, "They're more worried about cleaning the radar than training us to use it. On a scale of one to a hundred, we spend 85 percent of our time cleaning the radar and 15 percent using it. I don't know what they're afraid of. We keep pushing the dirt around from one place to another. The other day a flag officer used a urinal and noticed it was dirty. He put a sign on it saying 'This urinal is dirty. Clean it.' A seaman put up another sign that said 'Stop pissing on the floor.' "

In the Air Force, not only were the planes not getting off the ground but the ground control crews were being punished for not maintaining them properly rather than being shown how to do the job in the right way. The situation became unbearable for many senior noncommissioned officers at RAF Upper Heyford in Oxfordshire, England, the home of the 20th Tactical Fighter Wing of complex F-111 fighter-bombers.

Senior Master Sergeant Frederick T. Gilbert decided to retire from the Air Force after twenty-four years of service. Why?

"I'm retiring because the Air Force is changing so goddam much. It's loaded with inspectors. More and more people are looking for mistakes, checking the wrench turners. We have more people checking wrench turners than turning the wrenches. We harass the men. Even as a supervisor they expect me to hang the guy doing the work, expect me to take his stripes away and punish him for doing his job. If a quality control inspector finds a loose screw, he writes it up, decertifying the last guy to make an inspection. An English friend of mine said, 'You bloody people wear your fucking airplanes out looking at them.' It's the same way throughout the Air Force in Europe."

A public information officer had introduced me to Sergeant Gilbert, and when he caught the direction of the conversation, he said, "Sergeant, it isn't quite as serious as you make it sound."

Gilbert answered, "Well, it is. And it's getting worse. Quality control is just like a Gestapo outfit. Every time you look around, you've got some guy looking over your shoulder. That's the way it seems."

Chief Master Sergeant William L. Franklin, who shared an office with Gilbert, agreed. "Some people get punished on their first offense," he said, "but I don't think the planes are any safer for it. All of this over-inspection might make the planes better in things that don't really matter.

"We're at the point now where we're saying if we never fly a plane again, it's okay, but you must follow the check list. Before, we were willing to forgo the check list to fly sorties. You must have the technical data on the plane right at hand when you're doing the job and you must go by the data. I know a man who was reprimanded for not following the data even though the book was wrong. Now that's counterproductive."

Counterproductive or no, that was the situation at Upper Heyford, and Colonel Richard M. Baugn, the wing commander, admitted it. "We're still having some abuses with our quality control program," he said. "Some of our people are overreacting, taking the brown shoe approach, going by the book, but it's against Air Force policy and this wing's policy to take disciplinary action in the quality control program. When someone's doing his job improperly," he said, referring to maintenance men who make mistakes, "he's not properly trained or supervised."

But instead of training or supervising the men properly, the Air Force, to protect its $15-million airplanes, several of which had crashed previously, resorted to punishment. It was easier to punish, apparently, than to train.

It was also easier to conserve than to train. What was true of F–111s was also true of the Air Force's huge, expensive C5A cargo planes, the world's largest operational aircraft. The planes cost more than $56 million each (twice as much as each of the Navy's newest destroyer escorts) and were originally designed to fly for 30,000 hours. But problems developed with the giant aircraft. Wings repeatedly failed fatigue tests at the Lockheed-Georgia assembly plant in Marietta, Georgia. The pylons that held the engines under the wings also failed. The landing gears could only operate for four hours before breaking down. For each hour the plane flew, ground crews had to spend 6.19 hours of maintenance, according to a General Accounting Office report.

As a result of all this, the Air Force determined that the effective life of its C5As was not 30,000 hours but only 7,000. Air Force Secretary Robert C. Seamans, Jr., told a closed hearing of a House of Representatives defense appropriations subcommittee on January 25, 1972. But he said the planes could still meet their strategic airlift mission of ferrying troops and equipment to an emergency.

138

"We have got to conserve it for that purpose," he told the congress-men, "and only fly it enough to have our crews current so that in an emergency we can use it." Thus training was cut down to only two and a half hours of flight a day without full fuel loads and without practicing touch-and-go landings that would put too much stress on the giants.

The crews, Seamans was saying, may not be as well trained for the missions as they should be. In fact they would not be trained at all for quick landings and takeoffs under emergency wartime conditions. But they would nonetheless be called upon to operate if those emergency conditions should suddenly occur.*

The reluctance of the Air Force to take risks with its expensive airplanes began to have an effect in the Indochina air war in 1972 after President Nixon renewed the bombing of North Vietnam. During Lyndon Johnson's bombing campaign of North Vietnam in 1965 to 1968, American Air Force planes rarely encountered enemy fighter planes in their runs over targets. The American pilots were subjected instead to the best antiaircraft defense in the world, a dense mixture of antiaircraft guns and Soviet surface-to-air (SAM) missiles. When the pilots flew low over their targets to achieve accuracy in dropping the bombs, they took the flak barrage. When they climbed to avoid the flak, they were subjected to the missiles. But seldom did they have to worry about Soviet Mig interceptors.

In 1972, that began to change. An American Air Force that had

---

* The C5A Galaxy was an ill-starred project from the beginning. It almost drove Lockheed out of business, requiring the government to come to the rescue with an unprecedented $250-million loan guarantee for the company. Originally the Pentagon planned to buy 115 of the 700,000-pound, 28-wheeled aircraft, but when the problems developed, when the production schedules lagged and when cost overruns skyrocketed, the Air Force cut the order back to 81 planes. Actually it will only get 79. Two burned in fires on the ground. It was designed to carry the Army's MBT 70 Main Battle Tank into battle, but that project, too, had problems and Congress killed it in December 1971 after $400 million had been spent. Congress told the Army to start all over again, giving it $20 million to spend in killing the program and another $20 million to start a new program. After the first 47 aircraft were put into operation, the wing problems were discovered and the planes were grounded for a time. In 1971, the Air Force convened a 130-man task force and appropriated $3.8 million to it to study ways of increasing the lifetime of the plane. The cut in the estimated lifetime effectively raised the cost of the plane by 450 percent over its already well-overrun (by more than $1 billion) cost. "Yes, I am disappointed in the airplane," Seamans told the House committee. "Not from the standpoint of its performance measured in terms of range, speed and requirements for landing, but from the standpoint of the structure itself. It was designed too close to the margin."

known absolute superiority in the skies now found itself challenged by North Vietnamese pilots flying Soviet Mig-21s, fast, maneuverable, lightweight but short-range aircraft. In the first six months of the year, the Americans shot down twenty-three of the Migs, but the cost was high—fifteen F-4 Phantom fighter-bombers were lost in the dogfights. It was as severe a drubbing as the Air Force had taken since World War II. (During the Korean War, it was shooting down Migs at the rate of eleven enemy planes for every American plane lost.)

In the meantime, Navy fighter-bombers, flying from carriers in the South China Sea, were suffering far fewer losses to the North Vietnamese defenders. In fact, they were shooting down Migs at the old eleven-to-one rate.

There were several reasons for this advanced by fliers. For one, the Navy's targets were all along the coast, which was not as densely covered by enemy radar monitors, whereas the Air Force planes were coming in from bases in Thailand and had to fly through the radar screen. Second, the North Vietnamese appeared to be concentrating their Mig-21s against the Air Force and sending up older, slower Mig-17s to fight the Navy planes. Third, the Air Force had configured and maintained its planes only to carry out bombing missions. The planes had originally arrived in Vietnam with no guns for dogfighting. Their only defenses against attacking planes were missiles, and often they did not work because, in the pressure of the bombing campaign, all the maintenance effort went into keeping the bombing systems in order. The Navy, on the other hand, sensitive to the danger to its big carriers from attack, did not let down its air defense guard and kept the planes capable of defense as well as offense.

Fourth, there was the training factor. To minimize its losses of aircraft and pilots, the Air Force simply was not giving flight cadets realistic training and practice in dogfighting technique. It had a policy, for example, of not allowing one type of aircraft to be pitted against another in a training exercise. This meant that a pilot in training could not learn the full potential of his craft in a realistic environment. Also, in its rush to teach fighter-bomber crews skills necessary in Vietnam, it gave short shrift to the aerial attack techniques while concentrating on teaching bombing.

Lastly, the Air Force had no good way of measuring just who were its really proficient fighter pilots and what comprised good fighter tactics.

"Too often, we measure proficiency after an exercise or a mission at the bar," one Air Force pilot told me. "The guy with the biggest mouth or the biggest fist becomes the most proficient. And out at the Edwards Air Force Base test range [where tactics are developed], we have placed our worst field-grade officers, guys who are not willing to jeopardize their careers by 'rocking the boat.' They're men for whom the golf course is the prime source of professional contact."

This officer, who had been an F-4 squadron commander in Southeast Asia and had flown several missions over North Vietnam himself, said that every time an airplane is lost in a training exercise, "more constraints are put on similar exercises in the future. And when you put on the constraints, you have to kid yourself. You have to lie and pretend you won when you didn't, or else you have to violate the constraints to get good training. In too many cases, the limits are not violated."

There was an attempt to correct this in 1972, but the impetus came from the Navy. It was building an air combat maneuver range in Yuma, Arizona, that would contain instruments capable of measuring from the ground the performance of twenty-four maneuvering aircraft or missiles in a circular range thirty miles in diameter. Thus, trainers would be able to tell from their monitoring equipment just how pilots were reacting in terms of armament use, maneuvering, fuel consumption and all other factors in the face of a sham attack.

"It will be an important device," the Air Force fighter pilot said, "if we have the honesty and integrity to use it. But that's a big 'if' because you've got the prestige of pilots all wrapped up in this thing. I expect that we'll find that our best pilots are only 30 percent of optimum and that our average pilots are only 10 percent optimum."

Though the men who need it may not be getting the right kind of flying experience, others in uniform do plenty of flying, even if they have no need for it. They draw extra pay that way. And many others are paid for flying even if they no longer fly. In all, according to Congressional testimony taken in 1972, 17,000 officers and enlisted men were receiving flight pay in nonflight jobs, including 4,300 in the Navy 1,600 in the Marine Corps, 6,000 Air Force men and 4,900 Army men. The rationale, of course, is that these men would be called upon to fly in an emergency. But the totals included 2,438 Air Force colonels and generals, 1,215 Navy captains and admirals, and 242 Army and 100 Marine officers of similar rank who would never be called upon to sit in a cockpit in wartime. They were receiving an extra $3,000 a year in flight bonuses.*

"After all," one Air Force lieutenant colonel testified, "I didn't ask for a nonflight job. And I was told when I became a pilot that I would always draw flight pay. It's like a contract."

The Air Force claimed that if it withdrew the pay, two of every three fliers would quit and that if only one out of every thousand quit, the cost of training replacements would be more than could be saved by eliminating the pay. That, of course, did not answer the questions of why nonflying fliers were needed in the first place and why it would be necessary to train fliers to take nonflying jobs.[9]

In Germany, I visited the 14th Armored Cavalry Regiment which guards the frontier between East and West Germany. If a new European war ever came, the regiment would be one of the first to make contact with the enemy. The regiment's commander is a self-assured, knowledgeable paratrooper and helicopter pilot from Santa Rosa, California, by the name of Colonel Egbert B. Clark, III. He was drafted in 1946 and came up through the ranks, commanding a tank company in the Korean War and serving with the famous 101st Airborne Division in Vietnam.

Colonel Clark knows the Army and works hard at solving those problems over which he has some control. For example, his regiment was one of the few units I found where any kind of physical training program was under way. He meant to get his troops into good condition.

When I asked him for permission to visit a training mission, he answered, "Certainly."

The next morning, after a standard guided tour to an "Iron Curtain" watchtower, Clark piloted his helicopter to a regimental garrison at Bad Hersfeld. In a parking lot, six tanks had been rolled out, and on a hill far away, a target was wheeling back and forth like a duck in a

* When a Senate committee held hearings in 1972 on the removal of General John D. Lavelle as commander of the Air Force in Southeast Asia for falsifying reports on the air war, it developed an interesting sidelight on pay procedures for high-ranking officers. Lavelle, the committee learned, had passed a physical examination certifying him qualified to pilot aircraft six months before his retirement. This enabled him to continue collecting the $3,000 flight bonus. Just before he retired, he took a new physical and was awarded a 70 percent medical disability, allowing him to collect 70 percent of his $27,000-a-year retirement pay tax-free. According to Defense Department sources, several generals have benefited similarly in recent years.

shooting gallery. The tank crews, I was told, were practicing the firing of guided missiles at the target. It developed that only one of the six vehicles had equipment on board to simulate the firing. The others were just for show. An officer explained the technique and then invited me to try my hand at firing the weapon. I clambered onto the tank, down into the turret, and began tracking the target though the scope. When I pressed the button to fire, nothing happened. The simulator was broken.

Throughout the services, there were stories about broken equipment that had made training impossible or meaningless. At the one training mission anyone could show me in a six-and-one-half-week tour, the equipment was broken.*

It was not a good advertisement for the combat readiness of the American military machine.

If improved training was the key to all the Army's problems in the 1970s, then the model to adopt for that improvement was centered in a small group of buildings nestled in a faraway corner of the Army's sprawling infantry center at Fort Benning, Georgia. There was nothing prepossessing about those buildings. They looked rather like a boy-scout camp—a series of low, white clapboard structures nestled in a stand of tall, shady pine trees.

They were the headquarters for the Army's Ranger Department, where generations of officers and men have gone to learn how to survive and carry on under the most rugged conditions. Beyond the physical requirements necessary for ordinary combat training, there was only one prerequisite for Ranger training. You had to know how to swim. Beyond that, in a few weeks, the Army would teach you how to scale cliffs, live in the jungle, endure desert heat, and negotiate a treacherous swamp. The Rangers gave you the will to live. They taught you how to survive, even under the most adverse conditions.

"Not everyone wants to live," Colonel David Grange, the head of the Ranger Department, said. "Some people just give up too easily."

* I was also invited to witness a display of weapons at a combat-ready American fire base outside Danang in South Vietnam and try my hand at firing them. Of the three weapons attempted—a machine gun, M-16 rifle and M-79 grenade launcher, only the machine gun fired perfectly the first time. The escort officer had to call for two additional rifles and three different grenade launchers before he found one of each that fired as expected. The weapons, he said, needed better maintenance.

Dave Grange reflects all that is good in the professional soldier. He is a man deeply committed to the task of passing a body of professional knowledge on to others.

"I've been in the Army twenty-nine years," he said, "and I can remain another eight. I think I will, because I enjoy what I'm doing. I like the job I've got now because every eight weeks I can see the results."

To win a Ranger patch at the end of the eight-week course is to be marked as a man who has taken the toughest the Army has to offer and survived. Grange is the man to administer the course. He fought as a paratrooper in three wars—World War II, Korea, and Vietnam. He served as an enlisted man for seven years after joining up in 1943, graduated from Officers Candidate School in 1950, and has attended all the Army's service schools. He commanded a platoon, company, battalion and brigade. He is now on his second tour with the Ranger Department.

"I've done the Pentagon thing," he said. "I've sent papers out of my office never knowing whether they were read or not. But down here I get real satisfaction."

In May 1972, Dave Grange and I discussed the turmoil of the Army, all the wasted motion, the preoccupation with social problems that almost made it seem as if the Army had forgotten its basic mission.

"You know," he said, "last week I had a four-hour course scheduled for some of the students in the basic infantry course out here at the rope rappelling tower. It's a terrific thing. The students really love it. It teaches them how to climb down a cliff. Gives them a feeling of real accomplishment. At the last minute, the course was canceled. Someone decided they had to have four more hours of race relations and so they couldn't get the rope rappelling. Can you imagine that?"

8

RACE: BLACK PING-PONG BALLS
AND WHITE

The Regular Army of the United States at the start of the Civil War was a very small organization—15,000 enlisted men and 1,108 officers. When the Southern states seceded, virtually all the enlisted men, whether their homes were north or south of the Mason-Dixon Line, elected to fight for the Union. That was not the case in the officer corps. Almost one third—313—broke their oaths to uphold the Constitution against all enemies, foreign and domestic, and defected to the Confederacy. Along with the commissioned officers, seventy-five West Point cadets from the Southern states either left the Academy or were dismissed when they indicated they would not bear arms against the Confederacy. Those decisions by the officers and cadets were made all the more conspicuous by hundreds of other Southerners who chose to fight for the preservation of the Union.

The Southern defectors left a bitterness in the Regular Army that lasted for decades. Years later, when the Regular Army veterans raised money for a monument at the Academy to the Civil War dead, they specifically excluded from remembrance Academy graduates who had given their lives for the Confederacy. The "War Memorial" is a tall, massive, polished granite column set on the edge of a high bluff overlooking the Hudson River. Atop the column the bronze statue of a winged female in flowing robes looks down on The Plain, West Point's quadrangle. She carries a wreath in one hand, a trumpet in the other. Around the base of the column and on cannons mounted on a balustrade appear the names of all the Regular Army men who gave their lives for the Union. On the column itself this inscription appears: "IN MEMORY OF THE OFFICERS AND MEN OF THE REGULAR ARMY OF THE UNITED STATES WHO FELL IN BATTLE DURING THE WAR OF THE REBELLION"

On May 29, 1971, President Richard M. Nixon, visiting the Academy to deliver an address, motored past the memorial and inquired idly into its significance of his host, Major General William S. Knowlton, superintendent of the Academy. The general explained how the column memorialized the men who had fought to preserve the Union.

The President reportedly responded with some remarks on how the War Between the States had now receded over one hundred years into history, that the wounds had been bound up and that the Academy should have a memorial to all its sons who had fought and died on both sides. A new memorial was needed, he said, adding, "I will come up here to dedicate it."

The general reportedly was not certain that the President was serious. Not long afterward, however, he received a call from a White House official who asked how plans for the new memorial were progressing. Knowlton then appointed a committee that quickly developed plans for a $70,000 monument conforming to the President's wishes. The theme was clasped hands.

In the fall of 1971, the 4000-man Corps of Cadets, returning to classes for a new academic year, learned for the first time about the memorial. Among the cadets were 146 blacks, many of whom for the previous two years had been struggling with the problem of resolving a conflict between emerging black awareness and their experiences at West Point.* At a time when thousands of other young blacks were taking to the streets in militant protest, these black cadets were submitting themselves voluntarily to the control of one of the institutions in society most repressive in its outlook toward individual rights, for

---

* Those cadets were the results of a vigorous recruiting program at the Academy, paralleling similar efforts at the Naval Academy and the Air Force Academy. In the previous twenty-one years, a total of only 96 blacks had matriculated at West Point.

whites as well as blacks. They were moving slowly in dealing with their problems.

West Point had never been a very easy place for a black cadet. One of the first, Johnson Chestnut Whittaker of South Carolina, who attended the Academy from 1876 to 1880, was completely ostracized. He was given his own single room when other cadets had doubles, spoken to only on official business and then curtly, and hazed when he tried to sit next to whites at mess or when he fell into formation. Whittaker recorded the solution to his problems in his Bible:

Try never to injure another by word, by action . . . Forgive as soon as you are injured and forget as soon as you forgive.

The solution did not work. On April 7, 1880, he was discovered bound tightly hand and foot, tied to his bed, bleeding from cuts in both earlobes (the tip of the left ear had been cut off), with tufts of hair cut irregularly from his head. After a cursory investigation, a Court of Inquiry ruled that Whittaker had himself written a warning note that presaged the attack, mutilated himself, bound himself and then feigned unconsciousness when found. The implication was that he either wanted to embarrass the Academy or sought some excuse for not being able to finish the course. Academy officials defended the ostracism (not because of his color but because he was not a gentleman, they said) and a subsequent decision to court-martial Whittaker (because he was a follower, not a leader, and should be gotten away from West Point, "where he does not belong"). Whittaker was court-martialed, convicted and released from the Academy. He was also fined and ordered imprisoned, but these penalties were suspended.*

From Reconstruction until the Montgomery bus boycott of 1956, forgive-and-forget was the dominant black philosophy toward oppression throughout society. The Reverend Dr. Martin Luther King's more activist ideas began to replace that. By the late 1960s, the more militant

---

* The Whittaker affair is explored in detail in "A Black Cadet at West Point" by John F. Marszalek, Jr., in *American Heritage*, Vol. XXII, No. 5, August 1971, p. 30. Marszalek notes that subsequent historians of West Point fail to give a full account of the affair and do nothing to rescue Whittaker's reputation. Writes Marszalek: "The record, however, speaks for itself and tells volumes about the long struggle of the American Negro against the bias, conscious and unconscious, of his white fellow citizens."

extensions of that philosophy, including the use of violence as a tool to show discontent, spread to the armed services.

In 1971, black militancy came to West Point. It was triggered by President Nixon's remark on the need for a new memorial. The new cadets were already uneasy in their surroundings, particularly over the fact that their social opportunities were more limited than those of the white cadets. There were few black girls in the surrounding Hudson River Valley communities, and the blacks found it uncomfortable to go to cadet hops and other social events with white girls. The first attempts at banding together came over the matter of easing social pressures. By midwinter of 1970–1971, the blacks had organized a "contemporary affairs committee" as a part of the Academy's Political Sciences Club. It had Academy sanction but had to be named a "committee" rather than a club because rules forbade organization of a club along racial lines.

Major Melvin Bowdan, one of the black faculty members, said: "The brothers began to find out there were a lot of other things of common concern besides just the social problem. They discovered that they shared feelings of subtle discrimination against them as black cadets."

Much of this resulted from the Academy's military aptitude-rating system in which one's peers, cadet superiors and already-commissioned tactical officers judge cadets in nonacademic matters relating to how good an officer each man will make.

In this system, Bowdan said, the best blacks and the worst, like the best whites and worst, achieved fair ratings. But the vast majority of average blacks always seemed to be rated worse than the average whites.

Jay Kimmitt, twenty-one, of Washington, D.C., a white cadet, described the problem this way: "The average white cadet can go through West Point keeping a low profile. The average black can't do that. He always stands out because of his color. The color is almost like a magnet. It's like one black ping-pong ball in a box of white ping-pong balls. The white ping-pong balls may have little spots on them but they're not seen. They don't count. People are always concentrating on the black ping-pong balls."

News of the plans to build the monument impelled the black cadets to abandon their low profile. Knowlton himself was not convinced that the monument was necessary. He invited comment from a number of groups, including the black cadets. The blacks broadened their discussion of the monument into consideration of all their grievances and finally decided to submit a petition covering many points. When the general heard of this, he sent word to the black cadets that the petition would be unnecessary. The cadets persisted.

After much discussion, more than ninety of the black cadets and eighteen out of twenty-two black faculty and staff members signed a petition of grievances against the monument and these other matters:

—West Point encouraged blacks to forget their heritage. The petitioners pointed out that it was Academy influence, they thought, which impelled the service's second black general, Benjamin O. Davis, Jr., '36, (his father was the first) to once remark to some more militant young blacks, "I'm your color but not your kind."*

—The Academy should have some black associate and full professors. It was noted that there were only six black instructors and six black tactical officers on the faculty.

—The Academy lacked a large enough number of black civilians in high-paying positions.

—Tactical officers refused to allow blacks to cut their hair attractively.

—The Academy had refused permission to Representative Ronald V. Dellums, the radical black congressman from California, to speak on campus.

—Only one black cadet had ever been named a permanent captain in the Corps, although others were qualified.

—The instructor teaching a black history course was leaving, and there were no plans to continue the course.

—Cadet skits put on at the end of summer training programs tended to ridicule black noncommissioned officers.

—Although one troop of the famous 10th Cavalry Regiment, a unit once commanded by General of the Armies John J. ("Black Jack") Pershing and consisting of all black enlisted men, was once headquartered at West Point, there was no memorial to the black troops. (There were, however, memorials to the unit's white officers.)

Cadet Percy Squire, twenty-one, a black upperclassman from Youngstown, Ohio, delivered the petition to Knowlton on a Friday afternoon in November 1971. The meeting lasted "about ten seconds," Squire said. "Knowlton looked at all the signatures and then said, 'I have to go watch a football game' or something like that."

* Davis graduated from the Academy in 1936 after enduring four years of virtual silence from his fellow cadets.

Although the general may not have wanted to discuss the matter with one of his cadets, the document did have an impact on him. In subsequent weeks, the haircut policy was modified, Dellums was allowed to speak at the Academy, promises were made to correct the summer skit policy, the black cadets were allowed to organize a benefit soul concert for sickle cell anemia, and plans were made to erect a plaque to the men of the 10th Cavalry.

Meanwhile, plans to build the new Civil War monument were dropped, despite the President's wishes. There were objectors in addition to the blacks. Officers such as General Harold K. Johnson, who had been chief of staff of the Army during the early days of the Vietnam build-up, opposed the memorial in debates in the Association of Graduates, the Academy's alumni organization. One of the arguments against the memorial was that in the Vietnam War, West Point had been increasingly troubled with graduates and cadets expressing a doctrine of "selective conscientious objection" or a refusal to bear arms only in the current conflict. How, the objectors asked, could the Academy or the Army deal punitively with these modern-day objectors and at the same time erect a memorial to men who were selective conscientious objectors in the nineteenth century? The monument idea was dropped in deference to this view despite the fact that the Association's governing board approved the idea by a seventeen-to-fifteen vote.

At the Academy some of the black cadets remained unhappy despite the decision not to build President Nixon's monument honoring white men considered traitors in their day. Instead of a mere inconspicuous plaque, they wanted West Point to build a full-scale, visible memorial to black soldiers.

"I would rather see a statue of a black sergeant major riding a horse," Cadet Squire said. "That would have a lot more impact than a plaque."

While the black cadets at West Point were slowly developing group activities to satisfy their awakening racial consciousness, the rest of the military experienced a black rebellion that in some places reached mutinous proportions.

Racial outbreaks were all the more striking because, in the public's eye, the services were among the few institutions in society which had succeeded in granting equal rights to all, regardless of race, creed or color.

It was generally thought that President Harry S. Truman had done away with segregation in the armed forces in 1948. Therefore the problem no longer existed. Throughout the 1950s, there were stories about equal opportunity in the armed forces—men were promoted on ability; housing problems had been solved; blacks serving abroad were treated better by host-country nationals than they were in the United States. That was the popular picture. It was unreal.

The reality was the exportation of racism by Americans overseas, resulting in the education of landlords to follow discriminatory policies in renting off-base housing as well as pressure on bartenders and women to refuse service and affection to blacks if they wanted business from the white majority. At the same time blacks were placed in low-prestige jobs inside the service where they had little opportunity for advancement and were suffering more severe punishment than whites for similar offenses. In some cases, discrimination against black Americans was even part of this country's foreign policy. The United States, for example, reached an agreement with Iceland limiting the number of blacks who would be stationed there.

In 1971, the Air Force's Air Training Command (ATC) at Randolph Field, Texas, published a study of racism and discrimination on its bases throughout the United States that best summed the situation up. And what was true of the ATC was true of all the commands in all the services. The ATC study said:

> Equal treatment *has not* been practiced in the ATC. Whites get letters of reprimand in their UIF [Unfavorable Information File] which is destroyed when they leave the base . . . and the black gets an Article 15 which stains his record permanently for the same offense. A white gets "personally reprimanded for his indiscretion" and told not to do it any more if he makes advances or pinches a married black waitress where you shouldn't pinch; a black airman is fired or has charges brought against him . . . if he does the same thing. A white airman is just "late" and gets chewed out if he returns from leave a day or so late; a black airman is charged with AWOL, served with an Article 15 and usually loses money or a stripe. These cases are not fiction; they are fact and we saw it. Unequal treatment is manifested in unequal punishment, offensive and inflammatory language; prejudice in the assignment of de-

tails, lack of products for blacks in the PX, harassment by Security Policemen under orders to break up five or more blacks in a group, double standards in the enforcement of regulations, etc. The cause of this is blatant supervisory prejudice in many cases, but for the most part it was the result of supervisory indifference to human needs . . . We heard numerous explanations from clock-watching technicians on why they couldn't provide for some of these needs but not one explanation or proposed solution on how they could solve the problems . . .

The correction of grievances should not stop at the front gate or be confined to the internal boundaries of the military installation. The correction process must extend to all civilian communities that are accessible to airmen and officers off that base. The passive commander . . . who condones or permits prejudices or de facto segregation that affects his people in the civilian community has lost all credibility with his men. And this includes a tremendous number of young white airmen and officers. Economic sanctions (possibly in the form of "Off Limits" action or termination of civilian business contracts) must be applied if necessary to right legitimate complaints of discriminatory or segregationist practices. And, in accordance with our very own AFR 35-78, it should be swift and without any foot-dragging delay. If fair and equal treatment cannot be obtained for all military personnel and their families, then the base should be closed and/or relocated. If the United States Air Force and Department of Defense mean what they say about equal opportunity and treatment of military personnel, then *we have no choice* and the civilian/military community should know it.[1]

Conditions such as these led to a series of explosive incidents of which the following are only examples:

Darmstadt, Germany, July 1971: A white sergeant takes offense at the doings of some blacks, enters their room with a gun, threatens to kill them. Apprehended, the sergeant is brought before his company commander who takes the gun, releases the sergeant. A few days later, a fistfight breaks out in a mess hall after whites try to drown out soul music from a juke box with country-and-western music they play on a tape recorder smuggled into the hall. One black is arrested. Others gather before company headquarters to find out why and protest. The battalion commander orders his men out in battle gear to surround protesters. Fifty-three are arrested, charged with disobeying an order to disperse. Charges are subsequently dropped against "Darmstadt 53" after much publicity.[2]

Fort McClellan, Alabama, November 1971: Fistfight between a black man and a white man breaks out in an enlisted men's club. Blacks leave the club in a bus which breaks down on the way back to barracks. They start to walk. A white off-duty MP drives his jeep through the group, knocking several down. Blacks, including some sixty WACs from the Woman's Army Corps Center on the post, rampage, breaking windows, damaging cars, attacking and threatening white GIs. The next day, many WACs refuse to go to work; fights break out between militant and moderate black WACs. Investigation uncovers seventeen Molotov cocktails in a guest house. Authorities arrest 115 blacks and jail them as far away as Fort Benning, Georgia, and Fort Bragg, North Carolina. As a result, ten black WACs and thirteen black enlisted men are discharged from the Army as unsuitable. Two black men are court-martialed and convicted. Thirteen black men are given nonjudicial punishment. Forty-six black WACs are transferred to other bases. The white MP goes unpunished, a spokesman at Fort McClellan saying that the Army is having trouble getting statements about the incident from those involved.[3]

Augsburg, Germany, October 1969: In moves resembling the midnight-knocks-on-the-door of totalitarian countries, ten blacks in 24th Infantry Division are summarily transferred to new bases—six in the United States, four to Germany. The blacks are transferred because "this command, from time to time, deems it prudent to remove individuals whose activities have been found to be prejudicial to morale, discipline or good order." They are members of a group that had been holding Sunday afternoon meetings on Negro history, music, neighborhood news from home and general complaints. One of the transferees is routed out of bed at 3 A.M. and driven to the airport. Why such an hour? So the man can make his plane, an Army spokesman answers.[4]

Berlin, Germany, August 1970: Dozens of whites and blacks brawl; MPs are stoned when they try to interfere; one policeman and seven GIs are hospitalized with injuries. Influence of black power organization is blamed.[5]

Hohenfels, Germany, May 1970: A hand grenade is thrown through a mess hall window during 1st Division training exercise. Ten men injured. On the same night, a series of fires breaks out in a motor pool. Ten blacks, including a Vietnam combat hero who had been honored in Chicago by Mayor Richard J. Daley, are charged.[6]

Hanau, Germany, January 1971: Near-riot triggered by death of black GI. Blacks claim he was pushed down barracks stairs by whites.[7]

Koza, Okinawa, April 1970: About one hundred blacks hurl stones, empty bottles and garbage at MPs trying to break up a disturbance outside a military base. MPs are forced to fire two shots into the air to disperse crowd.[8]

Koza, Okinawa, August 1971: In protest over exclusion from bars where only whites are served, a group of twenty black airmen enter Club Venus, sit one to a table, order one drink and stay several hours without reordering. Next night, four blacks enter Club Orbit and occupy every other stool at the bar. One night later, sixteen blacks occupy tables at Club Orbit, ordering one drink each, remaining two hours. The owner shuts down; an Okinawan breaks a bottle and a barstool menacingly. Other owners and bartenders gather outside. The next night, after midnight, twenty to forty blacks gather in night-club district, enter Club Orbit, begin breaking tables, chairs, bottles and bar. Okinawans, three hundred strong, retaliate. Blacks are hunted throughout the area; eleven are attacked and injured; four privately owned vehicles are damaged. The melee continues for three hours.[9]

Kin, Okinawa, November 1970, March–June 1971: Black marines repeatedly protest discrimination, block mess hall lines with prolonged black-power ritual handshakes ("dapping"), create disturbances in barracks, inflict "pains of the death of one thousand knives" on a black noncommissioned officer who is rescued before hundreds of subcutaneous knife cuts do serious injury. In uneasy settlement, Marine officers allow blacks to wear jackets with clenched-fist sign of black power on the back, and grant permission for blacks to exchange black-power salute on base.[10]

Washington, D.C., January 1972: Over five hundred black civilian employees, servicemen and patients at Walter Reed Army Hospital rally in Martin Luther King Day program to protest job discrimination and racism at the hospital. White officials concede validity of complaints but say "gap is constantly narrowing because we are working to narrow it.[11]

Washington, D.C., March 1971: A black Marine patient beats a white Naval corpsman who, the marine charges, called him a "nigger" in a men's room at the enlisted men's club at the Bethesda Naval Medical Center. This triggers a fight between whites and blacks outside the club, exposing simmering racial tensions of many months' standing at the hospital. The club is closed. Surprise raids uncover weapons in lockers of enlisted men. "Kids like him [the Marine patient] are just not going to turn the other cheek any more," a hospital official says.[12]

Travis Air Force Base, California, May 1971: Twenty-four are injured in race-rioting involving 500 blacks. Police "detain" 135. Fire breaks out in transient officers' barracks. Blacks submit a list of fifty grievances after the incident, most of which can be registered as easily by whites.[13]

Detroit, January 1971: A nineteen-year-old black GI, home on leave from Fort Knox, Kentucky, is waylaid by men he describes as "black radicals." They beat him, burn him with cigarettes, pour boiling water on him and set his uniform afire, saying "You're a pig in a pig's uniform and we're going to kill you."[14]

Camp Lejeune, South Carolina, July 1969: A thrice-wounded white Marine corporal dies of massive head injuries sustained in an assault by black marines. In a series of fights thereafter, fifteen whites are injured by thirty to fifty black marines of the 2d Marine Division. Authorities report 160 assaults, muggings and robberies on base between January and August, 1969.[15]

Fort Benning, Georgia, February 1970: A number of black soldiers waylay and assault whites making telephone calls from an outdoor booth on Kelley Hill, a remote area reserved for the 197th Light Infantry Brigade. Military police report brawls with increasing frequency in the area. "Kelley Hill may belong to the commander in the daytime, but it belongs to the black Spec Four after dark," goes the saying at Fort Benning.[16]

And so it went in dozens of places around the world—almost wherever American military installations were situated. In Germany alone, during the year October 1970 to September 30, 1971, there were fifty-four instances in which large groups of blacks marched to commanding officers demanding an audience to express grievances or present demands.

Throughout the nation and the world, fact-finding teams from the Defense Department, each of the services, Congress, and organizations such as the National Association for the Advancement of Colored People, the Congress on Racial Equality and the Urban League criss-crossed with each other, gathering up information, weaving together a tapestry of racism within the services. Even before all the studies were finished, the fabric had many patterns.

A compilation of statistics by the Defense Department illuminated the difficulty blacks confronted in reaching the highest grades in both the officer and noncommissioned officer corps. In 1949, 11.8 percent of Army privates and their equivalents in the other services were black. At that time, only 2.2 percent of the E-7 grade, then the highest-ranking enlisted grade, were black, reflecting the lack of opportunity in the segregated military establishment which had just come to an end. But by 1970, that picture should have changed. Many of those men entering the service in 1949 and the years immediately thereafter should have achieved the highest enlisted grades in the coming two decades. The numbers showed they did not. By 1970, when 13.8 percent of all privates and the equivalent were black, the number of black E-7s had risen to 10.8 percent. But, at the same time, the services had added two more enlisted grades at the top, and in these grades, the percentage of blacks fell off sharply. The black percentage in E-8 was 7.1 and in E-9 it was 3.6. Though blacks qualified in a constant ratio to whites for all the lower enlisted grades, they were excluded when it came to the very top jobs.

In the officer corps, the picture was roughly the same. In 1970, 2.2 percent of all officers were black, and that was a figure that remained approximately constant from warrant officer up to lieutenant colonel. At the colonel level, however, the number dropped off sharply to .6 percent. By percentages, there were less than one third as many black colonels as lieutenant colonels. And there were less than one tenth as many black generals as lieutenant colonels.* Clearly there was little room at the top for blacks.

---

* The following table shows the percentage of blacks by grade in the officer corps of each of the services in 1970, just as black militancy was starting to take hold in the armed forces. Since then the services have taken steps to promote a greater number of blacks to the highest grades. The table was compiled from

In addition to showing how unqualified blacks were deemed for higher rank in all the services, the statistics pointed out other phenomena. They showed how the Navy, in 1970, still had not lost its image as the most discriminatory of all the services—the only one in which blacks were not represented in the enlisted grades in roughly the same proportion as blacks in the general population.* They indicated a discrimination against blacks in the Marine officer corps that began not at the colonel level but at the grade of major. Though there were proportionately as many black Marine second lieutenants as there were

---

figures supplied by the Office of the Deputy Assistant Secretary of Defense for Equal Opportunity Affairs. (Navy equivalent grades are, from top to bottom, admiral, captain, commander, lieutenant commander, lieutenant, lieutenant junior grade and ensign.)

	Army	Navy	Air Force	Marines	All Services
Generals	.2	.0	.2	.0	.2
Colonels	1.2	.1	.4	.0	.6
Lt. Cols.	4.7	.3	1.2	.2	2.3
Majors	5.2	.5	1.7	.3	2.6
Captains	3.7	.6	2.2	1.4	2.4
1st Lts.	2.5	.6	1.4	1.5	1.7
2nd Lts.	1.7	1.2	1.2	1.9	1.5
Enlisted Men	13.5	5.4	11.7	11.2	11.0

* Blacks have served with distinction in the Navy going back to the days of the Revolutionary War and the War of 1812, during which one sixth of all naval personnel were black. A black seaman won the Medal of Honor in the Civil War and another, a former slave, commandeered a Confederate ship which he sailed out of Charleston harbor and turned over to the Union with its entire crew. Segregation entered the Navy at the time of the Spanish-American War and grew ever stronger. By 1920, the Navy only permitted Negroes to enter the service as messmen. The policy eased a bit in World War II when some blacks were allowed into general service, and sixty black officers were commissioned. All but four resigned at the end of the war. It was not until 1949 that the first black graduated from the United States Naval Academy. In 1945, 95 percent of all stewards in the Navy were black, the rest being Filipinos, Guamanians, Samoans and other Oriental peoples. When blacks were freed of steward duty, the United States concluded, in 1952, an agreement with the Philippine government to enlist Filipino nationals. Between 1952 and 1968, 19,468 Filipinos were recruited for mess duty. Few of them worked their way into other occupations. "We have not been successful in getting large numbers of Caucasians to volunteer for the rating," the Navy said in defending its policy of recruiting dark-skinned foreign nationals for the mess jobs. In other areas, the military has never been bashful about coercing men into taking jobs that had to be done. The information for this footnote was taken from *Report of the Director of the Recruiting Division's Informal Study Group on Minority Recruiting for the U.S. Navy*, Bureau of Naval Personnel, Washington, D.C., August 1968.

Army second lieutenants, there were seventeen times fewer black majors in the Marines than there were in the Army on a percentage basis.

The statistics also showed a bleak prospect for the future, even if the services did want to increase the percentage of blacks in the chain of command. The evidence was that bright young black men who might make good officers were turning their backs on military service. The indication of this was in the Army officer corps where, proportionately, there were almost three times as many black lieutenant colonels as second lieutenants. The lieutenant colonels were men who, after the desegregation order of 1948, saw better opportunites for themselves in uniform than in civilian life. In 1970, however, young black college graduates were finding far greater opportunities outside the services and thus were not choosing careers in uniform after fulfilling minimum service obligations. Their decisions were hastened by the feeling that to enter or remain in the service, they would either have to endure manifestations of racism or sell out to a white-controlled establishment. Major Melvin Bowdan, the West Point instructor, at the age of thirty-six had made the decision to remain in the Army. A Californian who had graduated from the University of Denver, he was a veteran of fourteen years of service in the combat arms in 1972. His experiences at West Point with the black cadets had awakened him to the situation he faced.

"I now realize," he told me one late spring afternoon at West Point, "that for years I have been treated as the 'house nigger' in the various units I served in. As a result, I had no self-respect as a black man or as a soldier. But now I am getting to know myself as a black man and as a soldier.

"It will be interesting to see whether I, as a noncareerist, will be able to talk to my peers, my subordinates and superiors and tell them what I think should be done about certain problems without suffering personally as a result. The question I'm asking myself is whether or not a man can survive in the Army who is not moved by artificial requirements.

"Right now we're making quick fixes. We're adapting but not changing, and so we've made no real adaptation yet. But I still have a strong belief in the system's ability to adapt. I doubt that any other society has the power to adapt like this one."

Quick fixes. In this regard, the services in 1971 and 1972 suddenly found many blacks qualified to wear stars. In those two years, the Army promoted eight blacks from colonel to general, giving it a total of nine general officers. It assigned the senior man among them, Major General Frederic E. Davison, to be the first black ever to command a division. During that same period, the Navy promoted the first black ever to reach the rank of captain to rear admiral. He was Samuel Gravely. And the Air Force, following the retirement of Lieutenant General Benjamin O. Davis, Jr., named two black generals. There was also one each in the Army National Guard and the Army Reserve in mid-1972.

There were other blacks who shared Bowdan's faith in the system. One was Army Captain Curtis R. Smothers who, in 1970, became the Army's first full-time black judge. He was twenty-eight years old at the time. Smothers graduated from Morgan State College in Maryland in 1965 and entered the Army with an ROTC commission. Under a special program, he went to Georgetown Law School in Washington and was later assigned to the Judge Advocate General's Corps in Europe. As a judge, he traveled a circuit throughout Germany from headquarters in Frankfurt and quickly discovered manifestations of discrimination and racism.

In December 1970, along with six other black officers and enlisted men, he signed a petition calling for a Court of Inquiry to determine whether the Army's commanding general in Europe, General James H. Polk, had been guilty of dereliction of duty for permitting discrimination in housing. Told by his superiors that it was unseemly for a judge to take such an action, Smothers said he replied: "The chief justice of the United States goes around making speeches advocating changes in laws. I'm not even doing that. All I'm asking is that existing Army regulations be enforced."

About the same time, he was interviewed by Mike Wallace for a television show. Asked if, in his estimation, the Army command in Germany was racist, he answered, for millions of home viewers: "We're judging by actions. By actions, yes."

A few weeks later, Smothers was advised that if he felt so strongly, he should leave the bench and take a job where he could do something about it.* He was transferred back to the Pentagon, where he occupied

---

* The Court of Inquiry was never convened, but the Army did conduct informal investigations, and in early 1971, General Polk suddenly retired from service, sooner than had been expected. There were many who said that the retirement

159

a small office, with little to do. Later in 1971, however, Frank W. Render, a black whom President Nixon had named deputy assistant secretary of defense for equal opportunity affairs, was fired after speaking out vigorously about the military's racist policies. Mr. Nixon appointed Donald Miller, a black personnel specialist from big business, to replace Render. Smothers, resigning from the Army, was named Miller's deputy. Smothers was no idealist seeking to win the hearts of men. He was far more pragmatic.

"If we begin to recognize that people simply do not do things out of love, do not do things because it's nice, good and right to be fair to all people, then we'll begin to make some progress," he told me. "If we look at the fact that people respond to situations for their own reasons and if you make it profitable for them to develop real successes in the area of equal opportunity, then we're going to get something done. In some respects the military has been ahead of the civilian system. It is certainly more capable of dealing with racial questions simply because of its ability to *order* people to do things. If we can get these efforts under way, we're probably going to see inroads made. Otherwise, it will continue to be just like in civilian society—a continuing polarization. But there will be a lot more potential for violence because in the military they already have weapons."

Like Smothers, Lieutenant Commander William S. Norman decided to remain in the Navy and try to help work the problems out. In 1970, after completing a tour as an instructor at the Naval Academy and another as an aircraft carrier pilot in combat in Vietnam, Norman had decided to resign from the Navy in protest over its racial policies. Asked by Admiral Elmo R. Zumwalt, Jr., who had just been named Chief of Naval Operations, to stay on, Norman did. As Zumwalt's special assistant for equal opportunity affairs, Norman, thirty-four, drew up a series of programs designed to increase the percentage of black enlisted

---

was not voluntary but was requested because of the general's attitudes on the race question. Smothers accused the general of violating Army directives by (1) refusing to comply with an order establishing equal opportunity councils and (2) not enforcing his own order to all units to post lists of punishments given for offenses. Such posting would have compelled superiors to mete out equal justice to blacks and whites by exposing any discrepancies. Polk was replaced by General Michael Shannon Davison, who quickly established a reputation as the "Zumwalt of the Army" and was generally mentioned as a favorite candidate to succeed Westmoreland as Chief of Staff. However, in 1972, President Nixon named General Creighton Abrams, the Vietnam commander, to that job.

men in the Navy to 12 percent by 1976 and the number of black officers to 5 percent, ensuring all equal opportunity. It was a delicate task that had Zumwalt's complete backing. He realized the Navy had a lot of catching up to do. But whether others realized it was another matter.

"It is unbelievable to me that any officer can believe that these problems can be solved by fiat from Washington," Norman said in late 1971 at the start of a tour of all Navy installations in the Pacific. "We must get the support of all echelons. We must make it so costly in terms of promotions, awards and assignments that people cannot afford not to cooperate. We're lucky that Zumwalt came along when he did. No one else in the Navy can do it. But what I worry about is, what happens when Zumwalt goes."

Within four months after assuming office as Chief of Naval Operations, Admiral Zumwalt, in November 1970, issued a Z-Gram calling for increased attention to the provision of equal opportunity for the minority groups in the Navy. More than two hundred different programs were devised. One was the establishment of a recruiting program for intelligent young blacks at the Naval Academy. Another established more NROTC units at black colleges. Others provided for more cosmetics used exclusively by blacks to be sold at base exchanges. One decreed the establishment in each command of a "minority affairs assistant" to advise commanding officers on problems relating to blacks, Filipinos and Mexican-Americans.

Two years after all this activity began, Admiral Zumwalt learned that little progress had been made. In the fall of 1972, a study group informed him that some of the minority affairs assistants had been so badly misused by their commanders that they never even received copies of directives from Zumwalt's headquarters ordering implementation of new programs. In many cases, commanding officers used the minority affairs assistants not to get at basic causes of racial tension but, in Admiral Zumwalt's words, "to slip over a 'hot spot' without getting at the cause."

Zumwalt's education did not come only from that study group. In October 1972, two of the Navy's largest aircraft carriers and an oiler were wracked by racial violence of the kind that had hit Army installations two years earlier. Aboard the aircraft carrier *Kitty Hawk*, en route to a combat mission in Vietnam, fifteen hours of racial fighting resulted in injuries to forty whites and six blacks. Twenty-five black crewmen were arrested as a result; no whites were. The *Kitty Hawk* fighting in which men used knives, forks, chains and any other available weapons was described as the worst racial disturbance in the history of the Navy. It apparently began over an incident in the men's room of a bar in the Philippines the night before the ship sailed into the combat zone.

A few days later, fighting between blacks and whites broke out on the oiler *Hassayampa,* which was tied up at Subic Bay in the Philippines. Blacks charged that white crewmen had taken money from their wallets. Fighting started, resulting in the arrest of eleven blacks. Once again, no whites were arrested.

Two days after the incident aboard the oiler, some 250 men aboard the aircraft carrier *Constellation,* which was on a training cruise off the coast of California, staged a sit-in on the mess deck of the 80,000-ton vessel. Most were blacks. They had heard rumors that 250 unskilled crewmen were going to be discharged, and they viewed this as discriminatory, since most of the men in unskilled jobs were black. They asked for a meeting with the skipper, Captain J. D. Ward. He refused to meet with them. Protest meetings were held daily for almost two weeks with the skipper refusing to attend. At the last meeting, Marines carrying M-16 rifles surrounded about 150 blacks, and it appeared that rioting would begin until, finally, the Marines were recalled.

At that point, Captain Ward had to break off his combat-readiness maneuvers and return to San Diego where he put 137 of the protesters, all but a dozen of them black, ashore without ever listening to their grievances personally. He had his first meeting with the dissidents after the carrier returned to port.

In November, fighting between blacks and whites broke out in the Navy Correctional Facility at Norfolk, Virginia, and on Midway Island, a remote station in the mid-Pacific. The Midway fighting, involving 130 men, stunned the base commander, Captain Samuel G. Anders. He said his base had "a good minority affairs program."

In response to the outbreaks and the findings of the study group, Admiral Zumwalt summoned more than eighty admirals and Marine Corps generals to his office in mid-November to read them a lecture.

"In my opinion," the admiral said, "the most destructive influence on the resolution of racial problems is self-deception. . . . It is self-deception to feel a[n equal opportunity] program is a reality. It is not."

He accused the admirals and generals of failing to make the programs work "wherever a 'real' change from hallowed routine was required," adding: "It is my view that these current racial incidents . . . are clearly due to failure of commands to implement those programs with a whole heart."

Zumwalt ended his lecture with a seven-point program reiterating what he had decreed to be the Navy's policy two years before. The new program was not accepted any more easily than the old. Many officers, refusing to give their names, spoke out against their chief for condoning "permissiveness" in the service. Modernization of the dress and grooming codes in the Navy and the sweeping away of other "Mickey Mouse" restrictions had lowered discipline and led the blacks to mutiny, they said.

The Defense Department seemed to be siding with Admiral Zumwalt. In the fall of 1972 an order was issued compelling all generals and admirals in each of the services to attend race relations seminars at the new Defense Race Relations Institute at Patrick Air Force Base, Florida.

One element of grave concern in the military's race problem was the training in violent methods that young blacks were learning in the service which they could put to use when they returned to civilian society. In 1970, Wallace Terry, II, a newsman on the staff of *Time* magazine, made a study of attitudes among black soldiers in Vietnam. Terry reported:

> A frightening number—schooled in the violent art of guerrilla warfare—say they would join riots and take up arms if necessary to get the rights and opportunities they have been deprived of at home.[17]

For every Smothers, Norman or Bowdan directing his energies toward working within the system to achieve equal opportunity and avoiding the kind of reaction that Terry had forecast, there were dozens of young blacks who tried and were beaten down by the system for their attempts. Some were simply given bad efficiency reports. Others were punished, even when legal charges could not be justified. Specialist Four Alfred A. Cason, a twenty-year-old black volunteer from Trenton, New Jersey, is an example. Cason enlisted for six years in January 1970 to avoid the draft, learn a trade, and as he put it later, "to perform my duties as an American citizen."

He was trained as a communications specialist, awarded a top-secret clearance and assigned to an Army Security Agency base in rural

Korea. When no one else would take the job, Cason was named his base's equal opportunity counselor in April 1971. In the following months the base became a center of racial conflict. One night in July 1971, Cason was in the camptown adjoining the base, trying to quell a disturbance that erupted into a night of fighting between black soldiers, whites and Koreans. The next day he was arrested and confined on charges that he was one of the leaders of the riot. He was charged with conspiracy, destruction of private property and assault and placed in pretrial confinement for ninety-two days. Then all charges were dropped, but he was nonetheless stripped of his security clearance and transferred out of Korea. While he was in jail, his Korean fiancée bore him a son. He was refused permission for leave to see the mother and child.

From his new station on Okinawa, Cason was having difficulty appealing the removal of his security clearance. As a result he could not do the work for which he was trained.

"So many people are getting screwed over and they don't know where to turn," Cason said. "We can only turn to our friends—the civilian lawyers and the newspapers—to get help. Society knows this army is all wrong. The leaders of the Army are afraid society will find out they don't know anything. That's why they're afraid of any kind of program that would bring real communication between the ranks. It would cut into their authority."

When Cason spoke those words, he was working with representatives of the Congress on Racial Equality (CORE) to try to win back his clearance and his assignment in Korea so that he could be near his fiancée and son. Although he was working outside the Army system, he was at least still in the service. Others were summarily discharged for their activism, receiving a full measure of harassment first. Yusef R. Sudah, née Charles E. Erby, of Washington, D.C., was one of these men.

Erby enlisted in the Air Force in 1966 at the age of twenty-one. He graduated with honors from a propeller repairman's school and was named "Airman of the Month." His commanding officers liked his enthusiasm and promoted him rapidly to airman first class. During those years, Erby became a black activist, which the Air Force found offensive.

At one point, a superior took a book Sudah had been reading on black history and threw it into a garbage can. His movements became so suspect that a noncommissioned officer followed him constantly to make sure no one talked to him at Langley Air Force Base in Hampton, Virginia, where he was stationed. He was pressured into cutting his Afro

164

haircut and intentionally assigned to punishment details. His superiors changed their estimations on written reports, saying he had a "socio-pathic personality" and was a "self-appointed legal protector of the Negro race." Finally he was given an undesirable discharge.

The American Civil Liberties Union petitioned the Air Force to revoke the discharge, and in 1972, the Air Force's Board of Correction of Military Records found for Sudah, ordering that he be given an honorable discharge. The board cited the "utter frustration and powerlessness" of black airmen and said the Air Force had illegally dismissed Sudah on trumped-up charges of shirking his duty after harassing him because of his hair style and interest in African history. The board accused the Air Force of brushing aside its own regulations and urged an "increased understanding of the pent-up feelings of utter frustration and powerlessness among . . . black airmen (who) attempt to assert and maintain (their identity) in the armed forces."[18]

Promotion, career opportunities and maintenance of identity among blacks were only part of the problem within the services. Others, as the Air Training Command study indicated, included inequitable standards of military justice, off-base discrimination in housing and recreational facilities, inadequate attention to the cultural differences of minority groups and the failure to accord minority-group members the same standards of human dignity shown to whites.

The military began to deal with these problems seriously in the early 1970s. In each of the services, orders went down the chain of command specifying that human relations or equal opportunity councils be established on all bases. Courses were given on race relations in basic training and all service schools. A special race relations institute was set up at Patrick Air Force Base, Florida, once the center for the nation's space program. Blacks were given access they never had before to the offices of commanding officers. PXs throughout the world began stocking a long list of cosmetics, clothing, tapes and records, and books aimed at black audiences. On bases preference was shown to blacks in promotion. At enlisted men's clubs, "soul nights," during which soul food and music were featured, became regular occurrences.

In Korea, Major General Robert W. Malloy led a Martin Luther King Day parade on his base. At Fort Meade, Maryland, the commanding general of the First Army met a deputation of black enlisted men on his front lawn to discuss problems. Hot lines were established on dozens of bases where enlisted men could dial a number and leave a recorded message for the base commander.

The steps were good beginnings even though they were taken years too late in reaction to a crisis rather than in perception of a problem that could have been avoided. Many steps were not taken, and this left bitterness to fester that could erupt in the future.

For example, authorities on Okinawa did nothing to try to do away with the "Bush" area of Koza. The Bush was a four-square-block area of the city to which after World War II all blacks had been segregated for their after-hours entertainment. Over the years nothing was done to give blacks equal opportunity in the white areas of the city. By 1970, the Bush had developed into such a strong domain of black militancy that whites could not safely walk its streets.

"It would take armed force to do away with the bush," Captain Don Donaldson, equal opportunity officer for Kadena Air Force Base, said, "and there would be a lot of bloodshed." Efforts to desegregate other bars, hotels (actually houses of prostitution) and restaurants in the white areas in the hope of luring blacks out of the Bush were denounced as tokenism. For the time being, at least, the blacks enjoyed the polarity, compounding the problem for the military leaders.

That polarity led to a new problem in the early 1970s—one of white backlash arising out of discontent among young whites over what they saw as excessive privileges for blacks. At Camp Hansen, one of the Marine bases on Okinawa, Private First Class Jeffrey Smith, twenty, of Salt Lake City, Utah, talked of his discontent.

"The blacks all walk around giving the black power sign, holding up the lines in the mess hall with their dapping and wearing black power jackets. I requested mast [a meeting] with my battalion commander to complain about the jackets. He said there was nothing he could do. So I went to my regimental commander and he said he could do nothing. Now I have requested mast with my division commander and I suspect that he won't do anything either. I don't think the blacks should be able to wear those jackets. I find it offensive. We're not supposed to be black marines and white marines. We're supposed to be all green marines.

"After I speak to the division commander, I'm going to write a letter to my congressman, but I suspect he won't be able to do anything either.

"And then, you know what I'm going to do? It's stupid, I know, but I'm going to put on a jacket that says 'white power' on it and I'm going to walk down the street and it will start a lot of trouble. Then maybe something will be done."

With little awareness of the fact, Jeffrey Smith, who was only two years old when the Supreme Court handed down its 1954 decision declaring school segregtaion unconstitutional, had set forth a scenario for white protest from peaceful petition to violence-inducing action that mirrored exactly the history of the black movement in the United States in the past generation. The white backlash in the services could easily lead to more violence unless even-handed leadership asserted itself.

And this leadership would have to address itself to problems among enlisted men that were common to both white and black.

9

HAIR AND HARASSMENT IN THE GARRISON-GHETTOS

It must have been an important subject. It was argued in the federal courts and in courts-martial. Officers and enlisted men were banished from one base because of it. Generals exchanged correspondence about it. Enlisted men returning from Vietnam were harangued by top sergeants over it. All the services wrote and rewrote regulations in an attempt to define its limits. Photographers labored to portray the rights and wrongs of it in full color. It was a preoccupation in countless conversations among professional military men.

The subject was the length of a man's hair.

The great hair hassle—over such matters as the shape of Afros, the length of sideburns, the taper of the fall on the back of the head, the amount of neck that should be seen, the droop of the forelock, the shagginess of a mustache and, in the Navy alone, the style of a beard— was a source of utter fascination to anyone interested in whether, or how, the military machine was going to recover from defeat in the early 1970s.

It was an important point of confrontation between the traditionalists in the services and those with a more progressive bent. It symbolized the premium the military put on appearance as opposed to substance. And finally, it was a test of whether or not the chain of command could function properly in executing any but the simplest orders.

In May 1971, every unit in the United States Army received a full-color, 27-by-17-inch, black-bordered poster titled "Army Haircut Policy" with the instruction that "this poster will be displayed on all unit bulletin boards, in offices and in barber shops." The poster had a block of text that read as follows:

ARMY REGULATION 600-20, SECTION VI, PARAGRAPH 5–39.

5–39. *Appearance*

A. The Army is a uniformed service. Therefore a neat and well-groomed appearance by soldiers is fundamental to the Army, and contributes to building the pride and esprit essential to an effective military force. A vital ingredient of the Army's strength and military effectiveness is the pride and self-discipline which American soldiers bring to their service. It is the responsibility of commanders to insure that military personnel under their command present a neat and soldierly appearance, and it is the duty of each soldier to take pride in his appearance at all times.

B. There are many hair styles which are acceptable in the Army. So long as a soldier's hair is kept in a neat manner, the acceptability of the style will be judged solely by the criteria described below.

C. Haircuts, without reference to style, will conform to the following standards:

(1) The hair on top of the head will be neatly groomed. The length and/or bulk of the hair will not be excessive or present a ragged, unkempt or extreme appearance. Hair will present a tapered appearance and, when combed, it will not fall over the ears or eyebrows or touch the collar except for the closely cut hair at the back of the neck. The so-called "block-cut" fullness in the back is permitted in moderate degree. In all cases, the bulk or length of hair will not interfere with the normal wear of all standard military headgear.

(2) If the individual desires to wear sideburns, they will be neatly trimmed. The base will be a clean shaven horizontal line. Sideburns will not extend downward beyond the lowest part of the exterior ear opening.

(3) The face will be clean shaven except that mustaches

169

are permitted. If a mustache is worn, it will be kept neatly trimmed and tidy. No portion extending beyond the corners of the mouth will fall below a line parallel with the bottom of the lower lip. Goatees and beards are not authorized.

(4) The wear of a wig or hair piece by male personnel, while in uniform or on duty is prohibited except to cover natural baldness or physical disfiguration caused by accident or medical procedure. When worn it will conform to the standard haircut criteria as stated.

(5) The photographs at the left illustrate various hair-styles, mustaches and sideburns which are acceptable according to these criteria. No style longer than the ones illustrated is permitted.

To the left of the text block were color photographs of six en-listed men, each in front, side and rear views illustrating a permissible hairstyle. Three of the men were black, three white. Three sported mustaches, three were clean shaven.

The poster was intended to settle in military fashion the problem of hair in the Army. Until its publication, confusion reigned. In some units, men were allowed to grow long hair. Transferring to others, they were ordered to get short haircuts. Some styles left a cap or hat precariously balanced atop a bushy head. On some bases, muttonchop sideburns were sprouting. The Army was coming to look like the United States Navy, where Admiral Elmo R. Zumwalt's Z-Gram against "Mickey Mouse" regulations had wrought a return to the early nineteenth century as far as grooming standards were concerned. Not only appearance was at stake. Hair was becoming an emotionally charged issue between young and old, and it was threatening a breakdown in the disciplinary system. Noncommissioned officers, weary of challenges from their young subordinates and not always backed up by their superiors, stopped enforcing grooming standards on many bases. When officers began demanding that enlisted men get haircuts, their orders were openly defied.

The poster set forth guidelines regarded by enlisted men and their superiors as liberal. Throughout the Army, barbers began cutting hair in conformity with the pictures. The shaved-sideburn look disappeared. Sideburns grew to the lowest part of the exterior ear opening. Hair fell over the forehead. Subdued Afros appeared. And then, in the summer of 1971, General William C. Westmoreland, the Army Chief of Staff, made visits to some bases in which he saw countless examples of violations of the regulation. The general, uneasy with the new regulation from the beginning, had approved it only as a concession to the men under him who were trying to build the new volunteer Army concept. He returned to Washington from these visits complaining about what he had seen, angered that the regulation was not being enforced.

As a result, Major General Warren K. Bennett, secretary of the General Staff of the Army, wrote a new memo on the matter which was distributed throughout the Army. Bennett's memo was issued on a Friday afternoon without any discussion with advocates of the liberalization. Men like Lieutenant General George Forsythe, who was then in charge of the Volunteer Army Program, returned to work Monday morning to discover a *fait accompli* that read in part:

DEPARTMENT OF THE ARMY
Office of the Chief of Staff
Washington, D.C. 20310

MEMORANDUM FOR: HEADS OF ARMY STAFF AGENCIES
SUBJECT: Appearance of Military Personnel

. . .

2. As a result of personal observations, inspections and reports, both in the Washington area and during trips in CONUS [Continental United States] and overseas, the Chief of Staff has determined that the limits of the new Army haircut policy prescribed in Army Regulation 600-20 are being exceeded by many personnel and that many commanders, leaders and supervisors in the chain of command are not demanding adherence to prescribed standards.

3. The resulting improper appearance of Army personnel is totally unacceptable, as well as damaging to the Army image. More disturbing, however, is the apparent ineffectiveness of the chain of command to enforce clearly stated policy.

. . .

5. AR 600-20 provides a clearly defined haircut policy, in words and pictures, that can be enforced. The exercise of judgment is required. Some criteria are quite clear (e.g., sideburns no lower than lowest part of exterior ear opening), yet are often violated; there is no excuse for non-compliance with

these precise standards. Of equal, even overriding, importance are the requirements that soldiers present a "neat and well-groomed appearance"; that " the length and/or bulk of the hair will not be excessive or present a ragged, unkempt or extreme appearance"; and that "the bulk or length of hair will not interfere with the normal wear of all standard military headgear." Finally, the criteria in AR 600-20 represent maximums—"no longer style than the ones illustrated is permitted." Thus, the posters and illustrations represent the outer limits of neatness and grooming required the day *before* a haircut—not the day after.

· · ·

WARREN K. BENNETT
Major General, GS
Secretary of the General Staff

Thus did Major General Bennett succeed in making the posters depict, instead of legally sanctioned styles, haircuts that were within a day of becoming illegal. To stay within the bounds of both the poster and the Bennett memorandum, all Army men would have required a haircut every day. Even then they would have been subject to harassment by their superiors ("You need a haircut, soldier"). Confusion returned. And now, still another general stepped into the act. General Ralph E. Haines, Jr., commanded the United States Continental Army Command at the time; he had charge of all the training and all the housekeeping functions on all the Army bases in the United States. Haines, like Westmoreland and Bennett, found long hair offensive and did not like the concessions implicit in the poster. So he put out this order to every Army installation in the nation on October 12, 1971:

UNCLASSIFIED

ATPER-PSD

SUBJ: REMOVAL OF HAIRCUT PICTURES (DA POSTER 600-20)

1. AT THE RECENT ARMY TRAINING CENTER COMMANDERS' CONFERENCE IT WAS DETERMINED THAT INSTALLATION BARBERS CONSIDER THAT THE ILLUSTRATIONS OF DA POSTER 600-20 DEPICT PROPER HAIRCUT STANDARDS FOR A PATRON UPON HIS DEPARTURE FROM THE BARBER'S CHAIR. THIS INTERPRETATION IS CONTRARY TO THE ARMY CHIEF OF STAFF'S GUIDANCE ON WHAT CONSTITUTES ACCEPTABLE HAIRCUT AND APPEARANCE STANDARDS.

2. THEREFORE, ALL DA POSTERS 600-20 ARE TO BE REMOVED FROM INSTALLATION BARBER SHOPS TO ELIMINATE THIS SOURCE OF MISINTERPRETATION.

Haines's order overruled that of a superior, General Westmoreland. And when a subordinate, even if he is a four-star general himself, overrules a superior in the Army, an explanation is necessary. So Haines wrote the following to Westmoreland:

HEADQUARTERS
UNITED STATES CONTINENTAL ARMY COMMAND
Office of the Commanding General
Fort Monroe, Virginia 23351

12 Oct 1971

Dear Westy:

While discussing haircut standards with commanders at my recent Army Training Center Commanders' Conference, it was determined that Army and Air Force Exchange Service barbers are interpreting the illustrations of DA Poster 600-20 as depicting haircut standards applicable to the patron upon departure from the barber's chair. Such an interpretation is contrary to your guidance addressing improved haircut and appearance standards.

Accordingly, and notwithstanding DA instructions to display DA Poster 600-20 in all barber shops, I have recently directed that the haircut poster be withdrawn from barber shops on CONARC installations. Additionally, I recommend that action be taken to remove DA Poster 600-20 from all barber shops Army-wide to eliminate this source of misinterpretation.

Sincerely,
RALPH E. HAINES, JR.
General, United States Army
Commanding

General William C. Westmoreland
Chief of Staff
United States Army
Washington, D.C. 20310*

---

* Haines's opposition to long hair stood in sharp contrast to his otherwise literal belief in the Bible. If religious art of all ages is any indication, Jesus Christ, his

Thus did General Westmoreland, the man in charge of directing the activities of some 850,000 men, and at least two of his key aides spend their time in 1971. It might have been considered laughable—indeed, people did try to laugh about it—had it not had such a devastating effect on the troops.

Consider the hair hassle first as a matter of military control over civilians. National guardsmen and reservists, whatever their motivations for joining up (many did it in the Vietnam War period to avoid the draft), are true citizen-soldiers. They are citizens who enlist for a specified time period and then attend periodic drills near their homes, training for duty in an eventual emergency. They are soldiers for just a few hours a week.

Bruce Friedman, a second-year student at the Harvard Law School in Cambridge, Massachusetts, was such a citizen-soldier in 1972. He was a long-haired citizen. He was a part-time soldier. He had no complaints with the authority of the Army to prescribe standards of appearance during the hours when he belonged to the Army. The stipulations of AR 600-20, Section VI, Paragraph 5-39 (4) notwithstanding—as General Haines might say—he purchased a short-haired wig to cover his long locks during drill.

When the Army ordered him to remove the wig, Friedman brought suit in Federal District Court in Boston. Judge W. Arthur Garrity, Jr.,

---

Old Testament forebears and his New Testament followers generally wore their locks long. Haines must have known this. He was a student of the Bible, and in 1970, he said he received the charismatic gift of glossolalia, the speaking in tongues. As Washington *Star* reporter Jerry Oppenheimer heard Haines describe it, the general was in Buffalo, New York, at the time, and "I experienced a bubbling up and a violent eruption of the Holy Spirit . . . The whole room was filled with the Holy Spirit and I was the number-one lightning rod. All of a sudden the Holy Spirit started coming out of my ears and eyes and nose, and I heard this voice coming out in some strange language, and then I realized it was my voice, and I knew I was on a special wave length up there." After that, Haines began crisscrossing the country making evangelistic speeches. Visiting a military base, he would call together leaders in the chapel rather than a secular office. Part of his message was that Washington is "the center of God's power" and that "our nation and our allies need whatever we can do to put God's unerring hand upon the helm of the free world." Haines was telling his audiences he "would rather be a private in the army of Jesus Christ than a general in the United States Army." Shortly after the *Star* published Oppenheimer's story on August 6, 1972, the paper ran an editorial suggesting that some consideration should be given to having the general's wish granted. A few months later, Haines retired.

174

ruled for the Army. It was a specialized community, the judge said, "governed by a separate discipline" which could, in effect, regulate Friedman's appearance even during the vast majority of the time when he was not under military control.

Different judges, however, saw the wig question differently. In New York, Eric Harris, a young reservist, also tried to cover his long hair with a wig, and like Friedman, he was banished from monthly reserve meetings. Harris also brought suit, and Federal District Judge Charles H. Tenney ruled in Harris' favor. As part of its argument in defense against Harris' suit, the Army harked back to the story of Absalom in the Bible, referring to the age-old, but not necessarily correct, interpretation that Absalom's long hair snagged in an oak tree, resulting in his capture and murder by King David's men.

The Army memo to the court said:

> The wearing of long hair, whether covered by a wig or not, has, since the Biblical days of Absalom, been subject to hazards. Additionally, even in weekly reserve meetings there is a likelihood that wigs may fall. While the bald and disfigured [who are permitted to wear wigs under AR 600-20] may suffer embarrassment in this eventuality, they unlike plaintiff will not instantly present an untidy or unkempt appearance.

Tenney handled that argument neatly. After quoting it, he said in a footnote to his opinion:

> While the Court appreciates the Government's metaphorical use of the Biblical story of Absalom, 2 Samuel, 18:9–15, metaphors are no substitute for facts and can often cut both ways. Cf. Samson and Delilah, Judges, 16:17–19.

The Friedman and Harris cases were not isolated incidents. At Homestead Air Force Base, Florida, south of Miami, Colonel Edwin Turner ordered "six or eight" reservists off the base because of the length of their hair. They were civilians working at the base only one weekend a month to fulfill their commitment. Turner himself, at fifty-five, had given up a crew cut for longer hair and sideburns to within a half inch of his earlobe. He considered himself "quite liberal in the matter of mustaches and hairstyles." In fact, he said that when he had visited his son once at a Marine Corps base, the son refused to accompany him around the post until he got a haircut. But the hairstyles of those six or eight men were the last straws in a long series of problems with the reservists.[1]

Then there was the matter of appearance versus substance. Specialist Five Harry S. DuVal was a twenty-four-year-old electronics warfare analyst at the supersecret National Security Agency (NSA) at Fort Meade, Maryland. NSA is a little-known agency that operates a network of spy satellites, aircraft and monitoring posts throughout the world, eavesdropping on the communications of friend and foe. DuVal had a top-secret research job in the agency, which, according to his colleagues and supervisors, he performed in an "excellent" and "original" manner. They found him "honorable" and "trustworthy."

But Captain Robert E. Caddell, DuVal's military superior, saw things differently. He thought DuVal's hair was too long and ordered him to get a haircut in July 1971. DuVal refused, asking for a lawyer, saying his hair was cut within the AR 600-20 regulations. But in the end, he got the haircut. Caddell wanted to go through with the court-martial anyhow. Caddell's commander dismissed the charges and simply gave DuVal a reprimand.

In November, Caddell struck again. He summoned DuVal one day and handed him a written order: "I, the commanding officer of Co. B, U.S. Army Security Agency Support Group, am giving you a lawful order to have your hair cut and your mustache trimmed to comply with the standards required by Army Regulation 600-20, Section 6, paragraphs 5–39."

DuVal retreated to the home of his girl friend, Margaret Campbell, for a trim. He said it was too late that day to get to a barber shop. The next morning, Colonel Herman Conrad conducted the inspection and determined that the regulation standards still had not been met. He ordered a court-martial.

In the meantime, DuVal's skills and knowledge were ignored, and he was detailed to a special platoon to mop and wax floors and scrape paint at Fort Meade.

A court-martial convened to hear "the United States vs. Harry S. DuVal" on December 1. Caddell told the court DuVal's hair was "ragged . . . excessive in length . . . extremely oily, greasy . . . not tapered . . . a hideous appearance."

DuVal's defense was that his girl friend had tried hard to shave his neck and scissor the locks to meet the standards.

The prosecutor said that if DuVal had really "been serious he would have gone to a barber or have his girl friend do more chopping."

The prosecution asked that DuVal be jailed for his offense.

After five hours of trial, the court found DuVal guilty, fined him fifty dollars and reduced him from specialist five (the equivalent of buck sergeant) to private.

A month later, his four-year enlistment up, DuVal left the Army.[2]

In San Antonio, Texas, Air Force Sergeant Gary T. Ace, twenty-one, of Bowling Green, Ohio, tried the wig cover-up for his long hair. Ordered to remove the wig, he refused, was court-martialed, fined four hundred dollars and busted for refusing an order in June 1972.[3]

At the Pentagon, Private First Class Robert W. Ledder, twenty-two, of Rocky Hill, Connecticut, graduate of Kansas State Teachers College where he earned a degree in data processing, was transferred from his computer analyst's job to fatigue work at Fort Myer, Virginia, because he refused to get a haircut. His hair conformed to AR 600-20, but his superiors wanted it cut even shorter.

"It took me three months to learn this job and I don't know what will happen to the system while my replacement learns the job," Ledder said. "I'm afraid the colonel and the general are more interested in how people look, rather than their efficiency."[4]

While all this was going on, the Army's modish advertising campaign for recruits featured a double-page magazine advertisement that showed a soldier in a barber's chair getting his locks shorn in conformity with the AR 600-20 poster on the wall.

"You'll find that today's Army is pretty relaxed about how you cut and style your hair," the ad read. "You'll discover we care more about your head than we do about your hair."

Referring to the Bennett-Haines interpretations, Specialist Four Winfred Anderson and Specialist Five Denny Wheelis at Fort Leonard Wood, Missouri, wrote to the *Army Times:*

"Either the man pictured in the . . . advertisement is supposed to be receiving daily haircuts, or the Army is misleading the public by presenting two versions of the haircut policy. Internally there is a crackdown on long-hairs. To the outside world, on the other hand, 'the Army is pretty relaxed . . .'

"We think someone should get their own head a little straighter."[5]

Hair was even the subject of interservice bargaining. Marine Commandant Leonard F. Chapman and Admiral Elmo R. Zumwalt, Chief of Naval Operations, struck a deal under which Navy hospital corpsmen serving with Marine units had to conform to the Marine short-haired, white-sidewall policy while marines working in Navy jobs could grow the beards and sideburns allowed under the Z-Gram regulations.[6]

Finally, there was the scene at the 90th Replacement Battalion at the Army's sprawling Long Binh base just north of Saigon in Vietnam. It was through the 90th that many of those leaving Vietnam after their one-year tours passed on the way back to the World and to discharge after fulfilling their obligations to the nation. Those who had served with combat units were used to certain relaxations in standards of appearance.

But first there were procedures to be followed at the 90th. The men arrived, checked all their personal belongings in a storage room and then assembled on a grandstand over which a wooden canopy had been built. Facing the grandstand was a lectern on which a copy of AR 600-20 had been posted. A sergeant mounted the lectern and stood relaxed, looking at the men, fiddling, smoking a cigarette, checking his watch. Precisely at 3 P.M., the time announced for the next briefing, he began:

"Gentlemen, may I have your attention please. Please listen carefully to what I have to say. It will save you valuable time . . ."

The sergeant then delivered his lecture on the "DEROS" (date of expected return from overseas) procedure. He told the men which documents they must have ready, how much cash they were allowed to carry, what uniforms to wear, how they got their flight numbers. Later, he spent several minutes on drugs, explaining the procedure in the "Pee House of the August Moon," a latrine a few steps down the hill through which, since June 1971, every returning soldier had to pass to give a urine sample showing his system was free of narcotics.

Finally, he came to the subject of hair, spending as much time on it as he did on drugs. "Gentlemen, listen carefully. If you don't, you may lose an hour in the procedure and that could mean you miss a flight . . ."

The sergeant talked forcefully on, reviewing the regulations about sideburns, taper, forelocks, length, mustaches, and then he ordered the men to line up behind the grandstand in two files. Two subordinate sergeants passed down the files, ordering some men out of rank to the barber shop, others to trim their mustaches a millimeter and others to brush their hair back.

Most of these men would be out of the service in a few days. Why did they need one last hassle over hair? Why leave them with one last bitter taste in their mouths about the Army?

An officer studied his toes, smiled, hesitated and then said: "I don't understand it either. But we get a lot of generals coming up here to watch the procedure. We get about one a week. And they see a man with long hair. They look at him and they think 'This man's going home. He's a disgrace to the uniform.' And so they put a lot of pressure on us."

Hair was not a new issue with the services in the 1970s. It has been an issue ever since the founding of the Republic. During Thomas Jefferson's Presidency, the Army was commanded by Brigadier General James Wilkinson, who comes down through history as a double-dealer and self-aggrandizer of heroic proportions. He was, for example, receiving a pension from the Spanish government, to which he had sworn an oath of alligiance, while he commanded the American Army. Adopting styles newly introduced in France after the revolution there, Wilkinson decreed short haircuts and the removal of queues by American troops. A Colonel Thomas Butler defied the order and twice stood court-martial. Thirteen days before the order of the second court to remove the queue was to become effective, Butler died, still defiantly wearing the long hair. He was reportedly buried with the queue protruding from his coffin. Professor Russell F. Weigley, a historian of the Army, uses the early hair battle to illustrate the low intellectual tone of the officer corps at the time, commenting:

> Such an officer corps devoted itself little to improving the soldierliness of the men . . .[7]

It is not unfair to make the same observation today. While the services preoccupied themselves with the hair matter, other problems deepened. For example, living conditions. From Groton, Connecticut to Gelnhausen, Germany, the enlisted men of all the services were, much too often, living in slums.

It is not an exaggeration to think of enlisted men's barracks as ghettos—raucous, run-down, odoriferous, anarchic and at times violent compounds where emotions stretch at times to the breaking point. Tens of thousands of young Americans in late adolescence and early manhood—at the most impressionable of ages—live unsupervised in those ghettos. At quitting time, the sergeants, lieutenants and captains who are the enlisted men's contact with authority disappear from the bases.

In most areas of the world, they retire to a normal homelife with wife and family that, for them, makes service life appear but little different from the life of any worker in a large organization. They are commuters living in the suburban housing developments on the bases. Throughout the world, the little ranch-type bungalows in which they live could be features of any American suburb—bikes on the sidewalks, tiny-tot swimming pools on the lawns, here a basketball backboard, there an outdoor barbecue, an auto in the carport, a television antenna atop the roof. They carry attaché cases to and from work, even in the combat arms. They lunch in clubs resembling small-town restaurants. By all military doctrine they are responsible for the physical and mental well-being of their men. They have abdicated that responsibility or have exercised it only superficially, such as when they demand a haircut, a shoeshine, a change into better-pressed fatigues, or a salute.

In 1971, a team investigating the race problem in the Air Force's Air Training Command hit the crux of the problem of the commuting commanders when it wrote:

> . . . all up and down the chain of command there is a tragic indifference to human needs. Problems of airmen aren't being listened to, or if they are, they are misunderstood.[8]

The vast majority of the enlisted men in the armed services over the past quarter century have lived in the ghettos, adjusted and survived, at least to the extent of not drawing the wrath of their superiors. But thousands have not made the adjustment. Some have deserted, some turned to drugs, others to drink, theft or vandalism. Some developed a bitter but sublimated disrespect for authority. Overseas, the problems of living in ghettos were compounded by the strangeness of the surroundings.

Colonel William S. Tilton, head of the facilities directorate of the Army's Engineer Command in Frankfurt, Germany, expressed his concern over the psychological effects of living conditions this way: "Take your very young soldier; what can he do? He probably doesn't speak the language and when he goes to the PX, he sees a family and it makes him homesick. Then he goes back to the barracks and lies there, surrounded by crumbling walls and faulty plumbing. If he gets lonely and desperate enough, he may go to the Gasthaus, or, here in Frankfurt, to the Kaiserstrasse [the red-light district]. He may get sucked into narcotics. For his own safety, he doesn't go outside the perimeter of the base, and he stays in the barracks. At least that is what we would hope. I can't hit enough the point that it is important to make the barracks livable."

Lieutenant Colonel Ronald C. Crowley, executive officer of the 3d Armored Division's support command in Germany, said, "If they live in slums, they act that way. If their surroundings are good, they respond."

The two officers were interviewed by reporters for *Stars and Stripes,* the official military newspaper overseas, for a twenty-eight page, hard-hitting series on housing that appeared in January 1972. The series paralleled a report that had appeared in the Washington *Post* the previous September. Both reports went into great detail about how American men were living in squalor in Germany. Most of the barracks dated from the pre-World War I era and were former Wehrmacht or German railway worker caserns. American forces took them over during the occupation years after World War II and have lived in them ever since. Little money was spent in upkeep partly for the reason that no one knew how long the occupation and then the stationing of American forces under the North Atlantic Treaty Organization agreements would last.*

So pipes filled up with mineral deposits and jammed or burst. (As one captain in charge of a unit in Frankfurt said: "I've got stalactites this long in the basement," stretching his thumb and forefinger apart as far as they would go. "The water from C Company flows down on B; the water from B flows down on A.") Nothing was done to fix the plumbing.

Paint began peeling. Nothing was done. Plaster fell out, and still nothing was done. Flooring came up. No repairs. Rats began skittering

---

* When the West German Army was reconstituted in 1956 as the "Bundeswehr," that force did not move into the old Wehrmacht caserns. Instead, they built new barracks, with partitioned rooms, handsome dayrooms, gymnasiums on the bases, nice landscaping and, at almost every casern, a pond built under the pretext that it was needed as a reservoir for fire fighting. Actually those ponds were swimming pools. The German officers did not suffer frustration in keeping their men busy and motivated. When there was nothing else to do, the Bundeswehr troops would change into specially issued athletic clothes (not part of an American uniform) and undertake physical conditioning. Other times, each man would take out his officially issued songbook and they would sing. In favorable weather, they swam in their reservoirs. Until recently Bundeswehr members could wear their hair at whatever length they wanted (secured and neatened by nets when they were in uniform) and were allowed not only liquor but attractive bars and lounges in their barracks. They were regarded as "citizens in uniform" with almost all the rights of citizens. Most professional American officers, watching the Bundeswehr experiment, felt the German fighters would acquit themselves at least as well, if not better, than the Americans in combat. For one thing, the Germans were in far better physical condition.

out of holes in the walls. And still nothing. Heating systems broke down. No repairs.

On top of this, there was absolutely no privacy in the Army barracks. Dozens of men lived in huge open bays on double- and triple-decked cots with nothing but a wall locker and foot lockers. They were ordered to keep their barracks clean. No brooms, mops or soaps were provided. ("They can get them, if they really want them, in the commissary," one battalion commander, who lived off base, told me. "The materials don't cost all that much.")

Lack of privacy makes itself felt in annoying little ways. A GI returning late from a carouse, looking for his bunk, flicks the light switch at the doorway to his bay. On go all the lights, waking up many of the more sober-minded men in his bay. And it also makes itself felt in big ways. The military has taken the easy way out in trying to make life palatable. For example, the PXs around the world offer a dazzling variety of goods at attractive prices. High-priced, high-quality, high fidelity stereo equipment is most attractive. Many GIs purchase components at half the price they would pay at home for inferior equipment. Each plays his stereo in the barracks. At night, any given bay is jarred by the cacophony of a dozen stereos, all turned to the ultimate volume, filling the room with rock and soul, Lawrence Welk and Rolling Stones, cantata and country music.

You could understand why a man might lie back on his bunk, tamp a chunk of hashish into a pipe bowl, light up and take a mild trip. Many do. And the Army command, in Germany, looked the other way. A battalion commander who had no trouble imposing such rigid control on his men that they would keep toilet articles lined up just so in a shaving kit, said with a straight face that to keep hashish out of the barracks, he would have to impose a police state, as if in many of its aspects, the Army was not already, and with justification, a police state for enlisted men.

Not only was hashish smoked openly but in October 1971, General Michael S. Davison, commander of Army forces in Europe, issued an order making hard liquor, which had previously been banned, permissible in the barracks. He issued the order almost clandestinely. Although it affected a goodly portion of 180,000 troops, it was never made public. It was allowed to trickle down slowly, by word of mouth.

"I came to the conclusion when I was in Vietnam that if you were to say, O.K., a guy eighteen years old is old enough to come to Vietnam and fight and die, he should be able to go down to the Class C store and buy a bottle of booze. His billet is his home; it's the only home he's got right now, and he ought to be able to take that bottle of booze back to his room and drink it in his room."

If the barracks were really homes—with all the comforts and convenience that word connotes—then hard liquor for a social drink would be one thing. But the barracks had the same relationship to a home as did a skid-row flophouse. And one could draw the conclusion that the Army command had thrown up its hands over the magnitude of the housing problem and said, in effect, to its men, "Sorry, there's little we can do for you, so go ahead and take your drugs and drink and try to forget the misery."

The allegation, of course, was vigorously denied. But when *Stars and Stripes* received a copy of the regulation change on hard liquor and sought more information from General Davison's headquarters in Heidelberg for a story, it was told: Do not publish anything. Why? "We don't want the American people to think the Army is debauching the morals of their children."

In September 1971, Lieutenant Colonel William Henry Harrison, a thirty-eight-year-old Kentuckian commanding the 2d Battalion, 48th Infantry of the 3d Armored Division, showed up one day in a barracks in Gelnhausen, Germany, which housed some men from his unit. He was wearing a pair of white cotton gloves. He ran his hands over some surfaces and found—dust. Captain Kenneth H. Williams, the company commander for the unit, was incensed, and shortly after Harrison left, he put out Policy Letter 31 to his troops which said in part:

EACH MORNING THE FOLLOWING WILL BE ACCOMPLISHED:
1. Barracks will be ready from 0700–1500 for inspection.
2. Bunks will be made properly.
   a. Pillow cases on each pillow
   b. 2 sheets per bunk
   c. Dust cover tight
3. Shoes will be arrainged [sic] in the following order:
LEFT Boots/Low Quarters/Civ. Shoes/Shower Shoes RIGHT
   a. Shoes do not have to be displayed unless desired
   b. BOOTS will be BUFFED at ALL TIMES.

. . .

6. All garbage cans will be emptied prior to 0700 each morning and will remain so until 0900 hours.
7. Only clean ash trays will be displayed during the time of inspection.

＊　＊　＊

11. All window ledges will be cleaned daily.
12. Latrines will be spotless.
  The purpose of this letter is to outline each man's duty. Being on guard or detail is no excuse for living like a pig.
  ALL PIGS WILL BE PUNISHED   "Kill THE PIGS"
                                        KENNETH H. WILLIAMS
                                        CAPT., INFANTRY
                                        COMMANDING

  The "policy letter" was more than Randall E. Decker, then private first class, of Anaheim, California, could stomach, and so he wrote to his congressman, Representative Richard T. Hanna, a California Democrat, as follows:

14 Sept. '71

Dear Sir:
  Two days ago our company was lucky enough to receive a surprise visit by one Lt. colonel who goes by the name of Harrison. This kind gentleman was appalled, yes, even astonished by the living conditions in which we lowly enlisted men (but I could have sworn I was drafted) exist. My, my such a profound discovery! In our barracks alone live twenty-four men in a space approximately thirty feet by forty feet. There is one electrical outlet. There are seventy-two people using one latrine. Was the good Lt. colonel disgusted at these conditions? Why, don't be silly! Of course not. Not when there was actually dust under some bunks and footlockers, or even (heaven forbid) dust on top of our wall lockers . . . those of us who are lucky enough to have them. But this was not all, worse yet, there was trash actually found in the trash can. And some bunks were even made up sloppily at that point.
  Well, needless to say, our company commander . . . was very, very, very upset.

184

For the next day, at morning formation, we, those of us who live in the barracks as well as those of us who don't, were informed of the fact that we are "pigs" and that the conditions in which we live cannot be tolerated since we had embarrassed our beloved leader. Our beloved twenty-three (or so?) year-old West Point graduate leader. . . .

We swept, we mopped, we cleaned, we emptied the trash can and placed it upside down, the position that all trash cans should be found. But, what of the trash yet to be thrown out? It can't go in the trash can? "Where else, but out the back window" say the sergeants. So out the third story window it goes.

The inspection. What did we find out? The name tags on one man's footlocker are much neater than the name tags on another man's footlocker. Oh yes, our writing table, which has no chairs, needs some little lamps on it. First sergeant made a note of that. (I know not if he made a note of the fact that the nearest outlet was fifty feet away, but I suppose that matters not, we'll never see the lamps.)

Without hesitation, we all dashed off to the dayroom for our class. An Army class is not like the classes I used to attend in school where I would learn facts, about people, about life . . .

Anyhow, at our class we learned (I suppose I must use that word) that we're all sloppy dogs, in dire need of haircuts. If we don't have our hair cut to satisfy His (beloved captain) specifications Article 15s will be given ("I must make examples of some of you or you will all think that I was only joking.") Imposing maximum penalty: we "will not be able to go out to get drunk" (like all Army men?) "for two weeks, besides being fined a minimum of $32." (for those who only make $134.40 per month.)

That's nice.

Which brings us to the question. With only 493 days before I ETS (get out, the dream of all GIs) I'll just sit back and contemplate Taoism (remember Laotze), and smile.

Yours (Literally)
PFC Randall E. Decker
APO New York

Hanna took Decker's bit of sarcasm and irony and sent it off to the Army for comment. Down the chain of command it went until it ended up on the desk of Major General William R. Kraft, 3d Division commander in Frankfurt. Kraft answered, noting "regretably" the truth of Decker's statements about living conditions. But it was only temporary, he said, because renovations were underway. (He neglected to say that the conditions had been temporary since 1945 and had not been worried about in higher circles until enlisted men like Decker began complaining with more or less violence.) He denied there was any harassment involved in the frequent inspections (which were conducted at odd hours) and ended saying: "The failure of a soldier to comply with simple appearance directives is indicative of a lack of self-discipline which could be crucial in combat."

Hanna sent a copy of Kraft's letter to Decker with a form-written "Memorandum" on which had been typed the salutation "Pfc. Decker." The memo read, as it apparently did for any inquiry from a voter to his office: "The attached refers to a subject in which you are interested, and is, therefore, referred for your information. Yours very truly, Richard T. Hanna, M.C."

In January 1972, I visited Gelnhausen and met with the men of Company B. By now they were living in a renovated barracks on which tens of thousands of dollars had been spent. From skid row they had advanced to, say, the living conditions of a boy-scout camp. There were now doors on the commodes in the latrines (not all barracks offer this feature), and some of the commodes actually worked. Wall lockers had been arranged to give every four men a modicum of privacy. But the stereos still blasted forth in the bays. The lighting system had not been changed. There was a desk for each four men—and a chair—but no lamp. And now, with the freshly painted walls, the men were not allowed to put up any posters. The *Playboy* centerfolds had to be mounted inside one's wall-locker door. Even with the renovation, the barracks could not, under any stretch of the imagination, be called home.

"General Kraft's reply to Congressman Hanna was a whitewash," Decker, now specialist four, said. "But what else could be expected? He probably believes everything he said. What he said came straight out of the Army regulations. What bothers me is that Hanna seemed to be satisfied with Kraft's explanations and expected me to be as well.

"When I wrote Congressman Hanna, I was in a state of depression, anger, frustration, et cetera, and the letter was meant to be sarcastic and humorous. I guess that was my means of keeping control. Apparently Hanna, Kraft and others on down the line were unable to understand this and took my letter to be a complaint about the various situations mentioned. This wasn't the case. Most important, my hidden complaint was with this whole authority situation—so many incompetent, child-minded people in the higher ranks. I don't like being told how to live, particularly by those I believe to be unqualified. I make a perfectly good civilian. And I know I'm not alone."

Decker also told how he made certain that Lieutenant Colonel Harrison saw a copy of Policy Letter 31. The colonel chewed out the captain (who was subsequently relieved of command), and a new letter was posted, minus the reference to the pigs.*

"I was disappointed," Decker said. "It was not the 'pigs' portion that annoyed me. On the contrary I found the 'pigs' portion enjoyable. Didn't Captain Williams realize that to us, the pigs are the authorities—himself in particular?"

In late 1971, the United States reached an agreement with the West German government under which the Germans would provide $186 million to repair the decaying American barracks. The agreement had fine print which stipulated that only German contractors and laborers do the job. As a result, in Germany's booming economy, the workers and contractors were not available. Under the best of conditions, it would

---

* Williams' temporary replacement was Lieutenant James A. Grupi, twenty-three, an "Army brat" who had graduated from North Georgia College, a military school. Grupi was well liked. He knew and sympathized with many of his men. "Our men need to be made proud," he told me. "They need to be given a sense of accomplishment. And they need better training. The basic training my company received was just lousy. The soldier today is a lot more intelligent than the ones before; they are a lot quicker to learn. We have to do away with the repetition idea in training that was designed with old-Army techniques. Too much formula instruction turns a guy off. I've been able to change quite a bit here in two weeks." Though professional in his remarks, Grupi did not *look* like a professional soldier. His hair, though short, was shaggy. He was one of those men for whom a military uniform did not do things. In January 1972, it became known that Grupi would be replaced. His men began talking about a petition campaign to keep him. "That's just not going to be, men," I heard Harrison tell some Company B members. "The Army has scads and scads of fine young captains who just must get command time. A year ago we were lucky to have a lieutenant to command a company. But that's not the case any more." Thus did the need for ticket punching take precedence over solving one little bit of the personnel turbulence problem.

take more than four years to complete the work. But conditions were not the best, and estimates ran to six or more years. Enough evidence exists on American military bases to prove that if generals were required to live as enlisted men do, even for only a month or so, it would not take six years to clean up the barracks.

Living conditions in Germany received the most notoriety in the early 1970s, but they were not by any means unusual for the armed services.

At Osan Air Force Base in Korea I spent an afternoon listening to the gripes of a half-dozen airmen and junior NCOs. Unlike many Air Force barracks these had no private or semiprivate rooms. (The Air Force over the years has shown more concern for amenities such as good barracks than the other services.) So crowded were the bays that the men lived with their civilian clothing hanging from the rafters. There were six commodes in the latrine for over seven hundred men. There was no toilet paper. Showers were clogged up. The furnace had broken down four times during the past year. There was one washing machine for their clothes. Nothing unlocked was ever safe from theft.

Airman First Class Ronald A. Harry of Eugene, Oregon, said: "There are two mess halls on the base. One has no knives and forks. The other has no salt and pepper. Supply is a continual problem. You have to steal a roll of toilet paper when you find one and hide it in your locker."

"We have killed mice, bugs and rats in these barracks," said Staff Sergeant Stephen J. Shishler of Mt. Ephrain, New Jersey, "and then, when we called the medics to complain, they only told us we're dirty."

For two hours the conversation ranged over a variety of complaints. Harry and his friends talked of purchasing Underwriter Laboratories-approved extension cords in the base exchange to solve the electrical outlet shortage, only to have their superiors veto use of the wires, or similarly, how they could not put up on their walls *Playboy* posters sold in the exchanges. Finally one of the men, taking a pull on a bottle of beer from the communal bar at the end of the bay, said: "You know, all of our gripes are hardly immortal. We don't gripe about anything but chickenshit."

And indeed, it was the "chickenshit" matters that were helping to render the services ineffective.

. . .

188

No living conditions anywhere were worse than those endured by a relative handful of Navy men in the middle of the Northeastern United States megalopolis. These were the carefully chosen crewmen of the Polaris nuclear submarine fleet, the men who maintain custody over an important part of the nation's nuclear deterrent. Every several years, each of the forty-one submarines must return to the Electric Boat Division of the General Dynamics Corporation for a complete overhaul. The procedure takes eighteen months. In the meantime, the crews must stay with the ships because of the nuclear materials on board. In any emergency, the crews are far better qualified than the factory men to deal with the problems.

The officers all bring their families to Groton, rent houses and live on shore. The enlisted men, however, must live in World War II-vintage troop-carrying barges, rafted together and tied to a bulkhead in the Thames River. There is no place for outdoor recreation. On their barges, they live in windowless, dungeonlike, airless space belowdecks in bunks that stand four tiers high. In a pathetic lounge area, there were two old upholstered pieces—the springs peeking through the leatherette covering—in front of a television set that did not work. No two chairs in the petty officers' mess area were alike. Ordinary seamen ate on picnic tables. There was absolutely no privacy.

Nuclear submarines are not known for the spaciousness and comfort of their quarters, yet Lieutenant Commander W. E. Richman, executive officer of the SSBN *Kamehameha,* said that for the sixty men of his crew living on the barge, life was much worse than it was at sea. At any given time, there are two hundred men living in the Groton barges.

"I really feel we're going to lose some good people because of this," Richman said. "You just shouldn't ask men to live like this twenty-four hours a day."

Commander Larry Nace, the *Kamehameha*'s skipper, said he had received fifty-two complaints about the living conditions. He worried that the situation would lead to drug, race and AWOL problems within his crew.

When Admiral Elmo R. Zumwalt, Jr., the Chief of Naval Operations, visited the nearby New London submarine base for one of his famous "rap sessions" with ordinary seamen, a delegation of submariners from Electric Boat came to make a simple plea to him. All they asked was a bus service to take the men back and forth from the

Groton yard to the New London base, a distance of about four miles, so that they could use the base exchange, the movie theater, bowling alleys and athletic fields.

"We're looking into that," Zumwalt told the men. "The problem is that Congress says we must first ask a private bus company to provide the service. If they refuse, then we can establish one."

The situation at Groton was as old as the nuclear submarine program itself, which dates back to the mid-1950s. An official at the Electric Boat Division said: "If we could get those barges declared substandard, then we could put the men up in a hotel or something, but every time they're inspected, they're declared habitable. The whole problem is money. There's just not enough of it to go around."

And so, in 1971, the Navy was just making a beginning, with the establishment of a bus service: a quick fix for a deep problem. At the same time, it was offering nuclear submariners reenlistment bonuses of up to $15,000, unmindful of the fact that money could not buy those men a better life.

Decaying barracks could be found all along the East Coast. Complaints of servicemen indicated the conditions were prevalent throughout the garrisons in the United States. Broken windows, inoperative heating plants, leaky roofs, lack of silverware and toilet paper, no privacy and, perhaps most important, the danger of theft, were constant complaints. In a military machine where transfers were so frequent, men did not get to know each other well, and thus the constraints against appropriating what belonged to one's neighbor for oneself were almost nonexistent.

In 1971, Congress enacted a pay increase that did much to bring military salaries into line with civilians. Under the new law, for example, the members of the Joint Chiefs of Staff, considering the value of all the services they receive in kind—cars, drivers, quarters, medical care, tax advantages, valet and maid service—receive $43,080 a year. A lowly private under that formula received $4,986.96, or when you take just his basic pay without allowances and without factoring in the cost of services which are free to him, $3,456 a year.

But money is a measure of affluence only when it can be used to improve living standards. Lowly privates living in the kind of conditions described above are impoverished, no matter how much money they earn.

Even with improved salaries there is hard-core poverty in the mili-

190

tary services. In Orange County, California, there were, in 1971, an estimated two hundred married marines receiving food stamps for their families from the County Welfare Department. To make ends meet, hundreds of marines moonlight as gas station attendants, ball park ushers and cleanup men and, in one case, as a radio station disk jockey. In 1970, the Navy Relief Auxilliary at El Toro Marine Air Station interviewed 3,000 marines with money problems and gave short-term assistance to many to meet emergencies.[9]

At the 1970 White House Conference on Hunger, it was reported that as many as 50,000 servicemen with large families might be living below the poverty line. These were all servicemen heading families of four or more and earning less than $3,500 a year.[10]

In 1971, Representative William A. Steiger, a Wisconsin Republican, did a study of poverty in the military and found:

—GI families on welfare in twenty-nine states.

—Welfare refused in twenty-one other states to GIs simply because they were in the service, even if they might qualify otherwise.

—Wives of 166,000 first-term enlisted men—over half of all first-termers—working to supplement incomes.

—134,000 first-term GIs moonlighting an average of nineteen hours a week for an average of $33 a week extra. "Senior military officials with whom I discussed this problem have complained about the effect of such moonlighting on the training and readiness of certain units," Steiger said.

—A "definite poverty cycle for GIs in Europe" who go into debt to bring their families overseas.

Steiger encountered a community services officer at Fort Gordon, Georgia, who gave him this picture of the "bleak subsistence existence" of many GIs:

> If you take the typical married first-termer, add his base pay, allowance, and subtract his taxes and savings bond payments, he has about $240 a month. You can rent a lousy place for $100 including utilities and roaches, but then you've got to add transportation and carfare because he's living off base— about $45–50 a month in payments for his car and another $30 for gas and repairs. If you are very frugal, and do all your shopping at the commisary, you can get by on $50 a month. So $230 is taken up, which leaves you $10 for recre-

ation—providing everything else is perfect. Of course, if the kids need dental care or glasses, forget it!"[11]

Large pay raises in 1971 and 1972 by the Nixon Administration have helped to alleviate such poverty but not wipe it out altogether. The pawnshops near American military bases continue to be consistently good money-makers.

In one of the exquisite ironies illuminating the attitudes of the nation's great institutions toward individuals, the Defense Department in the 1960s did not see the problems of poverty within its own organization but did recognize those outside, within civilian society. Robert S. McNamara, Defense Secretary until early 1968, diverted his attention from the Vietnam War in 1966 to take a look at poverty and decided the services could help do something about it. So he organized "Project 100,000," a program under which each of the four services would be given a quota each year of substandard men—in either physical or mental capacity—and train them up to usefulness, not only for the military but for work in civilian life later on. The total of such men trained each year was to be 100,000.

The program was launched with great fanfare and statistics were issued, even from the White House in August 1968, to show how successful it had been. Actually, Project 100,000 proved of little use either to the men taken into the service under it or to the services themselves, unless it helped to provide a few thousand more men to carry rifles in Vietnam. But they could have been gotten in other ways.

Statistics for use in criticizing Project 100,000 are scarce, but its failure was widely talked about in the services. Project 100,000 people were described as malcontents, troublemakers, racial agitators (well over a third of the men in the program were black), drains on the time of superiors and unable to handle their fair share of work. They appear to have gotten into more trouble, to have become the butts of bullying NCOs and ultimately to have been administratively discharged from the services much faster and much earlier than men who complied with the standards.

"It's a revolving door for them," one Navy officer said.

Figures compiled by the Defense Department in 1968 but not generally released showed that Project 100,000 enlistees or "New Standards Men," as they were euphemistically called, did reasonably well in training for infantry, gun crews and allied specialties. They were, in other words, good cannon fodder. But in categories such as medical and dental specialists, 28.6 percent of all Project 100,000 trainees were flunking as opposed to 1.8 percent of others in the Army. When the Navy trained administrative specialists and clerks, 36.4 percent of Project 100,000 men flunked out as opposed to 1.8 percent of others.

Though it might have been McNamara's laudable intent to make a contribution to society, the services apparently were not following through. And in the meantime, attention was being diverted from personnel problems of far greater significance in each of the services.

In December 1971, the Defense Department quietly dropped the enlistment quotas for lower mental and physical category people, and Project 100,000 died a quiet and little-noted death.

In its place, emphasis was being put on Project Transition, a program to train military men in the services for usefulness outside. Transition was a follow-on to 100,000, an attempt to make the New Standards men—and others—fit for society.

There was need for that. In 1970 and 1971, unemployment rates among "Vietnam Era Veterans," to use the Labor Department terminology, ranged significantly above the rates for nonveterans in the same age group. In June 1971, the unemployment rate for veterans in the twenty to twenty-four age group was 13.7 percent. By June 1972, it had dropped to 9.9 percent, still well above the national average. Overall, the June 1972 figure showed improvement, standing at 7.2 percent as opposed to a 6.5 percent rate for nonveterans in the same (twenty to twenty-nine) age group.

It took a long time for the men who fought the war to work themselves back into society.

There was a relationship between the poverty, the garrison-ghettos, the harassment and the primary source of manpower for the services—the draft. Congressman Steiger touched on that point when he wrote:

> The draft survives as a last vestige of the ancient custom whereby the rich and powerful forced the poor and weak to provide service at subsistence wages. Conscription has been justified by the Supreme Court as a valid power of the State in times of "grave emergency or national peril." But the recent legislative history of military pay makes it plain that the

primary function of conscription has been to depress military compensation to a point where a disenfranchised minority of the citizenry has been compelled to bear a grossly disproportionate share of the costs of defense."[12]

There is a corollary to that statement: The United States has been militarized on the backs of its mostly poor, relatively uneducated young. Though society as a whole has paid—and paid dearly—to support the high cost of defense, these millions of young, even those who did not have to pay with their lives, paid far more.

That much can be said about the effect of impoverished living conditions the military machine imposed on most of the individuals within it. The machine's blindness to the conditions, for so many years, also had a drastic effect on itself. Just as civilian institutions for years ignored poverty and the downtrodden until crises developed that became preoccupying, so did the military. Civilian society got its superhighways, trips to the moon, its magnificent airports, its trips abroad, its new suburban houses, all the while allowing the impoverished inner cities to decay. Similarly, the military got its aircraft carriers, planes, tanks and rockets, all the while allowing its garrisons to decay. The same explosion out of frustration that hit the inner cities is now beginning to make itself felt in the garrison-ghettos.

10

DOUBLE STANDARDS IN THE FREAKED-OUT MILITARY MACHINE

The Air Force lieutenant colonel commanding a squadron of F-4 Phantom fighter-bombers in Southeast Asia did not have an easy job. First of all, he functioned as the executive vice-president of a business with $100 million worth of assets. As day-to-day director of operations for that business, he had to make sure the raw materials (fuel, bombs, ammunition, spare parts) arrived at the airfield to keep the assembly line running and that the productivity of his three hundred workers remained at peak levels day after day despite intricate vacation and holiday schedules. The lieutenant-colonel-executive-vice-president also functioned as the playing coach of a professional athletic team competing in a most unusual league. The lieutenant-colonel-playing-coach had little control over the strategy of the game or even the tactics. Game plans came from higher up in the form of targets to be hit, and the type of ordnance and attack methods to be used. The team's unseen front-office men, sitting in air-conditioned offices hundreds—or even thousands—of miles away were calling the plays and dictating the execution. But the lieutenant-colonel-executive-vice-president-playing-coach had to brief the team, motivate it and lead it in combat. If those were his only jobs, you could say with assurance that he earned his pay. Not only did he run the business, but in a typical year-long tour, he would be in the front seat of that supersonic machine almost every other day, exposed to antiaircraft shells, surface-to-air missiles and occasional Migs, bombing the Ho Chi Minh Trail system in Laos or its feeder roads in North Vietnam, taking his life—and the lives of his employee-teammates—in his hands each time he eased back the stick to lift his craft off the runway.

But there was still more to the job of the lieutenant colonel. He also functioned, in the 1970s, as the headmaster of an isolated boy's school, looking out for the morale and welfare of his troops, isolating and removing from his squadron those troublemakers who might influence the rest of the organization to fall down on the job. Maintaining good race relations was an important part of the lieutenant colonel's job in the 1970s. Keeping the accident and venereal disease rates down were others. And so was the drug problem.

One day in late 1971, a lieutenant-colonel-executive-vice-president-playing-coach-headmaster returned to his office after leading a mission over the Ho Chi Minh Trail to find this letter in his in-box:

> . . . I am Robert's mother. I'm writing to you in hopes that you can talk to Bob and straighten him out. Also if you would take the time out to answer my letter, to let me know how he is and how far along on drugs he is. We haven't heard from him since the first of December. I am very concerned about him. I don't know how he got started on this thing, but I hope it will end before he comes home.
>
> I love him very much and I don't think anyone will ever know how it tore us apart when we learned of this. Please write me and tell me where he is, how he is and if he is really trying to be cured of the thing. I will be forever
>
> Grateful

Millions of mothers have sent their sons off to war in this century, but it is only the most recent who have had to add drugs to their catalog of worries. Tens of thousands of commanding officers acting *in loco parentis* have had to exercise often conflicting concerns over individual welfare and group effectiveness, but only the most recent have had to worry about the effects of mood-changing drugs. In the past, those effects were caused by alcohol, and because alcohol was a well-advertised, socially acceptable mood changer, the services lived with the problem. In fact, by offering beverages at prices far below those on the open market, the services encouraged the use of alcohol. But narcotics, uppers, downers and marijuana were a new phenomenon, lacking in social acceptance, creating serious crime problems on the bases, sending back into society thousands of young men with physiological and psychological dependencies they did not have when they left home, offering (unlike alcohol) little hope of cure for those who were addicted.

Where did the responsibility of the services lie in dealing with the drug problem? The argument developed into one between those who said that the responsibility of the institution was most importantly to itself (to maintain peak combat efficiency) and those who said it was to the individuals (to rehabilitate the users before returning them to society).

Robert's lieutenant colonel, unlike most, was mindful of both responsibilities. This was his answer to the mother's letter:

> I received your letter yesterday. It was a very proper and thoughtful statement of a mother's love and concern for her son's welfare. Robert is in my squadron and I know him to some degree.
>
> About two weeks ago, he voluntarily came into my office and we discussed the drug situation and his particular susceptibility to it. He says he got involved in drug taking including marijuana, speed and LSD some time ago and that it became much worse when he was at George AFB [in California]. He feared the possibility that he would get hooked on heroin here, since it is easily available from the hundreds of locals who work in the barracks area. Actually, about 1% to 2% of Air Force personnel here get involved with heroin, according to very extensive clinical tests. But for someone who has taken drugs, somehow a strong temptation exists. I considered the risk of Robert going on heroin to be quite high.
>
> He is unhappy with the service and feels that everyone is bugging him, a particularly frequent symptom especially among marijuana users. Actually, he has had a couple of very minor scrapes with the more senior sergeants, etc., but nothing to be upset about. His haircut and appearance have been continually below USAF standards by his own choice. However, he has always reported to work on time. His skill and knowledge tests are excellent, among the best of

100 crew chiefs in my squadron—so he has a good mind but a bad attitude. He asked to be administratively discharged from the service since he dislikes military life and is concerned about drug exposure. I agreed to do this after investigating the situation. I really cannot use a disgruntled and confused man on my combat squadron flight line where lives are at stake every day. I expect Robert will leave here for (honorable) administrative discharge on 20 Dec. He has failed to accomplish service to the country in a satisfactory way, but if he can rebuild his life I have taken action to help him. He *must* stay away from the USA drug scene. I don't know if he has the self discipline to do this or not. He is smart enough I'm sure, but also has a sort of cynical contempt for authority. Many others do too and conditions here are poor although thousands of us live and work effectively here in spite of the situation.

In closing, I have tried to take action in Robert's best interest. As the father of four children I deeply understand your concern.

Sincerely,

That was the response of a thoughtful, concerned, humanitarian squadron commander caught on the horns of a dilemma, trying to do his best for both the institution he served and the individual he commanded. Under another leader, Robert's case could easily have developed into one in which he was ridiculed and abused by his superiors before he was sent home. Robert went home with a fighting chance to conquer his problem. So did thousands of other young men in 1971. In fact, when the leadership of the services discovered the extent of the drug problem in the ranks, it decided that it could do little more than discharge the users. Amnesty programs were offered in all the services, and the enlisted men began taking advantage of the programs to get out.

Typically, they would turn themselves in as drug users, and their commanders would order general discharges under honorable conditions. Many who were not drug users—save for use of marijuana, which was pandemic—turned themselves in in the hope of securing a discharge. In the past, many a disgruntled serviceman feigned homosexuality to get out of the service. Now they were feigning drug use.

Some Navy figures were indicative of the problem. In 1964, the Navy released 1,586 men for homosexuality and only 42 for drug use. In 1970, the figures were 5,672 discharged as drug users and 479 discharged for homosexuality. In the first six months of 1971, the Navy had 3,972 drug-use discharges and 225 discharges for homosexuality. Extensive medical checks began to turn up many among those applying for discharges who were not drug users, the Navy said.[1] When the services discovered just what was happening, they tightened up the restrictions on drug-related discharges measurably.

This is not to suggest that drug usage in the military in the 1970s was a phantom problem, a situation that some young men took advantage of to wriggle out of their obligations of service. Quite to the contrary, in a few short years, the use of narcotics, marijuana and mood-changing chemicals became a problem of overwhelming proportions within the military machine, just as the problem had already overwhelmed civilian society. And, just as civilian society was at first slow to recognize the extent of the problem and then unable to come to grips with it, so was the military.

Drug use, in fact, appeared in several worrisome places such as the service academies, a Nike antiaircraft missile crew in Florida with a capability for firing nuclear weapons, and among the elite marines guarding the United States Embassy in Saigon. In 1973, the Pentagon even had to transfer twenty-eight marines and eighteen Navy men providing security at President Nixon's Camp David, Maryland, retreat and twelve sailors assigned to the Presidential yacht *Sequoia* because many among them were smoking pot. The services dealt with drug use first as a disciplinary problem, severely punishing those apprehended. In a few cases in the 1960s, men were court-martialed for the mere possession of marijuana. Usually, however, such an offense resulted in a discharge as undesirable. Young men with this type of discharge, returned to civilian life, found the going rough. They were unable to obtain jobs, could not enter schools and were denied veterans' benefits.

The experience of a young Navy enlisted man stationed on Guam in 1967 is an example. He had previously experimented with LSD. And then, one night while he was assigned to a mine repair detachment, he "dropped a tab of acid." It was not a particularly good trip, and the next morning, concerned that his LSD use might impair his work, he reported the incident to his commanding officer. The commander referred him to the Navy staff judge advocate who in turn referred him to the Air Force. Within two hours after he spoke to the judge advocate, he was ordered to report the next day to Treasure Island, San Francisco, where he was processed out of the service with an undesirable discharge. As a result, for five years he was unable to obtain a job or gain entry to a college. In 1972, he and his parents were still appealing to have the discharge upgraded to honorable, without success. And meanwhile, the youngster's life was a shambles. In 1971, Defense Secretary Melvin R. Laird had ordered the services to review the undesirable discharges of any veterans who appealed them after mustering out for drug abuse, but there was no great rush to the appeals boards, perhaps because of experiences like those of the young Navy man.

Four years after that youngster's experience on Guam, Commander Herbert T. St. Omer Woolley, a member of the Navy's Judge Advocate General's Corps, and Lieutenant Commander Lee H. Beecher, a physician, had this to say about experimental LSD use:

> . . . Clearly an individual who chronically uses LSD is unpredictable and therefore undesirable in terms of the military. It is not clear, however, that every individual who used LSD in the past is thus rendered unfit for any further military duty. On the contrary, experience indicates that LSD users later have been able to perform their duties well and without difficulty. There is much to be learned about long term effects of LSD and further research is greatly needed in this area.[2]

Woolley and Beecher were, respectively, the legal adviser and medical consultant to the Pearl Harbor Drug Awareness Control Unit. Their study, based not only on intangible experience but also on a scientific survey of 8,000 Navy men stationed in Hawaii, was a major contribution to the body of knowledge concerning drug use in the military. But the implications of the study were overlooked with disastrous effects by those trying to deal with the problem.

The study pointed out that military men use drugs for three reasons: to get "high," to be "in" and to get "out."

But why the need to get "high"? According to the Woolley-Beecher study, this was the reason:

> Getting high is one way of dealing with depression or disappointments. Military personnel under stress may return to

drugs to find a release for their tensions and a respite from their fears.[3]

Woolley and Beecher said the services find the most difficulty treating the men who use drugs to get high. The two officers despaired of treating chronic heroin or morphine users at all. And for the others, they suggested that the only route to rehabilitation was through strict control of social life and the exertion of group pressure against drug users (using the Synanon and Alcoholics Anonymous models), the substitution of less dangerous drugs (for example, methadone for morphine and heroin), and the use of drugs which turn a high into something unpleasant (such as the use of Antibuse to make a drinker nauseated). They conceded, however, that all these approaches were basically incompatible with the idea of military service and suggested that Veterans Administration Hospitals are better centers for dealing with this type of drug abuser than the military services.

Their argument stopped short of recommending that the military take steps to reduce tensions and lessen fears. In the bureaucratized structure of the military, men dealing with drug problems were supposed to confine themselves only to those problems and not cut across lines of authority exercised by others. Thus, if tension was created by barracks living conditions such as those military men suffer throughout the nation and the world, the men dealing with the drug problem could do nothing about it. If fear was heightened not only by the prospect of having to fight but by a handful of more immediate problems, the men dealing with drugs could do little more than point out the component of fear involved when a user turns on.

But if the military is really going to attack the drug problem, it must think seriously about prevention. Effective prevention involves changing many aspects of military life. It would help to prevent drug use, for example, if troop leaders and commanders were to spend more time with their men, rather than deserting the garrisons for the comfort of their own homes like so many commuters deserting the big cities in the late afternoon rush hours. It would help to prevent drug use if barracks were made more livable. It would help if work were more meaningful.

Woolley and Beecher recognized some of this when they talked about the users motivated by the desire to "be in."

This motive for drug abuse [they wrote] can be reduced as

the military permits its enlisted personnel to feel less estranged from the society of young people encountered in civilian life. Liberalization of attitudes regarding styles of hair and civilian clothing is an example of an approach which will help reduce this sense of estrangement. As officers demonstrate their desire and ability to better understand the social problems of enlisted men, there will be a reduction in the motivation for "anti-establishment" groups who now come together for the purpose of expressing discontent or dissent with the military, using drugs as a ritual analogous to holding Communion.[4]

Once again, the Woolley-Beecher idea stopped short of prescribing a complete prevention program. In past years and in other military establishments, the services had created their own "in-groups"—units with proud traditions and cohesive spirits, teams to which the members belonged with enthusiasm, groups of friends who were willing to fight and die for each other. In today's services, unit designations are meaningless. Personnel turbulence is so great that men come and go almost without getting to know the men bunking next to them. Officers are so bent on furthering their own careers, so interested in having their tickets punched, that they have little interest in serving with one unit for more than the absolute minimum period of time. Throughout the services, concerned young professionals lamented the breakdown in unit identification. Army men pointed wistfully to the old British regimental system in which a man remained with his regiment throughout his career, earning a promotion only when a vacancy within that regiment at a higher level became available. Navy men talked about how ships' crews were assigned in the British Navy from commission to commission. That is, a man joined a ship when it came out of dry dock and stayed with that same ship until it went back into dry dock for a complete overhaul several years later.

In this manner, peers became hard and fast buddies able to give each other support during hard times, willing to stick up for each other in adversity, helping each other surmount difficult personal problems. Superiors were truly able to act as surrogate parents. They knew their men as individuals and were able to anticipate and ward off problems. The mark of a good noncommissioned officer in the pre-World-War-II Army was his knowledge of his men. The NCO knew when an enlisted man was not getting mail from home or sending home the money expected from him. He knew if drinking habits were changing or if other personal problems were developing. By the time the drug culture took hold in the American military machine, that kind of rapport between men had long since disappeared along with the concept of unit identification. In some divisions where there were over 50,000 job changes in a year, there was little chance to make true buddies. And this, indeed, was an important factor in allowing the drug culture to take hold.

The interaction between the introduction of drugs and personnel turbulence helped drain the military of morale. Men "turned on" to escape or to protest. Then, to support their use of drugs, even in areas like Vietnam where the drugs were cheap and readily available, users resorted to thievery. They stole from their barracks mates, and the resulting lack of security made morale even lower. No locker, no matter how strong the lock, was safe. No article was without value. In towns like Fayetteville, North Carolina, outside Fort Bragg, and Wrightstown, New Jersey, at the gate of Fort Dix, pawnshops bulged with items ranging from expensive stereo sets, televisions and cameras down to blankets, knives and forks, and combat boots, much of them stolen by junkies to earn money for their drug habits. In South Vietnam, those lucky enough to work in offices kept their expensive belongings there because their quarters were insecure. In 1971, there was hardly an American military office from the Delta to the DMZ that did not have one or more expensive tape recorders, record players and tuners resting on desks, tables and file cabinets. It was not so much that the military men liked to listen to good music as they worked. It was more that they wanted the equipment to remain safe until they could pack it up and ship it home. Only offices were secure from thieves.

Just as the military missed the opportunity it had as an authoritarian institution to enforce standards of racial equality, it missed the opportunity to provide an environment for its troops in which morale would remain high enough to discourage the use of mood-changing drugs.

It treated drug users as instigators of bad morale instead of as victims of the conditions that produced bad morale. Woolley and Beecher wrote:

> In many cases, drug use has become a symbol for discontent with the military and an expression of dissent. In these situations, drug use reflects a low morale. The causes of the

discontent and dissent which have led to low morale should be explored and clarified. Forums should be developed for airing grievances and discussing leadership and personnel problems among and between officers and enlisted men (to the lowest pay grade). A straightforward acknowledgment should be made that morale problems do exist. Clarifying the causes of low morale often suggests their solutions.[5]

In failing to clarify the causes of low morale, most of those in command positions in the military thus applied a double standard of loyalty. They expected their troops to remain loyal to the institution despite all the pressures generated by living a ghetto existence. At the same time, the officers showed a tacit disloyalty to the institution by refusing to recognize and try to correct those conditions. And they expected the troops to maintain their loyalty under circumstances that were by far more adverse than they themselves had to endure.

Meanwhile the commanders established a double standard for dealing with the "drug" problem as opposed to the alcohol problem. In 1971, the General Accounting Office issued a report in which it estimated there were 150,000 alcoholics in the services. If that number were true—and it was open to dispute—then alcohol would have been a far more serious problem than drugs.

Yet alcoholics were treated with deference by the command, mainly because by the time individual drinkers became a known problem, they had built up a great deal of seniority in the services. Alcohol was the drug of the professionals—the career NCOs and officers for whom the services had, in a variety of ways, made drink cheap and available. Once again, Woolley and Beecher:

> Alcoholism is still the number one drug problem for industry according to the Employers Counsel of the State of Hawaii. Yet, while the military services are attempting to discourage the use of "drugs," they are subsidizing the consumption of alcoholic beverages through officers' clubs, enlisted men's clubs, and military retail liquor stores. Tables 3 and 5 indicate that 86% of Navy personnel drink, 34% use alcohol 11 or more times in a week—but less than 3% consider that they have either a moderate or great problem with their drinking. Even today there is a tendency to regard the old expression "drunk as a sailor" euphemistically. Contrast this to the

attitude about being "turned on" with "pot" or some sort of hallucinogen.

* * *

One reason that the alcohol user in the military is treated differently than the drug abuser is a widespread belief, particularly at command level, that the drug user is likely to be subversive. The associations of drug use with criminality, insanity, and immorality should be viewed against the backdrop of this belief. Yet, there is little hard data to substantiate such associations.

* * *

There is a popular belief of a definite correlation between the toxic drug state and crime; however, a cause-and-effect relationship has not been proved by scientific studies—except for alcohol.[6]

This passage is not quoted as an argument for prohibition in the services. The use of alcoholic beverages is far too much a part of American life for one to argue the case for abstention at the present time. But on the other hand, one can argue against making alcoholic beverages so cheap and easy to obtain in the military. In March 1972, the Pentagon adopted a policy of treating alcoholism as an illness, and in line with this policy, it decreed that arrested alcoholism was to be no bar to promotion, to the granting of a security clearance or to special assignment.

Brigadier General John K. Singlaub, deputy assistant defense secretary for health and environment, commenting on the new policy, said, in the words of the *Army Times,* "the directive would have no effect on 'happy hours," Class 6 [liquor] stores and similar fixtures of service life."

Singlaub told the newspaper: "This is no temperance movement. But at the same time we (are making) an effort to try to deglamorize any social events that abuse alcohol."[7]

The deglamorization, however, was not going too far. Singlaub said he did not feel it necessary for any advocates of temperance to use the new directive as an excuse for cutting out traditional drinking activities at the service clubs. One of those activities is the practice of offering drinks on a two-for-the-price-of-one basis at specified times. These are drinks already sold at rock-bottom prices. Thus in many clubs, at some hours during the week, an officer or NCO could buy two big martinis for forty cents. With bargains like that, it was easy for the leadership to remain freaked out.

Nowhere is the double standard regarding alcohol versus other drugs better documented than in the case of Air Force Master Sergeant Walter T. Perkins. Perkins was the top-ranking noncommissioned officer in the intelligence division of the Air Defense Weapons Center at Tyndall Air Force Base, Florida. As such, he had access to information about new weapons development, tactics and techniques used in intercepting enemy aircraft, and intelligence on the weapons and tactics of potential enemies, including the Soviet Union. By October 1971, he had completed eighteen years in the Air Force, all of them in intelligence billets. He had served in Japan, Turkey, South Vietnam and Thailand as well as the United States.

By October 1971, he had developed a serious drinking problem. A later investigation by a lawyer representing Perkins showed he was spending from six to eight dollars a night on drinks at the Tyndall noncommissioned officers' club. The lawyer found that many of Perkins' NCO colleagues were drinking similar amounts. The price for those drinks was forty cents each. Perkins was also buying large quantities of package whiskeys at the base exchange and in downtown Pensacola. In all, he was drinking at least a fifth of whiskey a day, according to the lawyer, Captain Clyde W. Russell, Jr.

All this drinking went either unnoticed or ignored by his superiors until Perkins was arrested on October 18, 1971, at the Pensacola Airport. In his possession were a ticket to Mexico City and an attaché case full of classified documents from the files in his office. Perkins was taking them to Mexico City to hand over to Russian officials.

At a subsequent court-martial, Perkins pleaded not guilty by virtue of temporary insanity due to alcoholism. The defense freely admitted that Perkins had planned a rendezvous with the Russians but argued he was not in his right mind when he undertook the venture. Perkins was convicted, sentenced to three years in prison, reduced in grade to airman-basic, fined $150 a month out of the $288 he would receive each month while in jail and given a dishonorable discharge.

"Yes, I guess basically it is fair," the sergeant commented on the sentence.

The point of the story, however, is that for years Perkins worked in an extremely sensitive job while his drinking problem was ignored. The defense introduced testimony at the trial which showed that at one point Perkins, while drunk, fell and broke his leg. It was set at an Air Force hospital, and a full leg cast was applied. The hospital report contained no information about the drunken circumstances surrounding the accident. A few days later, drunk again, Perkins fell and broke the cast. It was repaired at the hospital, but once again no entry was made in the record about any drunkenness. The use of marijuana made one a security risk. Standing up for one's civil rights or racial equality made a person a security risk. Homosexuality was grounds for lifting a security clearance. But heavy use of alcohol was no problem until the drinker stepped seriously out of line.

The presumption in the military was that 95 percent of those people who used alcohol did not "abuse" it. On the other hand, by application of the double standard, even a one-time use of any narcotic, marijuana or dangerous drug "or the illegal or wrongful possession or sale of same" was considered "drug abuse" by the Navy.[8]

If there was any salutary effect of the drug problem in the military it was that the service leaders were forced to confront the alcohol situation. But that was no solace for thousands of young men who were hooked on other drugs. By 1971, no serviceman was immue from exposure to the drug problem. On shipboard, on flight lines, in stateside bases, throughout the Far East, in Germany, Spain, Africa and the Mediterranean, pills, pot and skag (heroin) were at least available; in many places, they were plentiful. In Congress and the press there were charges that the United States government was looking the other way as high-ranking South Vietnamese generals and officials made money in the drug trade. There were even accusations, such as by Alfred W. McCoy, author of *The Politics of Heroin in Southeast Asia,* that raw opium was being transported from the growing areas in Burma and Laos to South Vietnam by the Central Intelligence Agency-controlled airline, Air America.

McCoy told a Senate committee: "In northern Laos, Air America aircraft and helicopters chartered by the U.S. Central Intelligence Agency and USAID [United States Agency for International Development] have been transporting opium harvested by the agency's tribal mercenaries on a regular basis."[9]

Thus the vagaries of international politics gave rise to another double standard in dealing with drugs. While one arm (the Bureau of Narcotics and Dangerous Drugs, or BNDD) of the government was struggling to reduce the illicit international trade in opiates, another (the CIA) was abetting it—to the detriment of American troops, who were the main targets of the drug trade. Although the BNDD estimated the annual harvest of illegal opium in Southeast Asia at 700 tons, a White House report in 1972 said that only 29 tons had been intercepted between August 1971 and June 1972. Columnist Jack Anderson charged that only 5 tons of that cache was actually opium. The rest, he said, was fodder, plant material and chemicals. The BNDD denied Anderson's charge.[10]

Once the drugs reached the market, investigators were zealous in trying to ferret them out. They were zealous but not always successful. In 1971, a battalion commander at Fort Dix, New Jersey, confided to me that he thought he had identified one of the men in his unit who was selling heroin to others. "But I can't prove it," the lieutenant colonel said. "I'm trying every which way to get him out of the Army. I'll even give him an honorable discharge if I have to."

At Fort Bragg, a black private first class, educated in the ways of the world in Washington's ghetto, detailed for me one evening how he had earned enough money as a pusher in the 82d Airborne Division to pay alimony to his first wife, help send his sister through college, support his mother, run an expensive sports car, maintain the payments on a house in which he and his new wife-to-be were going to live, and furnish it.

"I don't need Uncle Sam's paycheck," the young Vietnam veteran, who claimed to be an *ex*-pusher when he talked to me, said. "My girl has asked me to stop pushing. But if things get bad, I'll go right back to it and I won't tell her."

The military was most successful in cracking down on the use of marijuana which, because of its bulk and because dogs could be trained to sniff it out, was easily detectable. But a marijuana crackdown was fraught with dangers in itself. Denied the pot—which was relatively harmless when used judiciously and over a short term—men turned to narcotics, amphetamines and barbiturates, all of which create physiological and psychological dependencies. The harder drugs, however, all had the virtue of being far more easily concealed.

As the drug problem grew in severity, particularly in Vietnam, there were indications that the commanders tried to sweep it under the rug. In the spring of 1971, before the drug crisis in the services exploded with full force on the public consciousness, the Army held a two-day workshop in Vietnam on the problem of drug rehabilitation. The workshop turned out a report estimating that perhaps as many as 25 percent of the lower-ranking enlisted men in Vietnam were abusing heroin. Surveys were presented at the meeting showing heroin use by 10 to 44 percent of some units in two different combat divisions in Vietnam.

The workshop report, according to then Captain John Eric Engstrom, was presented to a smaller committee which was to pass it up to higher authorities, including General Creighton W. Abrams, Jr., then the commander of all American troops in South Vietnam. But the command was apparently not interested in hearing that the drug problem was serious, and so, after prodding, the subordinates sent a watered-down version of the report to the top.

Now an attorney in Wichita, Kansas, Engstrom, who revealed the incident in August 1972, said: "The thing I object to most is that the Army ignored the drug-abuse problem for so long. We tried to tell senior officers we had a time bomb that would explode in the U.S."[11]

Within a few weeks of that workshop in Vietnam, the time bomb exploded. Representatives Morgan F. Murphy, an Illinois Democrat, and Robert H. Steele, a Connecticut Republican, completed a probe of the world-wide drug problem and charged in June 1971 that heroin addiction was reaching epidemic proportions. Steele, a former CIA agent, and Murphy, who had been a Marine Corps officer, estimated that 10 to 15 percent of all GIs in Vietnam were addicted to heroin. They called for the "total mobilization of all our national resources to combat the scourge of the 'white plague.' "

The Murphy-Steele report leveled some of the same charges as McCoy about drugs moving on Air America and about corrupt officials of friendly governments in South Vietnam and elsewhere taking part in the traffic. It also, however, pointed the finger at active-duty and ex-U.S. servicemen as key figures in the international trade.

> Heroin is smuggled into South Vietnam from Bangkok by Thai soldiers either returning from leave or those beginning a tour of duty in South Vietnam [the congressmen said]. Many of these soldiers travel in U.S. military aircraft . . . Finally, some heroin is thought to be carried in by American military personnel returning from R. and R. [rest and rehabilitation].[12]

At another point, the report said:

> Recently American citizens, mostly ex-military, have moved to Thailand and have entered the business of smuggling heroin to the United States.
>
> According to U.S. narcotics agents, the Bangkok operation is led by ex-serviceman, William Henry Jackson. Jackson operates a place called the Five Star Bar in Bangkok, which is patronized chiefly by black U.S. servicemen. According to the narcotics agents, Jackson is assisted by other ex-military men, some of whom have moved from Europe to Bangkok. According to the agents, the Jackson group recruits patrons of the Five Star Bar as heroin couriers to the United States and utilizes other active duty military personnel to ship heroin to the United States through the Army and Air Force Postal System . . .
>
> BNDD agents in Bangkok are of the opinion that Jackson is probably paying a Thai legislator for protection.[13]

On May 6, 1971, the United States Bureau of Customs bolstered the congressmen's charge that the military postal system had been used to transport narcotics into the United States. It announced that in the months of March and April, 1971, alone, 248 seizures of narcotics coming through the mails had been made. On April 5, 1971, the bureau seized a package at Fort Monmouth, New Jersey, that had been shipped from Bangkok, containing seventeen pounds of heroin. The package had a street value in the United States of $1.75 million.

The Murphy-Steele report raised the specter of active duty and retired military personnel trafficking in drugs in much the same way that other noncommissioned officers and their cronies were working other areas of crime. That story will be detailed in a subsequent chapter.

Clearly drugs in the military was becoming not only an issue to the services but one of strong political overtones at home. The White House moved quickly to show it was on top of the problem.

On June 17, 1971, President Nixon labeled drug abuse "America's public enemy number one" and announced a massive, White House-directed campaign against the problem. He appointed Dr. Jerome H. Jaffe, thirty-seven, director of the Illinois drug abuse program, as special consultant to the President for narcotics and dangerous drugs.

Overnight, a program to combat drug abuse in the military grew.

Every American serviceman leaving Vietnam had to submit to a urinalysis showing he was clear of narcotics, barbiturates or amphetamines. Every large military base in the world developed a rehabilitation program. Within months, the military, with satisfaction, was releasing figures showing that the hard-drug problem was not nearly so severe as Murphy and Steele had claimed. The urinalysis figures showed that "only" some 5 percent of those leaving Vietnam in 1971 were drug dependent. This in itself was a seriously high number. It meant that roughly the same percentage of men in Vietnam were heroin dependent as there were alcoholics in the United States civilian population. But at the same time, the low urinalysis figure took no account of those men who were able to remain free of heroin for the three to five days it took for their systems to be purged so that they could produce heroin-clear urine. There was strong motivation to pass the test. A positive urinalysis meant being left behind, going through a detoxification program and then a rehabilitation program before receiving a discharge from the service. Clearly, if a GI could do it, cold turkey for a few days was far more preferable. Thus the urinalysis tests must be considered minimal figures in describing the problem.

The military had little more success than other agencies with rehabilitation. Many men distrusted the "halfway houses" to which drug users could turn themselves in for rehabilitation with a guarantee of amnesty. The houses were staffed in many cases with sincere men and women who lacked experience in treating drug users and could not make up for this lack with their enthusiasm.

The Veterans Administration established forty-four drug treatment centers around the country, but because many servicemen had been given undesirable discharges they were not eligible for treatment at the centers. Others, who were forced into VA treatment programs as a condition of discharge, were noncooperative because they felt they had no problem. Drugs themselves were readily available in some of the centers.

Treatment facilities on a few bases aroused resentment from drug-free servicemen who felt users were being mollycoddled and given special privileges. The services ignored advice that the best rehabilitation for selected users might simply be reunion with their families, since, even with heroin dependencies, some of the problems were not nearly as acute as the mainlining heroin addiction common in the nation's ghettos. (Mainlining is injection of heroin into veins. With the highly diluted heroin sold domestically, this quickly becomes necessary to a user in the United States to maintain a high. In contrast, very pure heroin was available to GIs in Vietnam, which could be smoked or sniffed to produce a high. Only some 10 to 15 percent of GIs in Vietnam injected heroin, and there is some evidence that smoking or sniffing does not produce as severe a physiological dependency as injection. Thus the feeling was that once away from the drug, smokers or sniffers might be able to forswear the habit.)

But despite the lack of success, the emphasis remained focused on rehabilitation. Attempts at prevention of drug use were limited to educational programs—some of them highly imaginative, to be sure—and cutting down on the source of supply.

But the real connection, as in the ghettos at home and among the disaffected youth, was between drugs and living and working conditions, between drugs and what had come to be known as "the quality of life." The military missed this point, or to say the best for it, it came to understand it far too late.

In one of the many little-noticed ironies that made up the American military experience in Southeast Asia, a Chicago *Daily News* correspondent filed a story from Long Binh in November 1971. By that time the Americans were pulling out of Vietnam at the rate of almost 20,000 men a month. The huge post, which once numbered over 40,000 men and covered an area twice the size of the city of San Francisco, was reduced to 23,000 and was on its way to complete shutdown.

But the newspaper learned from the Navy, which awarded all construction contracts in Vietnam, that the following projects were planned, under construction or just completed at Long Binh:

—A collegiate-size swimming pool with attached bath house, $465,000.
—A 475-seat movie theater, $450,000.
—Three handball courts, $35,000.
—A hobby craft shop, $71,000.
—A twelve-lane bowling alley, $276,000.[14]

The story quoted an Army spokesman as saying the new facilities were necessary to help combat drug abuse and boredom even during the reduction of forces. That raised the question of why such facilities were not provided during the heyday of the build-up to help prevent the problems of drug abuse and boredom.

A good part of the military's drug problem resulted from a lack of any genuine interest of commanders in morale, troop health and welfare. They were more interested in the institution—in keeping it well stocked with a basic resource, manpower—than in the well-being of the individuals themselves. This was a cause of the drug problem and, ultimately, a cause of the institution's defeat. To live beyond its means, the institution mortgaged its future with drugs, slot machines, alcohol and fancy PX items to maintain a modicum of serenity but not true morale among its troops. It also used sex.

11

THE YOBO CULTURE

Korea is the Siberia of the American military establishment, the far-away, forgotten place for which 33,629 Americans died in a war a generation ago. No one really intended that the military machine sink into a state of debilitation and uselessness in Korea after that war. It just happened that way. The machine sat idle, waiting along the DMZ and in the rear base camps for years, protecting the farthest boundary of the Pax Americana. The men, fed continually on tales of danger to the Free World from Red China and the brutality of the North Koreans across the line, waited for an attack that never came. And while they waited, they sank deeper and deeper, imperceptibly each day, into a state of depravity.

The institutionalization of extramarital sex was the key part of that depravity. Air Force Technical Sergeant William T. Judy and his family, living in a Washington, D.C., suburb in 1971, were among its victims.

At first glance, it had all the characteristics of an attempted gangland murder. Mrs. Barbara Judy, thirty-six, flicked the left-turn indicator on her white Buick one Saturday morning in January 1971, and—kahboom—the midmorning peace of a residential intersection in Arlington, Virginia, was shattered by an explosion. A stick of dynamite had been wired under the hood of her car and set to detonate when she used the signal.

The explosion blew a hole in the dashboard and almost tore the

214

hood off the big car. Mrs. Judy escaped with only leg wounds. William, fourteen, Deborah, thirteen, and Matthew, seven, her three children accompanying her on a weekend shopping trip, were not hurt.

Mrs. Judy's husband, the sergeant, was at work at the time of the explosion, supplementing his service income with a job at a nearby supermarket. He drove to the scene where the police examined his car and found a bomb wired to the right-turn signal. The police impounded both cars.

Arlington Detective Clyde H. Hall, an Army veteran who had once served in Korea, was assigned to the case. That afternoon, at the hospital where Mrs. Judy was having two steel fragments removed from her leg, he questioned Sergeant Judy and learned that the husband, an electronics communications repairman in the Air Force, had served a thirteen-month tour in Korea that had ended a year before.

During the interview, Hall casually asked Judy if he had done much "running around" with Korean women.

"Just like most of the GIs," Judy replied.

The next day the police discovered that the bomb in Judy's car was a decoy. The wiring had been installed so that it could not detonate, unlike that in his wife's. Continuing the investigation, Hall learned from neighbors that, despite Judy's denials of marital problems, there had indeed been difficulties. Still later he discovered that while serving in Korea, Judy had met a Korean woman nicknamed Sandy with whom he had fallen in love. He had written forty-one love letters to Sandy after he returned to the United States. Judy had also been sending her $50 a month, had borrowed $1,200 from a credit union to pay the legal fees for a divorce, had rented a post-office box in a nearby town to receive Sandy's mail and had, in October 1970, made a month-long trip to Korea to visit Sandy after he received word that she had been unfaithful. He told his wife he had been detailed to Korea for temporary duty. Actually he took leave from his job to make the trip and arranged with a fellow sergeant to cover up for him in case his wife should inquire.

Judy was indicted for the attempted murder of his wife. The prosecution said the motive was his love for Sandy. At the trial he denied the charge and his wife backed him up. While they awaited the verdict, the two held hands. He was convicted and sentenced to a year in prison. He could have gotten twenty years as the maximum sentence.

The local press in the nation's capital treated the Judy case as just another sensational crime resulting from a rocky marriage. There were thousands of servicemen living in the area who knew better, who knew that behind the bizarre attempt at uxoricide was concealed a bigamous way of life in which tens of thousands of American servicemen, enforcing the Pax Americana around the world since the end of World War II, have indulged.

Nowhere is that way of life more blatant than in Korea—the land of the Yobo Culture.

Yobo, the GIs tell you, is the Korean word for "honey." A yobo, in the GI terminology, is a Korean prostitute whose affections, services and home a GI buys on a prolonged basis, at a fixed rate per month, depending on the GI's pay grade. Your yobo not only sleeps with you. She keeps house for you, does your laundry, fixes your meals, accompanies you to the local bars and movies, and goes shopping and sightseeing. Some yobos even shine your boots and keep your field gear in shape for inspections. In return you keep her well supplied with American cigarettes and whiskey, some of which she smokes or drinks herself but most of which she sells in the black market to supplement her income. A particularly smart yobo collects, from time to time, information which she can also sell in the black market at a price—not necessarily information involving military security that would be of use to an enemy (although one must assume some of this goes on) but information regarding base openings and closings that would be of value to real estate operators and other entrepreneurs who are parasites on the American military economy in Korea.

GIs, noncommissioned officers and officers liked the yobo culture. Not only did it give them some semblance of a home life in an area where they were not allowed to bring their own families except under unusual conditions, it also allowed those Americans living in the yobo culture to break free of the monotonous life on military bases in rural Korea after working hours—to escape the dreary barracks that had been hastily thrown up for temporary occupation a generation before and which were still serving.

The American military establishment as an institution aided and abetted the yobo culture for one very simple and important reason: When soldiers confined their sexual attention to only one woman, it helped to keep the venereal disease rate down. And, like fancy goods in the PXs and cut-rate alcoholic beverages in the clubs, it was a cheap way of keeping morale high. Finally, the Korean government liked the relationship. Yobo relationships were arranged in the hundreds of little bars established in shanty towns outside the gates of the bases. The bars, in turn, were licensed by a tourist administration in the Ministry of Interior. The ministry also operated the Korean Central Intelligence Agency. American officials, tracing this relationship and noting the participation of the girls and the bar owners in the black market, theorized that the Korean CIA controlled organized crime in the Republic.

It took money to support a yobo. The girls—or their mamasans, the madams who controlled strings of yobos in the camp villages—knew the pay scales in the American military and charged accordingly. A private paid $90 a month (out of $134.40 before the 1971 and 1972 raises) to his yobo. The rates went up to $130 a month for senior enlisted men. Payments by officers probably ran higher, but the information presented here comes from enlisted men who were ignorant of the relationships at the top of the chain of command. They did know, however, that the relationships existed. In Seoul, I was told by one military man that the commanding general of one large unit in the area regularly brought his yobo to the officers' club and to parties on the base. A quick-witted yobo could serve as wife, lover, housekeeper and valet to two GIs at once, providing they worked on different shifts.

Yoboing was an open phenomenon in Korea. It was not something done furtively, even by married men, because everyone—at least it seemed like everyone—was doing it. Estimates by various enlisted men and one sociologist working for the Army in Seoul were that anywhere from 20 to 60 percent of all the married men stationed with the American forces in Korea had yobos. A much higher percentage dealt with prostitutes on a less frequent basis. The practice was so open that one military policeman who worked on the vice squad took public umbrage when his yobo was subjected to a shakedown by the Korean authorities. They found American cigarettes stashed illegally in her house and extorted a bribe from her instead of pressing charges. The MP wrote to an English-language newspaper in Seoul:

I have been stationed in Korea for about eleven months as a military policeman. For approximately nine months, I've performed regular military police duties at ASCOM [Army Support Command] and for the past two months in the vice section of the ASCOM PMO [Provost Marshal's Office] . . .

For the past six months I have had a Korean girlfriend

who, because of her identity as a "business girl" has been the target of organizations like "Chonmae-chong" (Office of Monopoly).

After describing the shakedown, the letter continued:

> In a house where an American sleeps, what else does one expect to find but American items such as American books, American magazines, personal letters, an American radio and American cigarettes? . . .
>
> Respectfully yours,
> Sp/4 William S. Fraser
> Co. A, 72d MP Bn
> U.S. Army-ASCOM District
> APO S. F. 96220[1]

When Fraser used the term "business girl," he was using the euphemism for "prostitute" understood by Americans throughout Korea. That he should publicly admit to such a relationship was interesting enough. But even more interesting was the reaction. An American missionary in Korea by the name of Eileen Moffet wrote to the newspaper to castigate not the Korean authorities but Fraser for living in what Miss Moffet assumed to be an adulterous relationship. She called Fraser an "openly admitted adulterer," which, by his letter at least, he was not. Another missionary, George Patton of the Presbyterian Medical Center in Seoul, was more sympathetic to Fraser but also assumed "that he is normal and was committing adultery."[2]

As seen by Americans in Korea, adultery was normality. The military leadership played a role in maintaining this normality that began with the inspection of yobos to make certain they were free of venereal disease. Medical inspection, however, was only part of the military's involvement. One of the principal duties of every base commander in Korea was the maintenance of a good relationship with the president of the local "Businesswoman's Society"—the head madam in town. The base commander of Osan Air Force Base, for example, greeted me in the officers' club there with a smile and an apology. "Too bad you didn't arrive an hour earlier," he said. "I just finished lunch with the head of the local businesswoman's society."

The woman represented the yobos and other prostitutes of Chicol village, a shanty town that had grown up outside Osan to cater to the thousands of Air Force men stationed there. It was in Chicol that Sergeant Judy met his Sandy while he was stationed at Osan.

Stars and Stripes ran articles reporting on the meetings between the Yongsan Post commander in Seoul and the president of the local "Rose Society." Since Yongsan was the headquarters of the entire Eighth Army in Korea and Seoul was the nation's capital, the ladies and the officials agreed on an even more euphemistic description for their professional organization.

At Camp Humphreys, about fifty miles south of Seoul, Colonel Frederick W. Best, Jr., the base commander, detailed how he had to spend hours every month in negotiations with "Miss Yi," the businesswoman chairman in the nearby village of Anjong-ni, to maintain, as the colonel put it, "safe, sanitary and nondiscriminatory" facilities.

Best assumed command of the base in July 1971, when Anjong-ni was wracked with the racial discord centered on the yobo culture. Black GIs were disturbed because they were forbidden entry to several of the bars in the vill' (as the camptowns were known in Korea) and because the Korean prostitutes would not cater to them as they did to the whites.

The situation was explosive. In the previous spring, someone had stolen fifty hand grenades from a weapons-storage bunker, and some of those had been used to booby-trap a helicopter, which was demolished in an explosion on May 22.* One enlisted man was seriously injured.

The command responded to the complaints of the black GIs by helping Korean entrepreneurs to set up an all-black bar on a dark side street in the vill', even having posters printed to advertise the opening

---

* Of the fifty stolen grenades, fifteen were detonated on the base, according to Sergeant Major Harvey Parrish. Violence, for a time, became a way of life. An NCO club was fire-bombed; officers were threatened. The black troops at one point barricaded themselves within a mess hall for a protest meeting and refused to come out. Ten of the grenades were eventually recovered. Some fourteen or fifteen black men were arrested and tried as a result of the incident. But still, not all the grenades were recovered. A $5,000 reward was offered for information leading to the arrest and conviction of others involved. Then the command offered amnesty, the guarantee of transport to a safe haven and finally an early discharge from service to anyone turning in grenades. In December 1971, fifteen of the weapons were still at large. There were also reports that some M-16 rifles had been stolen. The command lived on tenterhooks. The ammunition and weapons on the base had been taken out of the spread-out bunkers and storage points and put under heavy guard in a few consolidated areas. That meant that in case of emergency, which is what the Army was stationed in Korea to counteract, the men could not get weapons and supplies as quickly as they should.

and donating several cases of beer purchased in the base PX. The blacks remained unhappy, and on the night of July 9, they went on a rampage through the vill' destroying practically all the bars. The riot lasted through the night and into the following day. Some of the black GIs had to go into hiding to escape retaliation by the Koreans. Finally, the American command had to send armed troops into the village to rescue the Americans. They moved through angry crowds of Koreans holding signs reading: "Niggers Love to Kill," "Niggers are Thieves. Beware," and "We Don't Need any Niggers. Go Back to Cotton Field."

The Army responded by placing Anjong-ni off-limits. To relieve the pressure among his men, Best allowed the yobos and other girls to come onto the base, even establishing a bus service for them from the town. Now the yobo culture had spread into the on-base clubs and even, in many cases, into the barracks where many of the girls spent the night with their contractual mates. They only had to show a card certifying them as VD-free to get onto the base.*

Though the girls continued to prosper, the bar owners and other businessmen did not. At first they tried to pull the girls off the buses and out of taxicabs in front of the main gate to the base. The tactic failed. Then they opened negotiations with the colonel. His demands remained "safe, sanitary and nondiscriminatory" service. Miss Yi paid him a visit. He would not compromise. Miss Yi and a local Korean legislator in a second meeting sought compromise. Still he would not compromise. Miss Yi, the legislator and the local Presbyterian minister sought an accommodation. Still no compromise from Colonel Best.

The colonel's demands meant the Koreans would not only have to change their segregated way of doing business—a practice that had developed over twenty years and was probably due in part to the attitudes white American servicemen passed on to the Koreans as they did in other parts of the world to Thais, Okinawans, Italians, Germans and Spaniards—but they would also have to make large expenditures to fix up their establishments.

Anjong-ni did not exist before the Americans built the camp. Over

---

* Technically, prostitution is illegal in Korea, but in fact, all prostitutes are required to carry government-issue cards, which must be kept up to date, showing they are free of venereal disease. Examinations are allegedly performed by officials of the Ministry of Health. Many a GI, however, has contracted VD from his yobo. The girls or their madams simply bribe the officials to issue the cards without examinations.

the years it grew into a ramshackle village of thatched huts and temporary buildings made of corrugated metal, wood, stone and castoff supplies from the American base. By day, it resembled any little Far Eastern village. Children in uniform made their way to and from school carrying book bags. Women did the marketing. Merchants tended their stores. Only the tailor shops, pharmacies (where amphetamines and barbiturates could be purchased without prescription), variety stores and bars catering to the Americans set it apart from hundreds of other villages in the country.

By night, the whole character of the community changed. The neon lights took over. The bars came alive. GIs and their yobos strolled the muddy main drags and disappeared into the dark alleys and culs-de-sac leading off them. Back in those alleys were the "hootches" where the yobo culture flourished, where hundreds of men were living off base. The unlighted alleys were the scene of fighting, of rape, of mugging. Several of the bars were situated in the alleys.

Best demanded that the barkeepers remodel their establishments so that each bar opened onto the main street. He demanded sanitary toilet facilities marked separately for men and women. He demanded that the girls all get legitimate and regular VD checks and that a clinic for this purpose be opened in the vill'. Most importantly, he demanded that the girls service all customers on a C.O.D. basis and that the bar owners play music, in sequence, to suit all tastes in regular cycles—jazz, country-western, rock, soul music, jazz, country-western, rock, soul music—throughout the night.

The bar owners continued to hold out. Best imported twelve buses from other bases in Korea to transport men to the camptowns of other, faraway bases to work off their frustrations when the blockade against the business girls began to work. But only 127 of the 3,000 men on the base rode the buses. "They wanted their own vill' and their own yobos," one of Best's subordinates said.

On August 9, the bar owners and businesswomen conducted a sit-in in front of the main gate to the base, effectively shutting it down. For thirty-six hours, no one entered and no one left. On August 12, the owners submitted a plan. On August 17 an agreement was signed by Best, Miss Yi and a representative of the bar owners. On August 28, after forty-two days, Anjong-ni was back in business. The yobo culture grew up once again with one significant change.

Best kept the vill' off-limits to his officers. "I can't have my officers shacked up with the enlisted men during the night and expect to have their orders followed during the day," he told me one evening in December 1971.

The colonel's problems were far from over. Despite almost nightly visits to the vill' which he made, despite continual patrols by junior officers and senior noncommissioned officers and despite a race relations program instituted by Miss Yi for the girls, some of them still sometimes balked at dealing with blacks. And this continued to create problems both on base and off.

"I spend all my time on this and what do I have to show for it?" Best said. "I have the cleanest center of depravity in all of Korea. . . . I sometimes wonder what I'll be fit to do after I'm finished in the Army. My answer to myself is that I'll be fit to be a madam."

He could talk so openly about his problems because they were far from unique. The military had come to terms with the yobo culture long before. Kunsan Air Base, headquarters for the 3d Tactical Fighter Wing, was built with a three-mile perimeter around it from which Korean civilians were barred for security reasons. There was only one exception, according to Norman Thorpe, the knowledgeable correspondent for *The Overseas Weekly* in Seoul. Thorpe said the American military cooperated with Korean entrepreneurs in building a vill' within the perimeter that had a population of 300, that is, 200 business girls and 100 supporting workers such as bartenders and maids. The Air Force, Thorpe learned, established a special alarm system in the vill' to alert servicemen off-duty for any emergencies and a bus service to pick them up in their hootches if they had to be hurried back to the base.

When I repeated Thorpe's story to American military officials, none denied it.

Not only did the yobo culture work to break down family relationships in the most obvious way—wife and children at home in the United States without daddy who was off living with another woman in Korea and even, in some cases, fathering a second family—but it also contributed to a corruption of the Korean economy in a manner that hurt the American military effort.

Obviously, the support of a yobo was expensive. Two households—one in Korea, the other in the States—were far more than servicemen could afford on their salaries. To help defray the expense, many of the yobo-supporters played the black market in cigarettes, alcoholic beverages and all kinds of other commodities. They also stole a lot and sold the goods on the Korean economy.

In June 1971, just before Anjong-ni was put off-limits, the men of Camp Humphreys purchased more than 9,000 cases of beer on post. Allowing for the summer heat and with past figures as a guide, 9,000 cases of beer were ordered for the last half of July. But the vill' went off-limits on July 10, and as a result only 4,800 cases were sold. Best thought that the overage represented the amount of beer going into the black market.

Camp Humphreys' police blotter was also a revealing document. Even the drug problem in Korea would not explain large numbers of thefts. Between mid-July and mid-November, 1971, reported thefts on the base made up a list twelve pages long. The list included cameras, tape recorders, radios, fans, refrigerators, watches, boots, clothing, blankets, two teletype machines, a telephone switchboard and an item listed as an "indicator group" valued at $11,328.00. Of course, not all the material was stolen by American servicemen. In fact, Best said, thefts by Korean workers on the base were so common that the command had even established a policy of checking refuse trucks hauling trash off the base. Often, concealed under the trash were valuable items. But much of the thievery did go to support yobos.

Some of the *reported* thievery actually never occurred. To help control the Korean black market, servicemen were limited in the purchase of luxury items at the PXs. Those items had value many times greater on the Korean economy than the service man had to pay. To circumvent the limitation, servicemen would sell their items and then report them stolen, making application for permission to buy replacements.

The black market situation was not unique to Camp Humphreys. An Army sociologist had this to say about the situation: "One of our researchers did a study on procurement policies here and found that the Army was importing three batteries each year for every vehicle it had in country. Figuring battery life at three years for a car or truck, that's nine times the number necessary. Yet all the batteries were being used. The mechanism was this: A person would get a new battery and then sell it on the black market. He would put an old battery in his truck, jeep or sedan and a month later come back for a second new battery. No one cared.

"Or another example. There are now 20,000 surplus Army vehicles in use on the Korean economy—jeeps and trucks that have been remodeled into buses and all kinds of other conveyances. No one imports parts for these vehicles. Yet you can go downtown and buy any part you need for maintenance. All those parts are being stolen from the military and no one cares."

As almost any serviceman stationed in Seoul would tell you, some stores in the downtown area sold goods stolen from the PX and still carrying their original PX price in dollars. The black market was so open that merchants did not even bother to remove price tags.

There was also a flourishing black market in MPC—the military payment certificates which the American command used as currency in an effort to control black-marketeering in Korean currency. MPC officially had no value on the Korean economy. It could only be used to make purchases in PXs, commissaries, clubs and concessions on the bases. Yet yobos, other prostitutes, taxi drivers, bartenders and others gladly took payment in MPC. They gave it to those authorized to make on-base purchases who in turn bought items not available on the Korean economy for the possessors of the MPC.

Yoboing in the camptown communities existed side by side with the good old-fashioned kind of prostitution that has been a feature of military life going back to antiquity. The services struggled mightily to control this situation as well in Korea but with limited success.

Prostitutes were allowed onto the bases, the only identification needed being a valid VD card. They could enter the service clubs in limited numbers, placing their cards in a special rack built for the purpose at the front door and taking a check for the card. Once the rack was filled, no more girls were allowed in. The on-base clubs were, perhaps, healthier environments than the clubs in the vill's. In the off-base bars, except in the rare situations like Colonel Best's crackdown, girls could come and go without offering the protection of valid VD cards. And the range of services they sold was awesome. To entice you to buy drinks, often watered, they sat on your lap and offered—forced upon you might be the better description—a free genital massage.

Then, if the serviceman expressed interest, arrangements were made. There was one price for masturbation, often administered in a back room, a higher price for oral copulation, for which rooms were reserved near the bar and still higher prices for different types of intercourse in the tawdry nearby hotels or in the girls' hootches.

Often these contacts resulted in the establishment of yobo relationships. Sometimes a yobo relationship developed into a legitimate marriage. Thousands of American soldiers married Korean girls over the years.

In many cases, the American husbands of Korean girls were transferred to Vietnam and left their wives and families behind. Some of the women went back to prostitution during the period their husbands were out of the country. Some even worked the on-base clubs openly.

In addition to whatever personal havoc was wrought in the lives of the American servicemen and their yobos, the yobo culture left a serious sociological problem in its wake for the Korean authorities to deal with. The problem was the offspring of the relationships. Orphanages were set up to raise many of those children abandoned first by the father who was transferred out of the country after his thirteen-month tour and then by the mother who had to go back to work. These orphanages were heavily supported by donations from GIs.

Because of the Koreans' prejudice, however, the orphanages would not accept children born of black American fathers and Korean mothers. These children were pariahs, abandoned to the streets, left to grow up on their own, rejected in their own country. You could see them along the streets and in the alleys of the vill's. By 1972, some of them were already in their late teens. In the flashing neon lights of the evening, they looked more Afro-American than Korean. Their gestures and mannerisms were those of the American South and the urban American ghettos. But their language was that of Asia, and as outcasts, there was nothing they could do except beg and pimp and ingratiate themselves with carousing Americans who, often enough, could spare a dime—or the Korean equivalent thereof.

Korea's yobo culture had its counterparts—though less highly developed —in other areas of the world. In Okinawa the procedure was called "ranching." In Thailand, they called it "bungalowing." During the height of the Vietnam War, GIs flying out of South Vietnam for one-week "rest and rehabilitation" vacations in cities of Southeast Asia and Hawaii were put into the hands of local travel agents who contracted with the American military to begin making arrangements on the vacation-bound aircraft.

A typical operation was that of Tommy's Tourist Agency in Bangkok. Tommy's is a Southeast Asian wartime success story. In 1965,

Tommy operated a bus that brought American GIs taking leave in Thailand from the Vietnam War from the airport into the capital. By 1971, that original bus concession had mushroomed into an enterprise taking up all the space in a seven-story office building on the fringe of Bangkok's downtown district. Tommy now operated tours, booked GIs into any of forty different hotels and operated as a concession the R and R center for the military. Tommy was also detailed to license hotels for the military to receive R and R guests and changed money for the GIs.

A room at one of the hotels cost $4 to $5 a night. That included air-conditioning, use of the swimming pool and service charges. For $25 a night or the flat rate of $125 for a seven-day week the hotel clerks supplied a room-with-girl.

In addition to the hotels, servicemen could meet women in the bars and night clubs, or at massage parlors. Bangkok had its "strip" of night clubs catering only to the GIs. Petchburi Road was situated on the fringe of the city, which kept all the activity isolated from the beauty of the downtown area, reserved for the more sedate—and free-spending— civilian tourists. A taxi driver taking you to Petchburi Road offered you a massage—"New Bangkok" or "Chinese"—dirty pictures, pornographic movies, voyeurism with lesbian acts or a prostitute. If he was a success-ful salesman, you never got to the night clubs. He, of course, received a commission on anything he sold. A typical massage parlor was located on a dark side street. You walked through an unmarked door and found yourself in something resembling a theater lobby with a glass-enclosed box office ahead of you at which you paid the price of admission. To the side behind a large pane of glass were dozens of young Thai girls, sitting in a small grandstand, all on display and waiting to be selected as your masseuse. Behind that glass, under the strong lights, dressed in bright silks, they suggested pieces of sweets in an old-fashioned penny candy case. They were all smiling to attract your attention.

At the clubs, the girls all wore numbered badges and danced with each other. You picked out a girl from the couples on the floor and gave the waiter her number. He brought her to the table for a closer inspec-tion, and after you bought her a couple of $1.25 drinks (and a couple for yourself), you struck a bargain. The going rate was $10 to $15 a night.

The services detailed a crew of thirteen sergeants to work as liaison men with Tommy's. They manned an office on the seventh floor of Tommy's skyscraper twenty-four hours a day to take care of complaints and emergencies and to brief incoming R and R groups. The briefers warned of all the con games—among other things, an American real estate outfit was busy in Bangkok peddling Florida swampland to unsuspecting GIs, young Thai boys dressed in boy scout uniforms were pickpocketing, older men impersonating females were mugging and the Thai women were luring servicemen to the marriage registrar where, upon signing a book, a GI found himself legally married (recognized by the U.S. government) and subject to a community property divorce settlement. After delivering these caveats, the sergeants got to the heart of the briefing.

As rendered by Staff Sergeant Gene Hilliard in late 1971: "There are approximately 1,000 bars located throughout the city. These bars have entertainment ranging from a jukebox to a small band to a floorshow. The drinks normally cost $1.25 on down, depending on what you're drinking. All the bars have female companionship available to sit, talk, drink and dance free of charge. It may cost you a drink or two but here there's no such thing as Saigon tea. These young ladies can really booze it . . . And when you get ready to leave one of these bars with a young lady, all you have to do is go over and see the mamasan, papasan or the first sergeant, whoever's on duty. Pay them anywhere from $10 to $15 and book up. She's yours for the rest of the night. . . .

"While we're talking about nightlife, I must tell you all . . . you stand an excellent chance of catching the old Victor Delta while you're here on R & R. For those of you not in the Signal Corps, that's VD. Venereal Disease. We strongly suggest you use all the preventative maintenance that Uncle Sam has taught you. This means more than just dipping it in the local beer, that's 18½ percent alcohol . . . Now all the girls working in the bars carry a little pink book like this. Gentlemen, this is not a ration card. This is a VD checkbook. Inside the cover of the book there should be a date stamped no more than seven days old . . . Don't be shy or bashful to ask the young lady for her pink book. She's in the profession just trying to make a little extra baht. She'll be more than happy to show it to you."[3]

There were two similarities between the situations in Thailand and Korea. For one, though there were an estimated 100,000 prostitutes in Bangkok, most of them carrying the little pink books, prostitution was illegal. That meant that in Thailand, as in Korea, the girls were subject to shakedowns by corrupt police and other officials and that the books did not guarantee VD-free business. Secondly, as Anne Darling put it in *The Overseas Weekly* story cited above:

> The Thai women have apparently learned about racial discrimination from the Americans. Several bar girls admitted that they were afraid of "dam-dam," the Thai word for black, and would refuse to sleep with them. So most brothers on R & R find their way to Jack's All American Star Bar, a hangout for in-country blacks, to meet women.

Unlike the generation gap that distinguished alcohol users from drug users, the lust for women transcended any age or rank barrier. This fact was brought sharply into focus in a little town on the Gulf of Thailand in late November 1971. Until the coming of the Vietnam War, Sattahip was a peaceful little fishing and resort village nestled in a lush landscape that resembled the French Riviera. It was 125 miles and at least three generations removed from the urban modernity of Bangkok. It was a village in which the water buffalo was still the principal means of transportation.

That all changed with the coming of the Americans after 1965. The Americans needed a secure base for the big B-52 airplanes used in bombing Vietnam and Laos. The base could not be located in South Vietnam itself because that would have subjected it to attack by the enemy. It had to be near the sea because the cargoes of fuel and bombs necessary to keep the huge Stratofortresses full (each plane carried thirty tons of bombs on a single mission) demanded a simple transportation system.

The Americans leveled a mountain and filled in acres of the Gulf of Thailand at a nearby village called Utapao. They built barracks, a swimming pool, clubs, hangars, shops, taxi-ways, jet-age runways and revetments. Up the harbor from Sattahip they built a special pier for off-loading the bombs from ships. They built fuel-tank farms to hold the gasoline and a pipeline to get the fuel from port to base. Now, huge trucks carrying the loads of bombs began to compete with the water buffalo for use of the newly paved and widened roads. The eight-engine bombers began their daily bombing missions, filling the skies with the

jet roar. American civilization did not grow slowly in Sattahip. It exploded onto the scene.

To construct this huge project—a modern American air base—the
American contractors hired thousands of Thai laborers from other parts
of the country. When the project ended, the workers remained behind.
They threw up a typical camptown and opened bars, shops, hotels, little
housing developments and taxi services. They imported prostitutes from
up-country.

Soon the Sattahip area had one of the largest crime problems in
Thailand. Americans could not ride the taxis alone because of the
danger of mugging by the drivers. They ran into trouble in the bars.
They were cheated in the shops. The exploiters were being exploited
cruelly.

In November 1971, Lieutenant Colonel Harry M. Sunk, fifty, of
Lockbourne, Ohio, arrived at Utapao for temporary duty. Sunk met a
Thai business girl in a bar and went home with her, to spend the night
and perhaps to make a bungalow arrangement. At the house, he was
accosted by the girl's pimp who demanded Sunk's money. The colonel
refused to hand it over. The pimp shot and killed the colonel.

All this happened just a few days after Field Marshal Thanom
Kittikachorn staged a coup in Thailand which did away with the limited
democracy that the nation enjoyed. Thanom was a determined law-and-
order advocate, and to show his sincerity, he went on nationwide radio
to order the summary public execution of the twenty-nine-year-old pimp.

Several thousand spectators, including many American servicemen,
turned out to watch the execution on a hillside overlooking the air base
and the beautiful Gulf.

"It is right that I will die," the pimp said as he was led to the execution site. "It is better to die than live in this life and be poor. Maybe
in my next life I will be a rich man."[4]

The American presence on the Gulf of Thailand contributed to
more than a simple rearrangement of a timeless landscape.

The yobo culture was ubiquitous. For example, there was Sydney, Australia, one of the cities used as an R and R center during much of the
Vietnam War. Ramsay Williams, a reporter for the magazine *Off Duty,*
wrote in June 1971 that "a new kind of Sydney swinger—the R and R
girl" had appeared in the King's Cross district of the city to compete
with the established prostitutes.

Charging $100 a week, the R and R girl gave more than the traditional prostitute's service. She served as tourist guide, girl-next-door substitute and hostess, according to Williams. He quoted one girl as saying: "The boys we pick up want company more than sex. If we stay with a guy for six days, we only sleep with him four or five times. If they want more we just leave. We take them around and show them Sydney, go to the night clubs, movies, shopping, lie on the beach."

In addition to their fees, the girls collected gifts of clothing and enjoyed the entertainment. Some found husbands.

By 1972, the yobo culture was even spreading to Generalissimo Francisco Franco's prim, proper police state, Spain. But the Spaniards were not committing their own women to the cause of keeping the world's policemen happy. Prostitution is illegal in Spain, and unlike others among the United States' allies, Franco means it, at least for Spanish womanhood.

So instead, Spanish bar owners have been working through British employment agencies to find nice English-speaking girls to come and work in the bars. The agencies advertised in newspapers throughout the British Isles for girls desiring "a paid vacation in the sun" as workers in hotels and cafés in the Spanish resort town of Rota.

When the girls arrived they discovered Rota, like Utapao, was the site of a huge American military base—this one devoted to the care and feeding of Polaris submarines, reconnaissance planes and supply facilities for the United States Sixth Fleet in the Mediterranean. Downtown Rota, a camptown, boasted fifty bars.

After undergoing VD tests, the girls were issued special three-month work permits that allowed them to work only as bar girls, enticing GIs to buy drinks. The pay, for a six-day week, was $28.50. To make ends meet, many of the girls established housekeeping arrangements with the GIs.

"We clean and cook and they give us a roof over our heads," one of the girls told a reporter. The British consul nearby did not find things too mundane. She reported at least four illegitimate children born over the past four years (raising a question about nationality, since the children were born on Spanish soil of unmarried foreigners), one girl murdered by an American GI (who was court-martialed and convicted), four bad LSD trips and numerous run-ins with police over unpaid bills and theft.

In the summer of 1972, the situation had grown so bad in Rota—dubbed "sin city" by the British press—that questions were raised in the British Parliament.[5]

The military might say that in sex, as in everything else, men in uniform only mirror the rest of society. That is the claim made to explain the problems of high drug use among the young in service and the racial conflict between whites and blacks. So you might expect that the military communities had their share of "swingers" living on the posts, just as "swinging" was reportedly becoming more and more widespread in civilian communities from coast to coast in the 1970s.

There was some evidence, never legally proven, elicited in a Florida court-martial room in 1972 that promiscuity was rampant on at least one Naval base.

Commander Andrew F. Jensen was, at forty-three, a chaplain with sixteen years of service to his credit. Married, the father of two children, Jensen had spent most of those years serving on ships at sea or with a Marine Corps amphibious unit. In 1970, he was serving as Protestant chaplain at Cecil Field, Florida, a Naval air station near Jacksonville, and the family occupied a home on base. As his wife, Mrs. Kathleen Jensen, explained it, the home was a devout one based on military organization. "Christ was the head of the house and Daddy was the CO," she said.

As base chaplain, Jensen performed the usual range of clerical duties—conducting religious services, meeting with church groups, counseling young men in trouble and counseling families with marital difficulties.

In the summer of 1970, one of the women he counseled was the attractive, blond, twenty-four-year-old wife of a Navy flier who came to him with the confession that she had been having an affair with another man at a previous duty station in Texas. The woman, Mrs. Mary Ann Curran, took her troubles to Jensen on the advice of her husband, she testified later at the court-martial.

As Mrs. Curran told the story, Jensen suggested that she transfer the emotional dependence she felt for the man in Texas to himself. And that started an affair, she claimed, that resulted in adulterous relation-. ships on eighteen different occasions in her home (after a Sunday church service), in motels and in other apartments in the Jacksonville area. Meanwhile, Mrs. Curran, a nurse, became friendly with the Jensen family, often baby-sitting when the chaplain and his wife went out, once nursing Mrs. Jensen when she was ill.

Mrs. Jensen told the court she considered Mrs. Curran a "close personal friend . . . I thought she considered me a very close personal friend."

During the period the chaplain was allegedly seeing Mrs. Curran, he was also, according to the court-martial charges, carrying on an affair with Mrs. Lora Gudbranson, thirty-eight, the wife of the base supply officer. Mrs. Gudbranson claimed she had had relations with Jensen on four different occasions in a motel near the base.

When Mrs. Gudbranson, a regular visitor to the chaplain's church groups, discovered that she was not alone in sharing Jensen's extra-marital affections, a sense of righteousness welled up in her. She confessed her sins to her husband and then preferred charges of adultery against Jensen.

After an investigation, the Navy charged Jensen and ordered a court-martial. He became the first chaplain in Navy history ever to undergo a court-martial and the first officer ever charged with adultery.

The chaplain pleaded "not guilty" to all the charges. The American Baptist Convention, his denomination, stood behind him, and to show its displeasure over not being allowed to investigate and take action in the case itself, it announced that it would no longer provide chaplains to the Navy. A source within the convention, who was never named, charged that the chaplain was being made a scapegoat for difficulties that had arisen between the Navy and chaplains in general, and that Jensen was charged to prevent him from "blowing the whistle" on a wife-swapping ring at Cecil about which he had evidence.

Jensen's lawyers tried to introduce testimony about the wife swapping in the trial, but the military judge, after hearing it privately, kept it from the jury. The Judge said the evidence was only hearsay and inadmissible.

Other chaplains closed ranks behind Jensen and testified to his high moral character. The two complaining women were denounced as self-confessed adulterers whose testimony could not be believed. One former chaplain testified that Mrs. Gudbranson had tried to seduce him. The witness, Joseph C. Simpson, told the court Mrs. Gudbranson came to him and talked of "free love" and ran her hand from his left shoulder slowly down to the belt line. Simpson continued: "She got two fingers inside the belt line and I stepped back. A counselee was to come in and see me about that time and that ended that."[6]

Jensen's wife stood by him and testified in his behalf. Notes he had allegedly written to Mrs. Curran were portrayed as notes to his family that the young woman had stolen while she spent the night in a guest room at the Jensen house. An alleged love letter in Jensen's hand was explained as the feelings of a young Navy enlisted man dictated to the chaplain and written down by him in a counseling session. Jensen's visits to motels, for which records were produced, were said to be attempts to get away from the pressures of his work on the base. He would go to the motels alone, he and his wife testified, to rest and to "air his body." During the period he was allegedly having the affairs, he claimed, he was suffering from a rash of infected chigger bites on his midsection that made sexual activity impossible. Airing out soothed the infection.

In his closing argument, Jensen's attorney, Jack R. Blackmon of Corpus Christi, Texas, likened the chaplain to Jesus, reminding the court that 2,000 years before, "a man called Jesus was wrongfully accused and put to death."

The court listened to the closing arguments and then retired to deliberate. Two hours later, they came back with a "not guilty" verdict. The date was Good Friday, 1972.

Jensen and his wife went to a nearby ice-cream parlor to celebrate on a malted. He was a teetotaler.

A few weeks later, Jensen granted an interview to F. T. McFeely, an Associated Press writer, and, asked to comment on adultery at Cecil Field, he responded this way:

> My lawyer had decided I shouldn't comment on that . . .
> It is a moot point now. There is no need to drag anybody into
> an issue we hope will die . . . The moral climate in the Navy
> is no different than in the rest of society. I'd hate to have
> every person who has committed adultery to be taken into
> court . . . Thousands of persons . . . have confessed adul-
> tery to me over the years. You hear of it in every ship's ward
> room. It comes in serious talks, in personal boasts and as
> jokes . . . I preach against it but adultery commonly goes
> on. It's not just in the military . . . I'd say that in civilian
> business, it's certainly more prevalent. Morality is high in the

Navy but most people don't consider adultery as conduct unbecoming an officer.

A few weeks later, Jensen was transferred to the Princeton Theological Seminary in New Jersey to study for a master's degree in theology.

To the extent that sexual relationships in the military community in the 1970s merely mirrored what was happening with the breakdown of long-established taboos throughout society, the military machine could not be faulted. The United States military machine is, after all, an establishment peopled in large part by citizen-soldiers. Cecil Field mirrored life in these United States, if the reports from inner cities and suburbia are at all accurate. But the Yobo Culture of Korea, and its counterparts in other areas of the world, was like nothing else known to man. And one is forced to wonder, considering all the hundreds of thousands of impressionable young Americans who have passed through it in the last generation, to what extent the military did not mirror the moral breakdown but fostered it in civilian society.

12

SHOULD WE COLOR THE BILL
OF RIGHTS KHAKI?

The men and women called to arms in the United States during the Cold War labored under the assumption that they were making the world safe for democracy, that they were protecting the time-honored virtues of life, liberty and the pursuit of happiness. For their pains, they subjected themselves to totalitarian control at a time when no one else in society was asked to make sacrifices. They themselves were denied the fruits of the democratic way of life.

By the 1970s, the disparity of this condition began to rankle, raising issues within the military machine that had seldom been raised before, that had never been raised before with such ferocity. The issues related to the rights of individuals within the system.

In 1971, Technical Sergeant Clarence Wirt, a veteran of thirteen years in the Air Force, went before a court-martial at Eglin Air Force Base, Florida, charged with refusing an order to trim his sideburns one quarter of an inch, the length they extended below his earlobe. Wirt was not a young malcontent for whom military service was a bitter interruption of civilian life. He was a professional, a senior noncommissioned officer who had chosen to make a career of military service. He was the kind of man the Air Force—and the other services—relied upon to keep the machine running smoothly, the kind of man who knew the value of strict adherence to regulations. He was the kind of man, then, expected to enforce haircut regulations, not violate them. He was not of the long-haired generation. Why had Wirt defied an order?

"If we are ever to get a career force, an all-volunteer military, we must make the individual count for something," Wirt said.[1]

To tens of thousands of officers and men, regulars as well as draftees, Wirt had defined the issue precisely. The military had reached the point where it had to recognize that the individual counted for something. In that regard the black movement in the services was only part of a larger, all-encompassing drive. It was not only on such mundane matters as living conditions that the disaffected dwelled. They also pushed for a greater share of the freedoms and privileges of American Democracy. They wanted the right to express opinions, to speak out on the policies they were called upon to uphold. To accomplish this, the enlisted men and a few officers developed a vigorous far-flung underground press movement.

Women, homosexuals, objectors to the Vietnam War, doctors, lawyers and service academy cadets were among those who spoke up for their rights. Tens of thousands, frustrated at their inability to make their protests fruitful, simply walked off the job. They deserted, melting back into civilian life or, as in the case of a few thousand, leaving the country. A few hundred resorted to the terrorization of their officers. The fear of "fragging" became a fact of life for leaders. A few dozen took part in sabotage and a handful started giving away military secrets. In truth, the soldiers in the military machine had become an important enemy of the machine. Most importantly, they demanded an overhaul of the military justice system. Even after a series of reforms, the system was still, in the 1970s, being used as an instrument by commanders to maintain authority over troops and keep them tightly disciplined. The reformers felt that the military justice system should be used only to determine who had passed beyond the bounds of legality and to punish them.

All this ferment was condemned by many senior commanders as an indication of the new "permissiveness" in American society. A generation of children raised under the precepts taught by Dr. Benjamin Spock, the senior commanders said, no longer yielded to authority without question. As Vice Admiral James Calvert put it when he became superintendent of the United States Naval Academy:

We accepted authority simply because it was authority. Today young men will respond to strong and effective leadership.
But it has to be strong and effective. It has to be done by men
who are more or less unimpeachable themselves.[2]

As an admission that his own generation, during its youth, was
willing to accept the word of superiors who were not "more or less unimpeachable," Calvert's statement illuminated the crux of the matter—the
difference in outlook between the young generation of military men in
the 1970s and all those who went before. But yet Calvert and his contemporaries continued to indict attitudes that were upheld by the Founding Fathers as virtuous. The idea behind a military establishment that
was part professional, part citizen-soldier, was that the short-time civilian, serving his hitch, would provide the leaven necessary to keep the
military in consonance with society. As long as the military's goals and
those of society were the same, the machine purred along smoothly. The
gears began to strip when society's goals (as expressed by "the people"
though not necessarily all "the leaders") diverged from those of the
military.

On Labor Day weekend, 1970, a small group of Navy men and their
wives, stationed at the United States Naval Station, Keflavik, Iceland,
appeared on the streets of that town and Reykjavik, the country's capital, to distribute to American servicemen Volume 1, Number 1 of the
Stuffed Puffin.

Puffin's purpose was stated this way on its attractively printed
front page:

The *Stuffed Puffin* is an assertion by its contributors that
the existing means for information, intellectual expression and
exchange of views for servicemen and dependents stationed
in Iceland is inadequate and that a publication such as this
one is one answer to the problem. It is our hope that it can
become an open forum to any opinion or personal expression
so that the admittedly narrow range of opinion reflected in
this issue might be broadened to a meaningful debate.

The five Navy men who published *Puffin*—three officers and two
enlisted men—had taken care to carry out the project within the con-

fines of a Defense Department directive regulating the unofficial press. That directive, issued on September 12, 1969, permitted unauthorized publications "by military personnel offpost, on their own time and with their own money and equipment." The directive also said:

> The fact that a publication is critical of Government policies or officials is not, in itself, a ground upon which distribution may be prohibited.[3]

A few days after 650 copies of the *Stuffed Puffin* were distributed, all five men received word that they were being transferred from Iceland. Shortly after that, the transfers were rescinded. The men were offered early separation from the Navy instead. The two enlisted men were soon discharged, one several months before his scheduled release date, ostensibly so that he could return to school, and the other more than one year early "for budgetary reasons." Similar action was taken against two of the officers. The third, Lieutenant William H. Laubenstein, III, a lawyer working on the Judge Advocate General staff at Keflavik and editor of the paper, was not discharged. Faced with a new directive from the Navy command on the island requiring clearance of all material prior to publication, he applied for permission to publish a second issue of *Puffin* and was turned down twice. He was told that the paper was detrimental to the mission of Navy forces on the island, grounds for which permission to publish could be denied under the Defense Department directive, and that publication was illegal under an Icelandic law forbidding publications in that country by other than Icelandic citizens. Despite this little-used law, the Navy published its own base newspaper, the *White Falcon,* which, the admiral in command told Laubenstein, the Navy considered a good enough vehicle for communication with the troops.

Shortly after Laubenstein submitted the second issue of the *Puffin* a second time in December 1970, he was transferred to Washington. The *Stuffed Puffin* was dead. A month later, Lieutenant Norman W. Pitt sent letters to the major newspapers of Iceland decrying the demise of the GI paper. As a result, he was called before his commanding officer and read an order prohibiting him from publishing any further articles without permission. He was also given a bad fitness report. Concerned about Pitt's action possibly stimulating others, Rear Admiral John K. Beling, commander of the Iceland Defense Force, as the American military presence on the island is known, wrote an article in the *White*

Falcon explaining why American servicemen stationed in Iceland could not publish their own unofficial newspaper. Pitt wrote a response which was never published. For his efforts, he too was discharged from active duty before his scheduled release date.

Several months later, Laubenstein belatedly received a fitness report from his commanding officer, Captain Lloyd H. Thomas, in Iceland. It said in part:

> Another area in which Lt. Laubenstein was a negative factor to the command was his involvement in the publication of an unauthorized newspaper . . . This paper . . . contained articles highly critical of the President and senior officers of the Defense Force in Iceland . . . This paper was considered harmful to the interest of the United States and NATO in Iceland and certainly gave aid and comfort to the Communist cause in this country.* By his action Lt. Laubenstein indicated he was a liberal, opposed to the military and the war in Vietnam.

Captain Thomas ended the report with the observation that, given his beliefs, Laubenstein should not have accepted a commission in the Navy. Actually, the lieutenant had little choice. After going through college and law school on draft deferments, he was faced with an induction notice. At that point, he enlisted in the Navy where he could practice his profession rather than serve as a draftee in the Army. The decision he made is the kind the Navy and the Air Force have relied upon for years to fill up their ranks with talented men. The captain's report also interpreted an officer's oath as compelling him to carry out

---

* Laubenstein is not the first military man to be put down on a fitness report with the charge of communist sympathies. Professor Jean E. Smith of the University of Toronto discovered that in June 1920 a young Army captain received a report in which his superior called him "inattentive in class" and a Bolshevik. That young officer demanded a court-martial, saying, "If I am inattentive, it is because of the poor quality of instruction. If I am a Bolshevik, that implies disloyalty and I demand a court-martial." The superior backed down somewhat, changing the report to read "inclined to be bolshevistic." The captain receiving that rating was Lucius D. Clay who, twenty-seven years later, as a four-star general, commanded all American troops in Germany and organized the Berlin airlift. He subsequently became a senior partner in Lehman Brothers, the Wall Street banking house. Professor Smith, Clay's biographer, says the report did not hurt Clay's career, as it would have today, because "promotion was strictly by seniority in those days and efficiency reports had not been inflated to the point where a single adverse comment proved fatal."

not only legal orders from above but also to follow the political and ideological views of his superiors. Many officers were unwilling to accept that interpretation of their obligation in the 1970s.

Publication of the *Stuffed Puffin* was part of a trend in the services. One compilation of unofficial publications in August 1970 listed fifty-seven such newspapers. The papers were, for the most part, poorly printed throwaways issued when funds were available, subsisting on advertisements placed by small businesses appealing to the counterculture, street-corner donations and funds from radical groups. Some lasted; others went under; new papers sprang up to take their places. In 1972, one was published at Offut Air Force Base, Omaha, Nebraska, under the nameplate *Offut Offul*. Offut is the headquarters of the Strategic Air Command, the keeper of a large part of the nation's nuclear deterrent. For a time, a paper was published by a Navy seaman in the Pentagon. It was called *OM*. Another vigorous publication in 1972 was *All Hands Abandon Ship* published by seamen at the Newport, Rhode Island, Naval base. At the Iwakuni Marine Air Station in Japan, a group published an irreverent newspaper called *Semper Fi*. The cover of that paper's January 14, 1972, issue was taken up with a cartoon showing Richard M. Nixon dressed as a barber looking on dolefully as Uncle Sam, inspecting a new white-sidewall crew cut in a mirror, says, "Now I really want out."

The underground press was not the only medium for dissident discussion and protest. In several places, groups of officers and GIs took ads in local nespapers protesting the Vietnam War.

In May 1971, a group of twenty-eight Army officers and one Air Force captain at Fort Bragg and Polk Air Force Base in North Carolina took an ad in the Fayetteville (N.C.) *Observer* protesting the Vietnam War. The ad said, in part:

> . . . We exercise our constitutional right to add our views to those who have already publicly spoken out. With them we demand the withdrawal of all American military personnel and advisors from that embattled land (Vietnam) by the end of 1971.[4]

Within days, seven of the Army officers, who were mainly doctors and lawyers, were encouraged to resign. Air Force Captain Frederick W. Ford, twenty-four, who had been a squadron section commander, was

240

transferred from his job, stripped of his top-secret clearance and given a meaningless administrative job for signing the ad. He did not take the transfer quietly. Instead he issued a statement which said:

> It is my opinion that this removal is a punitive action to harass and intimidate me into not exercising my constitutionally guaranteed right to express freely my opinions on the crucial issues which confront this nation. It seems to me strangely illogical and inconsistent, if not illegal, that an Armed Forces supposedly dedicated to preserving this country and its freedoms will so quickly seek to deny those same freedoms to the very men called upon to preserve them.
>
> Nothing in my oath of office as an officer requires me to give up my rights as a citizen as a prerequisite for military service.

Ford's argument may not have helped him, but it could have carried some weight in higher echelons. In fact, the service leaders might have come to realize that, in giving honorable discharges to dissenters, it might be creating a big loophole through which many in the service could find a convenient way out of uniform. The following month, thirty-eight doctors and dentists at Fort Knox, Kentucky, repeated the Fort Bragg ad in the Louisville *Courier-Journal*. Another group at Fort Jackson, South Carolina, placed the ad in the Columbia (S.C.) *State*. Local authorities began taking action similar to that at Fort Bragg, but the Pentagon intervened, saying the men were within their rights. The exercise of free speech had begun to work.

One of the most important dissident groups was known as the Concerned Officers Movement (COM). It was important because many of its members had key jobs, considering their age, in the military establishment. For example, there were chapters at two of the nation's five ICBM bases: Minot and Grand Forks, North Dakota. The Washington chapter, at one time, included two Navy officers who served as intelligence briefers to the Chief of Naval Operations and another officer on the staff of Vice Admiral Hyman G. Rickover, the man in charge of the Navy's nuclear submarine program.

COM chapters held monthly meetings, took part in protests of various kinds, published a newsletter and generally tried to promote these principles:

> Paramount in the program of COM is a fervent opposition

241

to the continuing military effort in Vietnam. COM decries the military policies that turned an internal political struggle into a nation-destroying bloodbath. The application of American military power in Vietnam was as unnecessary as it was unworkable. There is no need to prolong the mistake. COM supports a cease-fire and the rapid disengagement of American troops from Southeast Asia.

COM further abhors the military mentality that promotes absurd measures like the body count; that leads to the indiscriminate slaughter of innocent civilians; that destroys land and villages and calls it victory.

COM is opposed to the preponderant share of national resources devoted to the military. While Americans go hungry, while cities decay, while our natural resources become more despoiled, the Pentagon is able to get billions of dollars for an ABM system that may not even work. National defense is important, but so are poverty, education, and the environment. It is time to reexamine our priorities.

Within the military structure itself, COM supports the free expression of dissenting opinion. . . .

COM advocates a full airing of questions concerning the quality of life in the military. There are many points that should be considered, from haircut regulations to enlisted-officer class differentiation, from low pay to the harassment of new recruits.

Despite the fact that many COM members were among the brightest young men in the services, the military machine reacted not by attacking the sources of the discontent but instead by forcing out the men who expressed it. Lieutenant Junior Grade Robert C. Brown was a good example. As a high school senior in Mansfield, Ohio, Brown, the son of a conservative Middle Western doctor, supported the candidacy of Senator Barry M. Goldwater for the Presidency. A well-brought-up anticommunist, Brown, in those years, took offense when the Reverend Dr. Martin Luther King, Jr., accepting the Nobel Peace Prize, condemned the Vietnam War. "He's a preacher and a civil rights leader," Brown thought. "He's got no right speaking out against the war."

In 1965, Brown entered Princeton to study aeronautical engineering. Slowly his views began to change. By 1969, when he graduated, he was a confirmed but quiet opponent to the war. He was not a conscientious objector. Instead he felt that if he tried to avoid military service it would only mean that someone else, without education, would have to serve in his place. He sought and received a direct commission in the Navy. He excelled at officers' candidate school and was one of a select few chosen to work in Rickover's nuclear submarine program.* Brown lengthened his enlistment one year to accept the job. He worked on nuclear reactor materials.

Brown joined COM in the summer of 1970, after President Nixon ordered American troops into Cambodia. He felt he could no longer remain silent. In September 1970, he appeared at a press conference with five other young officers to speak out against the war. Four days later, he was transferred out of Rickover's office into a job where he was given nothing to do. At the same time, owing to the relentlessness of the system, he was promoted from ensign to lieutenant junior grade. Four months later he received a phone call from the Bureau of Naval Personnel. "How would you like an early discharge?" the voice asked.

"Do I have any choice?" Brown responded.

"You can get out now or you can wait ninety days."

In April 1971, Lieutenant Junior Grade Robert C. Brown received

---

* The officers serving in the Navy's nuclear submarine program are an elite, carefully chosen group. No officer enters the program without submitting to an interview by Rickover himself. The admiral keeps a tight personal control over every aspect of research and development, construction and operation of nuclear-powered ships. He has his own emissary at each nuclear installation or on each ship submitting weekly reports directly to him, by-passing the normal chain of command. He is isolated even from supervision by Admiral Zumwalt, exercising as much autonomy in the Navy as the late J. Edgar Hoover did in the Justice Department. He personally reads every letter going from his office, often making little changes in them. The job interviews, now that so many officers are necessary to run some one hundred nuclear craft, have long since developed into a quick ritual. All applicants are briefed beforehand on the procedure by subordinate officers. They are shown a diagram of Rickover's office and given instructions on how to enter, which chair to use, how to exit after the session. They are also warned to be prepared for surprises. Brown, a baby-faced young man with silky blond hair, was asked by Rickover: "Did anyone ever tell you you're cute?" He answered: "Yes, sir, my girl friend." Rickover then summoned his four secretaries and asked them to vote on whether Brown was cute. The ensign won, 3–1, and got his job. Another applicant's interview consisted of Rickover telling him: "Say something that will make me angry." Still another's session consisted of Rickover asking the young officer to sing his favorite song. When the officer performed poorly, the admiral summoned the secretaries to give him inspiration and ordered him to sing it again.

an honorable discharge from the United States Navy. He had served only one year and four months of his four-year commitment. The Navy did not seem to care. The following fall, Brown entered Harvard Law School, showing how times had changed. A generation before, in the heyday of Senator Joseph R. McCarthy, such dissent would have crippled his career. In the 1970s, the other great and venerable nongovernmental institutions in society shrugged it off as inconsequential. The services could not grasp the meaning of that point as an indication of how far out of step they were with society.

Although the Vietnam War was certainly the great catalyst in generating protest, dissent was not limited to that point.

In Alaska, seventeen enlisted men and one officer (out of a total crew of sixty-four) on board the Coast Guard cutter *Confidence* were reprimanded and fined in October 1971 for expressing support to a Canadian group sailing to Amchitka Island to protest an underground nuclear test there. While the cutter's commander parleyed with the Canadians in an Aleutian village, the eighteen handed the protesters a message that read:

> Due to the situation we are in, we, the crew of the *Confidence,* feel that what you are doing is for the good of all mankind. If our hands weren't tied by these military bonds, we would be in the same position you are in if it were at all possible. Good luck. We are behind you 100 percent.[5]

The men were fined one hundred dollars each and reprimanded for "conducting themselves in uniform in such a manner as to bring discredit upon the Coast Guard." The officer was also charged with conduct unbecoming an officer and given three days' restriction to the ship.

In Washington, Army Captain Donald J. McCartney, assigned to the National Security Agency at Fort Meade, Maryland, was rankled in August 1971 by a column in the Washington *Post* by Kevin P. Phillips expressing fear that the nation was losing superpower status. The Russians, Phillips wrote admiringly, are not questioning the Soviet Union's invasion of Czechoslovakia in 1968; they are proud of it. Phillips suggested United States citizens should emulate this attitude. "If this is what it takes to be a 'Super-Power,' let us hope America is saved from that status," McCartney wrote.

Even the service academies were not immune from protest. In

1970, a group of midshipmen at the United States Naval Academy in Annapolis, Maryland, objected to the rule requiring their compulsory attendance at religious services. When the Academy refused to do away with the rule, the midshipmen brought suit in federal court. They were represented by the American Civil Liberties Union, which brought a class-action suit against compulsory chapel attendance at all three service academies. Defense Secretary Melvin R. Laird was named as the defendant.

During the trial, Admiral Thomas H. Moorer, who was then chairman-designate of the Joint Chiefs of Staff, testified that "an atheist could not be as great a military official as one who is not an atheist." The district court upheld Moorer's view and the constitutionality of the compulsory-chapel requirement, drawing a distinction between "attendance" at such services and "worship." But a three-judge appellate court panel in Washington reversed the ruling, saying that compulsory chapel attendance amounted to state-established religion and was thus a violation of the Constitution, and in December 1972, the Supreme Court concurred.[6]*

The traditional relationship between organized religion and the military was also under attack as it related to conscientious objection. Thousands within the services were seeking conscientious objector status as a way out of uniform. And tens of thousands declared themselves C.O.s to avoid military service.

Before the Vietnam War, conscientious objection was practiced by a handful of Americans—members of the Quaker and Mennonite religions and a few other groups designated, by Selective Service, as "peace churches." The test for conscientious objection was strict, and although a few Catholics, Protestants belonging to the larger sects, and

---

* When it received the chapel case, the circuit court of appeals in Washington issued a restraining order compelling the academies not to punish the complaining cadets for refusal to attend chapel while the case was under consideration. Despite the order there was harassment of the cadets. One of them, Midshipman David L. Osborne, received fifty demerits when he did not attend, as required, a Calvary Methodist Church service in Annapolis. Osborne, to make a point of his right to choose his own religion, attended a Billy Graham service on the Academy grounds instead. When he asked his superiors if the court order did not protect him, he was told its effect was "none whatsoever." He was confined to quarters and ordered to march off the demerits at the rate of three hours per weekend. When his lawyers challenged the punishment in court, the Academy relented and canceled it. Officials told the judge it had been imposed by "computer error."

Jews did sometimes pass, the numbers were small indeed. A nonbeliever stood no chance at all. But in rulings handed down in 1965 and 1970, the Supreme Court changed that. The Court decided that one did not have to be a member of an organized religious group to be a conscientious objector; in fact, he need not even believe in a Supreme Being but could arrive at his C.O. status on temporal ethical and moral grounds.

In the year from June 1970 to June 1971, draft boards throughout the country received 110,000 applications for C.O. status and granted 35,000 of the requests. In 1970, the services received 2,943 requests for C.O. status from men already in uniform and granted 1,572 of the requests, or more than half. Of those granted, 875 were discharged outright and 697 were assigned to noncombat roles. Clearly, Selective Service and the uniformed services were taking a far more lenient view of conscientious objection than they ever did in the past. And similarly, so were the courts for those who refused induction either because they were denied C.O. status or for any other reason.

In 1972, the Administrative Office of the United States Courts did a study which proved embarrassing to the government. It showed that over a five-year period, the conviction rate in criminal cases had dropped markedly, particularly against alleged violators of the selective service laws. The government, the study showed, was prosecuting larger numbers of young men who sought to avoid service but winning fewer of the cases. In those it was winning, the punishments were growing lighter. Indeed, many of the convicted were simply placed on probation, meaning that the courts were, in effect, exempting the majority of those convicted without any real punishment.* Putting the brightest possible face on things, Selective Service said that 75 percent of the cases dismissed resulted from accused agreeing to submit to induction. That almost made it seem as if cooperation were the byword of the nation's young.

* Here are the figures compiled by the Administrative Office of the United States Courts as published by the *New York Times*, April 1, 1972:

	1967	1968	1969	1970	1971
Prosecuted	996	1,196	1,746	2,836	2,974
% not convicted	24.9	34.3	48.4	63.7	65.2
% dismissed	22.5	29.6	42.8	55.4	57.2
% convicted	75.1	65.7	51.6	36.3	34.8
% of convicted sent to prison	89.0	73.8	60.5	43.8	36.4
% of convicted on probation	10.4	26.0	38.8	55.7	62.7

Actually that was not the case, and no examples were better than those of Lieutenants Cornelius Cooper, Jr., and Louis Font, West Point graduates. Font, a member of the class of 1968, was the first West Pointer to seek conscientious objector status.[7] Cooper, class of 1969, was the first West Pointer to have such status granted. Font, who graduated thirty-first in his class, was named a distinguished graduate and sent by the Army to Harvard for graduate study, became a selective conscientious objector. He did not disapprove of all wars—only the one the United States was waging in Southeast Asia. The Army refused to recognize his claim and he appealed to the federal courts. Meanwhile, he was ordered to Fort Meade, Maryland, where he was made a barracks inspection officer. Font applied himself to the tedious job with the diligence that had made him a distinguished graduate at the Academy. He turned in a 106-page report documenting slum conditions in the enlisted men's barracks. The report cited dozens of violations by the Army of its own regulations. A team of Army doctors later pronounced the barracks uninhabitable. The result was a series of confrontations between Font and his superiors which resulted in charges being filed against Font for willful disobedience. In the meantime, Font made public accusations of war crimes against Major General Samuel Koster, the former West Point superintendent who had also been ordered to Fort Meade to await the outcome of the My Lai investigation. Koster was the commander of the Americal Division at the time of the My Lai massacre.

As legal proceedings ground on and Font received a more and more favorable press, the Army adopted the typical "quick fix" solution to its problem. It gave Font an honorable discharge on the basis of "substandard performance." The solution to the problem, thus, was a failure to confront it.

Cooper's was a more traditional case. One of the few black cadets at the Academy, he was the son of a World War II Army sergeant who had distinguished himself carrying supplies through enemy lines to relieve troops trapped in the Battle of the Bulge. Cooper's father remained in the service after World War II, and Cooper spent part of his boyhood on military posts. Later the father joined the Los Angeles Police Department, becoming chief of the community relations unit before retiring. Cooper considered medicine as a career but opted for West Point because of the military influence in his life combined with a sense of social responsibility and the potential contribution he could make as an

247

officer. His views began to change at the Academy. An outstanding student in philosophy, he applied his teachings in his senior year during a course on national security when he was assigned to read Herman Kahn's *On Thermonuclear War* and Defense Secretary Robert S. McNamara's statement before the House Armed Services Committee supporting the 1969 defense budget. Cooper later wrote of the experience in his application for C.O. status:

> I felt that for all the differences between Herman Kahn and Robert McNamara . . . both men were guilty of the same error. Death, human death, remained an abstract phenomenon for them. Otherwise, they could not discuss so academically the deaths of millions of people, they could not postulate an endless number of scenarios about the utility and flexibility of nuclear war . . . This mindlessness is the ultimate immoral act because it is much too clean . . .

Following graduation, Cooper went through the artillery officers' school, paratroop training and the Ranger course at Fort Benning, all important tickets to gather in a new personnel file as the basis for an outstanding career. He was troubled by what he saw as discrimination against Laotian officers in the Ranger course and discomfited when a harassed classmate made a bayonet assault on him in the middle· of an obstacle course. But the ultimate disenchantment came in the summer of 1970 when, stationed at Fort Bragg, his unit was alerted for possible duty during the Jordanian crisis. He filed as a C.O. saying:

> I am moved to this application by the unassailable fact that my moral convictions are entirely inconsistent with the duties I am called upon to perform as an officer in the United States Army. To do otherwise would be the height of irresponsibility and would bring personal dishonor . . . To do otherwise would destroy my conscience and personality.

Cooper was discharged, but not before a number of recriminations were made, including an editorial in the New York *Daily News* denouncing him as a "conchie" who should be required to pay back every last penny of the cost of his education. He returned to California to study medicine.

The Air Force vigorously tried to recover funds it spent on the education of men who subsequently claimed conscientious objection.

In October 1971, it presented a bill for $53,575 to Lieutenant John McCullough, twenty-four, of Salem, Oregon, for the cost of his Air Force education. The bill came after a federal court in effect granted McCullough C.O. status by ruling that the service was holding him illegally after the Air Force refused to recognize his C.O. status. McCullough subsequently sued to have the Air Force's bill for repayment voided, and in August 1972, a federal judge ruled in his favor. Similar attempts by the Navy to recover funds have failed.

One young man who did agree to repay a $3,500 Air Force ROTC scholarship was Leonard A. Erickson, Jr., of Tacoma, Washington. The Air Force gave him the stipend while he attended college on the agreement that he would serve four years on active duty. Erickson subsequently became a C.O., and the Air Force granted the status after he signed a promissory note agreeing to repay the funds with 6 percent interest. Once it had extracted the promise to pay, the Air Force apparently had no interest in handling the fifty-dollar checks Erickson made out each month to the "U.S. Treasury" and sent to the Litigation Division, Judge Advocate General, Department of the Air Force in Washington. The first several checks were not cashed for months. Then, when Erickson, who had returned to graduate school at Stanford, ran into some financial troubles and missed two payments, he never heard from the Air Force. C.O.s other than Erickson had refused to pay back scholarship money, claiming the Air Force was attempting to bribe them for their beliefs or force them into abandoning them. The Air Force in turn said a man's willingness to pay established the validity and depth of his beliefs. From the manner in which it subsequently handled the Erickson payments, it would appear that the Air Force was more interested in seeing whether a man would pay than in the payments themselves. That's another way of saying that in its statistics-consciousness, the military machine had convinced itself that money was a measure of a man's sincerity, just as body-count was a measure of battlefield success. Both measures were specious.

Indirectly related to conscientious objection were the high absent-without-leave and desertion rates, particularly in the Army and Marine Corps. Many of those who went AWOL and deserted did so because the services would not grant them C.O. status. Some did not even bother to apply out of the feeling that their applications would be summarily rejected. Whatever the reason, tens of thousands of American young men walked away from their obligations, left their camps and took their chances. A few hundred emigrated to Sweden; a few thousand took up residence in Canada; many more simply returned to their homes. Not only were deserters welcomed abroad but churches in this country offered them sanctuary, and in Berkeley, California, the city council passed by a 6–1 vote a resolution giving asylum to deserters. The measure banned city employees, including police, from helping authorities find deserters and draft resisters. Among the deserters was Scott Udall, son of former Interior Secretary Stewart L. Udall. Drafted in August 1969, young Udall had completed basic training and was in advanced individual training at Fort Gordon, Georgia, when the My Lai massacre story became public. In early November 1969, he left Fort Gordon and was listed as a deserter on December 3, 1969. The young man went to Canada as a "landed immigrant" and planned to become a Canadian citizen.

"He made his decision and went," Stewart Udall said. "When I could see that he was very serious about it and it was a matter of conscience with him, we supported him fully."[8]

Scott Udall was one of 89,088 deserters from all four services during the fiscal year 1970. In 1971, that number climbed to 98,059. Incomplete figures for 1972 show 58,410 deserters. The desertion rates in 1971, particularly for the Army, were record-setting, surpassing those of 1944 when, during the height of World War II, 6.3 percent of all the men in the Army deserted.* The 1971 rate was 7.35 percent.

Even at those high rates, there was some indication that the services were understating the problem. The Army, in particular, which for years had a rock-hard policy of listing as a deserter every man AWOL for more than twenty-nine days, began carrying many men AWOL for several months before transferring them to the desertion rolls. And many others were given administrative discharges as undesirable.

It was not only the Vietnam War that caused the desertions. The Army offered other reasons, some of which reflect not on the individuals who deserted but on the military machine itself. The Army's five main reasons for desertion were family and financial problems, inability to adjust to regimented life, personnel turbulence, poor leadership and "inappropriate values."[9]

---

* The high number of World War II desertions were mostly from combat zones. The 1971 desertion rate reflected defections mostly from noncombat areas, particularly the United States.

These reasons were presented to a House of Representatives appropriations subcommittee by Lieutenant General Walter T. Kerwin, the Army personnel chief in 1972, as he made a plea for $4 million to be used in hunting down AWOLs and deserters.* Kerwin told the committee that he thought both the AWOL and deserter problems would be reduced in coming years as the Army took in fewer draftees and draft-motivated enlisted men. His statement was contrary to a study of just what makes a deserter or AWOL that the Army itself had done in troop units stationed in Europe and at the Fort Riley, Kansas, stockade.

The study showed that the typical AWOL is not a draftee but a volunteer. He is also white, single, not a high school graduate and has served honorably in the Army nine to twenty-four months. He had, in the words of the study, "little or nothing to distinguish himself in civilian life—and very possibly came from a broken home. Frequently he joins the Army in search of some alternative to a future that seems less than promising." Six out of seven such men, the report went on, complete their tours of duty honorably. In other words, the typical absentee has the potential to make a good soldier if handled right. He is not the kind of "bad apple" which can be screened out beforehand.[10]

Commenting on the study, Army Captain Hamilton I. McCubbin, who helped write it, took the Army to task for "covertly" condoning

---

* Lieutenant General Kerwin's request was for funds in the 1973 budget. The previous year, the Army used $4.8 million to round up AWOLs and deserters. As with other military programs, the money apparently was not being spent very effectively. When I visited "personnel control facilities" (PCF) at Fort Dix, New Jersey, and Fort Meade, Maryland, two of nine such units placed around the country to collect absentees and deal with them, I learned that by far the largest number of men turned themselves in voluntarily. The Fort Dix PCF was so overcrowded and so run down that men who turned themselves in to straighten out their problems went AWOL from the PCF. The Army was just as happy. It did not have room for them anyhow. The *New York Times* of January 12, 1972, quoted an unnamed Army officer at Fort Lee, Virginia, on absentees this way: "There is little effort to find these guys. Why, if the Army went around trying to pick up all the AWOLs, they'd just have to shut down all their operations." The *Times* story told of one deserter who traveled to three different bases before he could finally find one that would take him in. On the other hand, I learned that at Fort Dix, roundup squads working in New York sometimes get the wrong man. In November 1970, they apprehended a man named Orlando Lopez on the sidewalks of New York. Records showed a man of that name was AWOL. Lopez was shipped off to the Fort Dix PCF, denying guilt all the way. He spent the day there while records were searched. In late afternoon the Army satisfied itself that it had the wrong Orlando Lopez. The officials at Fort Dix took up a collection among themselves to raise $2.40 for Lopez's bus ride back to the city.

desertion and absenteeism as part of the reaction to the Vietnam War and for failure in previous years to take steps that would prevent absenteeism. The study showed, he said, that improvement in job satisfaction, leadership and the attitudes of commanders could help prevent men from going AWOL and deserting.[11] In other words, the problem was the Army's, not the individual's. The problem was one more telling indication of the machine's defeat in the 1970s.

None of the traditional policies of the military were sacred in the steadily growing drive for civil rights. Along with all the other protesters, homosexuals stood up for their rights. In the years since the end of World War II, the number of homosexuals discovered and discharged by the services hovered between 2,500 and 2,700 each year. Roughly half of them were in the Navy and Marines. All four services have regulations prohibiting homosexuality or homosexual tendencies among their men. The reason, as the Army put it in a Senate hearing in 1966, was this:

> The Army considers homosexuals to be unfit for military service because their presence impairs the morale and discipline of the Army and that homosexuality is a manifestation of a severe personality defect which appreciably limits the ability of such individuals to function in society.[12]

Until the 1970s, the services routinely handled discovered homosexuals administratively. That is, they were not court-martialed but processed out of the services instead by boards of officers convened under other regulations. Almost all the men thus handled were granted undesirable discharges, very few of them raising any complaints. The effect of this was a subsequent denial of veterans' benefits; in addition, the discharge document made it difficult to obtain a good job.

Then the Gay Liberation Movement went to war. More and more homosexuals refused to accept the undesirable discharges, demanding hearings. Some even claimed that despite their homosexuality, they were fit for service. David Addlestone, a lawyer with the Lawyers Military Defense Committee, supported by the American Civil Liberties Union Foundation, said he knew of at least three men retained by the Air Force despite the discovery of their homosexuality. Two were stationed at Cam Ranh Bay in Vietnam in 1972, and one was a veteran of nineteen and a half years' service, stationed at Griffiss Air Force Base, Rome, New York, in 1967.

In 1972, the American Civil Liberties Union had a growing list of cases in which it was fighting the services' attempts to grant undesirable discharges. Franklin E. Kameny, the activist president of the Mattachine Society of Washington, noted that homosexuals were more and more refusing to cooperate with military authorities in engineering their own undesirable discharges, and refusing to live as second-class citizens in the military (without satisfactory social lives), they were turning themselves in as gay and demanding honorable discharges. Kameny foresaw the time, in the not too distant future, when homosexuals, openly declaring their sexual preference, would bring actions to compel the services to enlist them.

But for the time being, they concentrated on attempts to bring justice to their discharges and the aftermath. Though present law leaves a gray area in the difference between an "undesirable" discharge and a "dishonorable" discharge, the Veterans Administration, Kameny said, has categorized all discharges for homosexuality "dishonorable." Thus the V.A. denies homosexuals benefits they might otherwise receive if they were granted undesirable discharges. A key part of the gay program involved working for a change in this regulation.

There was one area in which the services gave at least the appearance of staying out ahead of a civil rights problem. That was in the treatment of women who, in 1972, were receiving, in some areas, far more than they asked of the services. Part of the reason for the increased solicitude by the leadership was pragmatic. As the time for an all-volunteer force approached, women represented an untapped talent pool that could be used if men did not sign up for the services in adequate numbers. Many a recruiting specialist, for example, looked longingly at the surplus of teachers in the job market and realized they had talents and skills that could be used in the services. Another part of the reason lay in the equal rights amendment to the Constitution passed by Congress on March 22, 1972, which, in its liberation of women, even made them subject to conscription and qualified them for combat. (Until the amendment is ratified, women are specifically disqualified from combat by law and regulation.) But the services had a long way to go in granting equality for women, and if the experiences blacks suffered in discrimination despite constitutional protections were any indication, the road to true equality for women would not be straight and smooth.

Numbering some 42,600 or 1.6 percent of all uniformed personnel in 1972, women were generally relegated to a list of specific jobs, ranging from cook and musician to typing, administrative work and running a switchboard. A few received billets in intelligence analysis and public relations. When Lieutenant Susanne M. Ocobock, twenty-three, of Grand Rapids, Michigan, became the first female civil engineer in the Air Force in 1971, that fact rated headlines. Women were allowed to "supervise" but not "command" men. Usually that meant they were given supervisory responsibilities in office jobs. Lieutenant Ocobock was supervising men out of doors. Though women worked with men in certain career specialities—intelligence, for example—they could not compete with men for promotions. They had to compete with other women.

In 1972, the House of Representatives Armed Services Committee, investigating the utilization of manpower in the military, uncovered a set of statistics that told a story of discrimination against women. Though there is one woman for every 66 men in the Army, the committee found only one woman brigadier general for 255 male brigadiers, one woman colonel for every 500 male colonels, and one woman captain for every 140 male captains. Only at the lieutenant level did women approach their proportionate share of rank.

Conditions in the Navy and Air Force were worse. The Navy had six times as many E-6 enlisted men as E-1s (the lowest rank). Yet women E-1s were twice as numerous as women E-6s. It had almost as many male commanders as ensigns, but there were three women ensigns for each woman commander. Though there was one woman in the Air Force for every 60 men, there was only one woman colonel for every 2,000 male colonels, and so on.[13]

One important reason for the disparity, of course, was that women chose not to remain in the services as long as men. That observation at once answered the question and begged it. It raised the question of why it was that so relatively few women decided to make military service their careers.

Part of the reason stems from the traditional female roles in society —housekeeper, wife, bearer and rearer of children—that appeared incompatible with a career in uniform. While adjustments in those roles were slowly made in civilian society to allow women to pursue careers, the services showed no willingness to make any accommodations at all until 1972. In fact, they built a barrier of regulations that made it more difficult for a woman to enter and remain in the services than men.

For example, a man could enlist in the services at the age of seventeen without parental consent and without a high school diploma. A woman had to wait until eighteen and be a high school graduate. Further, she needed parental consent up to age twenty-one. She had to take a different intelligence test than a man and score higher on it. A man went through basic training without any instruction in grooming or in standards of sexual conduct. A woman received instruction in both these areas during her training. A married man was entitled to a dependent's allotment for his wife, whether or not she had a job. A woman could get such an allotment for her husband only if she could show proof that he relied on her income for more than half his support. Most importantly, a pregnant woman or, if she were in the Navy or Air Force, a woman with a minor child as a dependent for more than thirty days a year, was subject to an immediate discharge.

Like blacks of bygone years, the woman accepted their status unquestioningly for decades after they were first allowed in the services in other than nursing jobs in World War II. Even as the women's liberation movement gathered momentum in civilian society, the women in the services remained docile. Their leaders—the handful of colonels and Navy captains, some of whom became generals in the late 1960s—had little interest in improving conditions. They, after all, had made it themselves. Like their high-ranking male counterparts, they had no interest in disturbing a system that had been so good to them.

But others were not as happy. In September 1970, Air Force Captain Tommie Sue Smith of Johnson City, Tennessee, a lawyer who enlisted after she was divorced, brought suit against the Air Force to compel it to allow her to take her eight-year-old son with her to the Philippines. Rather than contest the issue, the Air Force hurriedly changed its regulations, establishing the precedent that women could have minor children as dependents. Under this new regulation, in 1972 it allowed eighteen-year-old Debi Hahn of Denver to enlist despite the fact that she had a nine-month-old dependent son.

In 1970, Air Force Captain Susan Struck, twenty-seven, unmarried, became pregnant while on duty at Cam Ranh Bay in Vietnam. The Air Force began proceedings to discharge her under the pregnancy rule. Unwilling, because of her Catholic religion, to have an abortion, she fought back in the courts, and though continually losing her case, she remained in service long enough to have her baby and give it up for adoption. Even after the child was no longer in her custody, the Air Force refused to retain her. In October 1972, the Supreme Court decided to hear Captain Struck's appeal, and six weeks later, the Air Force suddenly reversed itself, deciding to grant Captain Struck a waiver, probably in the hope that the Supreme Court would then drop the case. The American Civil Liberties Union was set to fight any motion to drop the case. An ACLU statement said:

> If a serviceman and servicewoman conceive a child, the serviceman is not even disciplined while the servicewoman is discharged regardless of who is responsible for the failure of contraception. If this is not discrimination, then nothing is.[14]

A similar case developed with Air Force Lieutenant Mary S. Gutierrez, twenty-seven, who became pregnant while serving in Incirlik, Turkey. Lieutenant Gutierrez, unmarried, wanted to keep her baby and remain in the Air Force. The services argued that pregnancy created a disability that hindered the assignment of women. The women said pregnancy was no different from any other condition requiring hospitalization and recuperation. The services, they said, made allowances for men suffering those conditions. They also argued that single men are allowed to keep dependents and have them travel to duty stations abroad with them.

Though the services showed little indication of wanting to deal with those problems, they did, in 1972, take some steps to make women more useful during working hours. During the second week of August, each of the services announced programs to expand the scope of women's employment. First the Army held a press conference to announce that it was increasing the number of jobs a woman could hold from 139 to 436 out of the 484 specific jobs it lists. All the still-forbidden occupations were combat related.

Then Admiral Elmo R. Zumwalt put out a Z-Gram establishing a study group to look at all laws, regulations and policies that must be changed to give women the opportunity to enter all Navy ratings and compete equally with men for promotions. The admiral said that the "pattern of assigning women exclusively to certain billets" would be eliminated. Ultimately, the admiral said, women would be assigned to ships at sea. And, he said, once the equal rights amendment to the Constitution was ratified, women would be able to take their places on the Navy's warships. In the meantime, he said, women would be assigned to nonnursing jobs on the U.S.S. *Sanctuary,* a hospital ship, in a pilot program.* By the end of the week, two women received assignments—one as a personnel officer on the ship and the other as assistant supply officer. For years the Navy had argued that women could not serve on ships without drastic modifications to give them berthing and bathing facilities. Now suddenly, it had found a way.

The Navy's program was followed by the Air Force which announced the assignment of Colonel Norma E. Brown to the command of the 6970th Air Base Group at Fort Meade, Maryland. The group, which numbered about 2,000, including only 14 women, provides support for the National Security Agency. Colonel Brown thus became the first woman in the services to command men.

The August 1972 announcements followed some attempts by the services to make it easier for a woman to become an officer. In 1972 the Army began allowing women to enter ROTC courses on ten civilian college campuses as a trial program. In 1972, three members of Congress—Senator Jacob K. Javits, a New York Republican; Representative Jack H. McDonald, a Michigan Republican; and Representative Robert N. C. Nix, a Pennsylvania Democrat—all appointed women to the service academies. The Javits and McDonald nominations were to Annapolis, Nix's to the Air Force Academy. All three women were turned down. But a Navy Z-Gram did order the opening of all NROTC programs to women beginning in 1973. And the Air Force Academy began planning for the admission of up to eighty women a year beginning in the fall of 1975.

All this activity came after the House Armed Services Committee had denounced the military for practicing tokenism in its treatment of women in the WACs (Army), WAVES (Navy) and WAFs (Air Force) as well as the Marines where women were known as "WMs" (for "woman marines").

The services had good reason to loosen their policies relating to

---

* The admiral's order did not run into universal approval—even from women. At the Norfolk, Virginia, Navy base, the largest Naval concentration in the country, dozens of Naval wives banded together to sign a petition objecting to the stationing of women on ships. A primary objection was the wives' feelings of threats from other women. Though they were resigned to the fact that their husbands might be unfaithful in other ports, they could not countenance temptation of their men, for prolonged periods, on duty. But beyond that, a policy of women-at-sea was abhorrent to the wives because it brought them uncomfortably to an examination of the worth of their own lives.

women. Since the military was composed of increasingly fewer combat men in proportion to the total force, a woman's talents could be utilized as easily as a man's. (Zumwalt, when asked by a reporter whether there were not some jobs that were too tough for women, replied that some women were capable of handling tougher jobs than some men and that these jobs would be open to women.) Thus the services were acting out of necessity as well as a sense of egalitarianism.

There were some parallels between the 1972 actions concerning women and President Truman's 1948 order desegregating the services racially. The 1948 order had the effect of leaving a lot of problems unsolved in a racial situation that went unrecognized. President Truman's order was widely thought to have solved a problem. It did not. There was the danger that the same thing would happen with the women. All the problems were not solved by the August announcements. But those announcements, plus the promotion earlier in the year of a few women to general officer rank, made it appear that they were. The possibility remained that woman militants might join or replace the black militants in uniform in the coming decade or generation if the future actions of the military leadership did not live up to the 1972 promises.

Though there have been street demonstrations and rioting, fraggings and well-mounted public relations campaigns, the focal point for the attack on the civil rights problem has been the military justice system. The resulting attention has illuminated a number of glaring defects in the Uniform Code of Military Justice, even though it was newly amended by Congress in 1968 to bring it more into line with civilian justice.

Creation of a disparity between the concepts of civilian and military justice was deliberate and has deep historical roots. Two American military heroes have spoken eloquently on the need, in the past, for a system of military justice that was closely tied to all the other tools a commander could use to maintain discipline within a unit. William T. Sherman, Commanding General of the Army, told a Congressional committee in 1879:

> The object of civil law is to secure to every human being in a community all the liberty, security, and happiness possible, consistent with the safety of all. The object of military law is to govern armies composed of strong men, so as to be capable of exercising the largest measure of force at the will of the nation.

These objects are as wide apart as the poles, and each re-quires its own separate system of laws, statute and common. An Army is a collection of armed men obliged to obey one man. Every enactment, every change of rules which impairs the principle weakens the army, impairs its values, and de-feats the very object of its existence.

General of the Army Dwight D. Eisenhower spoke on the same subject before a meeting of the New York Lawyers Club in 1948:

> . . . I should like to call to your attention one fact about the Army, about the Armed Services. It was never set up to insure justice. It is set up as your servant, a servant of the civilian population of this country to do a particular job, to perform a particular function; and that function, in its suc-cessful performance, demands within the Army somewhat, al-most, of a violation of the very concepts upon which our government is established . . . So this division of command responsibility and the responsibility for the adjudication of offenses and of accused offenders cannot be as separate as it is in our own democratic government.[15]

As those statements make clear, a troop commander regards the imposition and maintenance of discipline as a matter of utter priority. Dilution of discipline cannot be tolerated. Thus, in the commander's view, military justice cannot afford the individual in the ranks the same rights he would have as a civilian. Civilian criminal law and the courts that administered it existed to punish transgressors. The Uniform Code of Military Justice, on the other hand, existed not only to deal with trans-gressors but to provide a quasi-judicial tool commanders could use to keep their men in line. The system was fitting for combat units in which, as Sherman said, armed men were obliged to obey one man. By the 1970s, however, the military machine was not composed mostly of such units. It was more an industrial bureaucracy than a pure fighting ma-chine. As a result, the UCMJ, as the uniform code was called, came un-der attack for these reasons:

First, despite the efforts of the 1968 reform in the code, there re-mained, the critics in the 1970s charged, far too much command influ-ence in the administration of justice. Prosecutors and defense lawyers were members of a unit commander's staff and beholden to him for their own progress up the ladder. The commander could bar judges from his base and thus exercise some control over who heard cases. He could play a role in the drawing up of panels from which members of the court—the jurors—were chosen.

Second, before cases ever came to trial, commanders could administer so-called Article 15s—nonjudicial punishment. Through this process, many enlisted men, unmindful of their legal rights to counsel and a full hearing, accepted punishment for alleged offenses of which they might be declared innocent in a trial.

Third, commanders exercised wide latitude in ordering men into pretrial confinement which had the effect of punishing them before their cases were ever adjudicated.

Fourth, in its emphasis on maintaining discipline, the system was one that was administered with few exceptions only against enlisted men. The number of officers brought to trial for offenses was extremely small.

These four deficiencies worked against all the enlisted men in the services. The fifth worked only against minority group members. The system, by its lack of blacks and other minority group members administering it, discriminated against blacks—or at least blacks perceived it that way. There were few black judges to hear their cases. There were few black lawyers to represent them. And in the highly polarized world of the 1970s, that only served to increase their distrust of "whitey" and whitey's institutions.

The experiences of Lieutenant William H. Laubenstein, III, the *Stuffed Puffin* publisher, in Iceland as a staff judge advocate, illustrate at least three of those conflicts. In the summer of 1970, Laubenstein was approached by Marine Corporal Harry Mebane, a black, who wanted to know if he had any legal remedy against his commanding officer. Mebane told Laubenstein that the commander had refused to assign black marines to guard duty at the main gate to the Naval station—the only attractive duty open to the marines in Iceland—and had refused to grant the blacks liberty passes to Reykjavik, the country's capital, on the same basis as white marines. Further, Mebane complained, the promotion of black marines above the rank of E-4 on the island appeared to be limited. Before talking to Laubenstein, Mebane had taken his complaint to his Marine commander. After repeated requests, the corporal saw the commander, but no change in policy was made. Then the corporal requested "Captain's Mast," permission to talk to the commanding officer of the U.S. Naval Station at Keflavik, Captain Lloyd H. Thomas. The request, contrary to Navy tradition of granting such meetings, was not honored.

Laubenstein advised Mebane to make a written statement concerning the alleged discrimination and convince his fellow black marines to do likewise to prepare a case for Thomas and Rear Admiral Mayo Hadden, the commander of the Iceland Defense Force. About the same time, the marines wrote to congressmen requesting assistance with their problem, according to Laubenstein. Before the lawyer could present their case, all the black marines were transferred off the island.

Laubenstein said the discrimination against blacks on the island resulted from collusion between the United States government and the Icelandic government. He recalls seeing a memorandum dated September 6, 1964, from the Icelandic government asking that blacks not be permitted to attend a country dance off the base.

Similarly, there was discrimination against Filipinos, he said, that was carried out with the help of the UCMJ. On at least two occasions, he claimed, the government of Iceland orally requested the Navy to transfer Filipinos off the island because of their involvement with Icelandic women. Before each transfer, according to the lawyer, Thomas gave the men nonjudicial (Article 15) punishment on "insubstantial charges" of misconduct such as violation of curfew and pass restrictions, and uniform regulations.

Laubenstein advised the Filipinos not to accept the Article 15 punishment and request a court-martial instead. The suggestion involved a gamble. If not acquitted, they could have received a stiffer penalty. The command, Laubenstein said, put pressure on the two men through their leading petty officer not to go through with the court-martial "for the good of all remaining Filipinos." The two men finally agreed, accepted their punishment and were transferred from the island.

Laubenstein, who was acting as any lawyer would in giving what he thought was best advice to a client, was accused by Thomas of trying to "clog the legal machinery" on the island rather than facilitate justice.

In some cases young lawyers are so much under the thumb of their commanders that they violate the traditional client-attorney relationship to help the commanders out. Under the guise of defending clients, they actually work for the prosecution. One case in point involved Army Captain Lewis S. Horton, a staff judge advocate with the 1st Division stationed in Augsburg, Germany, in 1971.

Horton had been advising a young black private by the name of Eric T. Thompson in connection with a general discharge the youth was receiving. While the discharge procedure was going through the paper mill, Thompson was implicated with two other soldiers in a theft on the base. The Army Criminal Investigations Division (CID) decided to arrest all three men simultaneously so that none would flee. They hit upon the idea of having Thompson summoned to Horton's office, an isolated location on the post, under the ruse that his lawyer wanted Thompson to sign some additional papers.

Thompson answered the summons and Horton kept him waiting in the office until the arresting officers arrived. Then, after charges were preferred against Thompson, Horton was named his defense counsel. At his court-martial, Thompson, who was also represented by a civilian lawyer, said he did not want Horton sitting at the defense table. After he told the judge why, the judge summoned Horton and this colloquy ensued:

JUDGE: You were holding him for the CI, so to speak?

HORTON: Well sir, the situation was that we were supposed to keep all these people here, and I know that they showed up, and the CID didn't show up, so he actually did come into my office, and it was actually that I was under the pretense of shuffling papers. It was just to avoid suspicion that I was in there, shuffling papers, yes, sir. I knew he was going to be arrested and I knew the CID was coming, and I knew the CID was late, and that's why I had to go ahead and bring him into my office.

• • •

JUDGE: Did it cross your mind that this situation could be in conflict when later acting as defense counsel?

HORTON: It did, and at the time I was against the idea. I said, "If you do that, you're going to breach the confidence of the JAGs [judge advocate general's staff] here representing especially the black troops." But the scheme had already been planned at that point, so to speak, and it was more or less, I guess, too late for the command to pull out of the plan. . . . But I was against it all along, and it never would have happened like it did if the CID had showed up on time. But as it happened, I feel like it was a breach of trust, so to speak, as far as the defense counsel in the 1st Infantry Division, and I thought it was bad all along. As I said before, it wouldn't have been so bad if the three individuals would have just showed up and been in the outside office, and then the CID would have been right there and could have made the arrest. But like it was, it was a goof-up, in my opinion.[16]

Interestingly, Horton felt there would have been no breach of trust and nothing wrong in tricking Thompson into coming to the office, allowing the use of the office and his name if he himself had not been physically involved. Subterfuge against a client, he was saying, was permissible as long as it went undiscovered.

With the system stacked against the soldier to the extent that defense and prosecution work hand in glove to fulfill the wishes of the command, it is little wonder that the soldiers refuse to believe that military justice is blind.

Young lawyers in the judge advocate general's office in Washington, doing research for a Defense Department race relations task force, discovered a wide variation in the severity of punishment given black troopers and white for similar offenses. For example, at Fort Hood, Texas, two blacks had narcotics charges placed against them. One, charged with possession and use of heroin, was given five years' imprisonment and a dishonorable discharge. The other, charged with possession and sale of heroin and marijuana, received a seven-year, eleven-month sentence and a dishonorable discharge. Both sentences were arranged in pretrial deals. A white soldier, charged with possession, use, sale and transfer of heroin also received a pretrial deal; his punishment was only two years' imprisonment and a dishonorable discharge. His military background, the young lawyers found, did not differ materially from that of the blacks.

Not only do the blacks get stiffer penalties when cases are adjudicated or on entering guilty pleas, but there are indications that they are also held in pretrial confinement far more often than whites.

Under the UCMJ, a commander can order pretrial confinement of a prisoner only if there is doubt that he will show up for trial, if the offense is particularly serious or if failure to confine the accused might endanger life or property. Army headquarters in Europe studied pretrial confinement figures for the twelve months from October 1970 to September 1971. In most of those months, the number of blacks thus held exceeded the number of whites. In one month, 65 percent of all those in pretrial confinement were blacks. In another month, the figure was 61 percent. In the best month, it was 48 percent. And this despite the fact that blacks made up only 14 percent of the Army population in Europe. The figures show that commanders, who are mostly white, consider blacks less trustworthy and more dangerous than whites.[17] Therefore they are held in custody more often than whites to await trial.

There were efforts underway in the 1970s to break down all this command influence while proving that the military machine could still survive without any resultant dilution in discipline. It could survive, the argument went, in the same way that other bureaucracies—big business, labor, the colleges and universities, the civilian departments of the government—had survived while still affording civil right to its workers. It could survive because, in a modern military machine, the number of men actually asked to shoulder rifles and work the will of one leader is but a small minority of all the men in uniform.

Dozens of young lawyers like Laubenstein, called into service to fulfill their obligations before entering private practice, were working within the system to try to force reforms. Many, like Laubenstein again, suffered harassment for it. (When Laubenstein, after his Iceland experiences, was transferred back to the Pentagon, he was put to work reviewing criminal investigation reports. When he applied for a job in the appeals section of the Navy judge advocate general's office, he was denied the transfer. His fitness report had rendered him unsuitable.) In the Army Judge Advocate General Corps, a group of young lawyers did band together to try to work reforms. Their first goal was to break down the system of command influence.

In addition to those working within the system, there were at least six groups of young lawyers working from outside, representing servicemen in the military justice procedure, making it more difficult for commands to work drumhead justice. These groups were the Lawyers Military Defense Committee, supported by the American Civil Liberties Union Foundation, which had offices in Washington, Cambridge and Saigon; the Center for Constitutional Rights of New York, which had lawyers working in Japan, Okinawa and the Philippines; the National Lawyers Guild, which had lawyers working at several bases in the United States; the American Civil Liberties Union, which supported a small staff in Europe; the Central Committee for Conscientious Objectors, which had a group of counselors traveling circuits of military bases in the United States advising men on how to file C.O. claims; and the National Association for the Advancement of Colored People, which sent black lawyers to Europe to help out accused black soldiers.

The outsiders were not always enthusiastically received. When the Lawyers Military Defense Committee set up shop in Saigon, they were at first refused access to the military transportation and communications systems run by the United States Army in South Vietnam. That meant they had to use commercial facilities and often did not hear of cases until well after their services were needed and could not get to the scene of a trial until after it had ended. The committee broke through that barrier and won rights to use the government facilities. Soon young civilian lawyers began showing up on remote fire bases throughout South Vietnam to counsel and defend their clients.

When Mark Amsterdam, a graduate of the Columbia University Law School, decided in 1970 to leave the Wall Street firm he had joined and take up a military practice on Okinawa with his wife under the sponsorship of the Center for Constitutional Rights, the two were not exactly greeted with open arms. The Marine Command posted pictures at the gates to all its bases with instructions to sentries not to allow them "aboard." The Army Security Agency, according to affidavits submitted with a suit filed by the center, set up surveillance equipment in a room near their office apartment. Criminal investigators established a guard near their office allegedly for the purpose of apprehending AWOLs. The two were denied access to the Army Law Library, except when accompanied by a military lawyer. A Marine staff judge advocate with whom they were working on a case said that since they could not come to his office, he was effectively denied the opportunity to cooperate.

Finally the center filed suit in New York, naming a range of defendants from Defense Secretary Melvin R. Laird and the individual service secretaries down to the staff judge advocates of the four services on Okinawa. After the suits were filed, the Amsterdams' troubles were cleared up. Though revolutionary in outlook—Amsterdam had become an outspoken admirer of Mao Tse-tung—the couple quickly earned the respect not only of enlisted men under charges but also of young officers sensitive to the problems of the enlisted men.

The military could have granted a better measure of civil rights to its men without causing disruption. By not doing so, it only created more problems for itself. As surely as generals and admirals misjudged the capabilities, goals and dedication of the people in Southeast Asia, they misjudged the capabilities, goals and intentions of the young men in their own services. Just as, it can be argued, the United States created its own enemy in Southeast Asia out of a people who could as easily have been friendly or at least of no concern to American interests, the generals and admirals created their own enemies out of American men wearing the uniforms of their own services. It need not have been that way. But the result of exploitation and repression was the consolidation of a beach-head within the services by young radicals who did not stop at calling for the mere reform of the institution. They began to press for its over-throw.

For example, Lieutentant Colonel Edward L. King, a retired Army officer, raised a call for doing away with the service academies. A former serviceman by the name of Andrew Stapp organized the American Servicemen's Union, saying: "We must band together in the fight for an enlisted men's union and show these brass gods who rule us that we are men and not dumb animals."[18]

The men who ran the military machine too often did treat the manpower within the machine like dumb animals, and to that extent, the problems they suffer today they brought upon themselves.

13

THE MILITARY MAFIA

To the typical GI, the oppression of impoverished living conditions and the repression of his individual liberties were palpable. He felt them night and day. If he was at all introspective, he could analyze the effects on his own well-being. If he had strength of mind and character, he could compensate and live, with varying degrees of dissatisfaction and discomfort, within the system. But he lived the life, nonetheless, of an exploited class. There were, in addition to oppression and repression, other forms of exploitation. They were more subtle. For years, they gnawed away at the system and the men within it while nobody noticed.

One was the kind of corruption that has been well known in county courthouses and city halls throughout the nation—cronyism, feeding at the public trough, stealing, cheating, favoritism, protection of the petty thieves by people in high places.

In January 1969, the Marine Corps sent a counter-mortar radar platoon to South Vietnam to help in detecting incoming mortar rounds that were, from time to time, chewing up the base camps and fire bases the Marines had established just south of the demilitarized zone separating North and South Vietnam. The platoon consisted of three teams, each operating a radar set. Each set was powered by an electrical generator without which the equipment could not work in the remote area. Each team had two backup generators to ensure the provision of power needed to keep the sets working.

In March 1969, one of the teams suffered 147 hours of complete shutdown from all three of its generators, rendering the radar useless. By the end of April, all three teams had shut down their radars because the generators were not working. In May, one team was shut down for 180 hours. During June, one team was completely shut down and another was off the line for 68 hours. In July, the command provided each of the teams with a fourth generator. In August, one team was shut down the entire month—all four generators inoperative. In September, one team was down seven days. In October, one team was down for 204 hours, another for 74 hours.

The enemy, of course, continued its mortar barrages throughout all those months. And men were dying from the blasts of the undetected incoming shells.

In October 1970, the Armed Services Investigating Subcommittee of the House Committee on Armed Services began an investigation of the generator problem. In July 1971, it held four days of hearings, and then it issued a report[1] from which all the following information is taken.

The committee learned that the failed generators were from a stock the Marine Corps began ordering from the Consolidated Diesel Electric Company (CONDEC) of Old Greenwich, Connecticut, in 1965. The Corps made the purchases after one of the most rigorous preproduction tests of generators it had ever conducted. Proper operation of the equipment, after all, meant the difference between life and death on the battlefield. The demonstration models supplied by CONDEC worked better than any other generators ever procured by the Defense Department. Eventually the Marine Corps contracted with CONDEC for 5,436 generators at a cost of $18,637,531. The first production models were delivered to the Marines in May 1967. There was a big difference between the production models and the sample generators on which the Marines had based their tests. On June 30, the Marines received word from the Defense Contract Administration Service that all thirty of the first sets were so poorly built that they had been returned to CONDEC. The problem was poor quality control, which CONDEC promised to correct. In August 1967, the Marines shipped two of the repaired generators to the Raytheon Corporation in Andover, Massachusetts, to provide a power source for radar equipment Raytheon was building for the Marines. Raytheon could not start the first set tried. Examination showed that loose screws were short-circuiting a printed circuit board. Finally the set did start, but it did not work well. A faulty transistor was discovered in the electronics. The second set had printed circuit board difficulties that required repair. Trouble continued to plague the two generators throughout the fall of 1967. In June 1968, one of the generators at Raytheon began to run overspeed, and finally it just exploded.

Meanwhile, other CONDEC generators had been shipped to an RCA plant in New Jersey for other radar tests. Those were so poor that RCA could not test its equipment. They found poor quality control in the CONDEC generators at fault. Fuel tanks split; wires frayed; circuit boards cracked and flaked; resistors burned out; the engines surged; the circuitry went out of alignment.

In spite of all the problems, the Marine Corps continued to buy the CONDEC generators and in fact exercised an option in November 1967 to increase the order.

In 1968, before the counter-mortar radar platoon arrived in South Vietnam, the Marines shipped 330 of the generators there for use by other units. By May 1968, all 330 generators were out of order.

In July 1969, CONDEC agreed to develop a "product improvement program" at its own expense. The program did not improve the product. In April 1970, the Marine Corps undertook its own program and developed a kit to improve the generators. Modified, the generators were now giving improved service. By then, the Marines were beginning to pull out of Vietnam. The improvement program cost $1.6 million. The Marines footed the bill.

What happened?

It turns out that CONDEC's lawyer in Washington was a man named Daniel Ross, a marine in World War II who later became an officer in the Marine Reserve Battalion in Washington. During that reserve service, Ross met and befriended two other marines, Jennings McLain and Ronald Gemmell. Called to active duty during the Korean War, Ross and McLain worked together in the procurement division at Marine Corps headquarters for about a year. Then, in December 1951, Ross returned to civilian life and began representing clients doing business with the Marines. McLain remained in the procurement division as a civilian after the reserve unit stood down from active duty, and eventually became director of the division. He retired from federal service in October 1969. In January 1970, he went to work for Ross on a retainer of five hundred dollars a month.

Gemmell was assigned to the procurement division in December 1952 and remained there, first as an active-duty officer until 1963 and then, after retiring from the Marines, as the civilian assistant director of the division. During that time, he became a partner with Ross in the Quorum Land Corporation.

Another employee of the division was Daniel Elmore, who got his job in 1962 after Ross suggested to him that he apply. Ross and Elmore maintained, over the years, business and social relationships. Elmore, for example, owned stock in a company represented by Ross that had contracts from the Marine Corps. Meanwhile, Ross had a highly placed associate outside the contract procurement division. He was Arthur Neuman, assistant counsel to the Commandant of the Marine Corps. Neuman went to that job from a position in Ross's law firm in 1967. His name remained on the letterhead of the law firm for ten months after he left. As assistant counsel to the Corps Commandant, Neuman purchased 200 shares of stock in CONDEC as well as 150 shares of stock in the Mite Corporation, another firm represented in Washington by Ross which had claims before the Corps. Among Neuman's duties was the rendering of legal opinions for the Marines on these claims.

In December 1967, after the trouble with CONDEC's generators was apparent, McLain, Gemmell and Elmore attended a meeting with several other officials to consider the award of a new contract for a series of bigger generators. CONDEC had been one of twenty-three companies asked by the Marine Corps to bid on the proposal. It turned in the third-lowest bid. The meeting was to consider all three bids. Present at the session was Daniel Ross, the only bidder's attorney allowed in the room. Ross summed up all the proposals and recommended that CONDEC receive the award. When Doral Hupp, another official, objected, McLain, the man in charge, ordered him to "shut up." Hupp subsequently wrote a memorandum describing the meeting for the file. The memo disappeared.

While all this was going on, Elmore was using a credit card and borrowing a car from another firm doing business with the Corps and represented by Ross. On a couple of occasions, Elmore and/or Neuman stayed in hotels at the expense of a Ross-represented firm. Elmore also owned stock in the firm, the G. C. Dewey Corporation. When the House Armed Services subcommittee asked to see the records of Elmore's stock holdings, he answered that he could not remember the name of his broker, who apparently had them.

Discussing this "tangled web of contractor influence," the subcommittee said it found "a flagrant disregard for the conflict-of-interest

statutes by several Marine Corps people, and, at least neglectful supervision by the Commandant, Headquarters, U.S. Marine Corps." Part of
the reason, according to the committee report, was Ross's influence in
high places.

Captain Thomas O'Brien, head of the Radar Section of the Technical Division (who himself accepted favors from a Ross client) told the
committee he once referred to Ross as "a shyster." Within thirty minutes
he was called before the quartermaster general of the Corps who, he
said, "gave me hell." According to the committee report:

> O'Brien also testified that Ross was reputed to be able to
> work irreparable damage to the career of a Marine Corps
> officer. He further stated that he believed Ross could influence
> the transfer of Marine officers. With such a reputation, it is no
> wonder that Ross was so successful in his dealings with
> Marine Corps personnel. That reputation also appears to have
> provided an umbrella as immunity for his protege, Mr.
> Elmore.[2]

In its report detailing all this, the House committee referred to the
situation as "petty corruption in low places." It said, "the persons involved might be classified as minor public officials, yet they effectively
controlled the spending of millions of taxpayers' dollars. Corruption,
however, requires corruptionists, and this report documents their method
of operation in the several Marine Corps procurement cases investi-
gated by this Subcommittee."[3]

You might wonder why the subcommittee did not go further in
looking into the operations of Daniel Ross and his friends. Why, for
example, did it not try to find out whether Ross really could influence
the careers of Marine Corps officers? How did Ross's associate come
to be named assistant counsel to the Marine Corps Commandant? Why
did the quartermaster general silence a complaining young officer?

One reason the subcommittee may have soft-pedaled its investigation is that John Russell Blandford, who was then still staff director for
the parent House Armed Services Committee, was himself the highest-
ranking man in the Marine Corps reserve. He held the rank of major
general and once admitted to an interviewer that, though he had worked
hard to achieve promotion as far as lieutenant colonel, the rest of the
steps up the ladder were probably conferred because of his position on
the committee.

271

When "Russ" Blandford retired from the staff director's job in 1972, he was eligible for two pensions, one from his twenty-six years of service on a congressional committee and one from his years in the Marine Corps both as an active-duty enlisted man and officer, and as a reserve officer. Blandford is only one of thousands of retired military men or reserves working on Capitol Hill or in the Civil Service who help to shade the distinction between the military and its civilian masters. In 1971, 118 members of Congress also held reserve commissions, ranging up to Air Force Reserve Major General Barry M. Goldwater, the senator from Arizona and 1964 Republican presidential candidate. Goldwater was one of fifteen senators and congressmen in 1971 who received military pensions for their service in the reserves in addition to their legislators' salaries.

In April 1971, a federal district judge, ruling on a suit brought in 1970 by the Reservists Committee to Stop the War, declared it unconstitutional for members of Congress to hold reserve commissions. Judge Gehard A. Gesell said the framers of the Constitution

> erected an inflexible barrier against Congressmen holding or being appointed to any other office under the United States. Moreover, given the enormous involvement of Congress in matters affecting the military, the potential conflict between an office in the military and an office in Congress is not inconsequential.[4]

The Judge, however, stayed an order requiring congressmen either to give up their elected offices or their commissions pending a government appeal. In late 1971, the Justice Department filed an appeal. In late 1972, the case had still not yet been heard by the Federal Court of Appeals, and the prospect, assuming a further appeal to the Supreme Court, was that there would not be a final determination of the case until late 1973 or 1974. Meanwhile, the military continued to enjoy the patronage of powerful men and women serving in dual roles on Capitol Hill. The 1971 *Congressional Quarterly* study showed that thirty-two senators holding reserve commissions included six out of twenty-four members of the Senate Appropriations Committee, ten of the sixteen members of the Armed Services Committee (including all but one of the Republican members) and two of the nine members of the Veterans' Affairs Committee. The eighty-six representatives in the reserves included twelve of the forty-one members of the Armed Services Committee, seven of the twenty-six members of the Veterans' Affairs Committee and four of the eleven members of the Appropriations Defense Subcommittee.

Throughout the Civil Service there were men such as McLain and Gemmell of the Marine Corps contract procurement division who were former military men. Many of them were drawing two government paychecks, one as a military retiree and another as a civil servant. They were in positions not only to influence defense decisions but also to hire friends and promote them. In areas of high military concentration such as Norfolk, Virginia, and San Diego, California, they made up as much as 20 percent of the Civil Service work force on military installations. They were present in large numbers in the Agency for International Development which administered the foreign aid program.

A House of Representatives manpower subcommittee began investigating this situation in 1971 and indicated it would hold hearings to expose the "invasion" of the Civil Service by military retirees. But somehow, the politically explosive subject was never aired, and in 1972, Bun Bray, the staff director for the subcommittee, who headed the investigation, resigned to take a lobbyist's job with the National Association of Supervisors, which represents workers in a supervisory capacity in the federal government. There was so little interest in seeing the investigation succeed that in more than a year of probing, the subcommittee could not even establish just how many retired military men worked in the Civil Service.

All that interrelationship between the military and its civilian master provided a fertile ground in which the seeds of conflict of interest—petty corruption by minor officials as the House report on the Marine Corps put it—could flourish like weeds in an untended flower bed. The gardeners really had little interest in keeping the bed free.

In this kind of atmosphere, other corruption—petty and grand alike—flourished. It even crept into that most sedate and respected organization, the USO. For generations stretching back to the earliest days of World War II, the United Service Organization, supported by Community Chest contributions, had been well known for its kindly women dispensing coffee, crullers and smiles to American GIs around the world with all the homey simplicity of the lady next door in small-town America. On April 14, 1972, Defense Secretary Melvin R. Laird released the text of a letter he had written to Congress indicating that those paragons of hometown virtue were no longer what they used to be.

Laird's letter disclosed that the Defense Department had uncovered evidence of fraud, currency manipulation and black market activities by USO officials in Vietnam involving "very substantial sums of money." The Defense Secretary said he was extending the investigation from Vietnam to all other areas where the USO operated and had asked the Internal Revenue Service to take part in the check. For its part, the USO issued a statement saying the illicit activities were those of "certain former USO personnel in Vietnam."

A few days after the Laird letter was released, Representative Les Aspin, a Democrat from Wisconsin, began issuing a series of statements making specific charges against USO employees. The Aspin charge included the following:

—a Marine Staff Sergeant, Lloyd Handy, admitted to a former U.S.O. professional staff member, that: "he and Bob (Robert Rawson, former director of U.S.O. in Northern Vietnam) had gotten 11 air-conditioners and sold them on the black market."

—cigarettes donated by local veterans organizations to the U.S.O. for free distribution to American GIs were sold on the black market.

—Robert Rawson allegedly stole gift packages sent to individual GIs in Vietnam. U.S.O.'s top official, Sam Anderson, was informed of Rawson's stealing but apparently nothing was done to stop Rawson.

—some air conditioners, instead of being sold on the black market, may have been illegally traded by U.S.O. personnel to American civilians and military officials.

—U.S.O. club's director in Dian, Floyd Seller, who constantly bragged about making a fortune in Vietnam, allegedly received kickbacks from concession owners.

—According to one former U.S.O. assistant director, "The GIs were being cheated blind." Allegedly, items in U.S.O. concessions were overpriced by as much as 300% to 400%.

—According to one of Aspin's informants, Richard Alexander, former director of Tan Son Nhut U.S.O., made over $2 million in Vietnam.

—An assistant club director was not permitted to examine invoices and inventories of an alleged illegal private concession run by Richard Alexander. A U.S.O. staffer who hoped to collect furniture for GI drug treatment half-way houses was barred access to U.S.O.'s warehouse on three separate occasions by Brian Sweeney, a top U.S.O. official. Normally, all U.S.O. professional staffers could inspect the warehouse.

In addition, Aspin leveled charges at the USO's executive director, Sam Anderson, quoting a Mike Moriarty, a former USO staff aide and security guard, to the effect that

—Anderson was made aware of the stealing of gifts and packages sent by U.S. companies to Vietnam;

—He [Moriarty] was told by two other U.S.O. officials—Judy Grenburg and Shirley Warner—that Anderson benefitted from a 35% rake-off collected from concessionaires by U.S.O. Saigon director Chuck LaMoy. He [Moriarty] personally saw LaMoy's books which revealed the 35% rake off;

—Anderson sponsored, either personally or with U.S.O. funds, a Vietnamese singing group, giving them $3,000 worth of equipment and automobiles valued at $10,000. While U.S.O. personnel used a broken down Scout, the Vietnamese singers had brand new cars.

And then Aspin released information based on a statement by Gloria Lentz, a former associate director of a USO club in Vietnam, charging that

—A rental agreement made by U.S.O.'s top official involved the payment of a $500 check and $500 in cash under the table. Half of the check was in turn given to the Viet Cong as protection payments by the Vietnamese landlord.

—Protection kickbacks were also paid to the Vietnamese national police commonly known as the "white mice."

—A well-known Vietnamese prostitute was kept on the U.S.O. payroll at an unusual high salary and regularly "visited" a U.S. advisory team next door to the U.S.O. club.

—Ms. Lentz saw an illegal gun exchange take place at a U.S.O. club in China Beach.[5]

"These allegations and Secretary Laird's announcement of a major investigation of USO seems to confirm that the American people, and particularly our GIs in Vietnam, have been victimized by a bunch of crooks," Aspin said. At another point, he added, "Alleged protection kickbacks to the VC and Vietnamese police as well as prostitutes and drug pushers on the payroll are clearly a misappropriation of the funds so generously given by the American people to the USO."

While there was evidence of this kind of hanky-panky with the USO, a House Armed Services subcommittee was also looking into irregularities concerning another supposed source of recreation for American troops —the service clubs, hobby shops and sports facilities operated on American bases for the benefit of GIs. Whereas the USO operated on a budget of only $6 million a year, the service-operated facilities did $6 billion worth of business each year. And their profits were supposed to be reinvested for the welfare of the troops. Instead, the subcommittee discovered that much of the profit was being sent back to Washington for investment by central welfare funds. In 1972, these funds had $137 million invested in gilt-edged securities such as Treasury bonds and instruments of the Export-Import Bank, the Federal National Mortgage Association and other government programs.

Though it might have represented sound business practice for an institution to treat its profits with such care, the funds thus invested were doing nothing to help the troops who had contributed the money through their purchases in the club system. Major General Leo E. Benade, deputy assistant defense secretary for military personnel policy, told the subcommittee that part of the problem was that no one could figure out how to spend the money. He said that of the $96 million which the Army had contributed to the central funds, $16 million came from local clubs and messes which wanted the money invested, and another $50 million had been made available to local commands, but the latter had not spent it. Apparently no one in the organization running the clubs and messes thought to suggest price decreases as an answer to the problem.

Meanwhile, the huge accumulations presented a temptation. Brigadier General James W. Gunn, chief of the Army Audit Agency, told the subcommittee that a recent (in 1972) audit of 298 service clubs showed that 209 had some kind of irregularity, ranging from a lack of controls to actual shortages. Between October 1, 1970, and March 31, 1972, there had been seventy-one "Blue Bell Reports" (serious incidents) regarding club funds.

Navy Captain Robert W. Thompson, acting auditor general to the Navy, said he had found relatively few problems in club management and slot machine controls. (Until 1972, slot machines were the principal source of income for the clubs. They were ordered out of the clubs as a result of the "service clubs and PX scandals," about which there will be more shortly.) Although there was no wide-scale corruption in the Marine Corps club and mess system, Thompson did point out such individual problem cases as these:

—unauthorized sale to a Vietnamese firm of seven air conditioners valued at $2,000.

—three cases of forged slot-machine jackpot payment certificates totaling $2,328.

—manipulation of slot machines.

—falsified pay records involving less than $100.

—illegal purchases of liquor.[6]

The testimony was enough to pique the interest of the subcommittee. It authorized a more detailed investigation which was still continuing in late 1972. Chances were, however, that it would not uncover anything as sordid as the PX, service club and black market scandals which the Permanent Investigations Subcommittee of the Senate Government Operations Committee uncovered in 1969, 1970 and 1971.

The Senate subcommittee's investigation lasted two years. Staff members pursued their leads in Vietnam, Japan, Hong Kong, Singapore, Thailand, Malaysia, Indonesia, the Philippines, Okinawa, West Germany and many American cities. They amassed thousands of pages of documents and affidavits. Then the subcommittee held thirty-five days of hearings, taking testimony from seventy-eight witnesses. When it was all over, the subcommittee published 1,791 pages of testimony, reprinted in seven slim volumes, that raise grave questions about the extent to which the notion of duty-honor-country has been abused by the men who run the military machine. That hearing record does nothing less

than paint a picture of organized crime within the United States mili-·
tary machine. It exposes a ring of military veterans ranging from generals down to top noncommissioned officers who protected each other,
enriched themselves, defrauded the government, worked at cross-purposes with the Vietnam War effort, received favors from civilians, helped
these civilians circumvent military regulations and cheated thousands of
GIs by controlling the slot-machine business in the services' enlisted
men's clubs. One of the many startling elements in all this was that the
organized crime ring enjoyed the protection of the United States Army's
top cop. And he gave that protection because he did not want to embarrass the Chief of Staff of the Army.

The "top cop" involved in all this was Major General Carl C. Turner,
who, in the late 1960s, was to law enforcement in the Army what the
late J. Edgar Hoover was to law enforcement in civilian society—and
then some. As provost marshal general of the Army, Turner controlled
not only all his service's criminal investigators (the Army's detectives)
but its military policemen (beat patrolmen) and stockades (jails and
prisons) as well. Turner was a figure so highly regarded that, shortly
after Richard M. Nixon assumed the Presidency with a campaign promise of restoring law and order, he enlisted the major general's help in
the fight against crime. On March 18, 1969, the White House announced Turner's appointment as chief of the United States Marshal
Services. It was to be Turner's job to revitalize the marshals, who had
been mostly political appointees previously, and make them into an
efficient force.

Before the appointment was announced, the FBI performed a full
field investigation on the general. It spoke not only to several of Turner's
associates in the Army but it reviewed his service record, checked Army
files for copies of criminal investigations against him, checked with the
House of Representatives Internal Security Committee (presumably to
determine if Turner had communist leanings), and cleared him with
the Office of the Secretary of Defense, the Central Intelligence Agency,
the Civil Service Commission, the Veterans Administration, the Internal
Revenue Service and the Secret Service. Turner, the FBI determined,
was clean.

In fact, he was not clean at all. For years, as an avid gun collector,
he had been clandestinely collecting confiscated weapons and reselling

278

them to a North Carolina gun dealer at a profit. In a typical transaction, he would ask the Chicago Police Department to turn over weapons it had collected from criminals, saying that he used them in lectures he gave about gun control to boy scout groups or that he planned to donate them to Army museums. Instead, the major general, perhaps after repairing them, sold them to the Pine State Gun Shop in Fayetteville, North Carolina.

After the major general learned that the Senate subcommittee was investigating his gun transactions, he amended his income tax returns from 1964 to 1968 to show that he had earned a profit of $6,800 in his gun transactions. The subcommittee never could learn for certain just exactly how much the major general did earn, because in July 1969, when the investigation was under way, the major general either lost or had stolen from him the record book relating to his gun dealings. He drew up a new book from memory just before he was called to testify before the subcommittee. But the subcommittee did determine from the North Carolina gun dealer's records that between April 1966 and February 1969 the major general received sixteen checks totaling $4,450.90 for gun transactions. Federal agents, according to the subcommittee report, found some indications that Pine State was in turn selling weapons to an organization of revolutionaries in Haiti. The subcommittee did not develop that point during its hearings.[7]

Just before the hearings opened, the chief marshal of the United States was fired by the Justice Department.* Subsequently, on the basis of information developed by the subcommittee, he was indicted for violating federal gun-control and income-tax laws. He entered a guilty plea on the gun-control charges and a no-contest plea on the income-tax

---

* The Nixon Administration was spared the embarrassment of learning about Turner's malfeasance at the same time as the public by Clark R. Mollenhoff, a Pulitzer-Prize-winning newsman who joined the White House staff with duties which included those of ombudsman. Mollenhoff learned that the Senate subcommittee was on to Turner through his well-developed contacts on Capitol Hill. Checking at the Pentagon, he confirmed Turner's culpability. But he also found that the military minimized the seriousness of the crimes. He then informed Turner's new employers at the Justice Department of the situation. They also minimized the crimes and the urgency of the matter. Mollenhoff persisted and was able to secure the firing of Turner and the well-publicized public announcement of the action before the subcommittee exposed the major general. Thus the administration was able to recoup somewhat on its blunder in not investigating Turner thoroughly enough in the first place.

charges and was sentenced to three years and three months in prison. On September 18, 1972, after serving one third of that term, he was freed on parole.

Turner's gun dealings were petty larceny in comparison with the tens or hundreds of thousands of dollars that others were making in organized crime within the Army, and though he went to jail for those gun dealings, he was far more culpable in the view of Senate investigators for his cover-up of the activities of others—Sergeant Major of the Army William O. Wooldridge, for example.

When Bill Wooldridge was sworn in as the first Sergeant Major of the United States Army in history on July 11, 1966, he was widely known as "a shining example" of all that is best in the military. The Army's Chief of Staff, General Harold K. Johnson, was so impressed with the new top-ranking enlisted man that he mustered the Old Guard and the United States Army Band on the Pentagon Mall to give color to the swearing-in ceremony, and he and Wooldridge reviewed the troops.

Little did the general know of Wooldridge's background. But even while the forty-three-year-old sergeant major was swearing on a Bible to uphold the Constitution of the United States, the Senate subcommittee record indicates he was scheming with several other senior sergeants in the Army to form a corporation that would sell food, beverages and other items to service clubs in Vietnam. The beauty of the scheme was that some of the members of the corporation were also the managers of the clubs which would make the purchases.

The Wooldridge group all came together in the early 1960s when they were stationed in the 24th Infantry Division at Augsburg, Germany. At that time, Wooldridge was the command sergeant major of the division. Other NCOs working in the division under him were Sergeants Narvaez Hatcher, William Higdon, Seymour ("Sandy") Lazar, Theodore ("Sam") Bass, William C. Bagby and John C. Nelson. Many of these men were "custodians"—executive directors or managers—of noncommissioned officers' clubs and chains of clubs at the time. In November 1967, Wooldridge, Hatcher, Higdon and Lazar formed the Maredem Company to sell goods to service clubs in Vietnam. At that time, Wooldridge was still Sergeant Major of the Army, Hatcher and Higdon were running club systems in Vietnam (Higdon at the huge Long Binh Post outside Saigon and Hatcher, all the clubs in the 1st Infantry Division) and Lazar, having retired from the Army a few months before, became the chief executive officer with headquarters in Hong Kong of Maredem at a salary of $24,000 a year. Bass, who also retired, subsequently joined Maredem as the firm's representative in Saigon.

But all this jumps ahead of the story.

The sergeants had been talking about forming such a corporation for years. A German auditor overheard some of them discussing the possibility in an Augsburg club in 1965. Even by then, they realized they had a good thing going.

The bread-and-butter portion of the Maredem sergeants' business in the early 1960s was gambling. At that time—and, in fact, until after the Senate subcommittee finished its investigation—clubs in all the services were supported by the revenue from slot machines stationed on the premises. The slots were played compulsively by men of all ranks, their wives, sweethearts and friends. Supposedly the machines were set to return most of the money to men in payoffs but to keep a "reasonable" percentage (30 to 40 percent in Army clubs, 15 percent in Navy clubs) to defray the cost of running the clubs. In that manner, the servicemen paid for the operation of the clubs themselves, and no funds came out of the taxpayers' pockets for this purpose. Realizing the possibilities for thievery in this setup, the services each established elaborate controls for the clearing of the machines and accounting for the proceeds. Jackpot payments, for example, had to be recorded, and the machines could only be cleared at specified times with at least two people present. The keys to the machines were carefully controlled so that, theoretically, no one could tamper with them.

It was against the background of all these controls that Sergeant Major Kenneth L. Parrent, newly promoted to his grade and newly assigned to an engineering battalion in the 24th Infantry Division in September 1963, walked out of his office in the Henry Caserne in Munich to survey his new domain. His gaze alighted on an American in civilian clothes carrying two buckets of coins. Parrent watched as the American walked to a civilian car, opened the trunk and placed the buckets inside. Stopping the man, Parrent asked for an explanation. The American identified himself as Sergeant William Higdon and explained that he had just cleared the slot machines in a nearby club and was taking the proceeds to be counted. Parrent said the procedure looked irregular. Higdon answered that this was the way it was done in the area. Checking with a superior, Parrent was advised that Higdon was "all right," and he let the sergeant go.

Within minutes, Parrent received a call from a man identifying himself as "Sam-the-hatchet-man," who told him he was "out in the field": that he was wrong to be suspicious of Higdon, who was Bill Wooldridge's boy. Sam-the-hatchet-man was Sergeant Major Sam Goldstein, Wooldridge's assistant in the 24th.

Because of his position, Parrent was named one of sixteen members of the Board of Governors of the 24th NCO club system. He soon came to realize that Wooldridge, on taking over as command sergeant major, had fired most of the men operating the 24th's NCO club system and replaced them with his own appointees. Hatcher was the operating head of the system. The board was merely a rubber stamp.

As Parrent sat at the meetings, he began to notice problems. Hatcher, for example, would bring up a $24,000 item for entertainment, saying "I need a motion; I need a second; I need a vote," to which the board would chorus, after each request, "You got it." It was only on the small items—$50 to $300—that Hatcher would permit discussion.

Troubled, Parrent, after he had been on the job a month or two, discussed the situation with Goldstein, who told him that kind of operation was needed on the board to run a smooth club system.

"When I left Goldstein's office," Parrent later told a criminal investigator, "it had not occurred to me that something was wrong with the system. I never gave it a thought that something might be wrong because to me Bill Wooldridge was a shining example of the best soldier in the United States Army and Goldstein, being his second in command, I had no reason to question either one of them."

Later, he did have reason to question. He saw wrong in the fact that he was not allowed to pay his bills when he visited the clubs. He thought it wrong that Hatcher, who held the grade of E-6, was chauffeured about in a club-owned car by an E-7. At one point, he discovered a $50,000 check paid to a firm in Liechtenstein for no apparent reason. At another point, after the board had voted not to use soft-drink dispensing machines sold by a firm called Carbo-Mix, he discovered that Hatcher had installed the machines anyhow. And finally, studying a financial statement which showed a $12,000 loss during a year in which over $1 million in revenue had been collected, he decided something was amiss.

Parrent wrote a letter to the board detailing all his complaints in 1964. He read the letter, he was thanked and then the meeting adjourned without any discussion. A few days later he was informed that the division inspector general had personally examined the club records and found nothing amiss. Shortly after that, about a year before his tour was to have ended, Parrent was transferred back to the United States. That was the beginning of five and a half years of harassment for Parrent. He was transferred from post to post as, somehow, word got to his superiors that he was unreliable. "My kids began saying to me, 'Dad, you can't be a very good soldier. If you're a good soldier, how come you are always being transferred so much,'" Parrent told me in 1972. At that time, even after Wooldridge and his cronies had been exposed and indicted, Parrent was still suffering, waiting out the time until he could retire in 1973 after serving in combat in three wars.

Only one man took Parrent's 1964 charges seriously. He was Major William L. George, the NCO club system's adviser. George read Parrent's letter and decided to conduct an informal investigation. He found some irregularities which, he later testified before the Senate subcommittee, he reported to Major General William Cunningham, the 24th's commanding general. Cunningham took no action.

Then, one Saturday night in the fall of 1964, after George completed an inspection tour of the division's NCO clubs with Wooldridge, Hatcher and two other sergeants, they all went to one of the clubs where one of the sergeants opened the safe and removed $1,000 in $20 bills. The group repaired to the Eva Bar in downtown Munich where they ran up a $700 tab for champagne and other drinks for themselves, entertainers and bar girls. The following Monday, George offered Wooldridge $150 as his share of the tab. Wooldridge refused the cash. George reported the incident to Cunningham, fearful that club funds had been used. The major general checked with Wooldridge and then told George that seventeen club sergeants had chipped in $25 each to finance the night on the town. George did not believe his commanding general.

He continued his informal investigation, concentrating now on slot machines. Tracing records of receipts back five years in the eleven clubs, he discovered that the gross of the one hundred slot machines in the system dropped from $60,000 a month to $30,000 a month at the time that Hatcher took over as the man in charge of the system. George compared this with bar and food sales which had not changed, and decided the drop-off in slot-machine receipts was significant. He found some machines that were fixed so that they would not register high-paying combinations.

He also took note of the fact that Hatcher's office was the equivalent of the commanding general's in plushness and that Hatcher owned a Cadillac. Another sergeant in the system drove a Mercedes, and still another, Bass, had two cars and had purchased a big diamond for his wife.

Repeatedly, George reported his suspicions to his superior officers. By now he was convinced that Hatcher and other sergeants were stealing $40,000 a month from the club system. The division chief of staff would listen and then either report to Cunningham or have George himself brief the major general.

Cunningham would listen and give a variety of replies: "Thank you, I will look into it." "Thank you, we will study it." "Thank you very much, you are doing a good job; keep it up."

But never would Cunningham order an official investigation.

At one point, George appointed a trusted sergeant to clear the slot machines for ten days at only one club. During that period, receipts rose from the $4,000 which Hatcher had recently been reporting for an entire month to $10,000 for the ten-day period. The trusted sergeant was offered bribes and women to forgo honesty, and when this failed, he was threatened. The ten-day test resulted in the relief of the club manager. George implemented reform measures, and subsequently Hatcher was transferred out of the club system. But no punitive action was taken against him.

During this period, George grew curious over how Hatcher had managed to remain stationed in Germany eleven years when the normal tour was three and rarely longer than five. He asked Hatcher, and the sergeant replied, according to George's testimony, " 'I would return to the States every three years or after a tour, go to the Pentagon, pay an enlisted man in the assignment section $300 to $500 for a return trip to Europe. I never stayed in the States between tours more than three or four months.' " George continued, "This may not be the exact words he used but the information is precise."[8]

Now George was making some headway. In January 1965, after serving seven years in Germany, Wooldridge was transferred back to Fort Riley, Kansas, where he became sergeant major of the 1st Infantry Division (which shortly thereafter shipped out to Vietnam), and Major General Edward L. Rowny succeeded Cunningham as commanding general of the 24th Division.

Several months later, George received an anonymous letter detailing how the slot machines were still being skimmed. On September 3,

1965, he intercepted a man identified in the hearings only as "Sergeant Jones," manager of the Sheridan Caserne NCO club in Augsburg, clearing a machine. Jones's tally was $654.10 less than it should have been. He was arrested, charged and three months later, court-martialed. Convicted, he was sentenced to a year in the Army stockade at Dachau and demoted from staff sergeant to private. After he served three months, he was released and transferred to Fort Dix, New Jersey, where, in September 1966, he was given a hardship discharge under honorable conditions after thirteen years of service.

As it turned out, George had apprehended only one of the little fish in the operation. Jones later told the Senate subcommittee how he got into the racket.

Wishing to supplement his staff sergeant's income, Jones had applied for a job as a master-at-arms in one of the clubs at a dollar an hour.* He subsequently rose through the ranks, becoming an assistant manager and then manager of the Sheridan Caserne Club, through appointments by Bass and Hatcher. As a manager, he was eligible to participate in the skimming of the slots. He got his cut for ten months before he was caught. He told the subcommittee that typically he would empty the machines in the club twice a week, each time reporting receipts for fifty dollars less than he actually took out. Bass would come by to pick up the money, allow Jones to keep fifteen dollars, and take the rest. Once, when Jones complained about his share, Bass told him, according to testimony, "this money took care of many people. He said that this was a good thing and as long as I went along, I would come out ahead."[9]

During Jones's tenure as a skimmer, Bass was replaced by Lazar, another partner in the future Maredem venture. Jones continued to

---

* Uniformed employees of the clubs, whether part or full time, received their Army salaries in addition to salaries paid by the clubs and set by the custodians. Hatcher, for example, in the grade of sergeant first class, including all allowances, received $5,760.82 a year from the government in the early 1960s. He doubled that by paying himself a monthly salary of $498.75 from the 24th NCO club system. This was at the rate of $1.75 an hour for 285 hours' work each month. He paid himself that salary even while on leave in the United States or as a patient in an Army hospital. This "legitimate" income was, of course, in addition to his take from skimming slots, taking kickbacks on purchases and pocketing money he took from the clubs to make repairs on facilities—repairs which, after he took the money, he would have done for nothing by Army personnel using Army materials on Army time. Hatcher would then secure receipts purporting to show that he had spent the money.

make his payoffs. He estimated for the subcommittee that the rake-offs, less the shares of the little men such as himself, from all eleven clubs in the division ran to $7,000 or $8,000 a week for the men "upstairs." At one point, Jones testified, all the club managers and assistant managers were assessed $200 each by Bass. The resulting $3,000 in contributions, he said, was presented to Wooldridge as a going-away gift.

When Jones was apprehended, he testified, he was warned not to implicate others in the slot-machine skimming. The other sergeants provided him with a lawyer who also told him to take the rap himself. He did. Another sergeant paid $600 of Jones's $700 legal fee.*

During the three months between the apprehension of Jones and his court-martial, Major George's life was not easy. He received threatening or abusive phone calls three or four times a week. One, at 2:30 in the morning, threatened, "You're dead, you bastard you." Another time, the caller, speaking to Mrs. George, related correctly the exact time the George children got off a school bus, and threatened them.

But the Jones case did convince Cunningham's successor, Major General Rowny, that a formal investigation was needed, as George had been suggesting for months. The Army's Criminal Investigation Division, at that time directed by Turner, was called in. CID Agent Irvin E. Beard, a warrant officer, arrived in the 24th Infantry Division in the fall of 1965 to begin his investigation of the clubs.

It was not an easy job. At that time, the eleven clubs employed 475 workers and did a business of $12 million annually in food, drinks, slot machines, entertainment and the like. The clubs were situated in the Augsburg-Munich area. To do a thorough job would have required a team of investigators. Beard was forced to work mostly alone with only occasional help. Not surprisingly, his efforts did not have high priority.

Beard began with Major George's allegations, the Parrent letter, another letter from a civilian supplier who felt the club system's management was dishonest, and the files of the 24th's own MPs. It turned out that the MPs had collected information of their own about club problems which had never been acted upon by Major General Cunningham.

---

* Because Jones had served his punishment and was trying to establish a new life in civilian society, Senator Ribicoff, the Senate subcommittee acting chairman, agreed to keep his identity confidential, using only his last name.

Jones's arrest and Beard's investigation made the slot-machine skimmers cautious. They made, the detective later testified, an "intense effort" to "slow down" the play in an attempt to show that Jones was the only culprit. Machines that had worked for years suddenly broke down. Club managers suddenly ran out of change. Reported monthly profits increased from $15,708.12 in the month before Jones's arrest to $41,651.60 after the arrest. Beard was not fooled.

From a statistical analysis of slot-machine records he determined that someone was stealing between $300,000 and $350,000 a year from the soldiers of the 24th. He discovered one revealing "coincidence" indicating how brazen the skimmers were. In the year 1962, gross receipts for the slots in the system repeated themselves, down to the penny, every six months thusly: January, $18,887.50, and July, $18,-887.50; February, $16,325, and August, $16,325; March, $16,945, and September, $16,945; April, $14,172.50, and October, $14,172.50; May, $19,150, and November, $19,150.

Beard estimated the odds at "20 billion to one" that such a coincidence could actually occur.[10]

It did not take Beard long to reach the conclusion that Major General Cunningham, the departed division commander, had covered up the situation in the 24th. Studying the records, he determined that the commanding general, even before Major George's informal investigation, had had ample evidence to call in the CID. The detective told the subcommittee he also "came to the firm conclusion that Sgt. Maj. William O. Wooldridge, the division sergeant major, had effective control of the club system and that all assignments to jobs within it had to be approved by him. He was well catered to by club personnel and obviously was a person of power and influence among them."[11]

While Beard was at work in the 24th, Bill Wooldridge was named Sergeant Major of the Army, moving into an office next door to the Chief of Staff. If Beard saw the press reports of that big day in Wooldridge's life, he must have chuckled at the irony. After Wooldridge reviewed the Old Guard and received the congratulations of such dignitaries as General Harold K. Johnson, Chief of Staff, and Army Secretary Stanley Resor, he moved to his new Pentagon office and held a press conference. "I hope to assist the enlisted men of the Army," he told the reporters. "I want to know if they have any problems, and I intend to listen to them."

Beard's job continued, with frustrations. Sergeant John Nelson admitted taking part in the skimming but refused to talk. He said the others in the ring might kill him. The detective found "expertly doctored records." He was stymied by the transfer of key figures out of the 24th. And finally, there was pressure from above, particularly after Wooldridge moved into his new job. Beard told the subcommittee:

> I was greatly frustrated by this investigation. There were roadblocks at every turn. I never had a regular staff to help me in checking out adequately the numerous allegations received. Investigators who were assigned to me were soon relieved, primarily because of the pressure of work upon all CID detachments in West Germany. I could not operate efficiently without more help in a case with so many widespread ramifications. I also encountered much resistance from officials who wanted the case closed and forgotten. Again, we were all aware of the "sensitive" nature of the case, particularly after Sergeant Major Wooldridge became Sergeant Major of the Army in July of 1966.[12]

On May 10, 1967, Beard traveled to Frankfurt to attend a meeting called by Colonel Henry Gibson, commander of the 15th MP Brigade, the detective's parent organization. The purpose was to consider the future of the Beard investigation. When Beard arrived, he learned that a decision had already been made. The case would be closed. His immediate superior had told him part of the reason was that a continuation would embarrass Generals Johnson, the Chief of Staff of the Army, and Cunningham, the former 24th commander. The primary consideration was, Beard said, the Wooldridge situation.

Beard went along with the decision, he later told the subcommittee, "partly because of my frustration and partly because I doubted that punitive measures would ever be taken."

The investigation was closed out in a strange way. Normally Beard would have written an ROI (report of investigation) that would have been forwarded to the CID's central records depository at Fort Holabird, Maryland (the location checked by the FBI in its fruitless investigation on Major General Turner), where it would be cross-indexed thoroughly. Instead, Beard was ordered to make his report on a Form 1932, a local commander's report of disciplinary action taken. A 1932 report is treated differently from an ROI. It is retained in the local unit's files, and thus the record would not follow the individuals involved throughout the rest of their careers. Beard filed all his working notes with the 1932 report at Augsburg in 1967. When the Senate subcommittee sought them in 1969, they could no longer be found.

The report of Beard's year-and-a-half-long investigation into the possibility that thefts totaling hundreds of thousands of dollars had occurred, was given the same stature as that on a stolen bicycle.

In late 1966, unbeknownst to Beard, who was still working on the Augsburg investigation, Major General Carl C. Turner, the provost marshal general, surfaced within the Army's criminal investigation circles as a protector of Wooldridge. The first incident occurred when a colleague of Beard's stationed in Washington, Warrant Officer Reis R. Kash, after reading a press report of Wooldridge's new appointment, ran a routine check of the sergeant major in the Fort Holabird CID files. He discovered that Wooldridge had a police record, a "rap sheet" in CID parlance, on file.

In 1943, while serving in a military police company in London, England, Wooldridge had been arrested for stealing eight dollars from two coin telephone boxes. He was court-martialed, convicted, sentenced to five months at hard labor, fined twenty-five dollars and busted to private. The file showed he had also been AWOL briefly on two occasions. It was a small and long-ago blemish on the shining example of all that was best in the Army, but Kash thought it was important enough to pass on to higher authority. He took the report to his superior, Lieutenant Colonel Jack G. Pruett, with the recommendation that Major General Turner and General Harold K. Johnson, the Army Chief of Staff, be informed of the file. Pruett took the file to Turner in April 1967 with the recommendation that Wooldridge be removed from his "sensitive position."

In 1969, that meeting resulted in this colloquy before the Senate subcommittee:

PRUETT: The reaction [of Turner] was that many people are accused of many things and that Sergeant Major Wooldridge was just a good old country boy and that was the end of the discussion, sir.

SEN. KARL MUNDT: Did you happen to tell the general that Jesse James was just a good old country boy?

PRUETT: Sir, I am an officer in the Army.

. . .

MUNDT: I don't know how colonels react to generals, I have never been either one, but did you raise any protestation? Did you say, "General, I think this is a kind of dangerous thing to do," or "This is unprecedented,". or did you just say, "Okay, sir"?

PRUETT: Sir, after you have spent your life in the service, you click your heels and obey your orders.[13]

The Turner-Pruett meeting took place during the same time period that Wooldridge had paid a visit to Vietnam and returned to Washington on the private jet airliner assigned to General Creighton W. Abrams, commander of American forces in South Vietnam. Unknown to Abrams, who was aboard the plane, eight or nine cases of contraband liquor had been smuggled onto the plane. Acting on an informant's tip, customs inspectors in Hawaii found the liquor and assessed not only the duties but penalties amounting to $500, which was paid by a group of sergeants, excluding Wooldridge, who were also on the plane.

Kash knew nothing of this incident until six o'clock one morning in April 1967 when, while he was on leave, he received a call at his home ordering him to report immediately to the Army Air Field at Fort Belvoir, Virginia, to meet Major General Turner. At this point Kash was upset over the Wooldridge case, but he did not suspect the extent of the cover-up in process. Part of his upset resulted from an attempt to get a second copy of the rap sheet at Holabird. When he asked for it, a clerk went to the files and discovered the Wooldridge dossier was missing. In its place was an index card saying it had been removed two years before. Kash knew that to be a lie. The dossier had been in the files a few weeks before.

When Kash arrived at the airfield, he joined Turner, and the two took off. Once in the air, Turner announced that the destination was Fort McClellan, Alabama, where they were to interview a sergeant major who had been with Wooldridge aboard Abrams' plane. Turner gave Kash a memo to read on the customs incident in Hawaii and informed Kash that he, Turner, had been ordered to make a personal investigation. Kash went along merely as a stenographer. Turner asked all the questions; Kash took notes in shorthand. Later, on the return flight to Washington, he transcribed his notes, and Turner took both the typed and shorthand copies. Kash never saw them again, a procedure he described as unusual. Normally those notes would have gone into an office file.

On their return to Washington, Turner ordered Kash to investigate and find out who the informant to customs was. Kash protested but was given an order which he went through the motions of obeying. "The business of trying to find out the name of the informant, there is no excuse or reasonable cause for that," Kash later told the Senate subcommittee in commenting on Turner's "unprofessional and improper" actions.[14] Turner himself told the subcommittee that he concluded Wooldridge was not to blame for the smuggling and that he "asked that publicity not be given to the incident in order to avoid pointless embarrassment to the Army."[15]

So Turner closed out the liquor-smuggling investigation, except for the determination of who had informed on Wooldridge, just days before the Beard investigation was closed out in Germany.

Perhaps as a result of the Beard-George investigation in Germany, the Augsburg sergeants decided that their good thing in Europe had come to an end. Sergeant First Class Narvaez Hatcher, for example, the veteran of eleven years in Germany, opted for a tour in the United States.

In the summer of 1967, Sergeants Hatcher, William C. Bagby and Theodore ("Sam") Bass of the still-to-be-organized Maredem Company; John C. Nelson, who had admitted participating in irregularities in the Augsburg clubs but was never punished; and Zane Fox, who did not figure in the Augsburg investigation but who was stationed there, were all assigned to Fort Benning, Georgia.

As Sergeant Major Kenneth L. Parrent had done in 1963, a Fort Benning sergeant major who sat on the NCO club system Board of Governors for that post noticed irregularities and turned a report over to the post CID. Warrant Officer Rex M. Harding read the material and received permission to begin an investigation. Harding organized his investigation with all the secrecy General Dwight D. Eisenhower used in planning D-Day. When the detective struck, on August 1, 1967, it took everyone by surprise.

The investigation uncovered a Hatcher scheme to ship fifteen cases of liquor belonging to the Fort Benning NCO clubs to Wooldridge in Washington aboard an Army aircraft. Harding's men also discovered that Hatcher had used club materials, club vehicles and club employees to build a fence around his new home in Columbus, Georgia. Bagby was implicated for attempting to get a civilian bookkeeper working in the clubs to alter records. Bass admitted falsifying liquor inventory records, saying he did it to have bottles on hand to give out as gifts to Fort Benning officials. The investigation could not find that any such bottles were ever given as gifts.

Harding's team never did get to the most intriguing allegation in the investigation. One of their informants told them that in July 1967, Wooldridge; Major General William Cunningham, who, after leaving the 24th Infantry Division, retired from the Army; Sergeant Seymour ("Sandy") Lazar; and Bagby, along with some other club-system sergeants, met in a private room at a Fort Benning NCO club to develop, according to Kash's 1969 testimony, "a system for manipulating Vietnamese piasters, American military payment certificates and green dollars."

Senator Abraham Ribicoff asked at the hearings:
Was this related to Vietnam?

KASH: Well, it was worldwide, as I understand it.

RIBICOFF: Piasters would have to be Vietnam.

KASH: Yes, sir.

RIBICOFF: Were subjects such as kickbacks, club operations, slot machine skimming and contacts discussed?

KASH: To the best of my recollection, again, sir, this was more or less a general business meeting. The thing that stuck in my mind was the investment of the money that was being generated by illicit activities.

RIBICOFF: What do you mean when you say "illicit activities"?

KASH: This was all in the framework of skimming slot machines, shorting on liquor, kickbacks, the whole procedure for illicit operations around food and liquor and clubs.

RIBICOFF: Has anything like this on a worldwide scale ever come to your attention before?

KASH: No, sir.[16]

After that Fort Benning meeting, there was some indication that a second meeting was held at a lake resort in northern Georgia to plan exploitation of the currency black market in South Vietnam. Needless to say, Harding was excited about his investigation and had every reason to believe that his superiors were interested in routing the corruption he was uncovering at Fort Benning. Like Sergeant Major Kenneth L. Parrent, Major William George and Warrant Officer Irvin Beard in Germany and Warrant Officer Reis Kash in Washington, he was to suffer a rude awakening.

In probing the Fort Benning corruption, Harding learned of the Augsburg investigation that had recently been closed out. With the permission of his commanding officer he routinely wrote to the Augsburg CID requesting a copy of the file. While awaiting the arrival of those documents from Germany, Harding's awakening began.

First he received an order from his commanding officer to delete Wooldridge's name from all the material in his Fort Benning investigation file. The detectives had to go through all their reports, penciling out Wooldridge's name. Some interviews had to be reconducted with neither the questioner nor the interviewee mentioning Wooldridge. Harding later testified that the demand for the deletion came from Major General Turner, the provost marshal general in Washington. Turner told the subcommittee that he ordered the deletion of Wooldridge's name because

> I was confident, based on a combination of my confidence in Wooldridge's preselection screening and my aversion to witchhunting, that my decision was just and that it served the best interest of the Army . . . I was apprehensive lest the Army Sergeant Major be smeared on unsupported accusations of another man . . . I certainly didn't want capricious, malicious, unfounded facts circulating throughout the Army on a man who represented 90 percent of our Army.[17]

From Turner's statement, you would think a CID investigation was as public as a court trial. Actually, it was being done very quietly and was a procedure that led merely to the determination of whether or not charges should be brought.

Three weeks after Harding began his investigation, he was summoned to Washington to attend an "interview"—not an interrogation—of Wooldridge.

Kash, who actually conducted the interview, described the whole procedure for the subcommittee this way:

On August 23, Colonel Pruett told me that he had received the following orders from Major General Turner relating to the Wooldridge matter: (1) That I would conduct an interview, not an interrogation, of Wooldridge; (2) that Harding would ask no questions; (3) that the interview would be restrictive in nature, because I was limited to the following questions: the flying of liquor destined for Wooldridge to Washington on a Government aircraft; a visit to Birmingham, Ala., by Wooldridge; and certain gratuities Wooldridge was supposed to have received at Fort Benning. I was told that Wooldridge could not be asked any questions relating to the Augsburg investigation. When I received these instructions from Colonel Pruett, Mr. Harding was not present.

I was extremely upset by the instructions and I so stated to Colonel Pruett. He told me that he shared my concern and frustration, but stated that General Turner had given him these orders.

Harding and I interviewed Wooldridge immediately thereafter, but we made no attempt to interrogate him. Wooldridge denied all the charges, making an entirely self-serving statement.

Harding, unaware that he was to be prohibited from questioning Wooldridge, waited patiently while I conducted the interview. Then Wooldridge read the statement, refused to sign it, took a copy, and left. Harding asked me in amazement, "What in the world is going on?" I answered, "It's a goddam fix."

Subsequently, I never discussed our interview of Wooldridge with General Turner.

As a result of my work with General Turner on the smuggling incident and my restricted interview of Sergeant Major Wooldridge, I formed the firm conviction that General Turner was in the process of covering up and "whitewashing" the case at Fort Benning involving Wooldridge.[18]

During this time period, Colonel James C. Shoultz, Turner's chief of staff, who was not directly involved in the Fort Benning probe but knew of it, thought he would be helpful. He had served in Europe from 1964 to 1967 and remembered that Wooldridge and many of the others involved in Fort Benning also figured in the Augsburg investigation. Like a good policeman, he mentioned the Augsburg record to his boss, Turner. The major general did not appreciate the help. He told Shoultz "that really Sergeant Major Wooldridge was a very simple fellow and people took advantage of him frequently; that he was just a good old country boy."[19] Then he threw Shoultz out of his office—"figuratively," Shoultz told the senators.

A few weeks after the Wooldridge interview, Harding, back at Fort Benning, received word that the Augsburg record would not be forwarded. For one thing, he was told, the principals in the case were not the same. The record was sent instead to Turner's office in Washington where it was marked "eyes only" for Turner, Pruett, Kash and a clerk-stenographer who did the filing. Turner ordered that it not be shown to anyone. With resignation, Pruett called Harding and told him that the Augsburg record was in Washington but that he could not see it.

All this happened in the fall of 1967. About the same time, Wooldridge, Lazar, Hatcher and Higdon were in the process of putting Maredem together. They must have felt pretty safe as they went about their business. They had the assurance of knowing that Army CID agents in Germany, Washington and Fort Benning had been firmly put in their place when they tried to expose the ring.

In January 1968, Harding shipped out to Vietnam, and on January 16, his successor closed out the Fort Benning investigation. At that time, Pruett made a third—and last—effort to have Wooldridge removed. By this time, he felt that the sergeant major should not only be removed from his position as top-ranking enlisted man in the Army, but he should be retired from the service altogether. Turner would not listen. Wooldridge's Pentagon term was coming to a close, and he was preparing to ship out to Vietnam to join the others of Maredem. Lazar, Hatcher and Higdon were already in country—Lazar running the clubs of the famous 1st Infantry Division, Hatcher assisting him, and Higdon in charge of the clubs at the 90th Replacement Battalion at Long Binh, the base through which all men entering the country passed on their way from "the World" to their new duty stations in Nam. In addition, Sergeant William Bagby, who never joined Maredem but was subsequently indicted with the other sergeants, was running the clubs in the 23rd (American) Division. This was the period of the build-up, and troops were arriving by the thousands. The clubs were busy places indeed.

. . .

For the get-rich-quick set of the 1960s, South Vietnam in the years 1965 to 1969, during the period of the American troop build-up, resembled nothing as much as the mining camps of California during the nineteenth-century gold-rush days. Whatever torture the war may have been for those who actually fought it and those on whose land it was being fought, South Vietnam was the land of milk and honey, the land of the big strike for tens of thousands of professional American soldiers, sailors and airmen bent on furthering their careers; for hundreds of American journalists pursuing the big story; for thousands of camp followers of several nationalities who brought the furs, diamonds, whiskey, peanuts, Hong-Kong-tailored suits, art objects and cuisine that the Army and all the other camp followers desired; for other thousands of American civilian contractors who built the bases, quarters, ports, pipelines, roads and communications networks on which the military operated; for the savvy Vietnamese officials who sold concessions to their countrymen to service the Americans; for the pimps and madams who recruited armies of prostitutes to serve the influx of men; and, finally, for bankers working from the shadowy street corners of Saigon to Wall Street offices to organize the spidery currency black market that was sucking the economy of the little country dry, working at cross-purposes with the huge American effort that was trying to save it. It was the land for the big wheeler, the land of the big expense account. Work hard. Play harder. Forget about tomorrow. South Vietnam was carnival-never-ending, perpetual theater of the absurd. Of course, not everyone shared in this excitement or partook of the manna. There were the Vietnamese whose ancestral lands, in many areas, were being transformed into moonscapes and free-fire zones. And there were the grunts, as that generation of American GIs were known, who lived in tents and barracks that could never keep out the monsoon rains or malarial mosquitoes and for whom war was hell even if they were nowhere near the enemy.

There was not much the leadership could do to improve morale through the expenditure of taxpayers' money. That was all going to arms and ammunition, for bases and communications to defeat the enemy. So instead, the command used the nonappropriated fund activities to pep up morale. A grunt might not have hot water to shave in regularly, but he did have a PX where he could buy cut-rate gems, fancy furs or discounted appliances to send back home or a high-powered stereo set to enliven the inactivity of his off-duty hours. He might not have a decent mess hall to eat in, but he did have a club on base where the booze

296

was cheap, the Vietnamese cocktail waitresses dressed in lace stockings, and slots held forth the promise of a thouand-dollar-or-more jackpot. He might not be able to shower in the latrine, but there was a massage parlor and sauna bath on base run by concessionaires where the young ladies, for a price, served you a drink, gave you a rubdown and, for an additional price, something more.

It was an easy-money kind of life made for the men—or women— with larceny in their hearts. And how they took advantage of it.

One of the first men to become outraged by the wholesale corruption was Cornelius Hawkridge, a Hungarian refugee whose ambition was to become an investigator for the United States government. Hawkridge went to Vietnam on his own in 1966 as a consultant to a United States foundation working on refugee programs. While there he entered the black market and made a profit of $50,000, which, he said, he subsequently spent in a probe of irregularities. He began by taking $1,000 to a black-market dealer in Saigon. The dealer gave him $1,600 in military payment certificates (MPC), the scrip that the American military machine used in South Vietnam to try to keep the black market in greenbacks under control. Theoretically, MPC had no value in the Vietnamese economy, since it could only be used by Americans. Actually, since many non-Americans had access to PXs where MPC was the only legal tender, it had great value. Hawkridge took the $1,600 in MPC up the street to the Saigon branch of the Chase Manhattan Bank and purchased traveler's checks. He took these back to the black marketeer and received $2,560 in MPC. He took those back to the bank—to a different clerk—and bought a cashier's check. He took this check for $2,560 back to the dealer and received $4,096 in MPC.

Through transactions such as these and others, Hawkridge discovered the existence of an account at the Manufacturers Hanover Trust Company in New York with the code name "Prysumeen." It was a key drop in the black market controlled by an Indian syndicate working out of Hong Kong.

Prysumeen was used this way: Someone—say, an American salesman, contractor or journalist in Saigon—wishing to purchase black-market piasters to pay his expenses would deposit dollars in the Prysumeen account in New York. A cable would be sent by the bank to the Indian bankers in Hong Kong confirming the deposit. Then the Indian bankers would cable their agents in Saigon, working out of bookstores or obscure offices, authorizing the issuance of piasters to the American.

The dollars that the Indian bankers thus earned were in turn sold at a much lower exchange rate to wealthy Vietnamese who could not otherwise accumulate hard-currency reserves abroad. Prysumeen was one of dozens of such coded accounts in American banks hooked into a network that spanned the globe and had drop points in such out-of-the-way places as the Sheikdom of Dubai, a Trucial state on the Persian Gulf.

Hawkridge complained about the practices in a letter to General William C. Westmoreland, which was ignored. He complained to the United States Agency for International Development, which was running the AID program in South Vietnam, and was ignored. He complained to other government officials, and finally, in the winter of 1968–1969, he took his complaint to the Senate Permanent Subcommittee on Investigations. The subcommittee, during the previous year, had just finished a probe of AID programs in South Vietnam which uncovered many abuses, among them AID's naïve purchase of an all-purpose elixir that turned out to be nothing more than bottled sea water. Senator Abraham Ribicoff had been acting subcommittee chairman for that probe. Ribicoff's staff had also been picking up evidence, perhaps originated by Hawkridge, from informants in the Johnson Administration. After hearing from Hawkridge, the subcommittee authorized an investigation, with LaVern J. Duffy, the subcommittee's assistant counsel, and Carmine Bellino, an investigator, as the leaders. The staff subpoenaed the Prysumeen records from Manufacturers Hanover. With those records as a beginning, it proceeded to unravel the whole story. At that time, it had no idea that military men might be involved in scandal. It was only investigating the black market in currency.

One of the deposits in Prysumeen, Bellino discovered, came from Southern California. He took a trip west, and looking into that deposit, he discovered the Maredem Company.*

By mid-1968, when Wooldridge, his Pentagon tour at an end, returned to Vietnam to become sergeant major for all American forces there under General Creighton W. Abrams, Jr., many of the Augsburg sergeants had been on the scene for almost three years. Maredem was a

* Duffy and Bellino both credit Hawkridge, who was never called to testify openly because some of his charges could not be documented, with supplying the original leads in the investigation. The information presented here about Hawkridge comes from an August 1, 1969, article about him in *Life* by Frank McCulloch.

going concern and the custodians of the clubs were already buying thousands of dollars worth of goods a month from themselves. In addition, they had forged strong working relationships with several other suppliers to the club and PX systems in Vietnam and were selling to them.

Even while he was back in Washington, Wooldridge had done his share. For one thing, the Senate subcommittee learned, between October 1966 and February 1967, he had written four "To Whom It May Concern" letters introducing salesmen for the firm of Tom Brothers & Company of Hong Kong, a firm that had sold civilian clothing and other goods to NCO clubs in Augsburg in the early 1960s. Tom Brothers was controlled by a Hong Kong family named Tung. The Wooldridge letters introduced Jimmy, David and Henry Tung and Peter Zee as salesmen for a firm that conducted "honest . . . business dealings" and sold good products. He signed the letters "William O. Wooldridge, Sergeant Major of the Army."

Senate subcommittee investigators found that on February 11, 1969, Tom Brothers paid Wooldridge $1,000. The check was deposited in a Wooldridge bank account at the Suburban National Bank of Virginia.

While Sergeant Seymour ("Sandy") Lazar was still running the 1st Division clubs in Vietnam (before he retired from the Army to become operating head of Maredem), he paid Wooldridge seven checks totaling $11,339 between December 23, 1966, and August 26, 1967. The sergeants also collected substantially from Frank Furci and James E. Galagan, two civilians who had firms selling to the clubs. In 1965, 1966 and 1967, Furci and Galagan sold $2.5 million worth of goods to Lazar's 1st Infantry Division clubs and those of the Americal Division, run by Sergeant William Bagby. During that period, the Furci-Galagan interests sent Wooldridge two checks totaling $4,544, which were deposited in a second Wooldridge account, this one at the First National Bank of Arlington, Virginia. The civilians also paid Lazar $1,114 which went to the Mechanics National Bank of Burlington, New Jersey. Two of these three checks were drawn on a Swiss bank account named "Fishhead" into which Furci-Galagan had deposited $362,000 drawn from a Milwaukee bank. The Senate subcommittee suspected that Fishhead was a secret drop point for transactions in the club systems in Vietnam.[20]

After Maredem went into business, it established accounts at the Banque Nationale de Paris in Hong Kong, the Crocker Citizens National Bank of San Francisco and the Beverly Wilshire branch of the Bank of America in Los Angeles. Its initial finances were $89,980, which came from a variety of sources. A $5,000 check from Frank Furci was deposited in the Bank of America account. Glenn Faulks, who sold bar supplies to NCO clubs and PXs from a Bangkok headquarters, wrote a $1,200 check which was deposited in the Crocker Citizens account. His checks were made payable to a George Schell, which turned out to be a pseudonym for Sergeant William Higdon, the custodian of the Long Binh clubs. A firm called Vanlaw Products wrote a $35.61 check which went to Crocker Citizens. It represented a 1 percent kickback on two orders sold to a club.

On and on went the list. Checks came from banks in Switzerland and Germany. Clinton W. Lininger, a former Wooldridge aide at the Pentagon who retired from the Army to go to work for Maredem, deposited $5,000 to the Los Angeles account personally. He put in ninety-three $50 bills and seventeen $20 traveler's checks.

Lastly there was a $13,415.86 check from the Long Binh NCO club system that was a story in itself. On March 30, 1967, the Board of Governors of the 1st Infantry Division club system empowered Lazar to purchase a walk-in freezer at a cost of no more than $7,000. The freezer, purchased at a cost of $9,000 from a firm represented by Furci, arrived the following summer, and remained with the 1st Infantry until January 1968. Then Hatcher, who had become Lazar's successor, shipped the freezer to Long Binh. Another of Furci's firms handled the shipment and was paid $225. At Long Binh, it was installed in a club operated by Higdon. The installation was done by Furci's firm, which received $590 for the job. Higdon then wrote a check for $13,415.86 in payment for the freezer and sent it to Maredem, which had never owned it.

It takes control to carry off a transaction like that, and the sergeants obviously had it. Meanwhile, Wooldridge, like any good strategist, was busy protecting his flanks and rear. In early 1968, he contacted an old Army lawyer friend, Colonel Richard F. Seibert, general counsel for the Army/Air Force Exchange Service in Dallas. Wooldridge told the colonel he was thinking of investing in a firm with three *retired* Army men who would be doing business with clubs and exchanges. He named Lazar (who was then retired) and Hatcher and Higdon (who were very much still in the service, running club systems). Was this, Wooldridge asked the lawyer, any conflict of interest? Seibert at first referred Wooldridge to the Army's Legal Assistance Office. Wooldridge persisted in seeking Seibert's advice, saying he did not trust his partners or their lawyers. Seibert relented, made a little investigation himself and then wrote Wooldridge a letter saying no conflict was involved. Wooldridge later used that letter to claim he had approval from the Army's Judge Advocate General's staff to enter the business. Seibert in turn told the Senate subcommittee he had given his personal opinion on the basis of "misleading, inaccurate and incomplete information" supplied to him. If he had known the true story, he said, he would have ruled that a conflict of interest was certainly involved.

Seibert had indeed been duped. About the same time he was rendering his opinion, the sergeants concluded a nice deal with an American civilian named Phillip M. Haar of Stanton, California. Haar owned a firm called Carbo-Mix that, in the early 1960s, did business with the NCO clubs of the 24th Division in Germany. In fact, it was dealings with Carbo-Mix that helped make Sergeant Major Kenneth L. Parrent suspicious of his colleagues in Augsburg in 1963. Carbo-Mix sold and serviced soft-drink dispensers and sold the syrup for them. In 1967, Haar was doing business in Vietnam, and Lazar, while still custodian of the 1st Infantry clubs, entered negotiations with him for a part of the business. Lazar wanted to sell the syrup. By January 1968, Lazar was out of the service and running Maredem. He reached an agreement with Haar in which Maredem would have exclusive rights to sell the syrup in Vietnam, paying Haar a one-dollar-a-case fee for each case sold.

It was a good arrangement. Maredem was also given office space in Haar's Stanton headquarters. Lazar could sell to the huge club systems controlled by his partners, Hatcher and Higdon, as well as those controlled by the friendly Sergeant William Bagby in the Americal. But Lazar's partners thought he had been too generous. Hatcher and Higdon flew to California from Vietnam. Wooldridge flew in from Washington, apparently registering at a motel under an assumed name. Former Sergeant Sam Bass, who was about to join Maredem as Saigon representative, joined the meeting. The sergeants pressured Haar into accepting only a fifty-cent fee per case. Maredem and Haar formed a jointly owned corporation, Macar Corporation, to run the soft-drink business. Wooldridge, Higdon, Hatcher and Haar flew to Las Vegas to celebrate their agreement. Haar picked up the tab for the trip. When

Wooldridge returned to the Pentagon, he submitted an expense account for nine days at $16 a day and was reimbursed by the government $122.25 for the trip.

Maredem prospered in the arrangement with Haar, but he lost money and eventually dissolved the relationship. Maredem was not unhappy. In a year's time, acting as a broker for other firms, it did $1,210,871 worth of business in Vietnam, 87 percent of which was in sales to the clubs controlled by Maredem partners Hatcher and Higdon, and with Bagby. Maredem's profits on the business came to over $120,000.

When Wooldridge, Hatcher, Higdon and Lazar were summoned before the Senate Subcommittee on October 23, 1969, to answer questions about all this, they took the Fifth Amendment 105 times. Anything they said, they told the senators, might tend to incriminate them.

Of all the sergeants involved in the machinations uncovered by the Senate subcommittee, only one, Higdon, was ever brought to justice in a military court. He was convicted on June 11, 1971, at Redstone Arsenal, Alabama, fined $25,000 and given a dishonorable discharge. Bagby was stationed at Fort Schafer, Hawaii. Hatcher, like Lazar, retired before anything became public. Wooldridge put in for retirement before the hearings but was denied permission. He was stripped of his command sergeant major's chevrons, relieved of his position in Vietnam, and the Army took back the distinguished service medal it had awarded him. In February 1972, he was allowed to retire on a pension of $783.90 a month after more than thirty years' service. In the mildest of rebukes, he was denied the retirement parade due a man of his stature and a certificate of appreciation for service signed by the Army Chief of Staff and the President of the United States.

At the time of his retirement, Wooldridge, along with Lazar, Hatcher, Higdon, Bagby, Bass and two civilians, Clifford and Irene Terhune, were under indictment by a federal grand jury in Los Angeles on charges of conspiring to defraud the NCO clubs. The indictments were returned on February 18, 1971. The trial was postponed many times and finally, on November 21, 1972, Lazar pleaded guilty to the charges against him. On February 18, 1973, Hatcher died. Ten days later, rather than face a trial which would have aired the situation completely, Wooldridge, Higdon and Bass entered guilty pleas. Mr. and Mrs. Terhune avoided prosecution by staying out of the country. (She was a British national.)

Federal District Judge Warren J. Ferguson set sentencing for April 30, 1973, and then gave the four ex-sergeants—Wooldridge, Lazar, Higdon and Bass—the opportunity to tell their stories before the Senate subcommittee in return for lighter sentences.

During the months of March and April, the Senate subcommittee, chaired no longer by Ribicoff but by Senator Henry M. Jackson, a Democrat from Washington, reopened the investigation. The sergeants cooperated. On May 8, 1973, a six-hour public hearing was held. Once a front-page story, the military corruption situation and its cover-up were all but ignored in Washington. The capital was engrossed in the continual exposé in the spring of 1973 of the Watergate scandal and the attempts to cover it up.

Wooldridge and his colleagues spread a chilling tale on the record. Higdon, for example, admitted to amassing, in less than two years between July 1967 and February 1969, a fortune of $301,498.15 which he deposited in his account (code-named "Seal") in the Foreign Commerce Bank, Incorporated, of Zurich. The former sergeant estimated that $100,000 of the total came from kickbacks he received for buying from proper vendors—including Maredem—and the rest came from black-market currency operations. While 55,000 Americans died in an attempt to make South Vietnam a stable nation, he was helping to suck the economy dry. Higdon admitted to receiving $60,000 in kickbacks from William J. Crum for purchasing pizzas and beer and allowing Crum to install his slot machines in the clubs under Higdon's control.

The sergeants told Senate subcommittee investigators how high-ranking officers helped cover up their business going back to the early 1960s in Augsburg. They detailed how, in September 1967, when Lazar and another sergeant were arrested in Dian for club-system larceny and black marketeering, Wooldridge intervened with the 1st Division's staff judge advocate, Lieutenant Colonel George B. Barrett, Jr. Barrett closed the case, saying there was insufficient proof of the charges, and allowed Lazar and the other sergeant, Ralph Myers, to return to the United States and retire.

In dropping the charges Barrett ignored evidence including large sums of currency and records of huge deposits by the two sergeants in Swiss and other banks. In April 1968, Barrett wrote a memorandum for the record which said that while the currency found did constitute a violation, Major General John H. Hay, the division commander, did not think criminal action against Lazar and Myers was appropriate. Thus was another general implicated as helping to cover up the illegal activities of the sergeants.

Wooldridge told the subcommittee investigators and then the senators a little bit about how such cover-ups are engineered. He detailed how the sergeants provided free wine, liquor, furniture, sporting equipment and women for the higher-ups. He said, for example, of Major General William Cunningham, the commander of the 24th Division in Germany: "He liked his comforts. He liked to be looked after."

In an affidavit for the subcommittee Wooldridge said that many senior Army officers, including General William C. Westmoreland himself, "knew of wrongdoings" in the club system but took no action.

"I think there was a lot of things covered up," Wooldridge said, "and I think what Washington was worried about is they couldn't afford to have some senior commanders have their names become involved or people who had served there previously . . .

"I believe there was a big cover-up, yes, sir."

Judge Ferguson deferred sentencing and forced the sergeants to talk in the hope that it would bring about reform. He did not make his point. The subcommittee closed out its interest in the scandal with that last hearing, referring the matter to the Defense Department for action. That was the same department that allowed Wooldridge to retire on a pension. Going on the Pentagon's past record, it had no stomach for a clean-up.

On May 29, 1973, the four surviving sergeants stood before the bench in Judge Ferguson's Los Angeles courtroom to hear their sentences.

The judge gave each of the men the maximum sentence provided by the law—Wooldridge, four years; Lazar, five years; Bass, two years; and Higdon, five years in prison—and then suspended the sentences after winning an agreement from the ex-sergeants to what must rank as one of the most unusual punishments ever meted out in an American court.

He made each of the men promise to work several years without salary for a charitable organization and to transfer all their assets, including the deposits in secret Swiss accounts, to the United States government. Wooldridge, in the only exception, was permitted to keep his small house in Junction City, Kansas, and all four were allowed to keep their military pensions. The judge also made them promise to turn over their entire estates, upon death, to the government.

"I want the defendants penniless," the judge said. "I want to make sure you don't have anything."

The ex-sergeants' attorneys complained that the punishments were unusual.

"This was an unusual crime," the judge answered.

Along with Major General Cunningham in Germany, Major General Turner in Washington and Major General Hay in Vietnam, the sergeants had another important protector-general.* He was Brigadier General Earl F. Cole. Earl Cole's biography reads like that of your typical country boy who made it big in the Army. Born in Madison County, Nebraska, in October 1919, he joined the National Guard in 1936 as an enlisted man. In 1942, he went through infantry officers' candidate school at Fort Benning, Georgia, but was never sent overseas during World War II. After the war, he spent a year in China, and then his career alternated between staff jobs and in-service educational assignments. He spent the Korean War period stationed in Europe, part of that time as an aide-de-camp to a general.

In the mid-1950s, Cole joined the circle of up-and-coming young officers clustered around William C. Westmoreland. During the period that Brigadier General Westmoreland worked in Washington as deputy assistant chief of staff for manpower control, Lieutenant Colonel Cole served as executive officer for Westy's boss. That meant that every time Westmoreland wanted to communicate with the boss, he had to go through Cole. After Major General Westmoreland became superintendent of West Point, Colonel Cole joined his staff as adjutant general. And after General Westmoreland became commander of the Military Assistance Command Vietnam (MACV), he summoned Brigadier General Cole from Washington to become deputy chief of staff for personnel and administration in the headquarters for the United States Army in

---

* Shortly after Cunningham left the command of the 24th Infantry Division in Germany, he retired from the Army and took a job with Pacific Architects and Engineers, a firm that had large-scale construction contracts in South Vietnam. Thus he became a part of the big-spending set, and Army investigators, noting his reported presence at the Fort Benning meeting with the sergeants discussed earlier, implicated him as a black-market currency manipulator. There was never any follow-up on the investigation.

Vietnam (USARV), one of the components of the MACV Command, Cole arrived in Saigon in June 1966 and remained until December 1968. Though he never served with a combat unit, he played the ticket-punching game well. He had even obtained his paratrooper's badge. Among his medals were the silver and bronze stars, an air medal, the distinguished service medal, the Army commendation medal, several Vietnamese decorations and—for a reason not cited in his biography—the Purple Heart.

As part of Cole's job, he had responsibility of running all the non-appropriated fund activities in Vietnam—the PXs and service clubs. It was from this position, in late 1967, that Cole decreed the appointment of Sergeant William Higdon as custodian for all the NCO and enlisted men's clubs on the huge Long Binh base near Saigon. Long Binh was a sprawling (sixty square miles) headquarters and supply area, representing a $100 million investment to the United States. Higdon, who had previously been running the smaller club system in the adjacent 90th Replacement Battalion, now had more than thirty clubs under his control, serving almost 40,000 men. But in addition to the clubs themselves, the club system also controlled a string of concessions—gift shops, clothing shops, a sauna bath and the like—which presented a variety of opportunities for commanding kickbacks. Cole named Higdon custodian over the objections of many subordinates who felt the sergeant was too much of a wheeler-dealer.* One of Higdon's first acts as Long Binh club custodian was to consolidate into the Long Binh system the two clubs of the 90th Replacement Battalion. Now he had a huge empire.

One of Higdon's key suppliers was William J. Crum, a business-man-adventurer whose life embodied the turmoil and tragedy of Asian history in the twentieth century, according to biographical information the Senate Subcommittee obtained. Crum was born in Shanghai in 1918 of American parents. His father was a Yangtze River navigator. After education in Beverly Hills, California, and at the San Rafael, California, Military Academy, he worked in jobs ranging from service-station at-

---

* As in Germany and Fort Benning, there was always some knowledge in Vietnam of what the sergeants were up to. It was just that they could never be nailed. One CID agent in Vietnam did try to begin an investigation, and he was aided by Warrant Officer Rex Harding, the conductor of the Fort Benning investigation, who himself had been assigned to Vietnam. Harding suggested to his colleague that he try to get the Augsburg file. The colleague wrote to Washington where, of course, permission to read the file was denied.

tendant to gold prospector and then went to sea. Partially disabled by muscular dystrophy and without the sight of one eye, he could not enter the serivce. He worked in the merchant marine in World War II, making dangerous runs in the Orient. In 1946, he appeared in Shanghai as agent for the Robert Dollar Lines. When the communists took over China in 1948, he was operating a radio station.

During the Korean War, he set up operations in Korea, selling various items to American service clubs and PXs. The parties at his house in Seoul were famous. Sergeants running clubs could always find free drinks, food, beds and women there and a perpetual poker game at which Crum regularly lost great amounts to those who gave him a lot of business. When they stopped buying from him, the Senate Subcommittee was told years later, the sergeants stopped winning. In fact, many ran up huge debts, and then they started buying again.

Billy Crum was as shrewd an observer of the international scene as any diplomat or statesman. In 1964, a year before the big escalation of the American effort in South Vietnam, when President Lyndon B. Johnson was publicly saying he would not send American boys to fight an Asian war while his planners were privately planning for such an eventuality, Crum moved to Saigon. He was in on the ground floor with a line of beer, liquor, slot machines, jukeboxes, pizza ovens and other goods and services he knew the United States military machine needed to operate efficiently overseas.

One of Crum's good friends was Brigadier General Earl F. Cole. Some testimony indicated the two had met in China after World War II. Cole denied this but testified he met with Crum some fifteen times during the thirty months he was stationed in South Vietnam.

Senate subcommittee testimony showed that Cole did far more than simply meet with Crum casually. Cole cleared the way for Crum to import goods ranging up to large automobiles duty-free. Cole gave Crum permission to store the illegally imported goods in areas on the Long Binh base. Cole paved the way for Crum to sell a string of gift shops he operated as concessions at Long Binh to the club system when he could not make a profit in them. The inventory was sold at retail prices, Crum realizing a $120,000 profit immediately. When Crum ran into trouble with customs inspectors, Cole wrote letters for him. When Crum felt he was not getting enough business for his Carlings Beer account, Cole, who by then had transferred out of personnel and administration into the pacification program, wrote a letter to the Army-Air Force

Exchange System headquarters in Dallas recommending that it buy more Carlings. When Crum's competitors—Furci and Galagan—began getting too large a share of the market, in Crum's view, he complained to Cole, and the Furci-Galagan headquarters was raided. They were fined $45,000 for various violations, which effectively put them out of business.

In turn, Crum did a few things for Cole. On one occasion, when Cole visited Hong Hong, one of Crum's firms picked up the tab. On another, Colonel Robert H. Ivey, the staff judge advocate at MACV, the command's senior legal adviser, asked Cole for recommendations on where to shop in Hong Kong. As a result, Cole initiated planning that eventually led to Ivey and his family being wined and dined, and put up in Hong Kong at the expense of Crum's slot-machine firm. Ivey paid only a small portion of the expense. Later Ivey was asked to render a ruling on the slot-machine firm's business in South Vietnam and ruled favorably for it. The colonel, appearing before the Senate subcommittee, said he had been duped by Cole.

> I find it unbelievable that a general officer would do something like this to anyone, much less to a friend [Ivey testified]. I feel it was a dirty, low-down trick . . . I have never knowingly committed an unethical or dishonest act. However, in view of the information brought to light by this committee concerning the activities of General Cole in Vietnam, it does appear that he did deliberately attempt to compromise me for the purpose of aiding Sarl Electronics [the slot-machine firm]. I have never in my 28 years of service been placed in such a position, nor do I ever intend to be again.[21] *

William J. Crum's activities were not going unnoticed by the CID. As the result of a CID investigation, Brigadier General Robert Ashworth, the Saigon headquarters area commander, sent USARV headquarters at Long Binh a memo in August 1967, warning that the Viet-

---

* Cole was a good guy to many people, including his secretary, Mrs. Catherine Gault. In 1968, on a base salary of $8,777.60, she actually earned $25,640.95. Most of the rest came in overtime authorized by Cole. She received the overtime even while on shopping trips to Hong Kong and on a visit to New York to consult her stockbroker. Cole and Mrs. Gault were indicted on charges arising out of this arrangement and convicted by a jury after a trial in a federal district court in Alexandria, Virginia, in January 1973.

nam Regional Exchange, which controlled all the PXs in country, was not properly regulating its concessionaires, particularly Crum and his slot-machine interests. Ashworth expected that Brigadier General Cole would handle the matter. There was no indication that Cole did anything about the situation, which continued to deteriorate.

Toward the end of the year, Major Clement St. Martin, a veteran enlisted man who late in his career had joined the officer corps, was transferred to Long Binh from MACV headquarters in Saigon. The transfer was made after St. Martin had published a letter to the editor in the *Army Times* criticizing his senior officers for inefficient records handling. The seniors took umbrage and shipped St. Martin out.

At Long Binh he was made officer-in-charge of all the open messes —the officers', NCOs' and enlisted men's clubs. After trying and failing to block the appointment of Higdon as custodian of the NCO-enlisted clubs, St. Martin was invited by Higdon to make a trip to Saigon. Higdon told St. Martin he would learn a little about the club system.

The two went first to Crum's villa where the major listened, he later testified, as Crum ordered Higdon to hurry the consolidation of the clubs at Long Binh and the 90th Replacement Battalion. Higdon said he was running into difficulty because someone was demanding an audit.

"——— it! I'll call Earl about this," Crum replied, referring to Cole.[22]

Then, after Higdon and Crum talked privately for about twenty minutes, the sergeant and the major left the villa and drove to the villa of Madame Tran Thi Phuong, who was known, because of her resemblance to the character in "Terry and the Pirates," as "the Dragon Lady." Madame Phuong was a very successful businesswoman who had plans, according to Cole's testimony before the Senate subcommittee, to build a huge house of prostitution at Long Binh, complete with a medical inspection facility for the girls. In the organizational structure, it would have operated as a concession in Higdon's club system.

Cole told the senators Madame Phuong was first recommended to him by Brigadier General William S. Knowlton, a member of General Westmoreland's staff who subsequently went on to become superintendent of West Point.[23] When Cole studied her plans, he realized that he could not authorize a bordello on the base, so he asked her to submit a new proposal. She came back with a plan to construct a huge steam bath and massage parlor, employing four hundred Vietnamese women. She was one of eleven bidders seeking permission to build such a facility.

309

Massage parlors and steam baths were common on bases in Vietnam. Many of them were houses of prostitution in disguise.

When Higdon and St. Martin visited Madame Phuong's home, she had not yet won approval for her venture. Higdon and Madame Phuong met privately for forty-five minutes while St. Martin waited in the spacious villa, studying the fine furnishings and works of art. Then the two reappeared, and Higdon announced that he and St. Martin would spend the night in Saigon, separately. They arranged to meet for breakfast the next morning, and Madame Phuong's brother drove St. Martin to a hotel.

On the way to the hotel the brother asked about Madame Phuong's chances of winning the concession, noting that she "was a very personal friend of General Cole" who "was going to help her obtain the contract." St. Martin answered that the club's board of governors had to award the contract.

The brother registered St. Martin, who went to his room. Within minutes a bellhop brought him a bottle of bourbon, ice and coke. St. Martin mixed a drink, and minutes later, a twenty-three-year-old Vietnamese woman appeared, announcing that she had been sent to spend the night with him.

St. Martin explained to the prostitute, according to his testimony later, that he was not interested. She said she would be in danger if she did not spend the night. They agreed that she would leave and both would lie to protect her. The next morning, when St. Martin checked out, the room clerk said he owed nothing for the room, drinks or entertainment. St. Martin, curious over how Higdon would write off the cost of a prostitute to the Long Binh club system, watched the records for the next two months but could find no indication that Higdon had ever charged the clubs.

At breakfast, Higdon asked, "How was your night, Major?"

"Fantastic," St. Martin replied.

"Were you pleased with the merchandise?"

"Ding-how," St. Martin answered, using the Chinese expression for "Number One."[24]

Breakfast was at the International House, a kind of service club operated under the aegis of the American Embassy in Saigon. St. Martin told the subcommittee he listened while Higdon illegally purchased 120 cases of San Miguel beer, a Philippine brand. The clubs were only allowed to sell American brands. He later learned that Higdon gave the beer to club employees to drink. It was never sold. In fact, St. Martin always found the refrigerator in his office stocked with cold Philippine and German beers. The beer Higdon purchased was delivered to Long Binh in an Army truck.

By the end of that visit, St. Martin was suspicious of what was going on. Back at Long Binh he began checking and discovered storage areas for club property to which access was forbidden without the permission of Brigadier General Cole. Among other things, Crum's illegally imported slot machines were stored there. Checking records, he found Higdon selling pizzas which he bought from Crum at fifty-five cents each while the officers' club sold similar pizzas it made itself at a cost of eighteen cents each. He also discovered that Higdon was illegally paying vendors with dollar checks for their goods. Regulations stipulated these payments were to be mailed out of the country to the home offices of the companies to avoid their use in black-market transactions. After Higdon gave the checks directly to the representatives in Vietnam, these salesmen could take them to Bangkok, which had a free money market, and exchange them for dollars. They would then smuggle the dollars back to Vietnam and convert them into Vietnamese piasters at the black-market rate. Finally, they would take the black-market piasters to Higdon's clubs and reexchange them for dollars at the lower official rate.

A typical transaction was this: Higdon would sign a $3,000 check and present it to a salesman for Crum's slot-machine firm. The salesman might then fly to Bangkok and cash the check, bringing the greenbacks back to Vietnam illegally. (Dollars were forbidden in the country except under controls.) The salesman would then exchange his illegal dollars for piasters at a black-market rate of about 185 piasters for each dollar. He would then take the piasters back to Higdon's club, which had a need for piasters to pay salaries to Vietnamese employees, and reconvert them to dollars (once again illegally, because dollars could theoretically only be exchanged at specified banks) at a rate of one dollar for each 118 piasters. In this way, the salesman would realize a $1,200 profit on the $3,000 check. He would then make the payment to his company for the bill owed by the Long Binh club system.

St. Martin told the Senate subcommittee that in the three months he was at Long Binh, Higdon issued $100,000 worth of such checks, on which the local salesman made a profit of $40,000 to $60,000. He suspected that Higdon was getting a kickback from the men who cashed the checks. There was this exchange in the hearings:

SEN. EDWARD J. GURNEY: By the way, did you have any evidence that he [Higdon] was getting a cut on this?

ST. MARTIN: The way he spent money, sir, I have no question he did.

GURNEY: From his high living?

ST. MARTIN: Yes, sir.

GURNEY: Obviously he had an outside source of income.

ST. MARTIN: Right, sir.[25]

A few weeks after the first visit to Saigon, Higdon invited St. Martin to make the trip again, the major testified. By this time, Higdon knew that the major was intent on making trouble for his operation, but he apparently still had hopes of co-opting him. And if St. Martin could not be brought around, Higdon and Crum could always count on Cole to get rid of the major as other generals had gotten rid of other troublemakers in the past. Cole's power over such matters at Long Binh was absolute. He was referred to in the hearings as a "Supreme Being" or the "second coming of Napoleon on the post." St. Martin told the Senate subcommittee he thought that if he had played along, he could have become Crum's executive assistant—Crum being the man who was really running the club system—with earnings of $10,000 a week.[26]

During the second trip to Saigon, the two once again visited Crum, who, St. Martin testified complained to the sergeant about difficulties in getting a new slot-machine contract negotiated. A lawyer at Long Binh wanted to put in a "performance clause" under which Crum's firm would have to give some free service. Crum did not like that and said he would talk to Cole about it. Crum also complained that Higdon, whom he treated as an employee, was slow in buying out a string of gift and novelty shops from other concessionaires, thus frustrating Crum's plans to sell half a million dollars' worth of dry goods stored in a customs warehouse. A Vietnamese customs collector was raiding the warehouse from time to time, forcing Crum to pay bribes.

"Bill," Crum said to Higdon, "the only way I can get rid of these dry goods is to have the gift shops under my control."[27]

From Crum's villa Higdon and St. Martin went to International House where, the major told the subcommittee, he watched Higdon purchase three sterling silver tea services at a cost of $960, paying for them in cash and getting receipts for $25 each. Higdon wanted two of the tea services to present to General Harold K. Johnson, Chief of Staff, and Wooldridge at a ceremony they would be attending marking the opening of a new club at Long Binh. The destination of the third tea service was never established. He needed the phony receipts in case questions should be asked about the lavishness of the gifts. Military personnel are not allowed to receive gifts of high value.

In addition to Crum, another outfit doing business at Long Binh was Tom Brothers, the Hong Kong tailors for whom Wooldridge had written letters of recommendation. They were running a Chinese restaurant, and St. Martin said he confronted them when he discovered they had imported two autos to South Vietnam duty-free, using as an excuse their need in the business. David Tung, one of the principals in the firm, replied, the major testified, that he would object to St. Martin's actions to Brigadier General Cole, "a personal friend."

About that time, St. Martin learned that twenty-two Datsuns addressed to the club had arrived at the port in Saigon. The club had not ordered them. He suspected that Crum's firm had hoped to import them duty-free, and began an investigation. But no sooner had he started than he was ordered by his commanding officer to stop checking into the matter.

On December 16, 1967, after he had been on the job only three months and the day after he began the Datsun investigation, orders came down transferring St. Martin out of Long Binh. Now St. Martin gathered together all the evidence he had compiled and confronted his commander, making strong accusations against Cole. Together St. Martin and his commander went to their commander, and St. Martin again told his story. The brigadier general to whom they talked, angered that another general outside the chain of command should initiate a transfer of one of his own officers, put a hold on the action.

Even with all the trouble St. Martin was making, Higdon did not give up, according to St. Martin's testimony. For a third time, he invited St. Martin to Saigon, stopping at International House to check on the engraving for the tea services and then going to Crum's villa where Crum spoke of the need to clear the Datsuns through the port of Saigon. At nightfall, Higdon suggested remaining in Saigon overnight and offered to provide St. Martin with the same prostitute. This time, St. Martin said he would spend the night at a bachelor officers' quarters. The girl came to his room. They went to dinner and window-shopped. St. Martin ‘learned that she worked for Madame Phuong's brother. She did not spend the night, but again both lied about it.

A few days later, Madame Phuong appeard in St. Martin's office to ask about the steam bath-massage parlor contract. St. Martin said a decision had not yet been made. She said Brigadier General Cole "wants me to get the contract."

The next morning, St. Martin arrived at work and found on his desk a memo saying the Board of Governors of the clubs had met and awarded the contract to Madame Phuong. Normally, St. Martin attended the board meetings. This time he had not been invited. The major signed the memo, thinking it "fruitless to argue" but intending to check with the board members to find out just what happened. He never had the chance.*

On December 31, 1967, the dedication of the new club took place, and the tea services were presented to General Johnson and Sergeant Major of the Army Wooldridge. St. Martin, who had hoped to attend the ceremony, arrived late, but subsequently he ran into Wooldridge at the bar. The major told the Senate subcommittee this conversation ensued:

> WOOLDRIDGE: You are the major who is doing some snooping around. Don't you know you can get hurt?

> ST. MARTIN: Considering what is happening, let me remind you a major still outranks a sergeant.[28]

At a New Year's Eve party later, St. Martin's commander informed the major that Cole had succeeded in having him transferred. Cole accused the major of making derogatory remarks about General Johnson at the club dedication and used this as the reason for the transfer. St. Martin denied the allegation.

The next morning, St. Martin testified, he was ordered to type up a report covering all his charges about operation of the Long Binh clubs.

---

* Madame Phuong opened the steam bath and took payment from the GIs in MPC, to which she was legally not entitled. She should have received piasters. She took the MCP to Higdon or other club officials, who exchanged it for dollar checks. The checks were then regularly mailed to a bank account at the Irving Trust Company in New York in the name of C. F. Hsiao, whom Madame Phuong later described to subcommittee investigators as her lover. Actually, he was the operator of a black-market drop account like Prysumeen, into which many others had made over $2 million in deposits between 1966 and 1969. All told, she was able, with the help of American military men, to smuggle over $500,000 out of the country. The checks went through the American military postal system.

As ordered, he gave this report to his commander, who in turn passed them on to Cole. In the afternoon, St. Martin was summoned to a meeting in Cole's office. He waited while Cole talked privately to a superior. Then St. Martin was called into the office, and Cole ran down St. Martin's charges, including those against himself, one by one, offering explanations. No one challenged him. The explanations seemed "reasonable enough" to the other officers in the room who knew nothing about the system. It was decided that St. Martin's transfer would stand.

After the meeting, St. Martin requested a private audience with Cole. During it, the major challenged the brigadier general to court-martial him for making false accusations in front of witnesses. Cole refused the challenge, telling the major he had made an "honest error."

During the meeting, Cole had promised an investigation of some of St. Martin's charges. It was apparently never carried out. On January 7, 1968, Major Clement St. Martin, like Sergeant Major Kenneth L. Parrent in Germany, was transferred. He spent his last months in Vietnam at Cam Ranh Bay, where it was impossible for him to make trouble over the doings at Long Binh. A protector-general had struck again.

Cole's tour as deputy chief of staff for personnel and administration ended later in January 1968, and he moved to a job in the pacification program, during which he wrote the letter to Dallas plugging Carlings beer, which Crum sold in Vietnam. The brigadier general moved from Long Binh to Westmoreland's MACV headquarters—the "Pentagon East" as it was known—at Tansonnhut Air Base in Saigon. Five months after Cole joined MACV, Westmoreland departed Saigon to become Army Chief of Staff in Washington. Cole stopped by to say farewell and left with Westmoreland's administrative assistant a sterling-silver cigarette case. There were eighteen names engraved on it and an inscription indicating the box was a joint gift of appreciation from the members of Westmoreland's MACV staff. Two of the names had no military title. One was W. E. Colby, a foreign-service officer helping to run the pacification program.* The other was William Crum. Westmoreland packed the case and after he returned to Washington, displayed it in his Pentagon office, thinking it came from all the men whose names were on the box.

* Although Colby was carried on the MACV roster as a foreign-service officer, he was really a CIA man. In May 1973, in fact, he became director of the CIA when President Nixon reorganized his administration in the wake of the Watergate scandal.

The Army later issued a statement saying Westmoreland thought the "William Crum" on the box was for the late Air Force Major General William J. Crumm (spelled with two m's) commander of the 3d Air Division on Guam, which provided B-52 strikes in South Vietnam. Crumm died in an air crash north of the Philippines in June 1967, and Westmoreland thought the other officers were memorializing him, although he was puzzled, according to the Army fact sheet, by the lack of title in front of the name. The fact sheet said Westmoreland returned the box to Cole in April 1970 on learning that Cole had purchased it through William Crum, the civilian salesman in Saigon, whose name was actually on the box. The sheet said: "General Westmoreland did not recall ever meeting or hearing of a civilian by the name of Bill Crum."[29]

All the indications are that Cole had a reputation among his friends as being expert on the good life in the Far East. Just as Colonel Ivey went to Cole for suggestions on things to see and places to stay in Hong Kong, Mrs. William C. Westmoreland approached Cole for help in purchasing a jade figurine. The request, General Westmoreland told Senator Ribicoff, came at a party attended by the Coles and the Westmorelands. Cole, whose record indicates he had trouble doing things in a straightforward manner, then wrote to the son of a Chinese restaurateur in Hong Kong asking for a figurine. The son was in the import-export business, Cole testified. The brigadier general had met him, he said, in the father's restaurant.

Several months later, according to Cole, an American soldier returning from a rest and rehabilitation trip to Hong Kong delivered to Cole a package containing a jade figurine with no bill. Cole delivered the figurine to Westmoreland's office and then wrote to "Mr. Chou" in Hong Kong for a bill, he said. It did not come. He wrote again several months later, and again there was no reply. While Cole was en route to his new assignment as commander of the European Exchange System in December 1968, he said, he again saw Mrs. Westmoreland, who asked for a bill, as she had before. From Germany, Cole testified, he wrote Chou for a third time with no results.[30]

Cole arrived in Nuremberg, Germany, in January 1969, to take over the European Exchange System. Late in the summer, news of the Senate subcommittee's investigation broke. The Army began its own investigation, and as a result, General and Mrs. Westmoreland flew to Germany, where the general personally relieved Cole of his command.

After the meeting, Mrs. Westmoreland, who had not yet returned the jade figurine, asked once again for a bill, Cole testified.

Cole was transferred to Army headquarters in Germany at Heidelberg, and then, after a wild weekend in October during which he disappeared, claiming he was offered a bribe of $50,000 to remain silent at the Senate hearings, he was apprehended by CID agents and transferred back to Washington. He put in a request for retirement, which was honored on July 30, 1970, after he was reduced in rank to colonel and stripped of some of his medals.

Though the Uniform Code of Military Justice contains provisions for trying a man for conduct unbecoming an officer, no proceedings were ever instituted against Cole.

In fact, efforts were made to stifle the Senate subcommittee's investigation of Cole's involvement. For one thing, John R. Blandford, the Marine Corps reserve major general who headed the staff of the House Armed Services Committee, made at least two visits to the Senate side of Capitol Hill to try to talk the Senate subcommittee into canceling its investigation. Meanwhile, Representative L. Mendel Rivers, then chairman of the House Armed Services Committee, which has been more a protector than a watchdog of the military, met with Ribicoff. Finally, Rivers wrote Ribicoff a letter. The letter, never before published, said:

February 25, 1970

Honorable Abraham Ribicoff
United States Senate
Washington, D.C.

Dear Senator Ribicoff:

You will recall that I talked with you on the telephone some time ago about Brigadier General Earl Cole, whose name had been mentioned by a professional entertainer in connection with the club investigations in Vietnam.

As you undoubtedly know, General Cole was summarily relieved of his command as head of the European Exchange Service and returned to Washington sometime after he was relieved, where he has been doing practically nothing since his return to the United States.

At the time we talked on the telephone you indicated to me that to the best of your knowledge there were no charges pending against General Cole, but that the Army had not yet submitted its report with respect to General Cole. I have since learned that the Army has no criminal charges or court martial charges pending against General Cole, and apparently the only statement containing any allegations against General Cole, submitted by a Major St. Martin, has been completely refuted.

I have received quite a few letters and have heard many comments by junior officers in the Army indicating that they no longer desire to make a career of the Army, simply because of what has happened to General Cole. They feel that if a general officer, who was doing an outstanding job in Europe, can be summarily removed and treated as General Cole has been treated, based upon rumors and hearsay evidence, then this can happen to them and they want no part of the Army as a career.

I am enclosing a copy of a letter I have received from Captain John S. Price, for example, who wrote me the other day and enclosed a copy of a letter he wrote to General Westmoreland. I hope that you will read Captain Price's letter. I call your particular attention to the last paragraph of his letter. The whole incident has had a very serious effect upon the morale of many junior officers.

In view of the above, I would deeply appreciate your advising me what disposition you plan to make in the case of General Cole.

I would very much appreciate your immediate reaction to this letter.

Sincerely,

/s/ Mendel Rivers

L. MENDEL RIVERS

Enclosures
LMR:jbs

When Cole brought Rivers' name up in the hearings, Ribicoff mentioned dryly that he had heard from the congressman but that the hearings would go on. For once, the power of the military lobby and its friends on Capitol Hill was stifled.

. . .

After Cole left Long Binh in January 1968, a new base commander, Colonel Edmund Castle, took charge of the post. Castle found the situation a shambles. Visiting the clubs, he found them disorganized, unsanitary and not conducive to military discipline. He told the subcommittee how, for example, rats scampered across his feet in the clubs and how Vietnamese women were found washing dishes on the floor in one area. The concession business was so badly out of hand that no one knew how many concessions there were. He discovered a barber shop concession operating in a latrine. Some concessions were mounted on skids so that, when they were raided by CID agents, the proprietors simply towed their shops to a new area. Madame Phuong's massage parlor was advertised by two huge guilded nude statues outside the door. Castle threatened to bust the statues up if she did not remove them. She replaced them with winged dragons. He stationed CID agents inside, posing as customers, and ordered all the doors and curtains removed from the massage booths. He also expelled the two hundred bar girls, and when Madame Phuong installed a huge, canopiea bed—she said it was for her own rest—he made her remove it. He took charge of the warehouse areas and tried to clean out all the illegally stored goods. At one point, he was offered a bribe to sell to Crum's slot-machine firm some used one-arm bandits that would command a good price on the Vietnamese market.

Toward the end of the tour, threats upon his life were becoming regular and he was assigned a bodyguard.

Crum did not restrict his contacts to Cole and the Maredem sergeants. His sphere of influence was far more widely diversified. Crum did business with the PX system as well as the service clubs, and as early as August 1965, two Navy officers who worked in the exchange system— Lieutenants Junior Grade Charles M. Foster and Kim R. Martiny— moved into a Saigon villa that Crum rented for them. In 1966, word of the arrangement came to the attention of the Army. Lieutenant Commander Julian B. King told the subcommittee that it was Crum himself who exposed the two officers because they had not given him enough business. Crum had his secretary turn the officers in for living it up in a Saigon villa while other men were dying in the war, King testified.

In late 1965, with the coming of the big troop build-up, control of the PXs shifted from the Navy to the Army/Air Force Exchange Service. When five Army/Air Force men arrived from the United States to take over the business, Crum was ready. He rented and furnished a villa for them. The group, including their leader, Lieutenant Colonel John G. Goodlett, Jr., moved right in. Thus Crum had the uniformed officer in charge as well as the civilian general manager, the chief for food branch and concessions, the chief for procurement and the chief for retail operations living at his expense. The arrangement was a real coup, which Crum, of course, recognized, writing this letter to a client, Mel Peterson, vice-president, international division, James Beam Distilling Company, Chicago:

> Dear Mel: I want you to know that Peter Mason and Dick Llewellyn, the two top civilians for the Army & Air Force Exchange Service, have arrived. I showed them the brand new house I am decorating for them and they are absolutely delighted.
>
> We are getting along like peas in a pod and they are real sharp operators, so I feel we are going to get a lot more action than we did in the past.
>
> Believe me, I am practically moving right in with these boys without jeopardizing our reputation. Got them a delightful 4-bedroom house which I'm doing the living room in natural rush rattan, installing wall to wall rush carpet and bamboo bar, etc. Also I include in the rent, the cook and two maids, utilities, and other local expenses, so they pay me in dollars once per month at quite a saving. The cook is a real pro and their cuisine will be only second to mine in Southeast Asia.[31]

Although that letter only mentions two men, it was not disputed at the hearings that the others moved in as well. The subcommittee could not determine how much the PX men paid, if anything, for the villa. Lieutenant Colonel Goodlett testified that he paid $100 a month to one of his villa mates but that he thought that went only for food. One of Crum's employees, who had previously lived in the villa, estimated it cost $2,000 a month to keep it up. In retrospect, Goodlett recognized his error, as these excerpts from his affidavit to the subcommittee indicate:

> I learned sometime in mid-1966 that the villa was being rented by William J. Crum. Mr. Crum was associated as a

vendor with Sarl Electronics [Crum's slot-machine firm], which supplied slot machines to the servicemen's clubs. He also represented Jim Beam liquor in Vietnam. When I learned that Mr. Crum was paying for the villa, I should have immediately moved out of the home and ordered the others to move out as well. But I didn't. By staying there I exercised a serious error in judgment.

. . .

My assignment as commander, Vietnam Regional Exchange, was the most demanding of my career. We were given the assignment on a very short notice of expanding in an incredibly short time a PX capability for 100,000 men to an exchange able to serve 450,000 men. We got the job done.

. . .

But I paid dearly. After several major operations I was retired with 60 percent disability by the Army. Now, in light of developments brought out by this Senate committee inquiry, it seems my reputation is going to suffer. And for this I have only myself to blame. But I can say—and I say it in truth—I did not accept payment or any other form of gratuity from William Crum. But I did live in his villa and that was a mistake.

. . .

In 1966, a sizable PX contract was awarded to Sarl Electronics for installing and maintaining juke boxes in Army/ Air Force Exchange System exchanges in Vietnam. As commander of the Vietnam Regional Exchange, I signed that contract. But the staffing was directed—and the recommendation to give it to Sarl—was made by Clarence Swafford. This was in keeping with his job description as head of concessions.[32]

Goodlett's successor, Colonel Jack Ice, lived in the villa for three weeks rent-free and later told the subcommittee he saw nothing wrong with the arrangement.

As the Senate subcommittee dug deeper and deeper into this morass, exposing the black-market currency manipulations that were sucking the Vietnamese economy dry, uncovering employees of the exchange system in other locations who were taking kickbacks, discovering that vendors to the clubs were shipping goods on military planes and ships, the services and other agencies of government took appropriate action to weed out—if not always punish—the wrongdoers, close loopholes and establish new ways of conducting their affairs. But outside the scope of the Senate's investigation and ignored by the services were the two basic problems from which everything else flowed.

First, there was the utter lack of concern the military leadership displayed for spending its budgeted funds for the welfare of its troops. It built slums for the troops and then allowed them to fend for themselves in improving their morale. And so, just as the unscrupulous have ever preyed upon slum dwellers, the Crums, Higdons, Coles and Wooldridges of this world were able to go to work.

Senator Charles H. Percy of Illinois, one of the subcommittee members, showed an appreciation for this problem as he interrogated Cole. After eliciting from the former brigadier general the fact that the troops were housed in substandard quarters at Long Binh, Percy turned to the use of clubs and sauna baths as maintainers of morale.

> Where [Percy asked rhetorically] is our sense of priorities? Instead of fixing up housing we build an elaborate sauna bath where the men spend their own money and come in with pictures of these lovely nudes from the outside. . . .
>
> In other words, we don't have the money to build housing but as long as the money comes out of the boys' pockets for slot machines, whisky or whatever, we spend their own money or advance it to build sauna baths. Then they pay a profit to the entrepreneur of the sauna bath who reaps a high profit, I assume, and it all comes from our own men out there. . . .
>
> How could the Dragon Lady provide hot baths, water for the sauna baths, and the whole United States Army, Navy and Air Forces couldn't get hot water? . . .

To which Cole replied:

> The person who made the decision on the type of facility and construction that would be made in Vietnam was not me. That was the Army's decision.[33]

The Army's decision. No individual had responsibility for the slums. So no individual with authority tried to do anything about them.

On any given problem in the military in the 1970s, you could trace the buck from desk to desk, from bureau to bureau, from department to department and never find out where it came to rest. It did not settle down on even the desks of the topmost generals, for when you asked them about the problems, they guided you along to the civilians controlling the Defense Department, to the White House and to the Congress.

Officers working within the system who persisted in trying to isolate and confront men of authority, ran into trouble, as did Major Clement St. Martin. While a generation of yes men ruled, the system could not take corrective actions. That point was summed up in this exchange between the major and Senator Ribicoff:

> SENATOR RIBICOFF: So your experience has been when you voiced your own personal opinion in the Army, you received punishment for it.
>
> MAJOR ST. MARTIN: Yes, sir. That was the first purple shaft, and the second one is when General Cole gave it to me.
>
> SENATOR RIBICOFF: You were learning slowly or fast that being frank didn't pay.
>
> MAJOR ST. MARTIN: That is right, sir.
>
> SENATOR RIBICOFF: It is pretty hard to buck the system.
>
> MAJOR ST. MARTIN: Not if you don't want to get promoted, I guess.[34]

Though specific quick fixes intended to deal with the specific issues raised by the Senate subcommittee hearings were subsequently made, there are indications that corruption involving American personnel in Vietnam continued. On July 19, 1971, four months after the hearings closed, a team of Vietnamese and American investigators representing South Vietnam's Customs Service, the National Police, the Army CID and U.S. Aid Mission Advisors appeared at the residence of Miss Hoang Thi Nam, directly across the street from the Vietnamese police headquarters for all the northern part of South Vietnam, in Danang. The raid lasted twelve hours, and when it was completed, the officials had collected three and a half stake-bed truckloads of goods including twenty-five air conditioners (two of which were delivered to the house by a pedicab while the raid was in progress), television sets, a motor scooter and dozens of other foreign-made items belonging to American military forces, purchased in PXs, received from Hong Kong or sent through the American military postal system to servicemen and American civilians. The inventory of illicit goods in Miss Nam's house and two warehouses on the property covered five and a half typewritten pages. The agents also found records indicating that she had a dollar bank account at the Guam branch of the Bank of America, containing some $2 million in deposits, when she should have been paid for any services she provided to the American forces in piasters. The raiders estimated her account was earning $100,000 a year in interest. When the agents asked her if she had any foreign accounts, she said she did not. When they asked her specifically about an account in a Guam bank, she again denied having one. When they showed her records indicating the account's existence, she said she had forgotten about that one. Records showed that practically all the goods in Miss Nam's treasure-trove had been originally purchased by Americans and then found their way to her house. USAID and CID reports on the raid called her one of four key figures in smuggling and black-market activities in Danang, South Vietnam's second-largest city. The other three included the wife of a zone customs chief and the wife of a Vietnamese Army officer in charge of the city's military security. Miss Nam was also said to be a very close friend of Lieutenant General Hoang Xuan Lam, the Vietnamese Army commander in Military Region One. (Lam was removed from his command almost a year later when his soldiers fled before the North Vietnamese invading Quangtri province.)

How had Miss Nam gotten away with all this? The USAID and CID reports contained almost identical explanations:

> It has been stated that the police did, in fact, attempt to raid the premises on two different occasions but in each case, there was a high ranking U.S. or Vietnamese General Officer present in her home as a guest and the raiding party departed immediately.[35]

It became fashionable in the 1970s for senior officers in the services to try to explain away some of the more publicized problems in their commands—drugs, race, desertion, discipline breakdown—with the assertion that the services only "mirrored society" and that of course the military machine suffered from the same problems that today's permissively educated and trained young were foisting upon civilian society.

If the idea of military-as-mirror is to be accepted, then it must be applied to the older professionals in the organization as well as the young. One must equate the failure of the Army, for example, to bring to justice men such as Cole and Wooldridge—or the generals involved in the My Lai massacre—with the mechanism that often allows an embezzling bank president or a big income-tax evader to go free while small-time bank robbers and automobile thieves go to jail.

It was not only in My Lai and in other corruption in Vietnam that men of position in the services went unpunished. Literally the sky was the limit. The ambitious reached for the moon.

So did some astronauts.

The Apollo 15 flight to the moon from July 26 to August 7, 1971, was a case in point. When the lunar landing vehicle *Falcon* settled down on the moon on July 30, 1971, it carried a cargo ripe for future exploitation on earth. Air Force Colonel David R. Scott, a West Point graduate, son of a general, and the mission commander, was carrying two watches that he had graciously agreed to take to the moon for a friend on a test run. He also had tucked away in a pocket of his government-issue flight suit a packet of 398 stamped envelopes on which he had, thoughtfully, placed commemorative stamps and taken to the John F. Kennedy Space Flight Center the morning of the flight for cancellation. The covers, as they are known in philatelic circles, were stowed away without the knowledge of NASA officials.

In addition, each of the other men on the mission was carrying some mail. Colonel James B. Irwin had, among other souvenirs, eighty-seven Apollo 12 covers belonging to Mrs. Richard Gordon, wife of a former astronaut. For some reason, those covers never made the Apollo 12 flight, and Irwin took them on Apollo 15 and then returned them to Mrs. Gordon, whom NASA described as a stamp collector.

Finally, along with some other miscellaneous authorized philatelic materials, Lieutenant Colonel Alfred M. Worden, who was the command module pilot, had 144 authorized covers, 100 of which were imprinted with a cachet showing fifteen phases of the moon and marked with launch and recovery dates by F. Herrick Herrick, a philatelist and friend of Worden's.

As a last item, the astronauts also carried a small statuette named

"Fallen Astronaut," which they left on the moon as a memorial to all astronauts—American and Soviet—who had perished in the exploration of space.

When the Apollo 15 crew returned to earth, they were busy men. They took most of their covers to the post office aboard the recovery ship, the USS *Okinawa,* bought stamps for them and had them canceled. Then, on the flight back to Hawaii, they each autographed all the covers. Finally, back in Houston, they had the unauthorized covers notarized as being genuine moon mail. Now Scott, working on a pre-arranged plan, mailed 100 of the unauthorized covers to Horst Walter Eiermann, a naturalized German who had once worked for the space program but who had returned to Stuttgart, Germany. Eiermann turned the covers over to a German stamp dealer, Herman E. Sieger, who proceeded to sell them for $1,500 apiece. Out of the $150,000 profit, the astronauts were to receive $7,000 each. Eiermann deposited the money in their names in savings accounts he opened in Germany. In February 1972, after the sale of the covers had been well advertised and began to attract attention, the astronauts returned the money to Eiermann. The former NASA employee then suggested they accept a set of stamps each instead of the cash. Initially, they accepted but then rejected the offer in April 1972. At the same time, Worden's covers had been given to Herrick—some as an outright gift, others to be held safely for the astronaut. Herrick started selling those which had been given to him and realized a $7,175 profit before NASA blew the whistle. In September 1972, NASA, after an investigation, said: "To date, no information has been developed indicating that there were agreements or arrangements between Herrick and Worden whereby Worden was to have received anything of value from any sale of the covers by Herrick."

Meanwhile, "Fallen Astronaut" was enjoying a rebirth on earth. Its sculptor, Paul Van Hoeydonck, signed 950 replicas of the statuette, which were then sold by a New York art gallery for $950 each. The astronauts said they had had a clear understanding with Van Hoeydonck, whom Scott had met at a dinner party, that he would not exploit the memorial commercially.

Their experience, then, with the statues was similar to that suffered by Admiral Alan Bartlett Shepard, Jr., who a decade before was lionized as the first American in space. On the Apollo 14 mission, Shepard carried 200 coins prepared at the Franklin Mint, a private mint in Pennsylvania. On his return, he sent 50 of the coins to the mint, which melted them down and mixed the metal with enough new materials to make 130,000 new coins. Those, in turn, were offered to new mint subscribers at nine dollars each. Shepard took no money from the transaction, and Donald K. Slayton, chief of flight crew operations for the Apollo program, accused the mint of breaking faith. "We had a gentleman's agreement" with the mint, Slayton said, never detailing what it was.[36] Neither was there any public explanation of what happened to the 150 coins Shepard retained.

The three Apollo 15 astronauts were removed from the astronaut corps, reprimanded and given notations for using bad judgment in their military officer efficiency reports, according to a National Aeronautics and Space Administration report issued in September 1972, from which this information is taken. NASA also turned the information over to the Justice Department for review. No action was taken against Shepard.

The NASA report also contained an appendix which revealed, for the first time, that fifteen out of the sixty-six Apollo astronauts had signed blocks of stamps, post cards and other material for Eiermann in the past at a rate of $5 per signature. Each of the men received $2,500. Five of them donated the money to charity. The others kept the money.

After the reprimand, Irwin resigned from service to become an evangelist—"to go with God," as he put it. He also went before the Senate Committee on Space and Aeronautics with his two colleagues to answer questions about the stamps. Their testimony was taken in closed session under a little-used rule that allows such private hearings on matters of national security or where the testimony "may tend to reflect adversely on the character or reputation of the witness . . ." The *New York Times* quoted a Senate official who keeps track of rules usage as saying he could not recall a similar usage in twenty years.[37]

Many were willing to dismiss the actions of the astronauts as indiscretions or bad judgment and not out-and-out corruption. However, the situation was at once more complex and more simple.

The complexity results from the fact that from the very beginning of the manned space program, NASA made it easy for the astronauts to capitalize personally on their experiences. The original Project Mercury astronauts, of which Shepard was one, were allowed to sign a lucrative contract with *Life* magazine giving that publication exclusive rights to their first-person stories. Then NASA brought them together with a Washington, D.C., attorney who helped them invest their earnings. Among the investments was a motel at Cocoa Beach, Florida, used heavily by NASA contractors, government officials and the press in the early days of the manned space flight program.

With such relaxed rules, when the astronauts moved to Houston, Texas, they were offered free homes in a new housing development, which they almost accepted. They received new automobiles at greatly reduced prices and could have gotten them gratis if a NASA official had not intervened. Shepard became a stockholder in a local bank. Astronaut James Lovell bought heavily into an airline that flew between the Manned Spacecraft Center near Houston and the Houston Airport. Even in the late 1960s, Scott was allowed to sign an exclusive contract with the *New York Times* for his personal story.

Thus, the space agency helped—and maybe even urged—the astronauts to capitalize personally on their experiences in spending the taxpayers' money. The complexity of the situation then results from the manner in which they were placed above the rules and regulations kept in effect for lesser mortals.

The simplicity of the situation is that they stretched the rules even further than NASA was willing to allow.

In this sense, they were no different from the Maredem sergeants or the generals who protected them; no different from the USO officials, the Marine Corps procurement men or the corrupt Vietnamese officials whose activities are detailed in this chapter. All of them had been encouraged by the system to take care of themselves. Sergeants down through the history of the Army were special people who received a cut on gambling in their units, who loan-sharked, who scrounged for extra comforts. These were perquisites allowed by the system. Generals were —and continue to be—a special breed of men who lived above the law.

Officials in the Vietnamese government the United States supported were given leeway in their own personal financial transactions out of the belief they had to be kept happy to help the war effort.

All this corruption was important not only in itself or even in the debilitating effect it had on those who were its victims. It was also important as an indication of the double standard the military maintained for the treatment of the powerful and prestigious as opposed to the ordinary people in the system. It appeared impossible to maintain properly the necessary discipline to run a military machine if key personnel were going to be allowed to take advantage of their positions while the little people were punished severely for refusing to obey the oftentimes capricious dicta of the powerful and prestigious.

PART FOUR

A GENERATION OF DECEPTION
AND SELF-DECEPTION

*He was tall and thin, with long sideburns and a glorious mustache. He
was modishly dressed, serious and, above all, he looked like the kind of
man who would say: "I now consider myself a pacifist. I have never hit
anybody in my life. I couldn't hit anybody. Can you imagine killing
100,000 Russians just because their* leaders *attacked the United States?"*

*The speaker was Ted Weihe, twenty-seven years old, a foreign
affairs graduate from Georgetown University, who had recently completed serving three years in the Strategic Air Command in a job where
he kept his hand on one of the nation's nuclear triggers. Ted Weihe was
a Minuteman Missile deputy combat crew commander, spending most
of his working hours sixty feet under the Missouri plains in a command
capsule waiting for an order that would signal the coming of Armageddon.*

*It was natural that Weihe should have joined the Air Force. His
father was a pioneer of the aviation industry. His older brother flew
fighter bombers in the Vietnam War and then became an airline pilot.*

*Weihe joined the Air Force ROTC program at Georgetown and
then requested an assignment on the East Coast when he graduated.
Without any apparent qualifications—he had taken no math or technical
courses in college—and hoping for an assignment in intelligence or as a
language officer, he found himself routed off to Whitman Air Force
Base, Missouri, to work with the ICBMs.*

*For the first few months, he was fascinated by what he saw in the
Orwellian world of knobs, dials, lights, teletypes and disembodied radio
voices that were the features of his life in the capsule. But the thoughts
of the potential destruction, in the monotony of the underground capsule, were not long in coming. After he left the Air Force, Weihe wrote:
"Under the almost maddening conditions of isolation and boredom, a
launch officer repeatedly mulls over his reactions to an actual launch
message. Daily he practices the launch sequence from receipt of message to the twist of his wrist above the launch key slot. Each time a part*

*of his mind dwells on his role at unleashing the destruction at his com-
mand. He tries to cope with the moral implications of turning the key
on millions of people."*[1]

The result of Weihe's coping was a decision, not conveyed to his
superiors, that he could not ever turn Armageddon's key. The conviction
led him into politics in 1968 as a canvasser for and supporter of then
Senator Eugene J. McCarthy, who was seeking the Democratic presidential nomination as a peace candidate. And he made some subtle personal protests. He began letting his hair grow to the limits of the Air
Force's regulations—and then some. Under his blue jacket, he wore a
tieclasp with the peace symbol on it. One day, in an emergency warfare
operations class, the air conditioning broke down, and the officers were
ordered to remove their jackets. Weihe's tieclasp was exposed.

He was immediately called from the room and asked for an explanation.

"Well," he recalled saying, "the SAC motto is 'Peace is our profession'; I could think of nothing more appropriate than this symbol which
for thousands of years stood for peace."

His superiors reminded him that the symbol was now used by
"subversive groups" and asked Weihe if he was a member of any such
groups.

"No," Captain Weihe replied.

"Are you sure?" the officer asked.

"Well, I did work for McCarthy, and many in his organization
used the symbol," Weihe answered.

He removed the pin and did not wear it again.

By the time Weihe's tour was coming to an end, he was spending
his time in the capsule figuring out ways of delaying a launch or making
it impossible if the order ever came. He also convinced himself that
almost all his colleagues in the capsules across the country would not
launch if the order came. And if they did turn the keys, he said, the
possibility of the missiles ever leaving their silos was low. Repeatedly,
he said, tests had shown such serious problems that, to the men who
operated the system, its credibility as a deterrent was seriously in
question.

As it was incapable of performing effectively in a guerrilla war in
Southeast Asia, so the American military machine might be incapable
of performing at Armageddon. Weihe was not alone in holding that
view. Many others, in a better position to document their beliefs, held
the same view. But they would not speak out.

331

14

THE BRIDGE AT THANH HOA

Large standing forces of the kind that the United States has maintained throughout the Cold War period of the 1950s, 1960s and into the 1970s are not in the American tradition. They are forces, garrisoned throughout the world, intended to protect the nation against *possible* threat. They are forces configured to take advantage of the old maxim that the best defense is a good offense. And thus they are forces that allow the nation's policy-makers to make full use of the Clausewitzian idea that "war is not merely a political act, but also a political instrument."

Clausewitz went on to say that war was "a continuation of political relations, a carrying out of the same by other means." In the hands of modern policy-makers, however, the idea was skewed ever so slightly, and war did not become a *continuation* of political relations. It became a *substitute* for political relations.

Big wars such as the Civil War in this country and World Wars I and II illustrate Clausewitz' point. The international body politic suffered a massive breakdown. The only continuation of the game the policy-makers were playing at the time was through a resort to arms.

Neither the Vietnam War nor the Dominican Republic intervention of 1965 conformed to the Clausewitzian idea. In these cases, warfare was used not as a continuation of political relations but as a substitute.

The United States, during the Cold War period, had transformed itself into a militaristic nation. It did so without considering all the consequences. Indeed, it did so without admitting the fact of its new

332

militarism to itself. It did so with an imperfect knowledge of the nature of the threat confronting it.

Although always an aggressive nation pursuing a manifest destiny, stretching out its frontiers, making its mark in the world, the United States was not, until after World War II, a militaristic nation on the world stage.

Within months after the Treaty of Paris was ratified, ending the Revolutionary War, Congress ordered the cutback of the Army to a mere 80 men and a few officers—enough to guard the military stores at West Point, New York, and Fort Pitt, now Pittsburgh, Pennsylvania. In 1865, the million-man Union Army was cut back to 57,000 in a year's time. This number was halved again in another ten years. From a World War II peak strength of 8.3 million in 1945, the Army was reduced to 593,000 men by 1950. The American people distrusted large standing forces at worst. At best, they saw no good use for them. They were traditionally unwilling to mortgage themselves for protection against a vague *possible* threat. They were, however, more than willing to defend themselves against an *imminent* threat.

This changed during the Cold War. For the generation after the Korean War, the United States maintained men in uniform numbering between 1.5 and 2.6 million. They garrisoned what was known as the "Free World," patrolling its borders and roaming the seas and skies. With impunity, they flew airplanes over the countries perceived as enemies, probing, photographing, collecting data on the military capabilities of those countries. They established military missions in dozens of smaller countries, importuning them to cast their lot with the Free World. By 1972, the draftee sons of draftees who had fought for Korea were garrisoning posts in that remote country. By 1972, the West-Point-graduate sons of West Pointers who had commanded battalions in the World War II liberation of Europe were themselves middle-aged men commanding battalions garrisoned in Europe. By 1972, Brigadier General George S. Patton, III, had succeeded his illustrious father of World War II fame on the rolls of the United States Army's generals. The Pax Americana had become a deeply rooted way of life.

The momentum was toward the continued perpetuation of that way of life. Politicians contributed to the perpetuation. It was part of the political dogma of the time that America had to remain militarily second to none to survive. Bureaucratic policy-makers contributed to the perpetuation. They had developed the Cold War ideas on which the whole system was based and could not, for this reason, easily change their minds. Industry and labor contributed to the perpetuation. Huge profits and vast numbers of jobs were involved in supplying the military machine with all the equipment and consumables necessary to keep it running. The great universities contributed to the perpetuation. They received huge grants and contracts which allowed them to expand facilities; faculty members appreciably increased their income with consulting fees paid by the government for their thoughts about the unthinkable. And finally, the military professionals contributed to the perpetuation. The larger the machine, the greater were the opportunities for the men operating it.

Military machine and operator became indistinguishable. Since the inanimate machine could not express itself, only the operators were heard. Not surprisingly, they saw that what was good for the machine was good for themselves. As the machine grew larger, their prestige, power and standard of living increased. This led easily to the perception that what was good for themselves was good for the machine. And, of course, the logical extension of that thought was that what was good for the machine was good for the nation. Given the powerful confluence of interests among military men, politicians, bureaucratic policy-makers, academics, businessmen and labor leaders, the machine outgrew its status as a Clausewitzian political instrument. It became an important entity in itself, one that had to be pampered and maintained like the nation's economy.

Mistakes could be tolerated but not the exposure of mistakes, for that might cast doubt on the utility and capability of the machine. This led to the toleration of the practice of always putting the best face on any situation, then to the encouragement of cover-up and finally to the widespread practice of lying.

Covering up and lying to the public were egregious enough. But the operators carried the practice much further. They covered up and lied in their dealings with civilians in the Defense Department, with the rest of the executive branch, with Congress and even among themselves. The term "CYA" became a well-known cynicism within the military.

It stands for "cover your ass."

Thinking men in uniform were troubled by the pervasion of the CYA syndrome. In 1970, the Army War College surveyed 450 of the finest officers in the Army to obtain their views on professionalism, and here, from the reports, are some of what the men who conducted the study called "representative comments" they received on the pervasiveness of the deception:

> MAJOR: My superior was a competent, professional, knowledgeable military officer that (sic) led by fear, would doublecross anyone to obtain a star, drank too much and lived openly by no moral code. He is now a Brigadier General!

> CAPTAIN: Senior officers seem to live under the standard of "Do as I say, not as I do." In my last assignment I witnessed senior officers doing things that if done by an enlisted man would result in courts-martial charges.

> LT. COLONEL: Juniors are just more idealistic. Seniors, except for *some* generals, tend to lie . . . steal . . . and cheat . . . , and no one makes this an issue.

> MAJOR: It is disturbing to me to observe officers in the middle grades lie, cheat, distort facts and take other measures to aggrandize their own personal careers. . . . Their conduct fools no one.

> COLONEL: The military requires success in everything. So success is reported. Training records, supply records are two cases in point. These lies lead easily to others.

> CAPTAIN: The majority of my associates were interested in keeping higher headquarters happy—false reports were the result. . . .

> MAJOR: . . . excessive emphasis on statistical data . . . Under such a system, the honest commander who reports his AWOLs, etc., get into trouble while the dishonest commander gets promoted.

The interviewers listened to and reported stories from men who admitted to carrying extra enemy weapons and planting them on dead Vietnamese civilians so that they could be recorded in inflated body counts. One young officer confessed he almost got into a fistfight with a South Vietnamese officer over the arm of a dead person so that he could report a better body count. Other officers admitted to falsifying AWOL records—actually reporting men who were absent without leave as being on approved leave to meet requirements from higher headquarters for low AWOL figures. .

One interviewer reported:

> The expression that they [the survey subjects] used was that senior officers appear to be deluding themselves and actually talking themselves into believing these false statistics, all the way up the line.[1]

By 1971, concern over the deception was leaking into the public prints. Navy Captain Robert H. Smith, a 1946 graduate of the Naval Academy and son of a Navy captain who was killed in World War II, published an essay in the *U.S. Naval Institute Proceedings* reviewing the troubles confronting his service at that time. The essay was awarded the Institute's Gold Medal Prize for the year. On the matter of self-deception, Smith wrote:

> . . . A climate is created wherein disagreement is stifled and where there are "party lines" to which all views must be subordinated in order that faltering programs will not be impacted. We relinquish the traditional and honored military reputation for plain speaking and we find that when we adopt the ways of the salesman or the maneuvering bureaucrat, our words are so taken, with wariness and doubt. No one has been long in the Pentagon without hearing the familiar, disgusted lament, "We've lied to 'em so often that now they don't believe a word we say." . . .
>
> The greatest danger, though, is that we can try to fool others only so long and then we start to fool ourselves. We can repeat our own distorted arguments only so many times, toil to bend all evidence to advance our cause, and we come to believe what we are saying. This way of operating diverts us from substantive consideration; the superficial aspects take our eyes away from facts and fundamentals. It breeds a cynicism destructive to the spirit. . . . So long as the system in which an officer matures is one that esteems the juggler of figures, and rewards men who can "sell" shaky programs over a man who stubbornly insists that a *bad* one be killed, then we will stay in trouble.[2]

The doctrine of CYA led to the development of the yes-man syndrome in the officer corps of each of the services. It permitted the exploitation of officers and enlisted men by the machine at the same time that it permitted a few men to exploit the machine. It permitted the cover-up of the war-crimes situation in Vietnam. It allowed men such as the Army sergeants, the Marine Corps procurement officials, USO officials and even astronauts to operate as long as they did without obstruction. It permitted barracks to go to seed. It permitted some men to sink into depravity and others into drugs and alcohol.

Finally, in the generation of deception that accompanied the Cold War, it permitted each of the services to deceive itself about its own capabilities. All the services thought they were manned, configured and outfitted to be used as political instruments. None of them were. In their efforts to live up to a mission they could never fulfill, they may have committed the most important error of all. They lost the capacity to defend the nation if, in the nuclear age, the time for defense were ever to come again.

That was the ultimate cost of the generation of deception which the nation paid.

What follows are some examples of how deception affected the ability of each of the services to perform its mission. First, the Air Force.

The city of Thanh Hoa, about ninety miles south of Hanoi in North Vietnam, sits astride the main North-South railroad in that country. The right of way runs from Hanoi south to the demilitarized zone between North and South Vietnam. As it works its way southward, the roadbed comes within miles of the Mu Gia pass, one of the gateways to the Ho Chi Minh Trail complex in Laos.

Thanh Hoa is a major junction along the North Vietnamese supply route, and the key feature in the junction city is a bridge. The Thanh Hoa Bridge was of sturdy steel-truss construction, 540 feet long and 56 feet wide. It rested on a concrete pier in the center and two heavy concrete abutments, one on either side of the river it crosses. The concrete roadway supported railroad track, two truck lanes and two pedestrian lanes.

When President Johnson opened the air war against North Vietnam in February 1965, the Thanh Hoa Bridge was, along with several other potential bottlenecks in the transportation system of North Vietnam, a primary target. During the first year of the war, Air Force and Navy pilots knocked out three hundred other bridges in the North, but they could never knock out the Thanh Hoa Bridge. They tried eveything up to three-thousand-pound blockbusters. They dive-bombed the bridge. They flew down the roadway at low levels, trying to "walk" their bombs onto the span. From time to time they might do some minor, easily repairable damage to the roadbed, but they could not pierce a span.

The Thanh Hoa Bridge stood, throughout the "first air war" from 1965 to the end of 1968, as a symbol of frustration for the Air Force and the Navy. They had sold air power as an instrument of surgical precision. It could be used, they argued, to cripple an enemy's lines of communications and war-making capacity while inflicting a minimal civilian loss, and at great savings in American lives and dollars.

The Thanh Hoa Bridge mocked that idea. As the planes returned for attack after attack, the North Vietnamese, seeing their opportunity, beefed up the antiaircraft defenses around the bridge. By the summer of 1971, the enemy claimed to have shot down one hundred American airplanes over that one target alone. Some American pilots believed the claim. Asked for official confirmation, Air Force headquarters in Washington refused to supply numbers. Once they said the numbers were classified. Another time they said the computers did not contain that kind of data. In Saigon, the American command admitted to the loss of sixty planes and the damaging of forty others in attacks on Thanh Hoa. Assuming all the planes were F-4 Phantoms or the equivalent, which cost some $4 million each, that would mean a loss of from $240 million to $400 million in aircraft alone, exclusive of the cost of mounting the missions or the cost in lives of crewmen, in an attempt to knock out one target. All they had to show for the effort from February 1965 to May 1972 was some easily repairable damage to the railroad tracks inflicted by a strike in November 1967. Otherwise, the bridge continued to operate.

On May 13, 1972, during the "second air war" ordered by President Nixon after the spring offensive of the North Vietnamese, the Air Force finally knocked out the bridge, using one of the new "smart bombs." The bomb was guided onto the target by a laser beam.

And then, what many pilots believed to be true was confirmed. The North Vietnamese made no effort to repair the bridge. It was not an important link in the transportation network at all. It had little military significance.

"There's a ford a few miles upstream," one pilot told me in the fall of 1971, before the bridge was destroyed. "It's not a legitimate target. They don't need it to move their supplies."

As a target, the bridge at Thanh Hoa symbolized the frustrations involved in the use of American air power. As a ruin, it symbolized the inflated expectations American officials placed on the use of aircraft. They saw airplanes as a swift, relatively cheap and clean way of bringing an enemy to its knees. They disregarded the lessons of World War II and Korea in reaching that conclusion in the 1960s. There is little indication that, in the 1970s and beyond, the added lesson of Vietnam will make much difference. At the top and at the bottom of the table of uses of modern day warfare, air power has its utility. It can be used to deliver nuclear weapons over intercontinental ranges with assurance that at least enough, though not necessarily all or even a majority, of the warheads will get through. Thus air power provides a deterrent. At the other end of the table, air power can provide the measure of superiority needed to hold a particular piece of territory for a limited amount of time. When officials write other missions into the table, they run into trouble. Air power alone—at least as it has so far been used—does not defeat an enemy. It does not destroy a war-making capacity. It does not materially affect the flow of supplies to the battlefield. It does not destroy morale. Even Israel, which has used air power more successfully than any other nation in the past twenty years, has found it necessary to invade her neighboring enemies to keep them under control. The doctrine, then, that the United States Air Force and the air arm of the Navy have adopted to justify much of their existence is open to serious question. The bridge at Thanh Hoa and many other features of the air war in Southeast Asia from 1965 onward attest to that.

The lessons of what air power could not do, learned in World War II and Korea, were ignored in Vietnam. Despite the awesome bomb tonnage dropped on North Vietnam in the two air wars, the one conducted under President Lyndon B. Johnson from February 1965 to November 1968, and the other begun by Richard M. Nixon in the spring of 1972, the United States did not stop the flow of supplies into North Vietnam from other communist nations or from North Vietnam to the battlefields in South Vietnam and Cambodia.*

---

* Although writers have recently begun referring to two air wars against North Vietnam, they are, of course, part of the same campaign. Though there were two periods of intense bombing, the North Vietnamese never really had complete respite from the American airplanes after President Johnson ordered a halt to the bombing on Halloween night, 1968, in the hope of advancing a negotiated settlement to the war. After that halt, the rules of engagement did permit so-called armed reconnaissance missions to be flown over North Vietnam. And these

By August 30, 1972, the United States had, since the beginning of the bombing in February 1965, dropped about three and a half times more tonnage of bombs, missiles, cannon shells and machine-gun bullets in Southeast Asia than all the Allies had expended in all the war thea-

---

missions were allowed to pursue a doctrine of "protective reaction." In a typical "armed recky" mission, an unarmed F-4 Phantom aircraft, carrying only cameras, was escorted to its target by at least two armed Phantoms—sometimes as many as sixteen. Under protective reaction, if the mission was fired upon, it was allowed to fire back. The doctrine also permitted the escorts to open up with their bombs and missiles if the enemy so much as turned on its radar to track the planes, under the assumption that the radars were connected with surface-to-air missiles or antiaircraft batteries which often fired automatically. The Phantoms carried instruments which told the pilots when the radars were switched on. Although "protective reaction" connotes a situation in which aircraft open fire when placed in jeopardy, the doctrine was stretched officially on a couple of occasions. At those times, the Pentagon announced that "reinforced protective reaction raids" had been conducted. These were large-scale bombing missions during the air-war hiatus, when the United States Air Force retaliated against North Vietnam for ground attacks that had taken place in South Vietnam. The raids had nothing to do with immediate jeopardy to picture-taking aircraft. General John D. Lavelle, who was relieved as commander of the Air Force in Southeast Asia for falsifying reports and exceeding the rules of engagement, stretched the doctrine of protective reaction even further. He allowed his pilots to make the assumption that certain enemy radar which could be monitored by the Phantoms was always turned on. In effect, then, he gave pilots a license to drop their bombs and fire their rockets on certain preselected targets without any clearance of those targets by higher headquarters. He was removed from his position because, to justify those raids, he encouraged the submission of reports from the field which said that the planes had been placed in jeopardy, and had forwarded those reports to higher headquarters. Air Force Sergeant Lonnie Franks, an intelligence expert stationed in Thailand whose letter to Senator Harold Hughes first exposed the falsifications, said that more than two hundred men were involved in faking the reports. The first of the twenty-eight unauthorized raids took place on November 8, 1971, while Dr. Henry Kissinger was involved in secret peace negotiations with the North Vietnamese. The raids lasted until March 8, 1972. The Lavelle case is a textbook example of how the practice of lying had become so deeply entrenched in the military. His subordinate officers accepted his commands without question. Major General Alton D. Slay, Lavelle's deputy, said he passed on the orders to falsify records out of the feeling that Lavelle must have had good reason for what he was doing. Lavelle's reason was that he was under orders to do whatever he could to block a build-up of enemy supplies for a new offensive in South Vietnam. On one occasion General Creighton W. Abrams, Jr., American commander in South Vietnam, authorized a raid that violated the rules of engagement. On another, Lavelle showed post-strike photographs of an illegal raid to Admiral Thomas H. Moorer, chairman of the Joint Chiefs of Staff, and Moorer voiced no objections. Though the military services pride themselves on maintaining a high standard of morality—West Pointers are taught, for example, "a cadet does not lie, steal or cheat"—Lavelle suffered only a mild rebuke. He ters in World War II. (Total tonnage dropped from planes in World War II was 2.05 million; the seven-and-one-half-year total in Southeast Asia was 7.5 million.)[3] Officials gave a threefold purpose for all this bombardment: (1) to halt or slow the flow of supplies to the battlefield; (2) to make the cost of the war prohibitive to the North Vietnamese; (3) to keep the morale of the South Vietnamese high enough that the American-supported regime would be maintained.

The bombing campaign was successful only in contributing to the third purpose. Without the American airplanes, the South Vietnamese effort would have collapsed. But that in itself was a trap, for the Saigon regime could only be maintained as long as American air power was applied. And the dosages of air power had to grow increasingly heavy to compensate for the withdrawal of American ground troops which President Nixon began in June 1969.

If air power was intended as a tool to shorten a war, the lesson of Vietnam was that the way it was applied did not accomplish such a purpose. In fact, by shoring up a regime that could not maintain its own viability, air power only helped to prolong the war. Going beyond that thought, the war exposed several deficiencies in the operating methods of the United States Air Force. Most important of these was the necessity of the Air Force to operate from completely safe, highly mechanized, heavily supported sanctuaries. The time had long since passed when Air Force leaders could station a few planes in a cow pasture of an aerodrome and expect them to carry out operations. A modern fighter-bomber base was an intricate industrial facility supporting airplanes containing engines of Swiss-watch delicacy and electronics of a sophistication similar to giant computers. It took a vast array of complex repair and maintenance facilities to keep those plants in order. The typical base in Southeast Asia, for example, stockpiled 70,000 different parts to keep an F-4 Phantom fighter-bomber wing in operation. The system was so complex that computers were needed to run it. The

---

was relieved from command and retired by the Air Force at three-star rank, one rank below the four stars he wore in his last job but still one rank above his permanent grade of major general. Congress subsequently ordered him retired at the rank of major general. But his retirement pay was set at the four-star level of $27,000 a year, all but $2,900 of which was tax-free. To accomplish this, the Air Force awarded him a 70 percent medical disability, despite the fact that just prior to his removal he was considered healthy enough to fly and was drawing flight pay.

58,000-pound Phantoms, resting on four small tires, exerted such force on the surface that the aircraft could not even operate on pierced steel planking for any sustained period of time. Heavy concrete runways were a necessity.*

It took 5,000 men to operate a fighter-bomber wing, and they lived in open, unprotected housing. The aircraft were all parked in open revetments when they were protected at all. The bombs for a day's mission were usually stacked in front of each revetment where, if one were exploded, the others would detonate as secondary explosions and themselves cause damage.

The engines were so delicate that the fields had to be kept as clean as a compulsive housewife's living-room floor. Even the smallest "foreign object" sucked up into the jets could cause trouble, and ground crewmen walked around with "FOD bags" (foreign object damage bags) on their belts in which they placed all stray nuts, bolts, sticks, pebbles or other foreign objects they found.

Even with all the equipment, the job of maintaining a complete fighter-bomber in the Vietnamese environment was often beyond the Air Force. On the F-4 Phantoms, frequently only those systems used for bombing missions were maintained. In other words, though the planes were called fighter-bombers, they were actually only bombers because the fighter part of the plane was not maintained. If the planes came under attack by enemy aircraft, the air-to-air missiles the American pilots carried for defense and the radar tracking systems were often inoperative, according to some pilots.

"The classic vulnerability of the sanctuary bases is virtually invisible to the current generation of unperceptive Air Force leadership," one young colonel said.

"We're lucky the North Vietnamese ran such a poor war," a squadron commander in South Vietnam volunteered. "Any Air Force with one tenth the power of ours, if they used it wisely, could cripple us. I've often wondered why the North Vietnamese did not. All they had to do was send one plane a week over Danang with area type munitions like the CBU-24 [the canisters of white phosphorus cluster bomblets used by American pilots], and they could have kept us out of action."

---

* To support a Phantom's weight, its tires had to be inflated to 275 pounds per square inch of pressure. Under the load of the plane, that pressure was put on the surface. It is roughly the same pressure a farmer uses in driving a fence post into the earth.

The squadron commander said that plane could have crippled the fields' communications systems, the electronics, the fuel supplies and caused enough casualties to bring base operations to a halt. Much of the damage, he theorized, would have been caused by the secondary explosion of the American bombs left exposed near the planes waiting to be loaded.

The reliance on sanctuary bases was so great that even during the height of the Vietnam War, before the American pull-out from South Vietnam, most of the air war was fought from sanctuaries in Thailand and on carriers stationed offshore with support from Guam, the Philippines, Okinawa and Taiwan, all locations immune from enemy attack. All these bases, of course, would have been vulnerable to another air power. One is tempted to think that, confronted by another air power, the United States Air Force and Navy would simply change their methods of operation. But the truth is that they could not. Revetments could be hardened to protect planes against direct hits, as they were in Europe after officials saw how easily the Israeli Air Force destroyed the Egyptian Air Force on the ground during the Six Day War of 1967. But beyond that, the bases must remain vulnerable simply because American aircraft cannot operate from less complex facilities. To do away with the sanctuaries, the Air Force must first rebuild itself with less sophisticated aircraft capable of operating from more widely dispersed, less complex fields.

Many other American pilots hold the view that the United States Air Force would not be up to meeting the challenge of another first-rate air power. They criticize the kinds of airplanes the service is ordering— planes which trade maneuverability for sophistication and firepower. They criticize the training given to pilots. They criticize the excessive centralization of supervision. Finally they criticize the rigidity of a system which will not allow all their criticisms to be fully aired.

Air Force Colonel John Boyd, who was with the Air Force Systems Command and an advocate of a new lightweight fighter in 1971, expressed part of the problem in these terms: "The Air Force claims, and with some justification, that it was successful in World War II. As a result there are many people around who refuse to overthrow the old ways of doing things. From World War II concepts we went to the idea that we must have a fighter plane that can fly in all environments under any conditions—that is, a fighter plane that can fly and fight in all weather and at night. It must also go faster than ever before.

343

"Operating under these assumptions, the Air Force has loaded very expensive electronics equipment into its planes and has gone from cheaper to ever more expensive alloys of aluminum and then to even more expensive exotic metals like titanium. It has developed avionics systems that cost, at the present time, fifteen hundred dollars a pound—far more valuable than gold.

"Now, when you start thinking about putting a thousand pounds of avionics into an airplane, that means you've got an investment of one and a half million dollars before you even get the things off the ground. Then you add the airframe and engines by manufacturers who make things run with precision clockwork, and you are up to the present time when the F-15 aircraft will cost twenty million dollars a copy.

"And now you have an airplane you are afraid to use in a hostile environment because it's so expensive. The Air Force is confronted with the paradox of having a lot of extremely expensive units it is in fact reluctant to commit to any kind of wartime situation."

A colleague of Boyd's in pressing for the lightweight fighter concept was Colonel Everest E. Riccioni. The two officers argued that the Air Force could build many more lightweight, austere, easily maintained fighter planes for a given amount of money than it was actually doing. The concept ran contrary to Air Force dogma. The service was not interested in spending less money for less complex planes. The momentum was toward spending more for even more assumed but not proven capability.

Finally the Air Force authorized construction of prototype models to test the Boyd-Riccioni concept. But Riccioni suffered for his advocacy. He was removed from the program and transferred to a tour in Korea. Many considered it an exile.

Riccioni, however, was used to such treatment. In 1966, while an instructor at the Air Force Academy, he wrote a book proposing a change in the tactical fighter system the Air Force uses. He called the book "Tigers Airborne—A Creative Analysis of the Aerial Fighter Operation." The Air Force refused him permission to publish the manuscript. In fact, it refused three times, once after each revision he made to meet the objections of reviewers within the Air Staff.

> What is disturbing [Riccioni wrote of his troubles with the book] is to have totally unqualified, yet presumptive individuals condemn me for the mere act of analyzing a problem. . . .

I am at a philosophical crossroad. Out of loyalty to my fellow pilots, my country, and indeed out of loyalty to my Air Force, I feel a deep commitment to publish this book. On the other hand, it is clear that the Air Staff will take aggressive action against me if I do. The Air Staff will never approve my book for the simple reason that before I could solve any of the problems, I had to first admit that the problems existed. In fact, it was frequently necessary to analyze "Why?" the problems existed before their legitimate resolution could be achieved. *Primarily it is the airing of these problems that the Air Staff objects to.* Regardless of the nature of the book or the personality of the book (which they have also found objectionable), it will not receive approval in this type of environment. I have taken with my commission the commitment to give my life for my country. It is a somewhat smaller sacrifice to destroy my career (future) for my country. It is (philosophically) discouraging that I must risk the sacrifice of my career to help my Air Force. It is a great disappointment to see the importance attached to petty criticisms and parochial views instead of looking for the insights, the ideas to be evaluated, the lessons to be learned, and the actions to be taken.[4]

Publicly, there were not many officers—if any at all—as outspoken about the failure of the Air Force's higher echelons to give criticism from the working levels below a full hearing. Privately, many officers made the same complaint.

"You tend to feed back what the command wants to hear," one fighter-bomber squadron commander said. "Even in communications the 'Pi Factor Effect' applies—a given piece of information will only get reported up the chain of command 3.14 levels without getting distorted." (The officer complained that the Pi Factor crippled the Air Force in other ways. "If you want to know the true cost of a new system, multiply the announced cost by 3.14," he said. "If you want to know how much force will really be needed to take out a target, multiply the estimated force by 3.14.")

He continued: "In Vietnam, our ability to detect, validate and strike targets was poor at best, and I'm not talking here about the problem of civilians dictating what strategic targets we should hit. It sometimes took so long to get permission to strike a target we spotted that, by the time we received clearance, the target was gone. If we had Migs airborne against us, with our system we could not get clearance to fire at them even though several agencies knew they were in the air. We installed a system to prevent us from shooting down our friends, and it worked to prevent us from shooting down our enemies also.

"It was all due to the inflexibility, cumbersomeness and centrality of command. There was too much of a division between the men who had the authority to order raids and the men with the responsibility to carry them out. Mediocre officers tended to migrate to the staff positions where they had authority.

"After we got airborne on a mission, if it didn't go as planned, if we could not hit our primary targets because of the weather or because we could not make a rendezvous with an aerial tanker, we ran into trouble. We needed to expend our ordinance, but often we could not get permission to hit a good target.

"Our laser-guided bombs were all expended on preplanned targets that we had to hit even if we saw better targets. We could not hit an antiaircraft gun firing at us without getting permission if it was outside our area of operations. We had to check with the Airborne Command and Control Center (ABCCC), which was frequently saturated with communications from other planes. Often it took from two to twenty minutes just to get a response, just to be told to stand by. Usually, after you made a request, ABCCC said it had to get clearance from the Seventh Air Force control room in Saigon. There they were reluctant to give clearance because of possible low-altitude reconnaissance missions or the proximity of forces or sensors on the ground that I might not know about.

"All of this would happen only when I could not hit my primary target. But one third of the time conditions at the primary target were marginal to unworkable.

"Another thing. We had no secure communications. All of our communications were in the clear, all of our moves were telegraphed. The enemy monitored our channels and knew just what we were going to do. They heard us talking to the forward air controllers and to the ABCCC. They listened in from the moment we took off. We learned at West Point that the success of military operations depended on mobility, firepower and shock—that is, surprise. Well, the way we operated, there was just no surprise.

"In the seven years we have been fighting there, nothing has changed. The self-correcting mechanism in the Air Force just isn't working."

Problems were discovered not only with fighter-bomber operations in Southeast Asia. The Air Force also brought the Strategic Air Command (SAC) into the picture—the force that had been carefully built in the 1950s to maintain the nation's nuclear deterrent, operating a fleet of long-range bombers able to drop megatons of explosives deep inside the Soviet Union as well as the ICBMs deployed in this country. SAC could not easily stay out of the war. To do so would have been to admit it had a declining priority in the never-ending squabbles for force and budget allocations within the Pentagon. So it converted many of its B-52s to carry conventional bombs. And then it developed a system for rotating its crews through the war in 120-day tours to give everyone in the command combat experience. The SAC system for giving everyone experience was similar to that employed in the tactical air force and the Army in its disregard for the question of whether some men might be better than others in getting the job done.

The B-52 fleet was the quintessential example of the reliance the Air Force placed on attack-immune sanctuaries. Those huge bombers flew thousands of miles from bases on Guam or Okinawa (for a time) or hundreds of miles from Utapao in Southern Thailand to hit their targets. They were supported by tanker planes flying from Okinawa, Thailand and Taiwan. Because of their vulnerability they were not exposed to intense antiaircraft or surface-to-air war-zone defenses for most of the war. Their sorties were milk-runs to undefended areas where they could drop their loads without fear.

As time went on, SAC grew unhappy with this role. SAC generals mounted a campaign within the military bureaucracy for permission to send the B-52s into high-risk areas, including Hanoi and Haiphong. That campaign coincided with a SAC budget request to build a new fleet of modern bombers—known as B-1s—to replace the fifteen-year-old B-52s. Some Air Force officers suggested that SAC wanted to demonstrate, by the heavy losses it knew the B-52 fleet would suffer, the need for the new airplane. When SAC's desires coincided with the Nixon Administration's determination to punish the North Vietnamese for what the President viewed as enemy recalcitrance at the negotiating table in Paris, permission was granted.

In mid-December 1972, the B-52s began flying missions against targets in Hanoi and Haiphong. The Air Force employed fleets of over one hundred fighter-bombers and other specialized aircraft as escorts to provide a sanctuary corridor to the targets for the eight-engine lumbering bombers. The tactic was successful only once. Then the North Vietnamese adjusted their air defenses, and subsequent losses, even with maximum defense suppression, were high. In the two-week period of saturation bombing, before President Nixon ordered it halted, fourteen of the B-52s, each carrying at least a six-man crew, were shot down, according to information released by the Pentagon. The enemy claimed even greater numbers of the planes had been destroyed.

Military spokesmen said the B-52s, each one capable of carrying twenty-eight to thirty tons of explosives (or, to put it another way, 108 five-hundred-pound bombs), were a weapon of great effectiveness. The Air Force spoke of the terror the bombers produced within the enemy ranks because they flew so high they could not be seen or heard and then unleashed their earth-shaking ordnance in a carpet pattern that no one below could escape. Privately, the government had a different assessment of the B-52s' effectiveness. In 1969, Dr. Henry A. Kissinger ordered a complete review of Vietnam policy after the Nixon Administration took office. He asked bureaucrats and the military to submit answers to a wide range of questions, among them, the question of how effective the B-52s were.

Defense Secretary Melvin R. Laird's staff furnished numbers to indicate the planes were not very effective at all. It estimated that it took about two and a half plane loads of bombs—some 275 five-hundred-pounders in all—to kill one enemy soldier. The Joint Chiefs of Staffs were more optimistic. They claimed every two plane loads of bombs resulted in five deaths.[5] Even at that rate, the kill-ratio resembled that you might expect if you were using a sledge hammer to swat flies. Yet the rhetoric claimed success, and the highest echelons of the Air Force, publicly at least, were not willing to admit anything else. In that kind of atmosphere, lessons were certain to go unlearned.

Military men are wont to separate the Vietnam experience from so-called conventional warfare, by which is usually meant the kind of war that would be fought between superpowers and their allies in Europe. Yet, for the Air Force and, as we shall see shortly, for the Navy, there are lessons to be learned from the Vietnam fighting that apply perfectly to future planning for European conflict.

The Air Force should be asking itself, for example, how it can expect to operate its fleets of fighter-bombers in Europe, where it requires the same kind of sanctuary bases it did in Southeast Asia but where it will not have anything near the immunity from air attack that it enjoyed during the Vietnam War. It should be questioning the training procedures it has used and the tactical fighting doctrine it has taught its pilots. Many of these questions are being asked throughout the Air Force, but whether they are getting important enough consideration at the highest levels is another matter.

Part of the problem results from the fact that for years, the Air Force has been run primarily by bomber-oriented men who did not concern themselves or the organization with the need for tactical fighter planes. These men assumed air superiority would always be on the American side. The assumption is not valid.

But there are questions which even bomber men should be asking themselves as a result of Vietnam: questions about the validity of the Air Force's mission to interdict the flow of supplies elsewhere in the world, particularly in Europe. Discussing the lessons of Southeast Asia, one Air Force officer raised this problem in a letter to the author, writing:

> The real threat, of course, is Europe, where enemy commanders are not so inept and where, for the first time in our life, we would be outnumbered.

Much has been said about the difficulty of the interdiction job in Southeast Asia. The Ho Chi Minh Trail through Laos has been portrayed as a labyrinthine complex of truck roads, foot paths and bicycle trails that are unproductive targets for the bombers. Of course that is all true. But imagine how much more difficult an elaborate system of autobahns and railways would be to interdict. Some specialists who have studied the problem have concluded that it would be as impossible to stop the flow of men and supplies from Eastern Europe to a war zone as it has been to stop the North Vietnamese, so elaborate is the network of roads and railroads. They argue that even tactical nuclear weapons could not do the job. Yet the conventional Air Force doctrine is that it could perform capably in a European war without much modification.

That view could prove to be a deception and a self-deception of fatal proportions.

15

DIOGENES AT PEARL HARBOR

When Admiral Elmo R. Zumwalt, Jr., talks appearances, he talks of a new Navy—a mod Navy in which ships are commanded by younger men, a concerned Navy in which the enlisted men are subjected to far less harassment from their superiors than in bygone years, a humanitarian Navy in which men of all races and colors are granted the opportunity to advance on merit, a compassionate Navy in which married men are allowed to spend more time than ever with their families ashore.

All this is most important if the Navy is going to recover from the self-inflicted defeat of the past quarter century. And it is to the admiral's credit that he has decided to concentrate on what he calls the Navy's "people problems." But none of this, in itself, will ensure the recovery unless the Navy, like the rest of the services, does away with the deception and self-deception it has been practicing in regard to its roles and missions. When Admiral Zumwalt talks roles and missions—the jobs the Navy can be expected to perform——he is as tradition-bound as any aged admiral of yore, despite the fact that he was the youngest man ever promoted to his exalted position.

He still thinks of his aircraft carriers and cruisers, his destroyers and landing ship, his submarines and airplanes as protectors of the Pax Americana. Zumwalt expects his Navy to

Provide strategic deterrence
Project American power overseas

350

Control the seas

Provide a continual overseas presence

He expects the Navy, in short, to perform tasks that are far beyond its capabilities if the service is to live within a budget that will not help bankrupt the nation. Of the four missions enumerated by the admiral, the Navy contributes its share to the nation's strategic deterrent most capably. Its fleet of forty-one Polaris and Poseidon submarines, cruising the ocean deeps with sixteen nuclear missiles each targeted on potential enemy strike points, are an effective counter to any Kremlin ideas about initiating a nuclear exchange. The Navy also has the capacity to carry out the second of the admiral's missions, the projection of American power overseas. It can adequately land a detachment of marines almost anywhere in the world to influence what the planners euphemistically call a "brush fire war," and (provided a carrier task force is available nearby) it can fill the skies over some trouble spot with a wing of fast-reacting aircraft that could, for the moment, change the balance of power in any limited conflict in conformity with Washington's wishes.

However, when the admiral talks control of the seas, conjuring up visions of maintaining security along the North Atlantic sea lanes that would carry men and supplies from the East Coast of the United States to the ports of the nation's traditional Western European allies, he is perpetuating a myth. The Soviet Union would enter any future conventional war with a fleet of perhaps four hundred submarines already in being—almost eight times as many as Nazi Germany had at the beginning of World War II, three times as many as the United States had in 1972—and that fleet could make a mockery out of any American attempt to run huge convoys across the Atlantic. Even short of attacking the convoys of merchant ships, the Soviet submarine fleet could prove a convincing, if not conclusive, menace to the warships of Admiral Zumwalt's fleet.

Finally, when the admiral speaks of maintaining an overseas presence, he is advocating a policy that runs contrary to the American goal of holding high its prestige on the world stage. The American presence overseas engenders either of two possible outcomes—or both. It provokes anti-American feelings, as it has done in Japan, Germany, Okinawa, Italy, and Vietnam, or it contributes to the political and economic instability of the nations in which it is exercised, as it has in the Philippines, Korea and Thailand. The admiral would argue that the Navy's presence is not an important factor in creating either anti-American or local instability, since it can be exercised by a fleet at sea.

The Navy speaks with great pride about the self-sufficiency of its two big overseas fleets—the Sixth, patrolling the waters of the Mediterranean, and the Seventh, patrolling the seas that wash the shores of the Asian mainland. One of the Navy's big selling points is that its aircraft-carrier task forces and other ships can be provisioned and maintained entirely while at sea and that the Navy does not need great forward bases.

The claim is overdrawn. In fact, both the Sixth and Seventh fleets are heavily dependent on a string of bases in their areas of operations, as are the ships of the strategic missile submarine fleet.

For all the vaunted power of the Sixth Fleet in the Mediterranean —President Nixon once called it the mightiest fighting force ever assembled by man—it could not exist without bases stretching from Rota, Spain, on the Atlantic Ocean side of Gibraltar, to Athens, Greece. The myth is that the Fleet, consisting of two aircraft-carrier task forces (each composed of a carrier and several supporting ships), electronic surveillance ships, destroyers, cruisers and supply craft, could operate indefinitely at the end of a supply line stretching back to the East Coast of the United States. The fact is that the Fleet receives much of its support from the shore bases in Spain, Italy and Greece. Land-based spy planes continually patrol the area, helping to keep tabs on the Russian warships in the Mediterranean and Atlantic. Supplies are stockpiled at the bases. Tenders tied up to piers in Naples and Rota do much complicated repair work that might otherwise cause a ship to make a passage back to the United States.

Beclouded by the myth is the fact that the Sixth Fleet—that mightiest of fighting forces—is ill conceived for its mission of maintaining a strong presence in the Mediterranean. If war between the United States and the Soviet Union should ever come, the Sixth would have to evacuate the sea almost immediately or else endure great risks to its behemoth carriers. Those big ships could easily become sitting ducks for the Soviet submarines, land-based bombers and missile-firing surface ships.

Just as the Navy of pre-World-War-II days was built around the battleship, most of today's Navy (excepting the nuclear submarine fleet) is built around the aircraft carrier. And just as the battleship passed its peak as an important weapon twenty-five years ago, the aircraft carrier is today in its twilight years. As a sanctuary afloat—the equivalent of one of the Air Force's huge sanctuary bases—the carrier still has some utility. It can bring huge amounts of firepower to bear on a nation that cannot give challenge with either air power, guided missiles or submarines. Thus, the aircraft carrier proves an effective weapon against a country like North Vietnam, Syria or Lebanon. But once the carrier is matched against a country which does have power in the air or undersea, the effectiveness of the huge American carriers is diminished sharply. They must expend much of their effort simply protecting themselves from attack. Planes that might normally be sent on attack missions instead have to fly a protective cover above their seaborne base, negating the whole reason for the task force's existence.

Despite all this, the Naval policy-makers continue to argue for newer and larger aircraft carriers for reasons that are not altogether cogent. Those reasons relate to the inability of a tradition-bound bureaucracy to recognize that the ideas and systems on which they have based their careers are now passé. The Naval planners see the carriers, with their necessary air wings and support ships, as one way to continue to capture billions of dollars in the perennial competition among the services to capture a "fair share" of the defense budget. Still other reasons relate to the high-ranking officer billets that a carrier-centered Navy offers. Carrier task forces are commanded by admirals surrounded by large "flag staffs" of high-ranking officers. Any large diminution of carrier task forces would mean a reduction in command and prestigious staff billets that would make the Navy a far less attractive force.

Admiral Zumwalt and the other Naval policy-makers, while expressing alarm at the growth, sophistication and competence of the Soviet Navy and concern over the increasing age of the United States Navy, nonetheless feel that there are few problems the Navy cannot solve without more of the same—more carriers, destroyers, aircraft, and amphibious landing ships. Not everyone who looks at the Navy comes away with the same feeling. Not even men wearing the Navy blue. Some are deeply concerned that the United States is unwisely building the wrong kinds of ships and preparing itself for the wrong kinds of missions. They are fearful that today's generation of Naval policy-makers may have deceived themselves into sowing the seeds of future disaster.

One of the most deeply concerned in the early 1970s was Captain Robert H. Smith, a modern-day Diogenes who, while he was stationed at Pearl Harbor as an antisubmarine warfare specialist, searched in vain for honest men. He could find few, as his remarks quoted in the previous chapter indicate, who were willing to give the truth its due. Captain Smith's prize-winning essay in the *U.S. Naval Institute Proceedings* not only indicated the lack of candor in the Navy. It was also a grim catalog of what he saw as the Navy's deficiencies. He wrote:

> Not high intrigue, but failure to do our jobs as naval officers —mostly good and patriotic men, meaning well and doing badly—has brought us where we are. The critics have us wrong. Only their anger is valid.
>
> With leaner times, and in the spotlight of the rising Soviet threat, bones are showing, which in less challenging and more abundant eras were not visible. What we see today are the fruits of decades of mismanagement and inefficiency in a sluggish and ill-organized bureaucracy—all at the service of leadership that has been thin on naval professionalism, weak in imagination, and slow to perceive vital, new, emerging strategic and tactical truths. The result is the unready fleet of today. Above all, it is a Fleet whose composition and tactical characteristics are fundamentally flawed, deficiencies cast in the mold in obedience of concepts of naval warfare that no longer serve. An allegedly "balanced" fleet, the balance is spurious, illusory, it is a balance primarily within itself and not in relation to its needs. Against the Soviet submarine threat the unbalance of its capability invites defeat.[1]

Writing for an important audience of professionals—the *Proceedings* is the most prestigious of all American military publications— Smith said that it was not enough to argue that the presently configured Navy has been successful in recent years. "Comparatively little was demanded of that Fleet," he wrote. "Size and presence were usually enough to achieve its purposes. It was not tested."

With these preliminaries out of the way, Smith got down to the specifics of his argument, indicting the decision to purchase forty-six new destroyer escorts, known as the 1052 class, as "the greatest mistake in ship procurement the U.S. Navy has known." Each of those new ships will cost $28.8 million. They were intended originally for use as antisubmarine warfare vessels, but problems were encountered in outfitting them for that purpose, and now they are billed as general-purpose ships.

As antisubmarine ships, they suffered from two deficiences, First, they were designed to carry a new, lightweight remote-controlled helicopter that could land and take off from a vest-pocket flight deck at the aft end of the ship. The contractor, however, could not provide a helicopter to meet specifications. So, despite the fact that twelve 1052s were already in service in 1971, they had no choppers they could carry. The aircraft were intended to take off from the destroyer on patrols to seek out enemy submarines. On at least one ship, the commander converted the helicopter hangar area into a spacious recreation space for his enlisted men. Now the Navy faces the necessity of beefing up the ships' superstructures to carry heavier aircraft.

Secondly, the 1052s were outfitted with a huge eight-thousand-pound sonar dome at the extreme front end of the keel, right below the bow. The dome is a large, fragile, onion-shaped bulb riding below the water line. Equipment inside the dome is intended to detect underwater movements at great distances. The system is tactically self-defeating. Sonar, like radar, works by sending out a signal which bounces off an object and returns, pinpointing the location of the object. Radar sends radio signals into the skies. Sonar sends sound signals into the oceans. Both types of signals can be intercepted by an enemy, allowing him to pinpoint the location of the sending device at the same time he is located. The 1052's sonar is intended for long-range detection, sending out signals to a distance far greater than the ships can do anything about if an enemy is found. An enemy submarine, then, picking up sonar signals from the 1052, needs only to stay out of the destroyer's range of combat operations to escape attack. Thus the new fleet of destroyers, instead of hunting out enemies, could actually be of service to them.

At the same time, the sonar dome created problems in basic seamanship which, though they might have been acceptable if the equipment functioned properly, were laughable as they applied to the world's foremost seafaring nation. The dome is so large that it makes even such a fundamental procedure as anchoring difficult. Other maneuvers, particularly bringing the vessel up against a pier, are rendered burdensome. In a conventional ship, a skipper usually angles up to a pier bow first and then reverses his engines to swing the stern around toward the dock. The sonar bulb makes that procedure far more complicated.

Most older destroyers in the Fleet have twin propellers to make them more maneuverable and to give them redundancy in the event that one shaft should go out of order. The 1052s have only a single screw (propeller) that not only lacks the redundancy but cannot generate enough speed to make the ships effective in antisubmarine warfare work. In fact, with a listed speed of twenty-seven knots, they were seven knots slower than World War II-era destroyers. Going further, because of all the electronics crammed on board the ship and because of the space that had to be given up for the helicopter, the designers could find room for only one five-inch gun, where earlier destroyers had four five-inchers. That rendered the ships less effective than older models as general-purpose surface vessels. (It is not unfair here to compare the new destroyer escorts with the modernized, late World War II-era destroyers. The ships were of comparable displacement and dimensions.)

Even this is not the end of the problems for the 1052s. Included in their design was the use of a new antiaircraft missile known as the "Mauler" under development by the Army. The Army ran into trouble with the rockets and abandoned the project. So the 1052s are awaiting the design, development and production of a new system. And finally, a new type of torpedo the ship was designed to carry is still not in production. Commander Stuart D. Landersman, commanding officer of the USS *Hepburn,* the first of the 1052s to go on active duty, who wrote praising the ship in the same *Proceedings* issue that carried the Smith article, said the new torpedo is "far in the future."[2] He converted the torpedo room into classroom space and a lounge area for his petty officers.

Even before Smith's article appeared, the 1052s were being regarded with a jaundiced eye by the professional mariners of the world. Here is what the international naval authority, *Jane's Fighting Ships,* had to say about the class:

STATUS: These ships are considerably behind schedule, partially because of shipyard labour strikes and delays in Navy acceptance. The Fiscal Year 1964 ships are taking 2 and ½ to 4 years to build; some FY 1965 ships were not to be laid down until 1970, more than four years after the FY 1964 ships.

These ships have been criticized by some authorities as being inferior to their foreign contemporaries. Critics note the delay in providing variable depth sonar and a helicopter capability, the minimal gun armament, and the use of conventional propulsion vice gas turbines or combination diesel-gas turbines.[3]

That *Jane's* comment appeared a year before publication of the Smith and Landersman articles. Yet the ships continued to come off the ways. And, in an added complication, the Navy went ahead with plans to build an additional fleet of huge new destroyers (cost: over $90 million each) that, according to Smith, is already inferior to Soviet ships under way. He wrote:

> We need , , . voices now, enough of them insisting, as only one example, that the U.S. Navy does not want the 963-class destroyers as presently conceived—that it makes no sense to plan to build a ship that even now, on paper (and the first of which is not to be delivered for years), is inferior to competitive Soviet ships which are already at sea. Such an obvious truth one would expect to hear being shouted from the roof of the Pentagon. But, as in the old fable of the emperor who had no clothes, where are the subjects to tell him?[4]

By 1972, confirmation of Smith's views on the way the Navy did business was surfacing. In the preceding years, the Navy awarded contracts to Litton Industries, one of the nation's largest conglomerate corporations, to build thirty of the 963-class destroyers with five large amphibious-warfare ships—39,000-ton craft that would outwardly resemble aircraft carriers but which would each be able to transport into battle a full reinforced battalion of 1,800 marines with all their gear, guns and vehicles. The LHAs, as they are known, would have a flight deck from which troop-carrying helicopters could take off to put men ashore and a bay from which could be launched smaller amphibious-assault craft carrying trucks, tanks and armored personnel carriers and berthing space for all the men. In essence, each ship would be a floating ground and air base.

And, as one might expect, such facilities are expensive. Each of the five ships was programed to cost $192 million, and the first was scheduled for completion in early 1973. Litton planned to build the ships at a new yard it constructed in Pasagoula, Louisiana, which would take advantage of new labor-saving, cost-cutting, assembly-line techniques borrowed from the aerospace industry.

By mid-1972, the program was in trouble. The first of the ships had slipped a year and a half behind schedule. The others were expected to be two years late. Litton asked the Navy to give it $400 milllion more than it originally contracted for to build the ships. Cost overruns were beginning to seep into the program as the company encountered problems such as original, unfounded optimism about the ease with which a pioneering technical job could be accomplished; continuing changes in top management drawn from the aerospace industry and inexperienced in shipbuilding; labor problems, including a strike, and a hurricane in the fall of 1971.[5]

Litton denied that the delay on the five amphibious ships would affect the destroyer construction program, but in Congress and even in the Pentagon, men who had gone that route before with defense contractors were dubious. In fact, pressure began to build up for a transfer of part of the destroyer contract to other shipyards, an approach which the Navy rejected out of hand.

The Litton problems were a classic example of another of Smith's charges—that the promises of defense-industry contractors cannot be believed. He wrote of the Navy's failure to take hold of modern technology in these words:

> . . . Several decades have been witness to a succession of failures of new systems that never met minimum demands of Fleet need, let alone original specifications of performance laid out for them. A recurrent theme has been that of costly, complex systems, insufficiently evaluated and prematurely introduced, proving to be miserable flops, with the inevitable, dreary follow-up of costly "fixes" and retrofits which seldom do much better. Training, operability, and technical support have been habitually slighted, as details to be taken care of later, once the hardware is in hand, but which in actuality never does catch up. Entire classes of ships—graceful and handsome as they cut the waves of those full page advertisements flaunted by the very contractors who have let us down —have been pretentious beauties, a facade behind which their ostensible capabilities are in disarray. . . . For all our extensive postgraduate programs, we do not have officers able to sift fact from fancy, to distinguish the core of reality from the colorful brochures, and to assess skeptically the promises of the men with their pointers and slides.[6]

Smith concludes with the argument that, contrary to what many military critics think today, the voice of the military has not been too strong; it has been too "faint and uncertain." He notes that it has become the mark of the successful military man to be able to think like a civilian and that the professional schools have reordered their curricula to make this thinking process take hold. There is some truth in the captain's argument, as it applies to all the services, particularly the Navy.

Admiral Zumwalt has thought like a civilian when it comes to dealing with the people problems in his service, and this is all to the good. He has also thought like a civilian policy-maker in espousing the inflated roles and missions of his service—roles and missions that thinking military men realize are beyond the grasp of any navy living within a reasonable—or even an unreasonable—budget. But yet, he and the service he personifies continue to campaign for more, and that must continue to insure perpetual defeat.

16

THE GREEN MACHINE

The note on which the preceding chapter ended—that military men in the past quarter century came to think too much like civilians—bears exploration, particularly as it refers to the Army. Within hours after the Paris Accords ending the United States involvement in the Vietnam War were signed on January 27, 1973, Defense Secretary Melvin R. Laird announced an end to the draft which had been a fixed feature of American life since 1940, except for a brief respite in 1947 and 1948.

Laird told senior defense officials:

> I wish to inform you that the armed forces henceforth will depend exclusively on volunteer soldiers, sailors, airmen and marines.

Thus did the Nixon Administration fulfill a promise, made in 1969 when Vietnam War-generated objection to the draft was at a peak, to end conscription and defend the nation with an all-volunteer force.

There are several arguments to be raised against an all-volunteer force. Of those, the one made most emotionally is that such a force, without conscriptees, would no longer represent the wishes of society and would contain no checks against rampant militarism among the professionals. The logical extension of the argument is that the United States, with an all-volunteer force, would heighten the danger of military dissatisfaction growing into military disobedience of its civilian masters and eventually into a military takeover of the country.

The opponents of the all-volunteer force would rely on a few thousand teen-age draftees and a handful of junior officers just out of college to forestall that possibility by, so to speak, "keeping the military honest."

That argument misses the point of what has been happening to the military in the past quarter century. Danger has come to American society not from an isolated, apolitical military machine but from a machine that has grown too politicized.

Only a few high-ranking military men, such as Navy Captain Robert H. Smith, have recognized the problem of politization. Another who has meditated on the matter is Brigadier General Robert G. Gard, Jr., who at forty-three, when he was promoted to general officer rank in 1971, was the Army's youngest general. Gard's is a military heritage. He was born at West Point, which is revered by professional Army men as the fountainhead and keeper of the service's traditions. He grew up on military posts, graduated from West Point in 1950 and matured during a combat tour in Korea and in the Cold War Army. In the late 1960s, he held a series of important staff jobs in the Pentagon and served a tour as a division chief of staff in Vietnam. An introspective man, Gard had the opportunity to think about the meaning of his experiences as a fellow at the Council on Foreign Relations in New York City from 1970 to 1971. During that year, he produced a perceptive article on the relationships between the military and American society which went deeply into the question of politization.

Gard traced the beginning of the military's politization to the prolonged truce negotiations begun in 1951 at Panmunjon to end the Korean War. "During these negotiations," he wrote, "armed combat lost its wartime autonomy. The objective of military operations ceased to be solely the destruction of the enemy forces in order to remove their capacity to resist; instead, the employment of force was closely controlled to convey a diplomatic message."[1]

From this time forward, Gard wrote,

> There evolved a new concept of natural security policy and strategy, requiring both in peace and war the orchestration with the military of other instruments of statecraft—political, economic, sociological and psychological. . . . Adjustments to the profound changes proved exceedingly difficult, particularly for the military.

At this point, Gard said, civilian participation in what had been the exclusive province of the military "grew swiftly." And, as the services began to bicker among themselves over a fair share of the budget, increasingly, the civilians in the defense establishment were called upon to settle disputes. "The result was that the military professional no longer was considered to possess an exclusive expertise," Gard wrote.

Although Gard did not say so, others hold that however difficult the military adjustment to this new role was, the services applied themselves to making it with traditional efficiency. The Army, in particular, sent hundreds of their best officers off to the top-ranking colleges and universities of the nation for graduate-level instruction in political science, the humanities and other studies. Many if not most of these officers unfortunately came to view their tours on campus as still another ticket to be punched and did little to broaden or deepen their minds. But a few, like Gard himself, developed an appreciation for the political, diplomatic and sociological problems impinging on the new military establishment.* Whatever benefits might have accrued from this—and there were many—also quickened the pace of politization. The military had grown into the largest and most powerful of the federal bureaucra-

---

* One of the most important mechanisms for educating the best minds in a generation of Army officers was the so-called Abe Lincoln Brigade, named after Brigadier General George A. ("Abe") Lincoln. A 1929 graduate of West Point, Lincoln won a Rhodes Scholarship and received two degrees at Oxford. During and after World War II, he served on the staffs of Generals George C. Marshall and Dwight D. Eisenhower. In 1945, at the age of thirty-eight, he was promoted to brigadier general. In 1947, he voluntarily took a reduction to the grade of colonel to become a professor at West Point. In 1954, he became head of the Department of Social Sciences there, a position he held until 1969. During those years he identified some of the brightest young officers in the Army and sent them off to civilian graduate schools for advanced education that would qualify them as instructors in his department. Most of those tapped were his best students when they were cadets. Once the tour as instructor was completed, the officers moved into positions of responsibility throughout the Army. Occasionally a Brigade alumnus would identify and recruit for future membership a bright young officer who was a non-West Pointer, and recommend him to Lincoln. Today there are about two hundred alumni of the Abe Lincoln Brigade on active duty. Others have resigned to take responsible jobs in the government. Some have gone into academic pursuits, business and the professions. They hold reunions regularly in Washington and, with justification, express great pride in their membership in the elite group. Gard is a member of the Abe Lincoln Brigade as are many of the other officers mentioned in this book. "The Army accepted Abe Lincoln's idea for simply training West Point instructors," an admirer said, "but I've always suspected that his real purpose was to provide the best education possible for the best minds in the officer corps." Lincoln himself left West Point and retired from the Army to become director of the Office of Emergency Preparedness in the Nixon Administration in 1969 and is now, pipe in hand and looking very professional, a regular fixture at the alumni gatherings himself. But the system he established continues.

cies. It had the best communications system. It had access to transportation. It had plenty of money to spend. The result was that, increasingly, in interdepartmental meetings, the military officers began to outclass their counterparts in the State Department.

There were dangers in this, and Gard recognized them, writing: ". . . military participation in the policy process involves a degree of political activity inconsistent with the nonpartisan tenets of traditional military professionalism."

Others, however, did not come to the same realization. There is a subtle but nonetheless important distinction between a general's willingness—even eagerness—to do the bidding of his civilian masters and that same general's passionate and public espousal of his civilian masters' cause. The espousal has been considered the highet form of patriotism. It may not be. The better part of patriotism for the professional officer today is the planning and building of a military machine that can truly defend the nation and serve as the foundation upon which the superstructure of a vastly expanded machine of citizen soldiers can be built quickly in time of great need.

The catch here is the term "defend the nation." The ramifications of that concept will be considered more completely in the concluding section. But it is important to say that the term should no longer include—as it has since World War II—the undertaking of a crusade by professional men against a political system of opposing ideological views. The military's leaders did crusade against communism, against the Kremlin, against Peking, against Hanoi and against Havana with all the zeal of the civilian masters—and sometimes more. The posture of military-as-crusader was—and is—inimical to the traditional role of the military in American society.

It was as crusaders that the military came most to think like civilians. And from this style of thinking, many serious consequences flowed. It led the Army and the Air Force, for example, to sanction the posting of thousands of their men as hostages in Europe and in Korea where they would have been ill trained and ill equipped to hold back a massive onslaught by an enemy. The men stationed in those places were not there for strictly military reasons. They were there for political reasons —to show the United States' sincerity in containing communism, to prove that if the Communist Bloc ever did try to expand its frontiers, the United States, despite the oceans separating her from the conflict, would become immediately involved.

Whatever the political reasons for the overseas garrisons, they symbolized poor military judgment. From the military point of view, it behooved the generals and admirals to insist on one of two courses—the maintenance of truly adequate, well-equipped, well-trained, well-motivated garrisons overseas, or the abandonment of those garrisons. That would have presented a much clearer choice to the civilian masters and to the American people who, in the democratic process, hold ultimate authority. Given a choice this clear, the electorate would have faced the necessity of opting for a fully mobilized garrison state, with all the privation and lack of freedom that involves, or a far less costly defense establishment stationed at home. The clear choice would have avoided the creeping militarism that has taken hold in the nation in the past quarter century, a militarism that allowed President Lyndon B. Johnson, building on the decisions of his predecessors, to slide the nation into a major war imperceptibly while few important voices were raised against the moves.

In the 1960s, Robert S. McNamara, the defense secretary to President John F. Kennedy and President Johnson, mesmerized the nation with his computerized systems-analysis approach to military policy which brought forward the assessment that the United States could fight "two-and-a-half wars" at once; that is, wars against two major powers and a limited war at the same time. Responsible military men knew the assessment was built on a set of arbitrary assumptions that, though they made for convincing computer readouts, bore little relationship to the real world. As it turned out, the "half war" that was Vietnam, in itself, brought the Army to ruin. And still, the men who ran the Army, thinking like civilians, raised no great objections. They realized the *political* constraints that made proper military choices unacceptable—choices such as a call-up of the reserves and mobilization of the American economy—and *accepted those constraints* without strong objection. The can-do attitude took hold so strongly that the military leaders believed that simply by thinking positively they could solve any problem, no matter what the restrictions. In their confusion, they transformed the concept of patriotism from loyalty to country into loyalty to the men running the country. It was an easy transformation to make but one that did grave damage.

There was—and is—an alternative course of action. Subordinates should have argued their points forcefully, pointing out deficiencies in equipment, faulty conception in planning, or misunderstanding of a threat. It would have been the better part of valor for subordinates to tell superiors what could *not* be done rather than acquiescing in the belief that anything could be done. Responsible officers should have been prepared to back their rejected opinions, when the issue was important enough, with their resignations.

When a professional in a position of authority can no longer do his job, either because he is not given the necessary tools or because his superiors do not take the considered advice he knows is best, he has no alternative but to quit. The men who led the services, particularly the Army, to the defeat this book documents did not take that alternative. Instead, they compromised their positions in taking into consideration the civilian points of view and ultimately tried to do their jobs without the necessary tools.

Self-preservation played an important part in their reasoning. First there was personal self-preservation. Military leaders live and work in positions of great power and authority. Resignation would mean deprivation of perquisites, of status and of earning capacity. "Maybe only basically insecure people join the military," one officer commented. "We feel that our reward for all our suffering will be in the retirement benefits." So a circular reasoning—what is good for me is good for the organization—militated against protest from the officer corps. This was the most important problem raised by the politization of the military.

But there were others. As previously mentioned, McNamara saw the services as a social tool, an organization through which the physically and mentally handicapped could be educated and trained to perform jobs that would benefit them in civilian society. That purpose was laudable, but the program created more problems than it solved for both the services and many of the individuals who were supposed to receive the uplift.

Politization also led the Army into the realm of domestic spying. Beginning with the use of the Army to restore order in Little Rock, Arkansas, during the integration of schools there in 1957 and at the University of Mississippi in 1962 when that campus was integrated, the Regular Army—as opposed to National Guard or reserve units—was called upon more and more to preserve or restore order on campuses and in the nation's cities. In fact, Regular Army troops were used twelve times to quell civil disturbances from 1957 to 1972 and were alerted for duty on dozens of other occasions. When the Army arrived at the University of Mississippi, the unit commanders found they did not even know the name or telephone number of the local police chief. They had no direct contact with Washington, the only open telephone lines then being in the control of the Justice Department. They did not know the location of the local fire department or hospital. Finally, they had no idea of just who the local troublemakers might be. Confusion in carrying out the mission was the result, and that same confusion was to be repeated the following year when the University of Alabama was integrated with Army help and then, to a lesser extent, during the Watts riots of 1965 and the Detroit riots of 1967.

After that, when it became apparent that Army participation in quelling urban disturbances might become a major mission, the civilians in the Defense Department assigned to the Army the mission of gathering whatever information it might need beforehand to maintain order in any of the nation's twenty-five largest cities.

And that's how the Army got into domestic spying in a big way. Along with charting the location of hospitals and fire hydrants, along with listing the names of police chiefs and mayors, overly zealous planners also set out on a hunt for the names of potential troublemakers. The hunt was indiscriminate. Soon the Army was listing names and compiling computerized dossiers on thousands of citizens from all walks of life who were considered possible troublemakers. The names of governors, mayors and lawmakers were included in the lists the Army drew up along with many others who were not so distinguished. At the height of the activities, the Army had 350 different records centers around the country where dossiers were stored and an elaborate system of publications—classified and unclassified—for the distribution of the information.

After investigating the activities, Senator Sam J. Ervin's Senate Subcommittee on Constitutional Rights published a report which said that "Army intelligence was . . . collecting, disseminating and storing large amounts of data on the private and personal affairs of law abiding citizens. Comments about financial affairs, sex lives, and psychiatric histories of persons unaffiliated with the armed forces appear throughout the various records systems."[2]

The intelligence-gathering led the Army into spying on public events ranging from civil-rights meetings to Earth Day observances. Dossiers were collected on citizens because of their political beliefs or associations. The name of one Massachusetts woman was filed away because, according to the Ervin subcommittee report, she had "written a number of letters to U.S. government officials, civil defense officials and newspapers. The letters are generally critical of Federal and local governments because of what she considers the futility of a Civil Defense program and the refusal of countries to disarm."[3]

Along with spying by agents, the Army put its supersecret Army

Security Agency (ASA), which is normally busy monitoring the radio transmissions of foreign nations and their military services, to work at intercepting domestic transmissions. ASA monitored walkie-talkie and other private radio transmissions at the Republican and Democratic conventions of 1968, the 1968 trial of Black Panther leader Huey Newton, the October 1967 antiwar march on the Pentagon, the April 1968 riots in Washington, and the 1968 Poor People's March on Washington. The monitoring activities, in violation of the Federal Communications Act of 1934, were approved by General William C. Westmoreland, Army Chief of Staff, and his predecessor, General Harold K. Johnson. The Army admitted publicly to monitoring of this type on only one occasion—during the 1968 Democratic Convention. But classified memoranda showed otherwise. The memos showed that the Army realized the possible illegality of its acts and asked the Justice Department for a ruling. Justice, then headed by Attorney General Ramsey Clark, would not authorize the monitoring because it was clearly illegal, but the department also refused to put its denial of permission in writing, thus giving the Army tacit approval for its operations.[4]

Clark's tacit acquiescence in illegality and the original order to the Army to bone up on twenty-five major cities are good indications of how the civilians led the Army increasingly into the political sphere. The Army, then, is not completely at fault nor was it originally cupable for its politization. But it did allow itself to be used improperly. As keepers of a proud tradition of integrity and honor, its leaders should not have rushed into such dangerous areas so wholeheartedly.

The Army was somewhat more leery about entering the area of civic action and guerrilla warfare in the early 1960s through the enlargement of its Special Forces program. Special Forces—the Green Berets—was composed of small units designed to fight "unconventional wars." Its men were trained at once as the most ruthless of killers and the most compassionate of human beings. They could kill and torture as required; They could also bind up wounds and build small public-works projects of value to backward villages. They were intended to win hearts and minds away from enemy guerrillas on the one hand, and seek out and kill those enemies on the other.

So impressed with the program was President John F. Kennedy that he gave the Special Forces members the right to wear the Green Beret as a symbol of their elite status and markedly increased the size of the program and the funding. Though reluctantly, Regular Army leaders went along with the program but did not miss the opportunity,

367

after the Green Berets murdered a double-agent Vietnamese, to under-mine and de-emphasize the program.

The result of this politization has been the arrival of the Army in the 1970s with no good clear view of what its future role will be. Navy and Air Force men, equally confused about their future mission, can subli-mate the problem in ceaseless activity. They can continue to fly their planes and sail their ships, giving themselves—and the nation—the illu-sion of accomplishing something, even if that is not really the case. But the Army, on the other hand, can do little but sit in its garrisons and make an attempt to remain well trained and ready without being able to answer the question: Ready for what?

An Army, for example, that would fight a future ground war against an insurgency in Asia would prepare itself in one way. An Army ready to fight a conventional war on the battle-weary Central European plain would have to prepare itself in another way. And still a third way would be necessary to fight for and hold the oil fields of the Middle East. A fourth way would be necessary in Latin America and a fifth in Africa. Is the Army to prepare itself for all these possible missions? The task, if it is to include the readiness of units, is clearly impossible within budgetary constraints and within the constraints imposed by the ultimate need to maintain a free and democratic society at home to nurture and improve the American way of life.

This problem of what the Army is for is at the bottom of all the other problems confronting the Green Machine (as draftees and profes-sionals alike call their service). The manner in which the policy-makers solve that problem will go a long way toward dictating the answers to all the others, from the prescription of a cure for the yes-man syndrome in the officer corps to the provision of living and working conditions for enlisted men which will help to solve the social problems in the Army.

How the Army and its fellow uniformed services solve those prob-lems is the task for the coming generation of professionals: the men who will steer the military machine through the nation's bicentennial and into the twenty-first century. Whether they will return the machine to a more traditional path is a decision that is not altogether within their exclusive power to make. There is, however, much they can do on their own and much more that they can do to convince the civilian leadership of the value of tradition.

PART FIVE

A GENERATION FOR TOMORROW

For thousands of American GIs, the allure of the Far East is summed up in the Itaewon section of Seoul, Korea. Set on a little hillside across a broad avenue from the Yongsan Military Reservation—the Eighth Army Headquarters in Seoul—Itaewon is a warren of ramshackle bars, music shops, hotels, souvenir stands, clothiers, pawnshops ("We Buy and Sell Everything. If There is Anything You Want, Ask Us") and storefront offices set up to help a GI in need ("Xerox, Typing, Visas, Passports, Marriage Certificates").

Even on a cold winter's evening, several days after payday, Itaewon is alive. The bars such as Sam's Place and the 007 Club shake to deafening rock music amplified over the loudest stereos money can buy or operators can steal from the PXs. A man walking through the door is taken in tow by a lively young Korean prostitute, and before he knows it, he is seated, has ordered two drinks, and the "business girl" is in his lap, rubbing his genitalia, making a business proposition. Here a group of young black GIs sit at one table, balancing a group of girls on their laps. One of the blacks wears a wide wristband on which the clenched-fist black-power symbol is embroidered. There is a similiar group of whites with their girls. Over the back of one chair, a white has draped a jacket with a huge Confederate flag sewn onto the back.

Blacks and whites together in the same "club." It was not always that way. Early in 1971, Itaewon exploded in a huge race riot that required tear gas, water, Korean police and American MPs to quell. The issue had been the businesswomen. They were refusing to provide their services to the black GIs.

Sergeant First Class Louis R. Luther, thirty-nine, of Youngstown, Ohio, and his wife and four children, ranging from four to sixteen, witnessed that riot from their bungalow across the avenue from Itaewon.

370

"The air was thick with pot," Luther recalled. "The prostitutes were taking the men out of the bars and hotels to put them into cabs to take them to the hospital. There was race rioting in the streets. The MPs were late in arriving."

Since that rioting, authorities have taken steps to avoid repetition. They have organized a "Promote Equality Action Committee' (acronym, PEACE) among the seven most prominent bar owners in Itaewon, they have tried to educate the businesswomen in the concept of equal opportunity for all customers, and they have set up patrol upon patrol. Squads of MPs patrol Itaewon every evening. In addition, members of a committee called GIT for Get It Together make their informal rounds to make certain that peace is maintained. And so does a "courtesy patrol."

The courtesy patrol is made up each evening of four senior noncommissioned officers charged with the duty of marching in and out of the bars regularly and frequently to "render assistance and enforce the required standards of dress, appearance, and conduct" among the young American revelers.

It was extra and distasteful duty for the sergeants—a duty they performed perfunctorily, ignoring most dress-code violations they saw, steering clear of any other problems.

Halfway through one evening of courtesy patrolling in December 1971, Luther, an administrative noncommissioned officer in the Yongsan Motor Pool; Sergeant First Class Leonard L. Fenner, forty-seven, of Sayre, Pennsylvania, who works in the baggage section at the garrison; and I sat in Luther's dreary kitchen eating liverwurst sandwiches and drinking beer. In the living room, Mrs. Luther and the children watched television, she sharing a can of beer with her eleven-year-old son.

Fenner was developing a distinct middle-aged spread. He spoke quietly, without passion, about the problems of a noncommissioned officer in the 1970s. "I was brought up to do physical labor. I was a line soldier most of the time, a combat engineer, but now I just don't have anything to do. I find myself drinking quite a lot here." (As he nursed a can of Black Label he did not partake of the liverwurst.) "I hadn't touched a drop in two years, but over here I drink quite a bit."

As he talked, I remembered a conversation months before with a group of young GIs at Fort Dix who were turned on to drugs. They had done it originally, they said, out of boredom.

371

Fenner continued: "I have a lot of Koreans working for me and a lot of bright young NCOs. I just sit behind a desk and do nothing but think of home, I guess.

"The Army got too lax. There used to be a time when the senior NCO was, well, a god. He was never seen. He never mixed with the troops. But he had authority. Then they took all his authority away and gave it to the officers. Now they want to turn the Army back to the NCOs to straighten it up, and it's too late."

"Do you really think it's too late?" I asked.

"Yes, I do," Fenner said, and he took another sip of beer.

"My assessment of the situation is that it's sick," Luther said. "We're ruining the moral fabric of our nation here with this constant separation of families. I've seen more families busted up here."

Luther, not a man to partake of the Yobo Culture, had brought his family to Korea at his own expense and was spending $250 a month for quarters that were barely above slum level by American standards. Why?

"I took them to Saigon, too, back in 1965. I just can't leave my wife back in the United States with all of this. My family needs me. My children need me. But there's no place for them here. There's a place for prostitutes and a place for WACs, but no place for my family.

"I'm for getting out of here. There's too much thieving going on. Everyone is a thief. You just can't trust anyone here. They hire Koreans in the PX, but my wife can't get a job. She'd work for a dollar an hour, but they won't hire her, and the Koreans are stealing them blind.

"I think we ought to get out of Vietnam too [this was said in 1971]. We can never defeat the Asians. Did you ever try to jump on an ant hill and kill all the ants? You can't kill them except by pouring gasoline on the hill and lighting it. We can't do it without using the hydrogen bomb. We wanted to clean up Asian yards, people's backyards all over the world, and back home our own backyard was going to hell."

17

THE GREENING OF THE MACHINE

In his youth, the celebrated French "Tiger," Georges Clemenceau, spun off an epigram that has bounced from orator's tongue to orator's tongue through the history of the past hundred years. It goes: "War is much too serious a matter to be entrusted to the military."

Like most memorable epigrams, Clemenceau's was about half true. The other half might be: "War is much too serious a matter to be used indiscriminately by civilians."

This must be said in prelude to a discussion of how the American military machine can recover from its self-inflicted defeat. The recovery can only be made by the military itself. But it cannot be made at all unless the civilian leadership of the Defense Establishment—the President, his Defense Secretary and his national security advisers—make some difficult decisions and adopt the resolve to live by them.

The defeat was made possible by a civilian leadership whose conceptions of the uses of military power were faulty. Those conceptions grew from the single idea that the spread of international communism could be contained with weaponry and with vast numbers of men to operate that weaponry.

The military leadership and their civilian allies received an almost unlimited license to develop system after system to mount on the modern-day successors of the ramparts. No one took the trouble to determine if those systems would really work. Belief in the supremacy of American technology—in its ability to solve any problem—was consummate. To challenge the dogma of technological infallibility by doubt-ing the efficacy of any single proposed airplane, ship, tank, rocket or rifle was to be labeled a heretic. Just as Galileo meant no challenge to the dogma underpinning the Church in the seventeenth century, a doubting officer today means no challenge when he criticizes a proposed new weapons system. But just as the Inquisition brought the famed astronomer to his knees and ordered him imprisoned, so do American military men suffer ruined careers for opposing the development of new weapons systems. Career advancement depends not on resistance to the purchase of new weapons, no matter how dubious their utility, but on participation in the campaign to urge ever more purchases.

The military leadership acquired a vested interest in building a vast plant and storing tremendous amounts of equipment with funds that should have been spent on personnel. The personnel, particularly enlisted men, were exploited as a virtually cost-free source of labor. If the transitory civilian leadership of the Defense Establishment—politicians coming and going with the changing tides at the ballot box—did not understand what was happening, the military leadership, with a strong tradition of professionalism, should have. It was the military leadership, then, that brought on the machine's defeat—not on the battlefield but in the huge bureaucracy it built—by compromising a deeply rooted tradition of loyalty in favor of a less than wholesome concern for individual careers.

In a sense, what happened in the military was not much different from what happened in other American institutions during the same period. The military adopted the corporate ethic, and in so doing, it let the competitive spirit run mad. This shift in outlook helped give the United States not a strong military machine but an overbearing one, a machine that threatened to suffocate American Democracy, not protect it.

These are the trends that must be reversed. Reversal can only come with a careful examination of the past and fundamental changes to prepare for the future. The reforms suggested in the following pages all result from the belief that the United States no longer has the protection of a superior *defense force* and that prudence dictates the need for such an organization.

Reform must start with the removal of the men who run the military machine from the political process and the restoration of true military professionalism. The accomplishment of this goal involves a restructuring of the leadership at the top of the uniformed services and the delegation of authority to the men in uniform to determine force structures as well as to select and develop new weapons systems. All this, of course, must be done within the limitations of national policy laid down by the civilian leadership of the government.

The restructuring suggested here would abolish the ineffectual Joint Chiefs of Staff and the bureaucracy that presently supports it. That organization would be replaced by a Joint General Staff composed of five four-star officers—one with a background in each service and a chairman—supported by a strictly limited number of junior officers. Once joining the Joint General Staff, all these officers would be completely separated from their services. They would even wear a separate and distinctive uniform. Owing no allegiance to any particular service, the Joint General Staff could, with an impartiality that is lacking today, reach conclusions in the best interests of the nation. The members of the Joint General Staff would bring a greater unity of purpose to defense planning than the nation has enjoyed at any time since World War II.

The men selected to work on the general staff should be selected not as leaders of men but because they show talent as politico-military analysts, international-relations experts and students of foreign cultures. Their promotions should be controlled only by their superiors on the general staff, not by the services in which their careers originated.

The Joint General Staff should prepare the annual defense budget after careful consultation with each of the services (but without giving the services any veto or logrolling powers), control the military intelligence community, devise unified systems of command and control, and keep current the nation's plans for use of the military machine in defense of the nation. The members of the Joint General Staff would not be the heads of their services, as are the present Joint Chiefs. In the present system, the Joint Chiefs of Staff do not always have the best interests of the nation at heart in reaching decisions. Instead, they compromise those interests in favor of protecting the strength of their services within the Defense Establishment bureaucracy. If the techniques of systems analysis which Defense Secretary Robert S. McNamara brought to the Pentagon are at all valid, then it is the professionals in the military establishment—the Joint General Staff members—who should be taught to use them, not politically appointed civilians more skilled in the art of bureaucratic infighting than in the art and science of warfare. If the military has failed in the past, this is more an indictment of the system than of the individuals in it, and the system should be corrected. It should not be layered over with yet another system composed of civilians. The military professionals on the Joint General Staff should be taught and encouraged to stand up to defense contractors with a healthy skepticism. They should be given the authority to make contractors produce what they promise just as any private-sector big businessman has the leverage to make his vendors produce. The officers should be able to make decisions on such politically sensitive matters as contract awards and base locations on the basis of what is necessary for the defense of the nation and on this basis only.* Finally, they should be sufficiently insulated from the political process that they have the authority to argue forcefully against their civilian masters when the civilians propose using the military machine in adventures for which it was not designed. They should be prepared to resign when their advice is rejected.

While the Joint General Staff kept busy with a unified defense policy, the Chiefs of the individual services, also four-star officers, would similarly be faced with a full work schedule. It would be the job of each service Chief to build his organization into one making the best possible use of the resources allocated to him by the Joint General Staff. It would be his responsibility to keep his men properly equipped, trained and prepared to defend the nation when called upon. The Chiefs of the services would continue to be selected, as they are at present, from the ranks of successful troop commanders. As leaders of men, they would be charged with the responsibility for making certain that their men are no longer exploited in the manner which they suffer today.

Along with the Joint General Staff and the Chiefs of Staff of the individual services, still one more four-star officer is needed in the reconstituted military leadership. He would be the Chief of Combined Operations. Working closely with the Secretary of Defense, he would, in time of need, direct and monitor all the nation's military operations. The Joint General Staff would play no role in these operations as a corporate

---

* Here, admittedly, the question of military reform entangles itself with Congressional reform. At present, contracts tend to be awarded and bases located in those districts represented by the powerful in Congress. In the best of all possible worlds, I would suggest a reconstitution of the armed services and appropriations committees in both houses of Congress to make certain that no facilities are placed in districts represented by committee members.

body, although its members, as originators of a plan under implementation, might be called upon for consultations. The service Chiefs would play no role beyond that of providing the resources for the execution of orders coming from the President, through the Defense Secretary and the Chief of Operations.

Such a restructuring means the delegation of far more authority to military leaders than they have had since World War II, with the stipulation that the authority be used only toward the goal of defending the nation. That restructuring can work only if the officer corps is thoroughly reformed. Reform must start with a drastic reduction in the number of officers in each of the services. The number of generals can be reduced, retiring dozens of traditionalists who have been resisting reform. Then, down the line, thousands of colonels and lieutenant colonels who are doing little more than occupying space and putting in time until early retirement can be retired. The reduction in numbers would help in the abolition of little bureaucratic empires working at cross-purposes with each other. Sinecures would be abolished. Creation of the Joint General Staff and the Chief of Combined Operations would allow the services to do away with many billets in the Pentagon on each of the service staffs that exist only so that each service has a man of rank to deal with his counterpart in today's Organization of the Joint Chiefs of Staff.

Similarly, true unification of operation would allow for the trimming of hundreds of jobs in the so-called unified command headquarters. At present these headquarters, which supposedly exercise a single command over men of all services in one area, are actually "layered" commands in which the representatives of each service in the headquarters pay more attention to their superiors in their individual services than to the superiors in the unified commands.

All these changes, though requiring more four-star generals at the top of the military establishment, would allow for a significant change in the Chiefs-to-Indians ratio throughout the services. The cutback in the number of officers, however, would provide only a foundation for other necessary reforms. Standards of professionalism must also be reintroduced. Career patterns should be revised so that officers can specialize in a particular job—troop command, supply, personnel management, automatic data processing, communication or intelligence, for example—and advance through the grades to the top in each of those subprofessions. Specialization should be introduced early in an officer's career, and with few exceptions, officers should be required to remain within their specialties.

Troop commanders in the Army combat arms, ship commanders and aircraft squadron leaders should be selected from that pool of men who truly enjoy command and who are talented at it. Command assignments should not be parceled out to as many men as possible on a rotating basis to give them all the requisite experience to become general officers. Incentives related to the achievement of satisfaction from doing one's job well should be created to substitute for the present incentives of promotion and decoration. Personnel policies should be revised to require the separation of many more officers much earlier in their careers —after eight to ten years rather than the present eighteen to twenty-two years—so that they can more easily seek full-paying jobs in the private sector of the economy or in other branches of government. These men should be separated with a lump-sum payment to help them in establishing themselves in new careers in their early thirties. This would cut down drastically on military retirement pay, which adds billions to the defense budget each year. At the same time, the far smaller number of officers who would be retained should be allowed to make longer careers in the service, perhaps up to thirty-five or forty years.

The present system forces most men out of service after eighteen to twenty-two years of service when they are in their early or mid-forties, a period in life when their financial obligations are the greatest. As a result, many of these men become preoccupied with planning a second career years before retirement and no longer have their minds on their primary job. At the same time, they clog up the system within the Army and make it more difficult for the truly talented to advance.

Men selected for the troop command specialty should spend their careers with troop units and not be called upon to serve tours in the Pentagon or in other higher headquarters staff jobs. Whenever possible they should be assigned to a particular division (or ship in the Navy and wing in the Air Force) and should advance through the grades in that division only, as one step in re-creating the kind of unit integrity that existed in the services before World War II and was based on the British regimental system. They should remain in their jobs not for periods of months but for years, looking at those jobs not as "stations of the cross" on the road to the top but as responsible positions in themselves where they perform a service.

With few exceptions, the Chiefs of Staff of the individual services should be selected from those in the command specialty. But the members of the Joint General Staff and the Chief of Operations should be selected from those who began their careers in other staff specialties.

The service schools, such as the Army's Command and General Staff School at Fort Leavenworth, Kansas, the Navy War College at Newport, Rhode Island, and the Air Force War College at Montgomery, Alabama, should be reoriented and perhaps even broken up into units that would provide specialized in-service training in each of the important specialties. Instruction could then be deeper, more intensive and of greater value to the men going through those courses.

Reform of the officer corps, including the reintroduction of a professional ethic, is the key to the reconstitution of the military machine as an effective fighting force. But much remains to be done after that.

The services cannot maintain a superlative defense force without a continuing source of high-caliber manpower. Though President Nixon's decision to end the draft for the active Army was a politically wise move, considering the draft's unpopularity in the 1960s and the turmoil caused by it, the services are now left in danger of recruiting men whose talents are marginal. Even with large increases in wages for men in uniform and with drastic reductions in the size of the armed services, the all-volunteer force will not draw the kinds of well-educated or skilled manpower necessary to run a modern, highly technical military machine. There is good reason to believe that without a draft, the services will be required to lower their requirements for numbers of men or else lower their standards to fill their ranks. Only an economic recession, when civilian jobs are hard to find, would change this assessment.

The draft is important not only in the number of men it generates itself for the military but in encouraging many other men to "volunteer" for service in the Air Force or Navy or those branches of the Army in which they can get preference by volunteering. Further, if the services are to become true defense forces, there is need for giving as many young men as possible a modicum of military experience so that in time of need, their training will not have to start from scratch.

Instead of being disbanded, the draft should be reinstituted and broadened into a program of universal service for all the nation's youth —women as well as men.

Rather than a draft simply to cover the needs of the military, a Universal Service Act requiring all young Americans to give a year of

379

their life for service to the nation, either in the military or in some non-defense-related pursuit, would be preferable. There would almost certainly be enough volunteers among each year's draftees to fill the needs of the military. The rest could be put to work in a variety of jobs designed to take care of unmet needs from the inner cities to the most remote wildlands. The draftees, to their benefit and to the nation's (and without circumscribing the prerogatives of organized labor or the private sector of the economy) could work in a numberless variety of jobs ranging from the education of youth to the provision of aid to the elderly. They could provide manpower ,and talent in the health-care industry. They could help conserve the nation's natural resources. They could work in antipoverty programs. They could work at home and, like the Peace Corps of the early 1960s, with great benefit overseas.

President Nixon's first defense secretary, Melvin R. Laird, and others have talked of using the military services in various civic-action capacities. Suggestions have ranged from allowing the Navy to run the Capitol Hill heating plant to using the Army in rural-development programs. Such missions would deflect the armed services from their basic job which is, to repeat, to maintain a force capable of defending the nation from external threat. Civic-action work would also serve to further politicize the services which, at present, are in need of depoliticization. Finally, the kinds of civic-action programs talked about could be performed far more efficiently by other government agencies drawing on the manpower pool made available by universal service.

A universal-service draft would be more equitable than any draft the nation has ever had, in spreading the obligation among all youth. It would encompass thousands of youths who are now deferred for physical reasons. It would mobilize a dynamic, idealistic manpower pool that would be more than willing to meet the challenges of such service provided they were given the necessary sense of purpose and feeling of excitement.

Functionally, such a draft would work best if it were applied to nineteen-year-olds or, at the option of the youths, to those who completed four years of college. Deferments should be granted to college-bound youngsters to obtain baccalaureate degrees in the interest of maintaining an adequate mix between the college-educated and the less educated in the draft pool, both for the purposes of the military and the nondefense-related activities.

The Universal Service Draft will only work properly if all the draftees are given the feeling that their service is meaningful. In the military, meaningfulness equals preparedness. That is, units must be ready at all times to defend the nation against attack. Training procedures in all the services must be revamped to make true preparedness feasible. This means the training not only of individuals but of units— teams of men in which each member knows his job, practices it constantly and can perform competently. Such preparedness can only grow out of a stabilization of personnel within units far different from the constant shifting from base to base that is the norm today. The key positions in these permanent units would be held by draftees who, after tasting military service, elect to remain in uniform as professionals. There will always be men and women drawn to the military life, and particularly if the services enthusiastically take some of the steps to be described below, their numbers should be adequate. At the same time, reserve and National Guard units could be filled by draftees who have finished their years of conscripted service and volunteer to keep some connection with the military. That would ensure that the men in these units have had at least the minimum of adequate training for their jobs, something that is not guaranteed in those units today.

Even with a draft, the services are going to need a cadre of professionals numbering in the hundreds of thousands who will be willing to make uniformed service at least a partial career. To accomplish this and to accord enlisted men in uniform the basic human dignity to which all Americans are entitled, a vast and expensive program is necessary to rebuild Army, Navy and Air Force bases, making them more habitable. Enlisted men are entitled to privacy, to minimum comforts far above those found in the slums in which they now live (college dormitories might be the desirable standard), to adequate recreational facilities and to a life-style not substantially different from that of their peers in such superficial matters as dress and grooming styles, and in such important matters as human rights.

There is no reason why standards of discipline in the services cannot be modified to suit the job. The standards necessary for men in the combat arms must remain rigid. Orders must be obeyed on command without discussion or dissent. But elsewhere in the bureaucracy that is much of a modern military machine, different standards can easily prevail.

The services must take cognizance of this fact if they are to continue to attract the types of manpower they need. Money alone will not serve as an enticement, nor should it.

Men willing to put on a uniform to defend democracy are entitled to the same human dignity and respect accorded civilians. That dignity and respect can be granted enlisted men without compromising the necessary standards of discipline in combat units. Only if it is given will the services solve their problems of drugs, depravity, dissent and racial turmoil.

The Uniform Code of Military Justice must be administered not as a disciplinary tool but as a true code of justice. This means that civilian defense counsel should be employed in far more cases—paid for by the military if necessary—and that standards must be established for the use of pretrial confinement. It also means that even further steps must be taken to remove command influence from the judicial procedure. Finally, the code must be enforced equally for officers as well as enlisted men right up to the rank of general.

A General John Lavelle, charged with violating the orders of his superiors, should be given his day in court and punishment if found guilty. It is not enough to say, as Air Force Secretary Robert Seamans, Jr., did in announcing that Lavelle would not be court-martialed, that the "interests of discipline" have already been served by the general's removal from command and retirement on a tax-free pension.* A Major General Samuel Koster, accused of covering up the My Lai massacre, similarly should be brought to justice. So should a Brigadier General Earl Cole, accused of granting favors to shady civilians in Vietnam and protecting corrupt noncommissioned officers. By refusing to court-martial these men, the military creates the impression, at worst, that such

* The Air Force itself apparently never had any intention of even looking into the possibility of bringing Lavelle to trial. Charges against him were lodged, under the Uniform Code of Military Justice, by Lieutenant Delbert R. Terrill, Jr., a twenty-five-year-old Air Force Academy graduate on active duty. Terrill charged the general with willfully disobeying a lawful order and criminally falsifying records. He called the decision not even to convene a Court of Inquiry to determine whether a court-martial was warranted "a slap in the face to every soldier who has ever worn the American uniform." The young officer continued: "In effect the Administration gives amnesty to men who disobey orders while denying any form of amnesty to our men in Canada." He could have added that the system gives amnesty to generals but denies it to enlisted men who, with alacrity, are routinely court-martialed for disobeying orders to get a haircut.

activity is even more widespread than one imagines; at best, it gives the impression that the military machine is so weak it cannot stand the dis-closure of the facts involved in such cases, whether or not the men are ultimately found innocent.

Finally, on the matter of military justice, no in-depth discussion has been included in this book of the searing question of war crimes in the American involvement in Vietnam. There are two reasons for this. First, the My Lai massacre and the trials resulting from it have already been well covered elsewhere. More importantly, the policies followed in the conduct of the war (the free-fire zones, saturation bombing, leveling of villages and dislocation of civilians) may have constituted war crimes in themselves. Officials have yet to address themselves seriously to this question. They should.

The question of war crimes should be addressed by the military, and a report should be made to the American people. In cases where men may have transgressed the military's own code of justice, the law of the land or international law, they should be brought to trial. If what war crimes occurred in Vietnam were only the acts of a few individuals, then they should be punished as any criminal is punished and as the World War II victors punished their vanquished in the name of civilization. If the crimes were not the acts of individuals but represented the norms of the system, then the American people should be exposed to that fact as well, as the Germans were exposed to the brutality they un-loosed on the world earlier in the century. The American people as well as the military machine must come to grips with this problem if we are not to tacitly condone the use of such terror in the future.

In keeping with the defensive rationale for the American military machine, the services should abandon all their overseas garrisons and bases. The Seventh Army should be brought home from Germany and the Eighth from Korea, where both forces have gone to seed in an atmosphere of boredom and frustration. The Air Force should give up its bases in Great Britain, Germany, Spain, Italy, Turkey, Thailand, Japan, Okinawa, Korea, Taiwan and the Philippines; the Navy should abandon its home ports in the Far East and the Mediterranean. The Marine Corps should withdraw its division from Okinawa and its air wing stationed in Japan. Only its men embarked in amphibious ships for extended training missions should serve outside the United States. Nuclear weapons and other pre-positioned stores should be returned to these shores. The rationale here is simple. The best that could be asked of these troops at the present time is that they fight successfully to cover their own withdrawal in the event that the Soviet Union sent its troops across what was once the Iron Curtain, or the North Koreans and/or Chinese came across the 38th Parallel in Korea. Those United States troops are not fighters; they (and the huge American communities surrounding them) are hostages, symbols of America's good faith. As ill-prepared hostages, they are hardly a credible deterrent to conventional war. It is a sad commentary on our nation's credibility rating in the world today that it cannot be trusted even among its friends and partners without surrendering thousands of men and their families as hostages.

All this can be accomplished only if the civilian leadership in the United States adopts the resolve to use the military machine in its one legitimate role—the *defense* of the nation when national survival is truly and unquestionably at stake. Adoption of this resolution in itself, if taken seriously, would reverse the militaristic turn that the nation took a quarter century ago. It would be recognition that foreign-policy goals can—and must—be achieved by other than belligerent means. It would give the foreign-aid expert primacy over the aircraft carrier; it would give the businessman seeking international contracts more importance than the bomber or the battalions garrisoned in far corners of the world; it would emphasize the importance of the teacher rather than the tank.

Such a resolution, then, would reestablish the legitimacy of the United States as a world leader through peaceful example. It would put the nation's leadership on its mettle to pursue the United States' vital interests abroad through political, diplomatic, sociological and economic means rather than with military tools. This, of course, is a moralistic approach to international relations, and it is fashionable these days to eschew moralism in discussing such matters. Washington is a city where the tough-minded man of action is revered. Discussion of right and wrong is considered woolly. More to the point in the councils of government is feasibility. Can it be done? That is the key question, not, Should it be done?

In this environment, the military has it all over any potential competitors. It can show results at once in terms of new airplanes lining the runways, new ships sliding down the ways, new battalions massing the field. Those units are seductive. They can be counted and their strength measured.

It is far more arduous and far less apparently successful, in the near term, to win friends and influence people overseas through other means. But the successes, when they do come, are far more lasting and far less burdensome to the United States.

The Japanese experience since the end of World War II is a case in point. Japan has had no difficulty pursuing her national interests abroad without a huge military machine. She has maintained a hand-some—to some, a disturbingly handsome—position in the American market; she is involved in joint commercial ventures with the Soviet Union; her salesmen and products are to be found throughout the world; she has even, now, begun to reopen her association with China on a peaceful basis. All this was accomplished without a meaningful military machine to back up her other initiatives. The tough, pragmatic policy-makers in Washington retort to this argument that Japan performed her economic miracle under the umbrella of the American military presense. That retort ignores the fact that Japan faced absolutely no threat.

The American military machine—strong, ready and willing to go to the nation's defense—must never again be used, as it has too often in the past twenty-five years, as a tool of repression, as an easy substitute for painstaking, peace-keeping diplomacy.

It is fashionable these days, in military circles, to blame the present defeated condition of the military on the Vietnam War. Once the United States was extricated, these circles held, the military could heal its wounds and recover.

That view was best expressed by one of the architects of American military policy in the 1960s, McGeorge Bundy, former national security adviser to Presidents John F. Kennedy and Lyndon B. Johnson and now Ford Foundation president, in a closed discussion at the elite Council on Foreign Relations in New York in 1971. Bundy said: "Extrication from Vietnam is now the necessary precondition of the renewal of the U.S. Army as an institution."

While extrication may have been a precondition, it is not the only one nor is it the most important. Renewal can only come after military policy leaders bring themselves to view the Vietnam War not as a cause of what went wrong in the military machine but as a symptom. It was a sympton of how the military machine came to be used in the wrong way. It was a symptom of how the men within the machine allowed them-selves and their organizations to be used.

Finally, nothing has been said in these pages about the use of nuclear weapons. This stems from the belief that the mutual deterrent represented by the silos and missile-carrying submarines is absolute and that no rational man would ever order the buttons pressed. Thus, contrary to the idea that the next great war will be over in a half-hour, there is every reason to think that, as we have in the past, we will recognize the danger signs of impending war, the build-up and finally the beginning of prolonged hostilities. The United States must be ready to mobilize for such a war, to fight it and win it. Today's defeated machine could not so perform, raising the uneasy possibility that, *in extremis,* it would be the United States that would press the first nuclear buttons if the world order ever broke down again.

We cannot let that happen. A strong, well-motivated, properly controlled, reasonably proportioned military machine, dedicated to the preservation of American Democracy but not the extension of a Pax Americana, would help stabilize world peace, whether or not those nations now perceived as our adversaries responded in kind.

SOURCE NOTES

PART TWO, CHAPTER 2

1. J. Glenn Gray, *The Warriors* (Harper Torchbook, New York, 1967), p. 183.
2. *Report of the Secretary of War's Board on Officer-Enlisted Man Relationships,* May 27, 1946 (United States Government Printing Office, Washington, D.C.), pp. 18–22.
3. Charts to accompany *Briefing on Quantified Judgment Method for Evaluating Combat Effectiveness from Historical Data.* Copyright, The Historical Evaluation and Research Organization, 1971. (Permission to reprint granted orally.)
4. "Making It in the Army," *The New Republic* (May 30, 1970), p. 20.

PART TWO, CHAPTER 3

1. Col. Everest E. Riccioni, "Tigers Airborne—A Creative Analysis of the Aerial Fighter Operation." Unpublished manuscript lent to author. (Permission to reprint granted orally.)
2. Comdr. Charles McIntosh, USNR (ret.), "Retention: The Talk and The Deeds," *U.S. Naval Institute Proceedings* (Sept. 1971), pp. 59–60.
3. Lt. Col. Robert Leider, "Why They Leave: Resignations from the USMA Class of 1966," Part III, Chapter 6, p. 9. July 6, 1970. Unpublished.

PART TWO, CHAPTER 4

1. *New York Times* (April 13, 1972), p. 1.
2. *Report No. 92–666,* Department of Defense Appropriation Bill, 1972. House of Representatives, 92d Congress, 1st session.

PART TWO, CHAPTER 5

1. Lt. Malcolm S. Harris, USNR, "Junior Officer Retention: A Lot of Little Things," *U.S. Naval Institute Proceedings* (March 1971), pp. 26–31.
2. Capt. Tom B. Thamm, "The Quiet Crisis in the Silent Service," *U.S. Naval Institute Proceedings* (August 1971), pp. 50–58.

PART TWO, CHAPTER 6

1. Henry A. Kissinger, "The Policymaker and the Intellectual," *The Reporter* (March 5, 1959).

PART THREE, CHAPTER 7

1. *Report of the Board for Dynamic Training,* Vol. II—Final Report. (Ft. Benning, Ga., Dec. 17, 1971), p. 26.
2. *Ibid.,* p. 45.
3. *Ibid.,* p. 49.
4. *Senate Report No. 92–962,* Committee on Armed Services, July 14, 1972 (U.S. Government Printing Office, Washington, D.C.), p. 133.
5. *Ibid.,* p. 132.
6. *Ibid.,* p. 135.
7. *Report of the Board for Dynamic Training,* p. 75.
8. Letter of transmittal accompanying *Report of the Board for Dynamic Training,* Vol. I, Executive Summary (Fort Benning, Ga., Dec. 17, 1971).
9. "It's Like a Contract: Millions Paid Yearly to Non-Flying Fliers," Washington *Star* (July 17, 1972), p. A-5.

PART THREE, CHAPTER 8

1. *Final Report: ATC Human Relations Team,* Headquarters Air Training Command (Randolph Air Force Base, Texas, July 26, 1971), pp. 3–4. Grammar and punctuation have been modified.
2. Thomas Culver, "Darmstadt 53; Race at German Bases," *Civil Liberties,* No. 283, Jan. 1972. American Civil Liberties Union, New York.
3. "McClellan Riot Results: Stiffer Penalties Handed to Men," *Army Times* (March 15, 1972), and "71 GIs, 68 WACs Arrested by MPs," *The Overseas Weekly* (Pacific Edition, Dec. 11, 1971).
4. "10 Negro GIs Reassigned for Remarks," Baltimore *Sun* (Nov. 14, 1969).
5. "Negro-White Troop Brawl in Berlin Hospitalized Eight," *New York Times* (Aug. 25, 1970).
6. "Black Soldier Goes on Trial in Germany Grenade Case," Baltimore *Sun* (Oct. 27, 1970).
7. "GIs Death Triggers Disturbance," Washington *Post* (Jan. 5, 1971).
8. "Black GIs Fight MPs on Okinawa," Washington *Post* (April 20, 1970).
9. "Report Reveals No Black-White Confrontation," Kadena *Falcon* (Aug. 25, 1971).
10. Author's interview with Col. Robert J. Perrich, commander of 4th Reg't, 3d Marine Division, Dec. 8, 1971.
11. "Walter Reed Blacks Launch Bias Fight," Washington *Post* (Jan. 14, 1972).
12. "Navy Probes Racial Fights at Bethesda," Washington *Post* (March 21, 1972).
13. "Few Ethnic Issues Involved in Travis Riots, Study Finds," Los Angeles *Times* (June 26, 1971).
14. "Radicals Suspected in Abduction: Black GI Beaten, Tortured," Detroit *News* (Jan. 25, 1971).
15. "Black Vs. White," *Armed Forces Management* (June 1970), p. 3.
16. *Ibid.*

17. Wallace Terry, II, "The Angry Blacks in the Army," San Francisco *Chronicle* (June 29, 1970).
18. William L. Claiborne, "AF Undesirable Discharge Reversed for Black Activist," Washington *Post* (June 30, 1972).

PART THREE, CHAPTER 9

1. "Reservists Ordered From Base: Long-Hair Turns Off Hospital Commander," Miami *Herald* (Sept. 14, 1971).
2. Details of the DuVal case were reported in "Colonel Cracks Down On Long Hair," by Jack Anderson, Newport (R.I.) *Daily News* (Nov. 17, 1971), and "Soldier Convicted of Not Cutting Hair" by Herbert H. Denton, Washington *Post* (Dec. 2, 1971).
3. "Sergeant Busted for Wearing a Wig," Washington *Post* (July 9, 1972).
4. John Matthews, "GI Loses His Job: Hairy Fight at the Pentagon," Washington *Star* (June 9, 1971).
5. "Two-Headed," *Army Times* (Nov. 3, 1971).
6. "Some Sailors Are More Equal Than Others," *Armed Forces Journal* (March 1, 1971).
7. Russell F. Weigley, *History of the United States Army* (The Macmillan Co., New York, 1967), p. 107.
8. *Final Report: ATC Human Relations Team,* Headquarters Air Training Command (Randolph Air Force Base, Texas, July 26, 1971).
9. W. B. Rood, "Money Problems Plague Married Marines: Military Life—Poverty for Many," Los Angeles *Times* (April 26, 1971).
10. Jeffrey Antevil, "Servicemen's Folks May be Going Hungry," New York *Daily News* (Jan. 1, 1970).
11. Rep. William Steiger, "Welfare, Extra Jobs Sustain GI Families," Washington *Post* (May 9, 1971).
12. *Ibid.*

PART THREE, CHAPTER 10

1. "Navy Reports Rise in Drug Discharges," *New York Times* (Oct. 10, 1971).
2. Comdr. Herbert T. St. Omer Woolley and Lt. Comdr. Lee H. Beecher, "Drug Abuse: Out in the Open," *U.S. Naval Institute Proceedings* (Nov. 1971), p. 23.
3. *Ibid.,* p. 20.
4. *Ibid.,* p. 33.
5. *Ibid.,* p. 34.
6. *Ibid.,* p. 25.
7. "Defense Prescribes Treatment: Punishment Out for Alcoholics," *Army Times* (March 29, 1972).
8. *Ibid.,* p. 19.
9. "Report Pessimistic on Screening Out Indochina Drugs," Washington *Post* (Aug. 2, 1972).
10. *Ibid.*
11. "Ex-Officer Says Vietnam Report On G.I. Addicts Was Withheld," *New York Times* (Aug. 16, 1972.)
12. *The World Heroin Problem,* House of Representatives Report 92–298, June 22, 1971. (Government Printing Office, Washington, D.C.), p. 21.

13. *Ibid.*, p. 20
14. Larry Green, "GIs Leave, Army Spends: Funds for Long Binh Fun," Chicago *Daily News* Service, Washington *Star* (Nov. 4, 1971).

PART THREE, CHAPTER 11

1. The Korea *Times* (Nov. 12, 1971).
2. The Korea *Times* (Nov. 18, 1971).
3. Anne Darling, "Bangkok: Wash the War Away on R & R . . ," *The Overseas Weekly,* Pacific Edition (Dec. 11, 1971). When the author checked this quotation at the Bangkok R & R Center, he was told by one of Hilliard's colleagues that the quotation was authentic.
4. "Col.'s Killer Dies in Public Execution," *The* (Bangkok) *Nation* (Dec. 3, 1971).
5. The account of the girls of Rota comes from *Newsweek* (Aug. 28, 1972), pp. 33, 34.
6. "Jensen Witness: Accuser Made Overture to Me: Teasing Episode Told Court," The Florida *Times-Union* (March 24, 1972). This account of the Jensen case is taken completely from stories that appeared in the *Times-Union* and Jacksonville *Journal.*

PART THREE, CHAPTER 12

1. "Sergeant Fights System," Washington *Star* (July 27, 1971).
2. "Annapolis Commandant's View of the Academy," San Diego *Union* (Aug. 8, 1971).
3. Department of Defense Directive 1325.6 (Sept. 12, 1969).
4. Fayetteville *Observer* (May 15, 1971).
5. "Coast Guard Fines 18 Who Oppose A-Test," Los Angeles *Times* (Oct. 15, 1971).
6. "Cadet Compulsory Chapel Out," Washington *Star-News* (Dec. 18, 1972).
7. The Cooper and Font stories are based mainly on "Professionals Protest: West Pointers Go CO" by Marvin M. Karpatkin in *Civil Liberties,* April 1971 (American Civil Liberties Union, New York) Karpatkin was Cooper's attorney.
8. "Udall Says His Son Fled Army to Canada," Los Angeles *Times* (Nov. 15, 1971).
9. George Post, "Over-the-Hill Gang Expensive: $4 Million Sought to Hunt Deserters," *Army Times* (Aug. 2, 1972).
10. George Post, "Study Shows: 'Most Likely' Awol Turns Up a Paradox," *Army Times* (June 28, 1972).
11. "Awol Studies," Letter to Editor by Hamilton I. McCubbin, *Army Times* (Aug. 2, 1972).
12. Colin J. Williams and Martin S. Weinberg, "The Military: Its Processing of Accused Homosexuals," *American Behavioral Scientist,* Vol. 14 (Nov. 1970), p. 203.
13. *House Armed Services Committee Report 92–58,* June 28, 1972 (U.S. Government Printing Office, Washington, D.C.), p. 14660.
14. "Air Force Reverses Itself on Pregnant Nurse Ruling," Washington *Post* (Dec. 12, 1972).
15. Both the Sherman and Eisenhower passages are quoted by Edward F. Sher-

man in "Justice in the Military," an essay in *Conscience and Command,* edited by James Finn (Random House, New York, 1971).

16. United States vs. Thompson, Army Court Martial No. 427121, tried at Augsburg, Germany, April 9, 1971, pp. 12–14.

17. *Unity is Power,* report for Conference on Equal Opportunity and Human Relations, Nov. 10–12, 1971, Headquarters, United States Army, Europe, Heidelberg, Germany, pp. K 7–10.

18. F. O. Richardson, *The GI's Handbook on Military Justice,* with introduction by Pvt. Andrew Stapp (American Servicemen's Union, New York, N.Y., Nov. 21, 1967).

PART THREE, CHAPTER 13

1. *Marine Corps Procurement Practices, Conflicts of Interest,* Report of the Armed Services Investigating Subcommittee of the House Armed Services Committee, Aug. 3, 1971 (U.S. Government Printing Office, Washington, D.C.).

2. *Ibid.,* p. 14.

3. *Ibid.,* p. 1.

4. "Court Opinion: Reserves Not for Members of Congress," *CQ,* April 9, 1971. (Congressional Quarterly, Inc., Washington, D.C.), p. 792.

5. Aspin's charges were made in a series of press releases issued from his office on April 20, April 25, May 4 and May 17, 1972.

6. The information about the welfare funds and financial irregularities in clubs comes from "Troops Short Changed? Welfare Fund Probed," *Army Times* (May 24, 1972).

7. *Fraud and Corruption in Management of Military Club Systems,* Report No. 92–418 of the Senate Committee on Government Operations Permanent Subcommittee on Investigations, Nov. 2, 1971 (U.S. Government Printing Office, Washington, D.C.), p. 60.

8. *Fraud and Corruption in Management of Military Club Systems,* Hearings before the Permanent Subcommittee on Investigations, Part 1 (U.S. Government Printing Office, Washington, D.C., 1969), p. 73.

9. *Ibid.,* p. 97.

10. *Ibid.,* pp. 44–45.

11. *Ibid.,* p. 46.

12. *Ibid.,* p. 46.

13. *Ibid.,* pp. 144, 148, 149.

14. *Ibid.,* pp. 186–187.

15. *Ibid.,* Part 2, p. 429.

16. *Ibid.,* Part 1, p. 189.

17. *Ibid.,* Part 2, pp. 429, 437.

18. *Ibid.,* Part 1, p. 179.

19. *Ibid.,* p. 168.

20. Senate Report 92–418, p. 73.

21. *Ibid.,* pp. 148, 151.

22. *Ibid.,* p. 161.

23. Hearings, Part 7, p. 1561.

24. *Ibid.,* Part 6, p. 1307.

25. *Ibid.,* Part 6, p. 1312.

26. *Ibid.,* p. 1340.

27. *Ibid.*, p. 1320.
28. *Ibid.*, p. 1332.
29. *Ibid.*, Part 7, p. 1791.
30. Cole's explanation of the jade figurine transaction appears in the Hearings, Part 7, pp. 1647–1648. A statement by Senator Ribicoff on how General Westmoreland had personally paid a visit to explain the matter appears in Hearings, Part 7, p. 1574. Ribicoff, telling the subcommittee and the press of the visit later, said he believed General Westmoreland's explanation.
31. *Ibid.*, Part 4, pp. 895–896.
32. *Ibid.*, p. 913.
33. *Ibid.*, Part 7, pp. 1559–1560.
34. *Ibid.*, Part 6, p. 1340.
35. The USAID report, dated Aug. 12, 1971, and CID report of Aug. 20, 1971, are in the author's possession. When I asked to discuss the matter with the CID investigator, who was stationed in Washington in 1972, he refused, after talking to his commanding officers.
36. "Ex-Astronauts Disregarded Warning Against 'Souvenirs,'" Washington *Post* (Aug. 1, 1972).
37. "Astronauts and Space Officials Heard at Inquiry on Exploitation of Souvenirs," *New York Times* (Aug. 4, 1972).

PART FOUR, INTRODUCTION

1. Ted Wye, "Launch on the Count of Three. One . . . Two . . . .," *Washingtonian* (May 1971), p. 67. (Weihe chose a simplified spelling of his name for publication.)

PART FOUR, CHAPTER 14

1. *Study on Military Professionalism*, U.S. Army War College (Carlisle Barracks, Pennsylvania, June 30, 1970), Appendix B. The study, conducted on the order of General William C. Westmoreland, Army Chief of Staff, was classified "for official use only."
2. Capt. Robert H. Smith, "A United States Navy for the Future," *U.S. Naval Institute Proceedings* (March 1971), pp. 22–23.
3. "'72 Bomb Tonnage in Asia Already Tops Last Year's," *New York Times* (Oct. 4, 1972).
4. Col. Everest E. Riccioni, "The Progress of My Book Through the Air Staff." Unpublished. A copy is in the author's possession. Emphasis is Riccioni's.
5. The figures used here were developed from "National Security Council Study Memorandum 1," which, though officially classified top-secret, was leaked to the press in the spring of 1972. A copy is in the author's possession.

PART FOUR, CHAPTER 15

1. Capt. Robert H. Smith, "A United States Navy for the Future," *U.S. Naval Institute Proceedings* (March 1971), pp. 18–19.
2. Comdr. Stuart D. Landersman, "Commanding Officer Comments: The New USS Hepburn DE-1055," *U.S. Naval Institute Proceedings* (March 1971), p. 102.

3. *Jane's Fighting Ships, 1970–71* (McGraw-Hill Book Co., New York), p. 454.
4. Smith, *op. cit.*, p. 25.
5. Richard Witkin, "Litton Plea Put at $400-million," *New York Times* April 19, 1972).
6. Smith *op. cit.*, p. 23.

PART FOUR, CHAPTER 16

1. Col. Robert G. Gard, Jr., "The Military and American Society," *Foreign Affairs*, Vol. 49, No. 4 (July 1971), p. 700. Subsequent quotations of Gard's are taken from the same article.
2. David Boldt, "City Leaders Monitored by Army in '69," Washington *Post* (Sept. 2, 1972).
3. Seymour Hersh, "Report Deplores Wide Army Spying," *New York Times* (Aug. 30, 1972).
4. Seymour Hersh, "More Army Snooping Under Johnson Is Revealed," *New York Times* (Sept. 1, 1972).

INDEX

ABOUT THE AUTHOR

STUART H. LOORY, of Dover, New Jersey, was graduated from Cornell University and the Columbia University Graduate School of Journalism, where he won a Pulitzer Traveling Scholarship. He joined the Newark *News* in 1955 and the New York *Herald Tribune* in 1959. After working as a general assignment reporter covering stories throughout the nation, a science writer and a Washington correspondent, he became the *Herald Tribune*'s last Moscow correspondent in 1964. In 1966, he won an Overseas Press Club citation for a series of reports from Siberia. In 1967, he became the White House correspondent for the Los Angeles *Times*. With David Kraslow, then that paper's Washington news editor, he co-authored in 1968 *The Secret Search for Peace in Vietnam,* an examination of the United States' attempts to secure a negotiated settlement of the Vietnam War. That work won three major reporting awards for the two newsmen. In 1971 he left the *Times* to take a fellowship at the Woodrow Wilson International Center for Scholars. In 1973 he became executive editor of WNBC-TV News in New York and later that year was named the first Kiplinger Professor of Public Affairs Reporting at Ohio State University. He has written numerous magazine articles.